Radicalism and Its Demise

The Chinese Nationalist Party,
Factionalism, and Local Elites in
Jiangsu Province, 1924–1931

Bradley K. Geisert

CENTER FOR CHINESE STUDIES
THE UNIVERSITY OF MICHIGAN
ANN ARBOR

MICHIGAN MONOGRAPHS IN CHINESE STUDIES
ISSN 1081-9053
SERIES ESTABLISHED 1968

Published by
Center for Chinese Studies
The University of Michigan
Ann Arbor, Michigan 48104-1608

© 2001 The Regents of the University of Michigan
All rights reserved

Grateful acknowledgment is made for permission to reprint copyrighted material:

"From Conflict to Quiescence: The Guomindang, Factionalism, and Local Elites in Jiangsu, 1927–1931," by Bradley K. Geisert. Originally published in *China Quarterly* 108 (December 1986): 608–703. © 1986 by The China Quarterly.

"Probing KMT Rule: Reflections on Eastman's 'New Insights,'" by Bradley K Geisert. Originally published in *Republican China* 9.2 (February 1984): 28–39. © 1984 by Republican China.

"Toward a Pluralist Model of KMT Rule," by Bradley K. Geisert. Originally published in *Republican China* 7.2 (February 1982): 1–10. © 1982 by Republican China.

Library of Congress Cataloging-in-Publication Data

Geisert, Bradley Kent.
    Radicalism and its demise : the Chinese Nationalist Party, factionalism, and local elites in Jiangsu Province, 1924–1931 / Bradley K. Geisert.
        p. cm. — (Michigan monographs in Chinese studies, ISSN 1081-9053 ; 90)
    Includes bibliographical references and index.
    ISBN 0-89264-139-8 (alk. paper)
    1. Jiangsu Sheng (China) — Politics and government. 2. Zhongguo guo min dang. 3. Elite (Social sciences) — China—Jiangsu Sheng. I. University of Michigan. Center for Chinese Studies. II. Title. III. Series.
    JQ1519.J53 G45 2001
    320.951/136/09042—dc21

        2001028315

For Ellen, Kevin, and Erik

Contents

Maps	vi
Acknowledgments	vii
Note on Romanization	xi
1. Introduction	1
2. Dramatis Personae: Local Elites and the Guomindang's "Would-be Elites" Before 1927: A Social Perspective	15
3. Guomindang Factions and Local Elites: The Early Period, 1924–1927	43
4. Jiangsu's Guomindang, 1927–1931: The Factional Background	69
5. Jiangsu's Guomindang, 1927–1929: Party-Elite Relations	103
6. The Party's Reverse Course During and After Rectification, 1930–1931	185
7. Perspectives	205
Appendices 1. The Evolution of Factional Conflict, 1927–1929	211
2. Factional Affiliations of Provincial-level Personnel	223
3. The Qidong Land Reform Movement	225
Notes	231
Glossary	305
Bibliography	313
Index	343

Maps

Map 1. Counties and county seats in Jiangsu Province   xii

Map 2. Regional divisions in Jiangsu   10

Acknowledgments

My Ph.D. dissertation, done at the University of Virginia in the late 1970s, provided the starting point for this book. While at the University of Virginia, I benefited from John Israel's instruction and advice, and since that time Professor Israel has continued to provide wise counsel and assistance in many of my endeavors—for which I am most grateful. The University of Virginia and the Commonwealth of Virginia gave financial backing, which not only partially paid for my graduate education, but also helped to make possible a year of research in Taiwan in 1976 and 1977. The Fairbank Center for East Asian Research generously funded a year of post-doctoral research and writing. I also received support from Northwest Missouri State University and Randolph-Macon Woman's College, some of the subsidy from the latter institution underwritten by the Pew Charitable Trusts. In 1989 the Mellon Foundation and the Chiang Ching-kuo Foundation funded my participation in a summer of language retooling at the Inter-University Center for Chinese Language Study in Taiwan.

Since I began this project in the mid-1970s, my views on the events recounted herein have evolved, and my ability to create a textured and, I hope, accurate picture has developed, largely because of the aid of numerous scholars, librarians, and archivists. In Taiwan, Professor Lü Fang-shang (formerly of the Guomindang Archives, later of Taiwan's Academia Sinica) not only helped to identify and make available many important sources, but he also helped me understand their historical context. In Nanjing, Professors Zhang Xianwen and Chen Qianping of Nanjing University similarly spent many hours helping me to gain access to significant materials, and Professor Yan Xuexi worked hard to help me gain entree to materials, patiently elucidating certain aspects of GMD-era politics and society. Xu Youwei, a professor at Shanghai Textile University, helped me locate relevant journal articles, and Lenore Barkan and Lloyd Eastman provided me with materials from their own personal stashes. Stephen Averill, Roger Thompson, and F. Garvin Davenport allowed me to use and cite their own unpublished papers. I am beholden to Stephen Averill for his skillful crafting of the maps in this book; I will never forget his patience with my piecemeal proofing and repeated revisions. Likewise, Carolyn Sherayko did an excellent job in her indexing of this book.

A number of individuals read and thoughtfully critiqued all or part of the manuscript at some point in its genesis: John Israel, Paul Cohen, Philip Kuhn, the late Lloyd Eastman, the late John King Fairbank, Guy Alitto, Kathleen Hartford, John Schrecker, Nelson Lankford, David Zweig, Fred Tiewes, and Benita Wong. Although I did not always take their advice, there is no question that their labors helped greatly to improve this book. Special thanks must go to R. Keith Schoppa, who read and commented on the manuscript twice—once, early in the revision process and, once again, much later in the game. I am also grateful for the many helpful suggestions of a reader—identity unknown to me—for the University of Michigan Center for Chinese Studies.

Another person who greatly aided in my understanding of the Jiangsu Guomindang is Robert Womack. He and I began researching the party in Jiangsu at roughly the same time. When we were working in Taiwan in the mid-1970s, we discussed our findings and our vision of the history of local party politics virtually every day. I can no longer recall which ideas were originally mine and which were his—so much did he influence my evolving understanding. We shared materials and cooperated in many ways. Moreover, he has helped me numerous times since that period of initial collaboration.

In the 1970s and early 1980s I was privileged to interview six individuals who played important roles in the Jiangsu Guomindang in the 1920s and 1930s. These persons gave unselfishly of their time; their knowledge of the provincial and local politics of the era this book treats was very important in shaping my understanding of my topic. In order to encourage my sources to discuss sensitive political topics, I promised them that I would not reveal their identities. In this book I honor that pledge by indicating in the notes only the times and places of the interviews that produced particular pieces of information.

This project has profited from research at the following collections: Alderman Library at the University of Virginia, the Library of Congress, Harvard-Yenching Library, Widener Library at Harvard University, the Guomindang Archives (in the 1970s when it was located at Daqijiao, outside Taibei, near Xindian), the National Central Library in Taibei, the Taiwan branch of the National Central Library also in Taibei, the Fu Sinian Library at Academia Sinica in Nangang, Taiwan, the Library of the Institute for Modern History at Academic Sinica in Taiwan, the Number Two Historical Archives in Nanjing, the Jiangsu Provincial Archives, Nanjing University Library, the library at the Xiyuan (at Nanjing University), the library of the History Department at Nanjing University, and the Longpanli section of the Nanjing Library. I am most grateful to the librarians and archivists at these institutions, many of whom have gone well beyond the call of duty to help me with this project.

Thanks must go to the *China Quarterly* for allowing me to use material that was originally published in my article, "From Conflict to Quiescence: The Guomindang, Factionalism, and Local Elites in Jiangsu, 1927–1931," *China Quarterly* 108 (December, 1986): 680–703. Similarly, *Twentieth-Century China* has kindly given me permission to use material from the following two articles I wrote, which were originally published in journals from which *Twentieth-Century China* descended: "Toward a Pluralist Model of KMT Rule," *Chinese Republican Studies Newsletter* 7.2 (February, 1982): 1–10; and "Probing KMT Rule: Reflections on Eastman's 'New Insights'," *Republican China* 9.2 (February, 1984): 28–39.

Finally, I wish to thank Ellen, who has supported me (both figuratively and literally) in all of my pursuits. On a number of occasions, work on this book meant my absence from home for rather long periods. Her cheerful willingness to forego my help in parenting our children during these intervals has put me in her debt. Likewise, her tolerance of the cluttering of basement, bedroom, and family room with books, photocopies, and other papers for the past two decades has made this work possible. Mostly, I am grateful for the confidence she has always placed in me—and the love she has shown me.

Note on Romanization

This book employs the Hanyu pinyin system of romanization for Chinese language terms. However, in a few cases it uses more familiar forms for the names of individuals and places, for example, Chiang Kai-shek, Sun Yat-sen, and Hong Kong.

The romanization applied to the name of one county in Jiangsu requires some explanation. Many maps and publications from the Republican era call two different counties in northwestern Jiangsu "P'ei," using the Wade-Giles system or "Pei," using modified Wade-Giles. However, the convention in the People's Republic of China is to call the westernmost of these two counties "Pei" and the easternmost "Pi." In fact, the standard pinyin romanization of the latter county name is now "Pi," the spelling I employ.

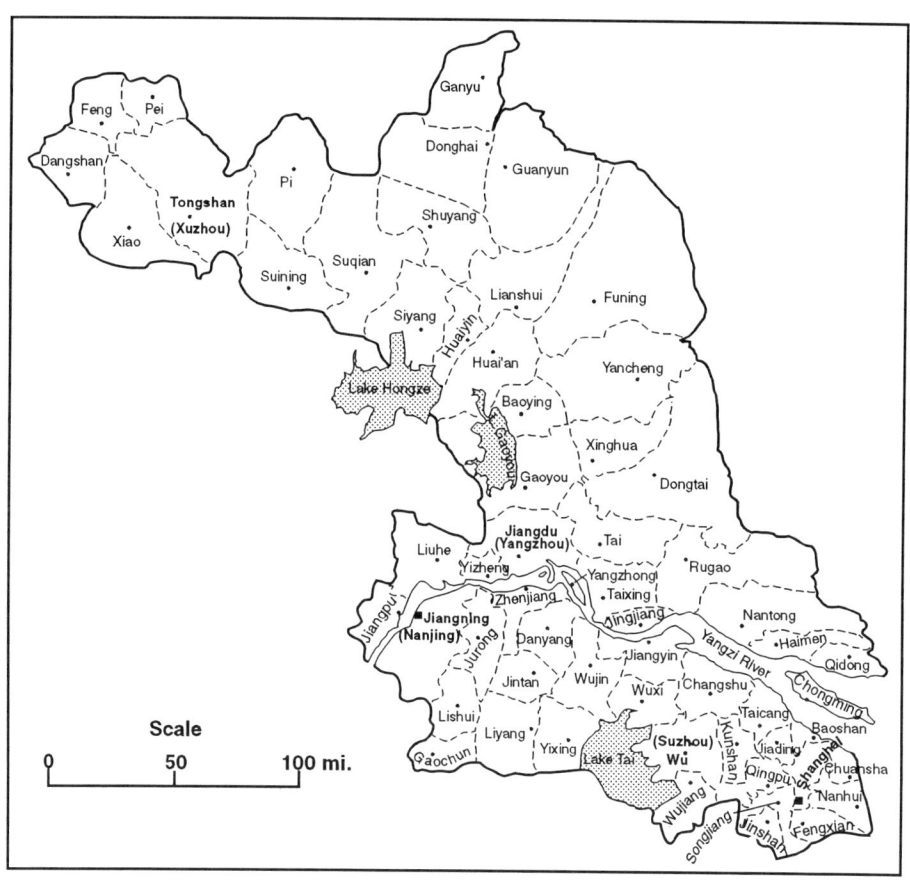

Map 1. Counties and county seats in Jiangsu Province

1

INTRODUCTION

> The manipulation and destruction of politics is . . . a fact that cannot be covered up. . . . The first step in restoring clean government is to get rid of the corrupt officials, local bullies, and evil gentry.
>
> Ni Bi, September, 1928[1]

Anyone familiar with modern Chinese history knows the importance the Chinese Communists have placed on thoroughgoing social and political change. Far less well known, however, is the radical complexion displayed for quite some time by the Guomindang (GMD, the Chinese Nationalist Party). Despite the conventional wisdom that the April 1927 purge of the Communists suddenly transformed the Guomindang into a consistent defender of the status quo in China, a sizable pool of young radicals remained active in the party. Attacks on local elites constituted a key ingredient in the radicalism of those activists. Although the Guomindang did eventually reject social radicalism, that change came later than 1927, and its causes went well beyond the purging of the Communists.[2] A focus of this study, then, is the rise of social and political radicalism in Jiangsu Province's GMD in the 1920s and that radicalism's demise by the early 1930s.

One of the tasks which the Guomindang had set for itself, even before it swept to power in central China in 1927, was to forge China into a powerful and cohesive nation-state. Its failure to accomplish that feat—thereby providing the opening for both the Japanese invasion and the eventual victory of the Chinese Communists—was, I believe, due in some measure to the GMD's approach to local politics and organization. As the Japanese invasion in 1937 marked the end of a decade of Guomindang rule in Jiangsu, the party in the province was, in many respects, weak. Although the intelligence and military components of the GMD regime had virtually destroyed the Chinese Communist Party (CCP) in the province, the Guomindang had not succeeded in engaging the political sympathy and loyalty of a broad cross section of Jiangsu's citizens. Nor had the regime spawned a network of durable and dedicated, party-led mass organizations that could energize and direct resistance behind Japanese lines and prevent collaboration of Chinese guerrilla units with Japanese forces.

The attention that this book pays to the Guomindang's relation to local elites will come as no surprise to anyone aware of the large body of scholarship which argues that the upper social strata of developing nations often impede the creation of strong and united nation-states.[3] In fact, many scholars consider Chinese local elites of the first half of the twentieth century to have been a problem to overcome.[4] Sometimes this study, too, describes parochial behavior of local elites. Nonetheless, it is only fair to note the important roles that some elites assumed in various efforts to reform local society. In fact, certain local elites spearheaded projects in the realms of education, local administration, industry, and commerce which might be classified by social scientists as modernization ventures.

Much of the recent research on Guomindang interactions with local elites has been inspired by the work of Lloyd Eastman and others who, starting in the 1970s, set forth a new view of the relation of the GMD regime to the society it governed. Whereas many earlier observers of Nationalist rule during the Nanjing Decade (1927–1937) had seen the Guomindang as a pliable tool of urban-based merchants—or at least a subset of them—and the rural landlord class, Eastman emphasized tension and conflict in the GMD state's relation to local elites. As he later refined his position, he argued that the regime was essentially "autonomous," meaning that it was "neither responsible nor responsive to" political groups and institutions outside itself.[5] The questions he posed and the debate that his work stimulated make it clear how essential it is to pin down the GMD regime's relation to the society it sought to control.

Since the mid-1970s, scholars concerned with the relation of the Chinese state to society have branched off in a number of directions. Prasenjit Duara, for example, has argued that Republican-era China was undergoing a process of what he calls "state involution." In his view the Nationalist state during the Nanjing Decade bolstered its extraction of revenues by relying on "entrepreneurial brokers"—persons who took fees in return for their administrative services—as tax collection agents and village officials. These tax farmers and new types of village officials did not rely on traditional sources of power, and partly because of the heavy taxes they collected (of which they took a cut), they could not command the loyalties of the communities in which they functioned. They became a predatory power at the village level and, as they grew in number, a swelling financial burden to the state. The state's mushrooming appetite for revenues, however, meant that the government had to increase its reliance on these brokers. Duara argues that although the state was involved in a project to penetrate society bureaucratically, its scramble for revenue to pay for that project was ironically undercutting the state's bureaucratic efficiency and power. Duara's "state involution" model provides a new lens through which to view administrative units and their interaction with society in parts of North China, but it concentrates primarily on relations of *government* to society. Duara gives little, if any, attention to the Guomindang as *party*. His analytic framework has limited application to this study of the party in Jiangsu.[6]

However, Duara also contributes ideas about the imbeddedness of local elites in a "cultural nexus" that includes religious practices and institutions. This attention to the religious dimensions of some local elites' power is an important counterbalance to prevalent conceptions of Chinese thought and society as predominantly secular. The present study parallels Duara in its concern with the religious nexus of some local elites and, like some of Duara's other work, probes an antisuperstition campaign pressed by Chinese intellectuals.[7]

Along rather different lines, many scholars have focused on what they see as the rise of a "public sphere" in late Qing and Republican China, a realm distinguished from the official and private spheres. In the view of these scholars, the late imperial state, by virtue of its minimalist, noninterventionist approach, left a sizable arena in which elites could found and manage institutions, forge initiatives, and "appropriate . . . local political authority."[8] Mary Rankin argues that late Qing "elite managers . . . developed autonomous ambitions that were not fully reconcilable with official supervision."[9] Some have gone so far as to find this "public sphere" to have been something akin to the "civil society" that many observers agree took shape in Eastern Europe in the 1970s and 1980s and helped to undermine the grip of the Communist states. In fact, the terms "civil society" and "public sphere" have been defined and used in many different and incompatible ways.[10] Given the cacophony of conflicting usages, the body of the present work describes the social and political realities in Republican-era Jiangsu without resorting to these expressions.

Bryna Goodman presents a perspective that transcends a simplistic either/or approach to the question of whether certain nongovernmental organizations were autonomous from the Chinese state in the Nanjing Decade. She holds that the relationship between native place associations in Shanghai and the state "is best understood as expressing not autonomy but shifting areas of partial autonomy, interpenetration, and negotiation."[11] The present work finds elements of control, as well as "autonomy, interpenetration, and negotiation" in the state's handling of merchant organizations.

The preceding brief description of relatively recent scholarly work is hardly comprehensive, but it should indicate that the question of the Chinese state's relation to local elites is still an open one. In fact, the present study's approach is to return to Eastman's original question of regime-elite relations in the period of GMD dominance, but to focus specifically on the party's social connections, rather than on those of the government. In fact, among published monographic treatments of Chinese state-society relations in the Republican era, few have focused in a sustained way on the party.[12]

Some of the historical incidents that this study considers provide support for the view that relations between the GMD and local elites were characterized by tension and mutual hostility. For example, much of the focus is on the party's assaults on particular local elites who were singled out to be prosecuted and punished as "local bullies and evil gentry." Attention is also given to the party's shift away from attacks on local elites, as well as to cases in which one or more groupings of local elites had special influence over a faction within the local party or enjoyed clout in the halls of a local government.

This work views the Guomindang regime as an entity of almost baroque complexity. The fact that the regime was not monolithic suggests that to understand it one must factor it down to its constituent parts and consider the societal relations of each element separately. It is important to bear in mind that although the Jiangsu GMD regime was a one-party state, and the government was supposedly a GMD-supervised entity, the party and the government in Jiangsu were for several years divided in perspective and direction. Far from being synonymous, the two institutions were often at loggerheads. From 1927 until early 1930, some segments of the party in Jiangsu and in many other places in the country retained much of the radical tone they had assumed in the period of alliance with the Chinese Communist Party. Until 1930 many party radicals were doing their best to overturn persons in the top stratum of local society, while, by contrast, local government bureaucrats were sometimes participating in mutually supportive transactions with those very same elites. Although this book at times touches upon the government and its social connections, its primary focus is the party and its approach to local elites. The government is a separate and complex topic that deserves full treatment in another study.

Not only must one at times distinguish between party and government, but one must also be aware of schisms within both institutions. GMD factions, especially prior to 1927, repeatedly differed on the question of treatment of local elites. Many historians have described in general terms Guomindang factionalism in central-level politics. However, few if any have examined the provincial and local underpinnings of the national cliques in the Nanjing Decade.[13] Beyond the vague assertion that Jiangsu from 1927 to 1937 was somehow a stronghold of the Organization Clique (often called the "CC Clique"), previous works have imparted little sense of the lower level structures that were underlying this and other important blocs within the GMD. One goal of this book is to trace the elusive provincial and, in a few cases, local networks of factionalism. Though national politics impinged on provincial and local party organizations, those subordinate reaches of factional webs were not simple mirror images of national alignments. From our provincial-level vantage point, the Organization Clique will appear less united and cohesive than it has usually been depicted.

Factional conflict drastically transformed the Jiangsu Guomindang. Far from being meaningless, the factional wars helped determine the political outcome of Guomindang rule. In 1930 one factional cluster, the Organization Clique, commandeered the GMD in Jiangsu, resulting in the abandonment of the radical attacks on traditional elites that the party had intermittently launched. Moreover, since factional competition, more than any other single force, impelled Guomindang politics, intraparty rivalry demands the attention of historians.

Beyond the need to distinguish among party factions, it is also important to consider differences of approach at the central, provincial, and county levels. Authorities and organs at the various administrative levels did not always see eye to eye on policies concerning local elites and other important matters. A fundamental part of the story of Jiangsu's politics during the Nanjing Decade is to be found in the attempts of the Guomindang's central apparatus to deal with what it saw as unruly and excessively autonomous provincial and local party branches. Among other things, the party center aimed to enforce its views on the proper approach toward local elites.

This study not only factors down the regime into its primary components, but also at times draws distinctions among subsets of the larger universe of local elites. Local elites were not alike in social, economic, and educational backgrounds, nor did they agree on politics. In certain counties the GMD branches embraced one set of local elites while attacking another. Thus at times, factionalism in the party intersected at odd and unpredictable angles with factionalism among local elites.

A few words are necessary to explain the organization of this book. Chapter 2 sets the stage by introducing the cast of characters in Jiangsu's local upper crust in the 1910s and 1920s on the eve of Nationalist rule. It provides a typology of local elites and analyzes the social foundations of a new counterelite that took shape in the 1920s, the local minions of the GMD. Chapter 3 scrutinizes the party from 1924 through 1927, when it was an illegal, underground body working to overthrow the warlord-dominated government of the province. During that period, the GMD's left wing, which favored the party's working alliance with the Communist Party, embraced a sometimes aggressive strategy of attacking selected local elites, while the anti-Communist right wing of the GMD generally shrank from such direct action.

Chapter 4 dissects GMD factional politics in Jiangsu from 1927 through 1931. Among other things, it charts the nature, origins, reach, and political strategies of the county-level factions that served as the unsteady foundation of the party. Additionally, it profiles provincial-level GMD factions and charts their ties to national-level counterparts. Most importantly, it explains a watershed event in late 1929 that led to the 1930–1931 party rectification, a wrenching process that helped bring about a shift in GMD policy toward local elites in Jiangsu.

Chapter 5 examines in detail the Jiangsu GMD's relation to local elites during the opening years of the Nanjing Decade, 1927 through 1929. The chapter traces the sometimes aggressive, sometimes timid provincial party policy toward local elites. It also imparts a textured picture of relations between the party and elites on the county (and sometimes, subcounty) level. Some readers may be struck by the considerable variety in the approaches of local party branches to local elites. In this early part of the Nanjing Decade some branches avoided confrontation with local elites, but many others saw attacks on selected elite targets as central to the GMD program. In a very few counties, local elites whose power predated GMD rule not only penetrated the party, but the very pattern of those older elites' factionalism was replicated within the GMD. More commonly, however, the activist leaders of local GMD branches styled themselves as a "new" ruling force which had set its face against older elites.

Chapter 6 argues that the party rectification, which took place largely in 1930 and 1931, fundamentally transformed the Guomindang in Jiangsu. The rectification put an end to assaults by local party branches against local elites. It also muddied the corporate self-image of the GMD. The defanged party was reduced to a colorless appendage of the government.

In a sense, this subordination of local party branches to local governments at the behest of the party's central apparatus may be seen as part of a larger trend toward expansion of the size and reach of the government's bureaucracy. Scholars have traced this trend to the era before GMD rule, but, as a recent work observes, "[u]nder the Nationalist regime, the process was accelerated, and the stranglehold of bureaucracy became tighter."[14] This drift toward bureaucratization and centralization of power counterpoised another long-term development: the late-Qing and early-Republican devolution of power from the central government to regional and local leadership. The growth of the power and autonomy of local elites since at least the Taiping Rebellion, and the central government's stratagems to counter that trend, provide essential frameworks for understanding twentieth-century China.

Although this book suggests that some of the Guomindang's political ways contributed to that organization's demise in mainland China, to focus exclusively on the party's failure would be distortive. It is simply not true that every wriggle and twist of the period's history points to the eventual demise of the party, still less to the victory of the Chinese Communists. Many riveting and revealing events of the era were not direct determinants of either CCP success or GMD failure. Thus, while tracking the Guomindang's approach to handling local elites in Jiangsu, we will be able to glimpse partial answers to other questions: Who were the local elites before the GMD rose to power? What sorts of people became GMD members and why? How did the GMD come to power? What role did the party play in grass-roots affairs? What animated its politics? And finally, what united and divided party members?

Jiangsu: Geographical Background

> In the north, people are wilder than in other parts. Bandits and robbers are quite common, and fighting is more favored than talking. In the central part, they are quite cautious and do not venture to do anything. They stay at home and starve and endure hardships rather than go out and search for a living. They are illiterate and superstitious and temples are numerous. On the south side of the river the nature of the people is quite different from that to the north. They like to talk and enjoy themselves. It is a richer part of the area which makes the people very delicate. They are clever and smart but cowardly.[15]
>
> An investigator for John Lossing Buck, 1937

As China's most populous and economically developed province, Jiangsu deserves attention in its own right. But it has representational value beyond that. Before the 1937 Japanese invasion, the GMD regime held Jiangsu, together with Zhejiang, its southern neighbor, longer and tighter than any other area. Warlords and Communists did not hamper GMD control there as seriously as elsewhere. Thus, in Jiangsu the regime had its best chance to implement its programs. The regime's performance in Jiangsu may be taken to represent its best case and may suggest how it might have ruled all of China, given the time and power to do so. Just as other historians have studied the CCP's leadership style in its secure base area of Yan'an, one can learn much about the Guomindang by examining its approach to politics in its relatively secure areas.[16] Although the cities of Shanghai and Nanjing are geographically part of Jiangsu, they are largely excluded from the scope of this study because they were administratively separate from the province during the Nanjing Decade. (For the locations of these cities and the counties in Jiangsu, see Map 1.)

Unfortunately for anyone attempting to understand Jiangsu in the 1920s and 1930s, the province was as complex as it was important. The vivid description given above of the inhabitants of the various parts of the province borders on the slanderous, but it also captures Jiangsu's diversity. Jiangsu displayed a multiplicity of local cultures, soil types, climates, agricultural products, and dialects. In its rich diversity as well as its demographic and economic significance, Jiangsu was the peer of many European nations. Although over 80 percent of the province's population of over thirty-five million lived in rural communities, Jiangsu also contained the most commercially developed and urbanized area in China.

The Chinese have traditionally spoken of the area north of the Yangzi as Subei ("northern Jiangsu") or Jiangbei ("north of the river") and the lands south of the river as Su'nan ("southern Jiangsu") or Jiangnan ("south of the river"). Complicating things further, some Chinese use Subei to refer only to the area from the Yangzi northward to the Huai, reserving the term Huaibei for the area extending north from the Huai.[17] Actually, Jiangsu crosscuts two major physiographic regions: the North China Plain and the Lower Yangzi area. One can further break down the Lower Yangzi region into core and periphery areas, with the core zone defined by a greater degree of urbanization and commercialization than noncore areas. (See Map 2.)[18] This study includes in the Lower Yangzi core all counties (*xian*) in which population density in the Nanjing Decade exceeded the threshold level of 320 persons per square kilometer. These are, in descending order of density: Shanghai (County), Wuxi, Taixing, Nantong, Yangzhong, Jiading, Jiangyin, Jiangdu, Zhenjiang, Tai, Nanhui, Haimen, Jingjiang, Songjiang, Danyang, Changshu, Jinshan, Rugao, Wujiang, Wu, Qingpu, Wujin, Taicang, and Fengxian. A handful of counties that did not reach the threshold level (Baoshan, Chuansha, Kunshan, Chongming, Qidong, and Yixing) are also included in the core zone because most of them were under the direct economic sway of China's foremost commercial center, Shanghai municipality.[19]

The core of the Lower Yangzi region includes much of southeastern Jiangsu and part of northern Zhejiang Province. Population density figures as well as nonstatistical information on urbanization and commerce suggest fairly sharp differentiation between core and periphery areas in the Lower Yangzi zone. Much of the available data relates to this core because Shanghai newspapers and other journalistic sources paid particular attention to this key economic area, which was tightly integrated with Shanghai.[20] This book, therefore, deals relatively little with counties in the Lower Yangzi periphery.

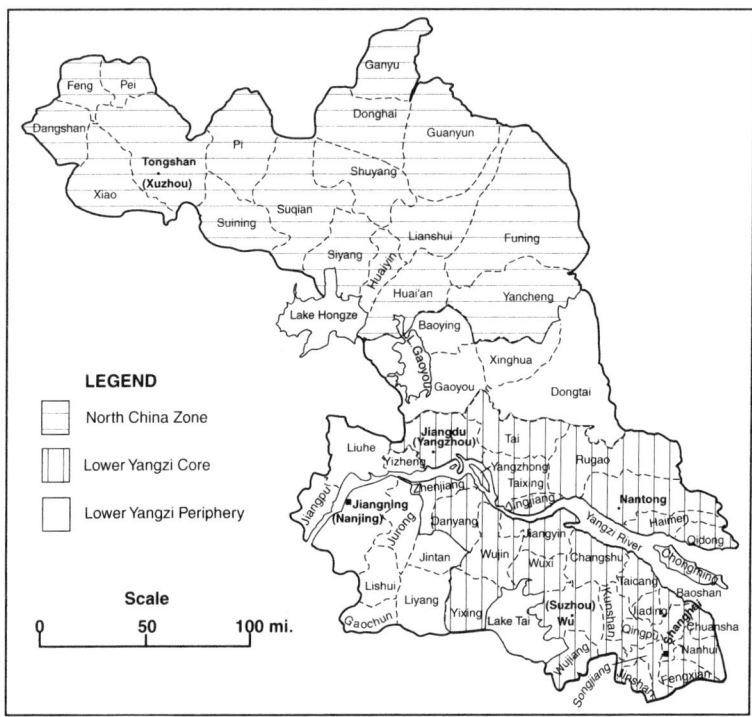

Map 2. Regional divisions of Jiangsu

In the northern half of the province, which lies within the North China region, population density statistics and other information do not indicate that any grouping of counties was predominant enough to justify dubbing them a core. The city of Xuzhou (Tongshan County) was a central focus of trade for much of northern Jiangsu and nearby sections of neighboring provinces, but there is no sign that the part of Tongshan County falling outside the city was particularly commercialized or urbanized, nor was Tongshan located at the center of a clump of especially commercialized counties. Cities in the North China section of the province were on average much smaller than those in the Lower Yangzi core.[21] In general, it is probably best to think of the North China area of Jiangsu as a relative economic backwater, though some cities, like Xuzhou and Haizhou, did punctuate the sluggish, overwhelmingly rural landscape.[22] Analyzing Jiangsu according to physiographic regions in this way dramatizes the lack of coincidence between the province and natural economic units. It also suggests the need for caution when generalizing from local evidence. While several examples of social or economic phenomena from the core areas in the south might give clues about the situation in other areas in the Lower Yangzi core, their predictive value for the North China area or any of the Lower Yangzi periphery is at best doubtful.

A widely known Chinese saying likens a broad area in the Lower Yangzi core to heaven.[23] Abundant and dependable rainfall not only painted the southern Jiangsu countryside in rich, verdant hues, but also made possible the agricultural abundance to which the proverb alludes. One of the most productive agricultural areas in China, the land south of the Yangzi was well suited to wet rice cultivation. However, the southern landscape was also punctuated by lands given over to cotton, wheat, barley, and mulberry trees, the leaves of which were the basis for silk culture, the economic sideline of two-thirds of southern Jiangsu peasants.[24]

Southern Jiangsu's economic core was the most urbanized and commercialized area in China. It contained eleven cities with populations of over 100,000.[25] Shanghai, China's premier port city, was administratively separate from the province, but its active and competitive markets deeply influenced the southern core's economy. The part of the core which lay south of the Yangzi was laced with countless navigable rivers, creeks, and diked canals, which kept transportation costs low. The core included modern silk and cotton textile mills as well as a dizzying variety of traditional Chinese industries, commercial concerns, and credit institutions.[26]

The highly commercialized nature of this core was reflected in local power structures and the distribution of social status. Oligarchies at the county and subcounty (township) levels there usually included many persons who owed their wealth and position to their own or their families' success in commerce or industry. One example of such an oligarch on the subcounty level was Chuansha County's Chen Weishan. Although Chen was from a poor family, he managed to obtain a lower exam degree in the latter years of the empire. He began to make his fortune as a factory manager in Shanghai, then set up several enterprises back in Chuansha, including a transportation company. Chen played a very active role in local politics, most notably as chairman of Chuansha's Changren Township Assembly in the late Qing and early Republican periods. He was also a township manager for several years. The local gazetteer records that a single word from Chen could settle disputes. Chuansha's gazetteer includes biographies of many merchants who were leaders at either the county or township level.[27] Many who had earned or purchased examination degrees in the imperial era combined traditional gentry roles—charity management, teaching, and direction of public works—with entrepreneurship. In fact, so-called "gentry-merchants" (*shenshang*) were among the most powerful elites in some Lower Yangzi core counties.[28] Also, most large landholding families in the Lower Yangzi core lived in cities and owed their wealth to lucrative commercial ventures.[29]

The spareness of the economy of the North China zone and its overwhelmingly agricultural nature stemmed in large part from the difficulty and expense of overland transportation. There were relatively few navigable waterways in the North China zone of Jiangsu, though the north was served by the Longhai Railway, which ran from Xuzhou east to Donghai, as well as by the Tianjin-Pukou Railway, which ran from Xuzhou south to Pukou (across the Yangzi from Nanjing). But the Tianjin-Pukou Railway bypassed most of Jiangsu as it dipped westward through Anhui. Even so, that rail line carried much of the long-distance freight that in early to mid-Qing times would have traveled down the Grand Canal. The canal, which had from the 500s extended from south to north in the province, was still an important waterway for those counties adjacent to it. But that artery had become badly silted in some of its reaches, making it too shallow and unreliable a transportation route for industry and commerce.[30] More important, some counties in the North China zone lacked any navigable stream, rail access, or decent motor road.[31]

Most of the Jiangsu countryside in the North China zone displayed the dusty yellow soil, dry climate, and treeless expanses that remain features of the rest of northern China and contrast sharply with the lush growth of the south. During the Nanjing Decade northern Jiangsu's crops—sorghum, wheat, cotton, millet, and corn—and its prevailing dry-farming methods identified it as a part of North China, as did its alternating cycle of frequent drought and flood.[32]

The endemic banditry and armed violence that Buck's investigator (cited earlier in this section) observed in the north were, at least in part, outgrowths of this harsh environment. Banditry and military service were just two of the survival strategies frequently embraced by peasants condemned by birth to the hard and austere life of the northern Jiangsu countryside.[33] Migration to the opportunities, both real and imagined, of the Lower Yangzi core was another.[34]

Introduction 13

The bleak ecology of Jiangsu's North China zone also affected society's elite strata. Fewer northern than southern Jiangsu elites were connected with commerce. But this meant that those in the North China zone who enjoyed a degree of business success had far fewer peers and less competition for position and status than merchants of similar wealth in the south. While the large-scale landlords of the southern core tended to have sizeable commercial holdings, most great landowners of the province's northern section had initially made their fortunes in political or military careers and depended largely on land rents and moneylending for their incomes.[35] Unlike the sedate, citified landholders of the Lower Yangzi core who relied on bursaries to collect rent from tenants on their scattered lands, quite a few of the great northern Jiangsu landlords lived in earthen fortresses in the countryside near their more concentrated land holdings and maintained their own armed bands. Not only did northern landlords exert a larger measure of direct political and economic control over their tenants than southern landholders, but they also exercised far greater autonomy from county government, taking advantage of the isolation afforded by difficulties of transportation and communication. In the Lower Yangzi core landlord bursaries often depended on government aid in rent collection, whereas most of the great northern landlords were able to handle tenants without government assistance, and some were so autonomous from outside help and interference that they were dubbed "local emperors" (*tu huangdi*).[36]

But if Jiangsu was diverse, China was far more so. Jiangsu was not, after all, a microcosm of China. While research on party-elite relations that encompassed the whole of China might be impractical because of the volume of data and variety of local structures involved, it is fair to question what one can learn from one province. What is the broader significance of phenomena and patterns of sociopolitical relations evident in Jiangsu?

The social patterns described in this book may well have little predictive value for areas far removed from Jiangsu. Social and economic structures must have been dramatically different in Guizhou or Gansu, just to name two far-flung provinces. But there is good reason to believe that the societal patterns that this study identifies do not always honor provincial boundaries. The portion of Zhejiang that falls within the Lower Yangzi core shares many features with southern Jiangsu, which is also part of that core. Similarly, the works of Elizabeth Perry, G. William

Skinner, and others suggest commonality of structures and tendencies within a North China zone that includes northern Jiangsu, northern Anhui, most of Henan, and Shandong. In other words, the North China and Lower Yangzi physiographic macroregions identified by Skinner may define the areas about which this study's discussions of social and economic phenomena may be most suggestive.[37]

Beyond this, however, the Guomindang, as *the* party in a supposedly one-party state that laid claim to all of China, thrust its tentacles into all corners of the country. It would, of course, be foolish to presume that the party's history in every other province replicated the experience of Jiangsu's GMD. In some respects, history as a craft—perhaps more so than the more purely social sciences—interests itself in the uniqueness of individual human experience as opposed to fitting that experience into grand models that purport to larger or even universal applicability. Nonetheless, some of the key threads of the story of Jiangsu's GMD extend conspicuously through the warp and weft of Guomindang history as a whole. These prominent features include pervasive factionalism, assertion of central control over the party by the Organization Department (and the Organization Clique) in the late 1920s and early 1930s, and battles over how to handle local elites and their interests.

2

Dramatis Personae:
A Social Perspective On Local Elites
And The Guomindang's "Would-Be Elites"
Before 1927

The 1910s and early 1920s have been called China's warlord period because of the dominance of military men, especially at the provincial level. However, that era might just as well be called China's "local elite" period because by that time local elites had come to exercise unprecedented power. Thanks to the decreased power and coherence of the central government, local elites acted as oligarchs. Throughout the first half of the twentieth century, these local oligarchs sometimes resisted measures decreed by central authorities to create national unity and to modernize China; nonetheless, the positive features and accomplishments of these elites should be noted. One historian calls many of them "urban reformist elites."[1] Some of them did reform, especially in localities in the Lower Yangzi core as well as in other relatively urbanized areas of China. In the last decade of the nineteenth century and early decades of the twentieth century, these local leaders energetically established and managed hospitals, newspapers, and Western-style schools.[2]

However, these elites were not universally popular. In fact, as a result of their costly reform projects, local taxes rose rapidly. This jump in taxes helped spawn a series of short-lived revolts against the elite-dominated local self-government system in 1911 and 1912.[3] Moreover, a sizable portion of the generation of youth schooled in the Western-style middle and normal schools, which older reformist elites had fashioned, had by the 1920s come to see the local oligarchies as corrupt, narrowly based tyrannies that did not have national interests at heart. It was from this new generation, which felt that existing local elites were selfishly blocking access to power, wealth, and advancement, that the Guomindang drew most of its members in the mid- to late-1920s.

Thus, part of the explanation for GMD hostility to the local oligarchs' rule is to be found in the social situation of the Guomindang members themselves in the 1920s. Most GMD members were from reasonably prosperous families, making it possible for them to see themselves as "would-be," even "should-be" elites. Most were young and, therefore, out of power. Most had obtained some Western-style education, supporting their self-image as rightful power holders. Not only did many of the members of this generational cohort whom the GMD recruited nurse their resentments into full-fledged revolution in the 1920s, but even thereafter many members of the GMD retained their distaste for the older local elites and the institutions they had managed. As late as the 1930s, one of the most damning criticisms that GMD spokesmen could think to hurl at party organizations was that they were acting like the old county assemblies.[4] County assemblies, which were elective self-government bodies in the era before GMD rule began in 1927, had been key mechanisms through which county elites had exercised their authority. Thus, when GMD leaders looked back on those institutions with venom and derision, they were expressing their distaste for older, non-Guomindang elites and their management of local affairs.

Local Elites Before 1927: Description and Typology

In this study the term "local elites" subsumes two largely, but not completely, overlapping groupings. First, it includes local political leaders—individuals who exercised power at the county level or below.[5] Second, it also embraces local economic elites—that is, the owners and managers of relatively large local business ventures, whether landed, industrial, or commercial. For the most part, they were the wealthy.[6] I do not presume any necessary correspondence between wealth and political power, though wealth was a very important factor in determining influence in the Republican era.[7] I am especially interested in the relations between the new GMD counterelite, which self-consciously styled itself as "modernizing," and the networks of local power that predated that group.

Certainly the gentry—holders of examination or purchased degrees conferred by the imperial government—were a chief component of local elites in the Qing and early Republican periods. When analysing these elites, upper gentry (holders of the *jinshi, juren*, and *gongsheng* degrees) can be distinguished from the lower gentry (*shengyuan* and *jiansheng*).[8] The position of the gentry in the localities was so commanding that scholars could say, not so long ago, that the "gentry *were* the local elite . . . ."[9] However, it is now clear that in late Qing and early Republican eras, nongentry also exercised local power.[10] The prominence of both gentry and nongentry was displayed in the composition of an assortment of institutions in Jiangsu's farflung communities.

Government-sponsored Institutions

Although my concept of local elites generally excludes bureaucratic officials, it includes leaders, and in some cases mere members, of an array of "government-sponsored institutions" that predated GMD rule.[11] On the eve of the Guomindang takeover of Jiangsu in 1927, these organizations included the local self-government bodies and professional associations (*fatuan*).

China's system of local self-government had first emerged as part of the whirlwind of reforms the Qing court embraced in its waning years. In the late 1890s and the first decade of the twentieth century, a variety of visions of self-government had caught the attention of Chinese reformers inside and outside of the halls of government. Varied and sometimes contradictory Western European notions of self-government competed with, and were at times combined with, more familiar Chinese statecraft conceptions of local initiative. Finally, however, the Qing Ministry of Interior, which came to dominate the framing of the regulations for local self-government in China, founded the dynasty's new enactments following Japanese models, which were in turn based on German models.[12] The German-inspired Japanese system had been designed to preserve the prerogatives of the Japanese emperor and the central bureaucracy, while putting into the hands of local communities matters of exclusively local interest; these were to be managed through election of local assemblymen.[13] Since returned students from Japan who worked in the Ministry of Interior helped draft the Chinese laws on local self-government, it is little wonder that those laws followed the Japanese model.[14]

The dynastic leaders had hoped that the 1909 legislation establishing local assemblies would, together with promises for higher-level assemblies and a constitution, take the wind out of the sails of constitutionalists and revolutionaries alike. The Qing court believed the new self-government bodies would bolster central authority at the expense of local elite autonomy "by incorporating local elite leadership into officially-sponsored (and, therefore, controlled) councils and assemblies."[15] However, these new bodies gave institutional recognition and support to the hitherto informal status of local elites, very likely augmenting those elites' influence and stature in their communities.[16]

After the establishment of the Republic in 1912, the local self-government apparatus underwent many changes. In fact, President Yuan Shikai abolished all assemblies in 1914 in reaction to the so-called "Second Revolution" aimed at toppling him. Although Jiangsu elected a new provincial assembly in 1917, county and subcounty asssemblies did not reappear for nearly a decade; thus, local elites had to revert to informal channels and professional organizations as frameworks for their activities.[17] In some parts of the Lower Yangzi core, the area of the province where local elites and government had become most interdependent, county elites' prominent public role was perpetuated in frequent formal conferences between those elites and government administrators.[18]

In response both to agitation by local elites for a greater voice in local affairs and to legislation by the National Government in Beijing providing for reestablishment of self-government, the Jiangsu provincial government in 1923 called local assemblies back into existence. Although some counties did not hold elections until 1924 (and certain localities never saw subcounty assemblies), many of Jiangsu's local elites again exercised power through assemblies. County assemblies (*yishihui*), containing on average twenty to thirty members, were chosen by a tiny electorate, which was kept small by tax qualifications. Each county assembly in turn chose half of the members of an executive council (*canshihui*) that served as an advisory body to the county magistrate. The magistrate chose the other half of the executive council's members, and he also served as the chairman of the council.[19]

The regulations that governed Jiangsu's county assemblies granted them greater legal authority than local assemblies in some other provinces enjoyed. Whereas assemblies in many provinces in the early 1910s had only the power to make suggestions that magistrates could easily ignore, Jiangsu's county assemblies had the statutory power to make binding decisions on public matters. Jiangsu's magistrates did not have unilateral veto power over assembly decisions. According to the law, a magistrate had to gain approval of the provincial assembly in order to set aside a decision of the county assembly.[20]

County assemblies not only had a hand in levying taxes and establishing local government budgets, but they also nominated local elites to posts on committees that handled charities, water control projects, and schools. They apparently had at least some power to block unwanted new exactions proposed by county magistrates. In addition, county assemblies settled disputes between institutions at the subcounty level and pronounced policy on a host of other problems.[21] In short, through the assemblies, local elites exerted a considerable measure of control over county affairs.

Below the county level, township (*xiang*) and municipal township (*shi*) assemblies echoed the form of their county-level counterparts. In some counties, especially those in the Lower Yangzi zone, these bodies elected unsalaried managers (*xiangdong* and *shidong*) and management committees (*dongshihui*) to handle day-to-day transactions.[22] In certain other localities, most notably those in the North China zone, township managers seem to have been appointed by county magistrates.[23] Some municipal townships were further subdivided into units overseen by managers (*dongshi*), though that title was sometimes applied to the aforementioned township-level personnel.[24]

The members of the provincial and national assemblies should also be considered county-level elites. Only the most prominent individuals on a local scene could hope to be elected to these bodies. In fact, laws restricted the franchise in provincial assembly elections much more severely than local assembly contests. Steep property-holding requirements and educational qualifications barred all but a tiny group (in 1909, 0.4 percent of the population) from voting for provincial assemblymen. While it might be tempting to exclude holders of provincial assembly seats from consideration as "local elites" because provincial assemblies focused on provincial and national issues, in fact these representatives spent much of their time in their home communities. Typically they could exert very marked influence over local affairs.[25]

As for county assembly members and their social background, very spotty data suggest that a large, but declining, percentage of them held lower examination degrees or purchased degrees from the Qing era. In Chuansha (in the Lower Yangzi core), the locality for which we have the most complete data on lower degree-holders, the percentage of county assemblymen holding earned or purchased degrees declined from 45 percent in 1910 to 23 percent in 1923.[26] This is not surprising, since degrees could not have been obtained after the 1905 abolition of the civil service examination system.

One of the chief causes for the declining number of degree-holders in the Chuansha assembly was the death of several prominent gentry in the 1910s and 1920s. Indications are that most county assemblymen were fifty years old or more. Many seem to have been in their sixties and seventies in the 1920s, though our spotty information probably exaggerates their ages.[27] Although available data do not prove that assembly elites constituted a gerontocracy, they do suggest that there was a profound generational difference between these established elites and the leaders of the various county GMD headquarters in the 1920s, most of whom ranged in age from their teens to their late twenties.[28]

Although there is less information available on subcounty assemblies in Jiangsu than for county-level bodies, it describes similar trends. For example, lower gentry membership in the Yuepu Township Assembly (in Baoshan County in the Lower Yangzi core) fell from 42 percent in 1909 to 14 percent in 1924.[29] However, not all townships displayed such a steady decline. For example, the percentage of seats in the Changren Township Assembly (Chuansha County, Lower Yangzi core) held by lower gentry fluctuated from 42 percent in 1909 to 14 percent in 1913, to 20 percent in 1924.[30] And a few townships, like Hengsha (in Chuansha County) seem never to have included any gentry members in their assemblies.[31] Ages of these township assemblymen roughly parallel those of the county assemblymen described above.

Since large gaps exist in the biographical data on assemblymen, the figures cited above may understate gentry control of these bodies. Nonetheless, the social genesis of most assemblymen who appear to have been nondegree-holders must be found elsewhere. Although a sprinkling of those without examination degrees were doctors, lawyers, educators, and military men, far and away the majority of them seem to have hailed from mercantile roots. This is especially true for the Lower Yangzi core area of Jiangsu where "gentry merchants," as well as some merchants who did not choose to pose as gentry, ruled the roost.[32]

In addition to the age differential that defined the generational distance between GMD activists and county elites, changes that had been occurring in the educational system in the early twentieth century divided the two groups. Whereas most of Jiangsu's GMD members had been educated in normal, middle, or specialized schools, relatively few assembly members received a comparable modern, Western-style, middle-level education.³³ In fact, such schools proliferated only after most of these elites were past adolescence and beyond the typical age of formal schooling. Except for occasional remarks to the effect that a particular person "studied hard" or the like, gazetteers are often silent about the education of assembly elites, leading one to the conclusion that most of these persons had followed the conventional educational route of the past by studying in private academies or with tutors. Something as new or unusual as modern schooling probably would have been noted by the biographers.

Despite the visibility of the township and municipal township assemblies and the local prominence of their personnel, in some localities, especially in the North China zone, managers at the subcounty level—*xiangdong*, *shidong* and *dongshi*—had greater authority over the day-to-day administration of township affairs. They were the persons who most often had to respond to demands by the provincial or county government for funds or other military provisions, and they were also the persons most often consulted by county magistrates. To be sure, magistrates also sought advice and aid from local elites who held no formal public position; they sometimes presided over so-called "gentry conferences," the purpose of which was to ascertain elite opinion on local questions and obtain elites' support. However, the managerial stratum of local elites was the linchpin of the administrative system at the township level in many counties. As one foreign observer explained the situation in Jiangsu's North China zone:

> There was a marked development of the power of the dungsih [*dongshi*] under tuchun [*dujun*, that is, "warlord"] administration. The reasons were easy to see, the power of the civil magistrates was continually on the wane [sic]. The magistrate could rarely get out to the country districts. As the military leaders increased in power they found it easier to make their levies for hay, carts, fuel, etc., direct [sic] upon the dungsih instead of going via the magistrates [sic] office as in former days—the dungsih was quick to take advantage of the change and promptly allied himself to the military authority. . . . His powers grew rapidly; he more often than not had a strong guard of soldiers around his own home and village. . . . Abuses did not wait to creep in but ran in full grown and we had the spectacle of the dungsih acting with despotic power. If a thief was caught and brought before him, the dungsih very promptly had him beheaded, and if ever accused of

overreaching his authority, he could plead that he acted in the public interest.[34]

Professional Associations

Many types of local organizations fell under the rubric of *fatuan*, which is commonly translated as "professional associations": chambers of commerce, agricultural associations, educational associations, lawyers' associations, landholders' associations, and others.[35] Like the local self-government system, most of these organizations had been established in the early twentieth century as a part of the late Qing reforms.[36] The chambers of commerce were generally the most powerful of these associations. Like all *fatuan*, the chambers had a dual character. On the one hand, they were able to speak to the government in the name of the local mercantile community, while on the other, the government relied on them as instruments of control over chamber members.[37] In a sense, membership in the county chamber was not entirely voluntary, because any merchant who did not join it had to apply to it for a license proving he had paid all applicable local business fees.[38] By 1911, most county seats in Jiangsu had a chamber of commerce, and in some cases, surrounding market towns established chambers as branches of the county-level body, though some market towns had independent chambers. Market towns' chambers themselves sometimes had branches in lesser market towns, an arrangement that reflected in institutional form the nested, hierarchical marketing system of rural China described by G. William Skinner.[39]

Officers of the chambers of commerce were important leaders in their communities.[40] Since county governments and local assemblies often asked the chambers to assume the financial burden for local projects of various kinds, the chambers and their leaders exercised a kind of "power of the purse," selectively accepting or rejecting such requests.[41] Chambers of commerce frequently were involved in decisions about capital improvements, public works, and local defense, as well as in the management of efforts in these realms.[42] In a few counties, the chambers had their own militia to maintain local order and defend merchant interests.[43] In essence, their power helped to propel certain merchants into the positions of influence that they enjoyed in the 1910s and 1920s. The chambers' provision of military funds for the warlord government in 1927 when it was fighting the Northern Expeditionary armies of the GMD turned some Nationalists against the local elites who ran these bodies.[44] The leadership of chambers of commerce, agricultural associations, local assemblies, and other government-sponsored elite organizations frequently overlapped, often giving the appearance of interlocking directorates.[45] The practice of some local elites holding several key posts in multiple organizations effectively reduced the number of prominent positions in government-sponsored organizations that other individuals could fill. It gave the local oligarchies the appearance of narrow, closed corporations. Resentment at the lack of mobility into the ranks of the powerful helped the Guomindang recruit forces for its revolution in the 1920s.

Unofficial Elites

Certainly not all influential persons held offices in the local self-government system, professional associations, or other officially sponsored bodies. In fact, many local elites exercised their power through private channels. This includes people like Suqian County's Shi Shanglin who, though he held no formal office, was said to have been able to "solve a local dispute, whatever its nature, with a single word."[46] In other words, some elites exercised power based more on networks of personal connections than upon formal organizational structures.

However, probably the most powerful unofficial elites on the county and township levels were those who could commandeer organizations to support their political and economic ventures. One traditional private institution that has received a good deal of attention by anthropologists is the lineage, a common descent group that held property.[47] Although lineages were found in all parts of the province, they were most powerful in the Lower Yangzi core area where some counties contained lineage holdings of around 100,000 *mu*.[48] There were, however, some lineages in the North China area of Jiangsu that were strong enough to propel some of their leaders into important township-level positions, as well as to fashion sizable local militia merely by mobilizing the lineages' own people.[49] Unfortunately, however, I have uncovered little if any information on the lineage connections of most local elites with whom the GMD was interacting in the 1920s and 1930s.

Militia were among the most potent of local organizations. Their growth in the late Qing and early Republican periods had facilitated the growth of local elites' power vis-a-vis the state. In fact, in many cases it was the very weakness of the state that had called forth these organizations in the first place. And although some militia were merely unofficial, ad hoc responses to disorder, most militia in the Lower Yangzi core area of the province were established and managed with the direct participation of the county government, local self-government organs, or other officially recognized elite institutions such as chambers of commerce.[50] Like many other institutions and practices, they are evidence of the blurring of public and private roles in the early Republic in the Lower Yangzi core area.[51]

However, though some militia in the North China area of Jiangsu also enjoyed government sponsorship or formal recognition, multitudes of militia there were privately established, managed, and funded; the county government played no role in the establishment of these private armed forces, except through its abdication of responsibility for maintaining order in wide areas of the northern countryside.[52] Banditry ravaged much of the North China area of Jiangsu, a fact which helps account for the growth of private military power to counter it.

Militia leaders in this area usually had substantial landholdings, and a few owned as much as 10,000 *mu* or more. They often lived in earthen castles inside stockades, some of which surrounded whole communities, and frequently their militia were composed of their tenants who lived in the vicinity of the fort. Although in the 1910s and 1920s, some militia leaders received government appointments as township managers, there was less interaction and cooperation between township elites and the county government in the North China zone than in the Lower Yangzi area. The government was simply less of a force in the relatively uncommercialized north than it was in the Lower Yangzi core, where the complexities of commerce and collection of rent for absentee landlords had not only expanded the public sphere, but had also forced county elites and the government to cooperate in mutually supportive ventures. Militia heads in the North China zone of Jiangsu were freer to use their corps autonomously to resolve local disputes, fight elites from neighboring communities, punish unruly tenants, and resist government exactions, than were the more government-integrated elites of the Lower Yangzi core.[53]

Local religious institutions provided a private organizational base for another genre of local elites. Religious professionals—monks, priests, and others—were not widely accorded prestige in China, and certainly not all of them were powerful. However, many of them were able to exert considerable power in local politics by virtue of their organizational ability, their demagogic prowess, or the wealth at their disposal. The strength and nature of religious bodies, not to mention religious belief, varied widely from county to county. However, there was no detectable systematic relationship between macroregion or economic zone and the prevalence of religious professionals or fervent religious belief.[54] Some local temples had large landholdings, greatly augmenting the resources that ambitious local religious leaders could employ to exert their power, with the largest temple landholdings being more common in the North China zone than in the Lower Yangzi area.[55] One investigator described a certain temple in Suqian County (North China zone) as follows:

> [The temple is] only nominally a religious institution; actually it is an economic and political power by itself. Together with five temples subordinate to it, the total temple land has reached 200,000 *mow* [*mu*], which would equal almost one-half of a small . . . [county] in southern Jiangsu. The chief monks who have practical monopoly of this land are busily engaged in rent collecting and . . . usury. They maintain big families, including many concubines, and their dwelling places are far grander than the Magistrate's bureau. They have armed Guards with rifles and big knives and their tenants are often conscripted for labor service. . . . Many of their tenants are utterly dependent upon them . . . and the monk landlords can easily organize them to oppose the local government if need be.[56]

Economic Elites

Wealth is a relative thing. The amount of wealth qualifying a person to be seen as "rich" depended in part on his community's position in the hierarchy of central places. Someone seen as fabulously wealthy in a dusty North China village might have qualified as only "rather well-to-do" if he had lived in a nearby market town, or as the smallest of fry if he had resided in a county seat or a regional metropolis.[57]

The top of the pyramid of wealth in Jiangsu, at least in the Lower Yangzi core, was occupied by the most successful merchants, industrialists, financiers and their families. We have already seen the key positions they held there at the township and, especially, the county level in the early Republic. Martin Yang has argued that the reason merchants enjoyed increased prestige and political power in this era was that they tended more and more to have received modern, specialized education and to organize their businesses in a modern way, two traits that the public supposedly respected.[58] However, available gazetteers from Jiangsu counties do not support the view that most merchants of local prominence in the 1910s through the 1930s had modern educations. Of the thirty-five late Qing and early Republican era merchants whose biographies appear in the Chuansha gazetteer (Lower Yangzi core), only four are unambiguously listed as having attended new-style schools.[59]

Merchants were a heterogeneous lot which included such varied sorts as silk cocoon merchants, restauranteurs, peddlers, opium smugglers, bankers, rice dealers, bus company owners, pawnshop owners, pig bristle exporters, importers of foreign goods, butchers, brokers, and electric utility entrepreneurs. Struggling small merchants, such as peddlers, could not in any sense be considered economic elites. And the interests of merchants, even those in similar lines of business, could diverge. For example, as Richard Bush has demonstrated, large-scale Chinese cotton mill owners favored easy importation of American raw cotton because its long fibers were essential to the fine yarn they produced. In contrast, small-scale mills used only short staple domestic fibers, and the owners of these mills had no interest in relaxed importation terms for cotton.[60]

Further complicating the picture, families often held mixed investment portfolios, which meant they did not necessarily define their interests in terms of only one sort of business or investment. And although we might tend to think of merchants and landlords as distinct types, perhaps 55 percent of the landlords in the Lower Yangzi core had commercial or industrial operations in addition to their land.[61] One of the favored forms of investments for landlords was pawnshops and other, more private types of money-lending. Eighty percent of the capital invested in Rugao County's eleven pawnshops had come from landlords, while 78 percent of the capital of Changshu's twenty pawnshops had been underwritten by landlords. In more intensely commercialized parts of the Lower Yangzi core, such as Wuxi and Songjiang, merchants provided most of the capital for pawnshops.[62]

At the bottom of the scale of central places, the village had as its economic elites a cast of characters that might surprise anyone familiar with the vast body of literature that paints the landlord as the king of the village. To be sure, land was one of the most conspicuous sorts of wealth a villager could hold; in rural China substantial landholding was one of the most obvious indicators of a person's status as an economic elite. Estimates of the minimum amount of land that would qualify a family in a North China village as wealthy vary from thirty to two hundred *mu*;

households in the thirty to fifty *mu* range were called only "comparatively wealthy."[63] But not all economic elites at the village level were landlords. In fact, a great many villages in the North China area of Jiangsu lacked any resident landlord. Philip Huang has argued that in the part of North China he studied, most village elites were actually "managerial farmers"— what others might call rich peasants.[64] (The distinction here is between "landlords," who made most of their income from *renting out* their land, and "rich peasants," who directly *managed the farming of their land* and used hired laborers to work it.) The same seems to have been true in some parts of northern Jiangsu.[65]

However, a second pattern common throughout the large North China area had landlords as resident village elites. We read, for example, about the village of Duanzhuang in Tongshan County, which had three moderate-scale landlord families: one held 400 *mu*, while the other two had 200 *mu* each.[66] In addition, the great militia lords of the North China area of Jiangsu seem usually to have been middle- and large-scale landlords resident in rural areas. Whether they lived in villages or in market towns at the center of a cluster of villages in which their holdings were scattered—and both patterns seem to have been common—they were able to use their armed forces to compel rent payment by their tenants.[67] Although a few sources refer to landlords in the North China zone resorting to government help to pressure tenants to pay rent, by and large these elites seem to have been far less reliant on the county government, and far more independent than elites in the Lower Yangzi core.

Furthermore, in the environment of the relatively isolated, backwater North China area, the resident landlords enjoyed a high degree of social deference from their tenants. We are told, for example, that tenants there were enjoined by custom from sitting or walking with their landlord. The gazetteer for Shuyang County reports that when the tenant visited the landlord's home, he was to squat at the front door on the ground with his knees to his sternum and his buttocks trailing behind his feet; in this submissive pose he had to look upward to respond to the landlord's queries because the landlord usually perched on a high stool or chair. The landlord in the north was also customarily able to demand unpaid labor service from his tenants.[68] It is no wonder that some have characterized the relations between landlords and tenants in some parts of the North China area as "feudal."[69] This contrasted with the Lower Yangzi core where the impersonal operation of the market had broken down many of the bonds of social deference.

In addition to the resident landlord households, the coastal portion of Jiangsu north of the Yangzi had a new genre of powerful landlord institutions: salt-land reclamation companies. The famous Qing and early Republican official Zhang Jian formed the first of these firms in 1901; by the 1920s between forty and fifty of them were operating from Nantong to Lianshui.[70] In other words, these companies operated in a zone that included the coastal portions of both the North China and the Lower Yangzi regions north of the Yangzi. For centuries, sand deposits had been forming new land along the eastern shores of this traditional salt production area. As the coast pushed eastward, many fields came to be located too far from the sea for economical evaporation of the sea water into salt. Salt-land reclamation companies purchased these wastelands in order to convert them to agricultural use, primarily cotton production.[71] The companies came to own gigantic tracts of land; altogether, they may have held as many as 15 million *mu*, though the figure may have been as low as 5 million *mu*. One estimate is that the companies owned fully 30 percent of all the land in the counties in which they operated.[72] Like certain other large commercial ventures in Jiangsu's North China and Lower Yangzi peripheral areas, many of these companies were dominated by elites from the Lower Yangzi core. For example, Zhang Jian and a number of wealthy persons from his native Nantong County founded and funded a high portion of the companies.[73]

The companies rented the lands out to over 50,000 tenant families.[74] Although originally the companies were responsible for collecting the rents and overseeing the tenants, by the 1910s a movement began for outright division of the lands among the stockholders, a process that was well advanced by the 1930s. As one observer put it, "What began as an effort toward collective ownership . . . resulted in private property on a huge scale."[75] And because a very few families had owned the bulk of the stock in the companies, far and away the greater part of the land after division was left in the hands of a minuscule number of very large-scale landlords. For example, when just one of these companies was divided in the 1930s, four families received on average more than 27,400 *mu* each, while some 451 families constituting over 75 percent of the stockholders received on average 35.2 *mu*.[76] Despite the new trend toward division of lands, most of the companies remained intact in the 1920s and 1930s.

In counties of the Lower Yangzi core which lay south of the Yangzi, we find few signs of "rich peasant" or "managerial farmer" elites, and although a high percentage of the villagers were tenants, large-scale landlords seem to have rarely resided in villages. In this area most landlords with moderate or large holdings lived in market towns or, even more commonly, in one of the county seats or in the city of Shanghai. One 1922 study found that 69.6 percent of the large-scale landlords in Kunshan County lived in urban areas, while 67.3 percent of those with medium-sized holdings lived in towns and cities; even 61.4 percent of the landlords with relatively small holdings were based in urban areas.[77] Another study revealed that landlord families constituted a significant percentage of the population in several Lower Yangzi core cities: Eight percent of the households in Suzhou were listed as landlords, as were 18 percent of those in the Changshu county seat, and 30 percent of those in the Wujiang county seat.[78] Absentee landlordism was the rule in most of Jiangsu's Lower Yangzi core, though there were some resident landlords with large holdings. Most villages there that have been studied—and this is admittedly a small sample—had no residents who would have been considered rich solely on the basis of their landholdings.[79]

In the mid-nineteenth century, urban-dwelling landlords, primarily in the Lower Yangzi core, devised a new institution, the bursary (*zuzhan*), to manage their far-flung land holdings.[80] Ever since the Yongzheng period, Qing law had officially recognized the landlords' right to rent payment, but legal support for landlords reached its most concrete form in government help for bursary rent collection.[81] A bursary's staff, which typically was responsible for managing the lands of several landlords, could depend upon government runners, land tax agents, and police to help press tenants for rent. In a number of Lower Yangzi counties the local government routinely jailed recalcitrant tenants and members of their families. The merging of public and private functions and the interconnection between elites and local government had gone so far in the Lower Yangzi core that bursary agents themselves kept on hand blank arrest forms that could be filled out and signed, authorizing the incarceration of tenants. In essence, bursary agents enjoyed quasi-police powers. In contrast to the situation in the province's North China area where the landlord-tenant relationship was frequently a diffuse, personal one, in the Lower Yangzi core the growth of absentee landlordism and bursaries was transforming the landlord-tenant relationship into an impersonal, commercial one.

Cleavages Among Elites

Considering the tremendous variety of institutions through which local elites exerted their muscle, it should come as no surprise that those elites were far from unified in interest or viewpoint. Sometimes local politics pitted one institution against another, for example the county assembly against a local temple.[82] The fault lines that divided local elites depended upon which issues were most salient at a particular moment, and those concerns could cut along several different planes.

In some cases, conflict took the form of fights between differing economic interests. For example, in the early- to mid-1920s, Wuxi silk cocoon merchants, via their cocoon bureaus, ably defended themselves against provincial attempts to impose new taxes on them as well as against silk weavers' attempts to saddle them with new regulations.[83] In other instances, conflict took the form of a feud, pitting one locality against another.[84] However, in certain cases, what looked like a feud was, in fact, a battle between different strata of local elites—for example, an urban-rural dispute or a fight between elites based in the county seat and those in the surrounding and sometimes not-so-rural market towns. Some commentators have argued that bad feelings between county and township elites were very common. One example of just such a situation was the long-standing political battle between Haizhou County elites and elites in that county's Southeastern Township. This conflict eventually resulted in the dismembering of the county in the late Qing, and creation of Donghai County (dominated by the old Haizhou elites) and Guanyun County (the bailiwick of the disgruntled township elites). One issue that had divided the two groups was the county elites' embargo of grain to outlying market towns during a flood-induced famine in 1904. Another was the question of which group would control the Haizhou County Assembly, established around 1908. Surprisingly, the township elites won that one. The dispute escalated when the county elites persuaded the county government to extract forced contributions to a flood relief fund from the township elites, who were much less well-to-do than the county elites. Ultimately the township elites successfully petitioned the province for the division of the county.[85]

Far and away the most common sort of dispute was factional. Competition for positions of power, such as those held by assemblymen, township managers, or chairmen of local educational associations, often boiled over into factional battles.[86] Social scientists have defined factions as noncorporate groups that engage in political conflict, the members being recruited on a variety of principles.[87] Many observers have emphasized the dyadic nature of factional construction. They see the building blocks of factions in the ties between two individuals who exchange favors and each of whom can expect the support of the other.[88] In this view, factions are chains of dyadic patron-client ties in which the key concern to an individual is his relation to another individual rather than his membership in the group, his embracing of group interests, or his adherence to group standards. However, one scholar who has studied Chinese factions has argued that "factions are sometimes more than the sum of the leaders' dyadic ties." Joseph Bosco, in his work on factions in Taiwan, has suggested that just as in physics anyone who wishes fully to explain the properties of light must consider it as both a wave and a particle, so one must, when seeking to understand factions in some Chinese contexts, view those entities as both chains of dyads and as groups. He notes that contrary to the prediction of those who view factions as nothing more than chains of dyads, factions in Taiwan outlive their leaders. In Jiangsu, factions also sometimes behaved as groups, though a great deal—perhaps most—of the time they appeared as chains of dyadic relations.[89]

Local factions were built on networks of personal "connections" (*guanxi*). As Andrew Nathan argues in one of his early works, *guanxi* are extremely important in Chinese culture; they are "rooted in the conception of the social order (*jigang*)," wherein each kind of relationship "involve[s] a distinct set of appropriate mutual behaviors, rights and duties."[90] Nathan lists types of personal connections upon which Republican-era factions were constructed: lineage, family friendship of former generations, locality, teacher-student, bureaucratic superior-subordinate, schoolmate, bureaucratic colleague, in-law, and sworn brotherhood.[91] In Republican China, lineage (or kinship) was generally traced through the male line, but Bruce Jacobs suggests that it is not enough to consider agnatic kinship as the basis for factional construction; affinal kin also provided building blocks for fabrication of factions. As Jacobs explains, this additional kinship network included "(1) the father's sister's husband's family . . . , (2) the father's wife's family, (3) the son's wife's family, and (4) the daughter's husband's family."[92] One might add to this list the natal family of the wife of the individual in question.

Jacobs provides a textured analysis of various kinds of *guanxi*, ranking them according to their importance in the formation of factions in post-WWII Taiwan. He also argues that particular kinds of *guanxi* have been most associated with factions at a certain administrative level. For example, he finds that teacher-student *guanxi*, though significant at the county level and above, was of little importance in villages and townships in which few people had received any education above the elementary level.[93] It is well to keep in mind, however, that Chinese culture is not static. Not only might the relative importance of different sorts of *guanxi* vary by administrative level and locality, but the very nature of *guanxi* and its strength can undergo transformations. Mayfair Mei-hui Yang has argued that *guanxi* virtually disappeared in urban China in the early 1950s, only to reappear in a new configuration in the late 1950s or 1960s. This new version of *guanxi*, she believes, took a particular form in reaction to the massive expansion of state controls (via the centrally planned economy) and the intense pressure on personal relationships created by the Cultural Revolution.[94] In Republican-era Jiangsu, teacher-student, schoolmate, and locality-based connections dominated factional construction at the county level.[95]

Factionalism permeates even the vocabulary of many accounts of Chinese local politics. For example, the vile-sounding term "local bully and evil gentry" (*tuhao lieshen*), which frequently occurs in sources on local politics in the 1920s and 1930s, is sometimes little more than one faction's tarbrush depiction of a member of an opposing local elite faction.[96] This does not mean, of course, that a significant number of local elites did not *merit* such derogation by their abuse of power. In fact, most sources on rural China in the late Qing and early Republican period record significant numbers of local elites involved in abusive activities, running the gamut from pettifoggery, tax engrossment, and extortion, to the use of physical violence and murder.[97] However, while some have attempted to identify "local bullies and evil gentry" with some specific segment of the local elite (for example, "the remnant of the lower rural elite of imperial days"), the term was sometimes applied to enemies among the local elite, regardless of their morality, education, source of income, or rural or urban residence.[98] The only consistent characteristic that I can perceive among persons labeled as "local bullies and evil gentry" is that they wielded power on the local level; they were dependably some kind of local elite.[99]

Some observers have suggested that factionalism among local elites was more common in the early twentieth century than it had been in the nineteenth. Information is fragmentary, and there is no source that allows a uniform comparison of the frequency and severity of local factional strife over the decades. However, anecdotal accounts do suggest an upsurge in factional schisms by the first and second decades of the twentieth century.[100] This observation fits nicely with the view of some social scientists that *guanxi* and factionalism are not unchanging and unique components of a static Chinese culture, but rather are best understood as phenomena that can be found in many societies and are largely dependent on the institutional contexts that motivate human behavior.[101]

Here we can only speculate why factional conflict among local elites may have grown in the early twentieth century, because facts about the origins of factions of that vintage are hard to come by. One plausible explanation for the posited increase is that the end of the civil service exam system in 1905 eliminated a qualifying bar to participation of many individuals in the competition for positions of political leadership, thus setting off a free-for-all among the ambitious. Members of the suddenly increased pool of aspirants for local positions found it necessary to mobilize acquaintances to impress magistrates who could make appointments to local offices. Such mobilization of friends and kin could also be used to piece together an electoral victory in the local self-government system.

Roger Thompson has posited that factionalism among local elites in the 1910s was largely the result of the local self-government laws of 1909, which he sees as badly suited to the Chinese rural situation. He contends that the Qing local self-government system was insufficiently corporatist in approach, and was thus inappropriate in China, where elites had seen themselves as part of a functionally defined "circle" (*jie*). In other words, educators were part of educational circles, businessmen belonged to merchant circles, and so forth. However, the self-government assemblies were not organized around such occupational groups. Although Thompson's book is a sophisticated analysis of the rise of local self-government institutions in China, his emphasis on the lack of corporatism in the self-government system as the reason for the rise of local factionalism seems overdone. Thompson does not demonstrate that a more corporatistic design for the local self-government system would have prevented factional schisms among local elites, and it is not obvious by what mechanism or logic corporatism would have precluded factional conflict. Thompson believes that the Qing local self-government system encouraged local elites to compete with each other for the attention and support of higher bureaucratic organs.[102] There is no conspicuous reason why a corporatistically arranged system could not have been subject to the same shortcoming.[103] In fact, we will see later that the GMD's adoption around 1930 of a corporatistically arranged set of organizations for merchants itself occasioned factional battles among merchants in some counties.

Still, the Qing government's adoption of the local self-government system may have been a prime factor in the factionalization of the local political area. Provincial and national political figures needed local backers who could generate electoral support so that allies would control provincial and national assemblies. Upper-level politicians recruited to their side local elites and encouraged them to activate their networks of acquaintances.[104] Furthermore, individuals who had never held political positions on the local scene and who lacked connections with the county magistrate could, under the local self-government system, make a run for office if they could mobilize a large enough network of connections.

Beyond the local self-government system, the plethora of other reforms decreed by the Qing government in the first decade of the twentieth century also framed and, to a degree, motivated factional friction. County magistrates and other administrators who chose to push reforms in education and other realms sometimes met resistance from local elites with a vested interest in the status quo. Qing and early Republican officials understandably sought allies from among local elites. This sort of situation, as well as those in which a group of local elites was more interested in change than was the government, fostered the growth of factionalism along lines that pitted more insistent reformists against those less interested in change. At the very least, the political environment in China motivated some local aspirants to pose as champions of progressive reform. In other words, China's predicament and the late Qing reform program provided justification and means for the "outs" on the local scene to challenge the "ins."

Education was one sphere which was particularly prone to factionalization. With the abandonment of the exam system, the Qing government called for establishment of secondary and primary schools modeled after Western educational institutions. Moreover, the new schools were patronage machines that headmasters, who hired and fired teachers, could turn to the political benefit of themselves and persons in their network of connections. As one memoir puts it, "To be a headmaster, one had to have the right kind of background; to be a teacher, one needed the requisite *guanxi*."[105] Both local elites who styled themselves educational "progressives" and those who fought change could find followers to attach to their personal networks. Stephen Averill has pointed out that "old learning cliques" and the "new learning cliques" that confronted them sometimes organized themselves into competing study societies—a rudimentary organizational form he sees as a stepping stone to the formation of political parties.[106]

This pattern in the late Qing and early Republic of groups styling themselves as progressive and pitting themselves against others they saw as resistant to necessary change is very similar to the lineup of forces that would appear in the 1920s, when activists of the reorganized Guomindang would pose as advocates of change against entrenched elites. Ironically, some of the elites the GMD would displace in the name of change had themselves earned their positions in the first decade of the twentieth century as the Young Turks of their own time. And to some degree, the Chinese Communists repeated the same process in the mid-twentieth century when they overturned the GMD. John Fitzgerald has focused on the *problematique* of "awakening China"; he describes one decade after another of national-level leaders in politics and literature who cast themselves in the role of "awakeners" of the Chinese masses to the concept of the Chinese nation and its imperatives.[107] Though accounts of conflict among local elites in the early twentieth century often put primacy on personal factors in the strife—for example, particularistic ties—the evidence also suggests that there were local versions of the evolution from one set of awakeners to another that Fitzgerald describes on the national level.

The Guomindang Counterelite

In the 1920s Jiangsu's county- and township-level elites faced a new enemy: a newly reorganized and reinvigorated Guomindang. The GMD's reorganization, which took place in 1923 and 1924, recast that party along the lines of the Russian Communist Party. This reconstitution was marked by the inclusion of Communists into the GMD and adoption of a propaganda line that castigated foreign imperialists as well as the warlords who ruled most of China. That propaganda line also let it be known that "organizations and individuals" that had "sold out the country and deceived the people because of loyalty to the imperialists and warlords" would lose their power and freedom under the new Guomindang.[108] Since all of the government-sponsored organizations manned by Jiangsu's established local elites appeared, in a sense, to be part of the warlord regime that controlled the province, those elites might reasonably have expected to become targets of the refurbished Guomindang. In fact, the party began to attract a phalanx of new recruits who itched to dispossess incumbent local leaders of their positions and power. This new Guomindang counterelite, though by no means homogeneous in composition, shared certain social characteristics that set it apart from the existing county and township oligarchies.[109]

In Jiangsu the reorganized GMD and its revolutionary movement were vehicles of a cohort of youth with a middle-level, modern education fighting for power and position against entrenched but ideologically insecure county and township oligarchs. In essence, the "would-be" elites of the GMD were using the party as a weapon in their "fight for the rice bowl." These young party members, although concerned about improving their political, social, and economic standing, were not completely self-serving. They were genuinely disturbed about the inability and apparent indisposition of incumbent Chinese leadership to unite the nation and protect it from imperialist depredations. Furthermore, many of the youthful party members were distressed by a host of domestic social ills that they felt were aggravated and perpetuated by the warlord-dominated governments and, as these youth saw it, the selfish and closed oligarchies that controlled Jiangsu.

Guomindang members after the reorganization could be characterized as mostly young, ambitious, and, in some measure, products of modern, middle-level schools. In the early 1920s, northern Jiangsu GMD leader Gu Ziyang and his associates in Xuzhou—men who would be responsible for building the Guomindang in many of the counties in northern Jiangsu—made a conscious decision to abandon the party's older efforts to press bandits into revolutionary service. Instead, Gu writes that they concentrated on bringing young students and school teachers into the party.[110] Gu's recruitment strategy was representative of the approach the party adopted throughout Jiangsu. GMD revolutionaries used schools as cover for their revolutionary activities. Although many universities and technical schools around Nanjing and Shanghai were used for revolutionary activities, the bulk of GMD membership outside those cities was associated in some way with normal and middle schools. Figures from 1929 suggest that at that time most of the Jiangsu GMD's members were between the ages of sixteen and thirty.[111]

Educational Level

Normal and middle schools were usually located in cities of some size, and most of the students in these schools hailed from more rural homes. These students, residing in dorms or other quarters in the city, kept in touch with friends and kin at home through letters and visits. After schooling was completed, graduates either went home or accepted teaching or other posts in locations lower in the scale of central places than the city in which they had received their middle-level education. Stephen Averill has pointed out that because of all this, the educational system constituted a "transmission line" through which "new ideological and organizational currents flowed from the cities to the county seats and market towns . . . ."[112]

We are fortunate to have party entrance and registration documents for members who joined the Songjiang County GMD in the period from February to June 1924. These sources reveal that of a group of 130 members, 26.4 percent were elementary or middle school teachers or principals, while another 18.6 percent were middle school students. The numerical sequence of the entrance and registration forms suggests that the original nucleus of the party organization consisted of teachers to an even greater degree than the figures above indicate, but that the county party soon branched out to include small merchants (17.8 percent), peasants (7.6 percent), and workers (7.6 percent). Overall, this admittedly small sample reveals that 43.4 percent of the members had attained middle-level educations, and information on another 20.9 percent is sufficiently ambiguous that they too may well have reached the normal or middle school level. Even this high percentage understates the role of middle schools and normal schools in the Jiangsu GMD, because the Songjiang County GMD, dominated by Communists, was apparently more active in recruiting peasants and workers than most other counties' GMD organizations.[113]

The lion's share of county-level party leadership positions were held by young men who had either recently graduated from middle-level schools or had started but not yet completed that schooling. For example, of the seven heads of departments in the Kunshan County GMD, five had graduated from normal school, while two had taken some normal school courses.[114] After 1927, the GMD membership continued to include persons with a secondary education; of the twelve leaders of the Feng County GMD on whom we have detailed information, seven had attained normal or middle school education, while two more had studied at the college level. Several of the Feng County leaders were teachers or principals in local schools, and because of their common interest in education, three of them in succession held the chairmanship of the county Office of Education for the ten years after the GMD rose to power.[115]

Economic Status

Beyond educational background, however, what does available data reveal about the economic and social standing of members and their families? Zhang Guotao (Chang Kuo-t'ao) ventured the opinion that "most KMT [GMD] members came from the ranks of middle class families . . . ."[116] Although there seems to be no small degree of truth to this view, a healthy slice of the GMD counterelite seems to have come from the upper end of the middle class. For example, one journalist noted that in 1927 between 80 and 90 percent of the members of the GMD in one Wuxi County market town were intellectuals from landlord families.[117] Robert North finds that most key Guomindang leaders were from the "upper or upper-middle class."[118]

The fact that a large percentage of GMD members in this period had completed or were pursuing middle school and normal school education tells us something about their families' economic standing. Thomas Curran has argued that most students at modern schools hailed from elite families. Middle schools, and even modern upper-primary schools, were concentrated in urban areas. Thus, students who lived outside these cities incurred for their families not only the cost of tuition and fees, but also significant room-and-board costs. Middle school tuition and fees were often particularly expensive, in some areas nearly equaling a typical peasant family's entire annual income.[119] Although some normal schools were tuition-free before the GMD swept to power, it took a certain amount of money to cover each student's room and board, not to mention the costs of books and supplies.[120] Even this small amount, two to ten *yuan* a month, was too much for landless peasants and most tenant farmers.[121] Of course, some students from less-than-well-to-do families garnered support from lineages or family acquaintances to underwrite their studies. Others held down part-time jobs.[122]

A late 1927 GMD Youth Department survey of the students at Huaiyin Middle School in Huaiyin County (North China zone) revealed that a plurality considered their families to be of "middle" economic standing in their villages or towns. Many of the answers were so vague that exact percentages cannot be given, but it is also clear that a significant minority of students, around a quarter of them, considered their families to be of low economic standing. A conservative estimate of the average annual income of the students' families based on the survey forms is 620 *yuan*. Using for comparison a report on income ranges in a county with similar economic circumstances, one can deduce that the economic ranking of the family of the average middle school student in Huaiyin County may have been above the sixty-eighth percentile when compared with all other families in the county.[123] Investigation documents on teachers at the school indicate that they fell into a similar economic bracket.[124]

The Songjiang County party entrance and registration documents also contain valuable information on the economic position of county party members' families. The average family property values and annual income were around 1,700 *yuan* and 340 *yuan* respectively, much lower than the averages for middle school students and teachers in the Huaiyin documents cited above. This annual income would place the average Songjiang GMD member's family below the fifty-third percentile when compared to other families in the county.[125] Apparently the figure was this low because the Songjiang party branched out to include quite a few peasants and workers. The income levels varied dramatically from one ward (*qu*) or precinct (*qu fenbu*) to another. The average figure for the original nucleus of the GMD organization in Songjiang (first ward, first precinct) was probably somewhat above the average for the county as a whole.[126]

Perhaps the best way of characterizing the economic standing of GMD members and their families is that employed by the Feng County leader who identified roughly half of the county party leaders after 1927 as members of the *xiaokang* class. *Xiaokang* translates as "of moderate means" or "well-to-do." One study applied the term to families of the sixty-sixth to ninety-ninth economic percentiles.[127] The rest of the Feng County leaders were split between those who came from poorer families—those who received financial aid to get through a tuition-free middle or normal school—and those whose families had considerable wealth.[128]

In comparison with the populace at large, most GMD activists were not particularly impecunious, but the economic status of many was insecure. Therefore, they were excluded from meaningful participation in a political system dominated by wealthy merchants, large landowners, and military leaders. In addition, elite status for youth and students in a local society that granted honor and status mainly to men of mature years was potential, rather than actual. The GMD revolutionary movement provided an opportunity for youth to gain positions of power and respect quickly, for people of moderate means (or better) to challenge the power monopoly of elites, and for teachers to attack a government that was often in arrears in paying their salaries because it placed higher value on military than educational expenditures. The GMD in its propaganda did not fail to play to these grievances, as when the Kunshan County GMD Congress in early 1927 berated the government for repeatedly decreasing teachers' salaries.[129]

There were, however, several variations on the pattern of alienated educators outlined above. For example, in Dantu (Zhenjiang) County the Guomindang, rather than starting in schools, began with the merging of the "Past and Future Weekly Lecture Society" (*Yiwei xingqi yanshuohui*) and the *New Zhenjiang News* (*Xin Zhenjiang bao*). Intellectuals and journalists from this association and newspaper had great difficulty branching out and attracting students and teachers. Their trouble stemmed from the close relationship between the government and educators in this county. The arrangement provided scores of students with government jobs and produced little of the frustration and insecurity in educational circles upon which the GMD in most localities fed.[130]

From 1924 to 1927 the Guomindang included both a left wing that favored cooperation with the Communist Party and a right wing that aimed to exclude all Communists from the GMD. The discussion above of the GMD's social composition applies to the pre-1927 leftists and the post-1927 party as a whole. The composition of the right wing of the GMD in pre-1927 Jiangsu differed somewhat from the model we have established.[131] The rightists depended far more on university and technical school professors and students than did the leftists. Nanjing's Jianye, Southeast, and Dajiang Universities apparently provided a sizable percentage of the members of Jiangsu's rightist GMD before 1927. Because only families with considerable wealth could afford to send their children to a university, the Jiangsu GMD's right-wing adherents were probably of higher economic standing than average members of the party.[132]

GMD members were self-proclaimed revolutionaries, and as such most of them held deep convictions about the proper political direction for the country. Their deepest aspirations for China were undoubtedly patriotic, but, at the same time, their own self- and family-centered desires to advance socially and economically conditioned their actions and policies. Using the party (and, later, factions within the party) as a mechanism for upward mobility, they attempted to do well for themselves as they did good for the country. Hostility to local political elites of the previous era was partially predicated on the certainty that if those elites were displaced, others—preferably the party members themselves—could take their places. And factionalism in the party was in part a fight for the right to be the ones to take the coveted places of the older elites.

The social status of party members was a relatively new one for China. Since civil service examinations no longer constituted the prime gate to elite positions, anyone with a little education and sufficient connections could aspire to elite status. So GMD members of moderate social standing and a middle-level educational could make their bid for remunerative positions of authority and prestige.

3

GMD FACTIONS AND LOCAL ELITES: THE EARLY PERIOD, 1924–1927

The roots of Guomindang rule in Jiangsu extend back into the pre-Northern Expeditionary period when the party was an illegal, underground, and revolutionary organization. During that period from 1924 to 1927, several warlords in succession ruled Jiangsu; some controlled only a part of the province, and others occupied parts of more than one province. Sun Chuanfang, the militarist who ruled most of the province from late 1925 through early 1927, also occupied Zhejiang, Anhui, Jiangxi, and Fujian. He became a prime target of the GMD and its anti-warlord Northern Expedition.

With the reorganization of the GMD and acceptance of Communists as members in 1924, the party grew rapidly. However, stiff competition for leadership positions and the inclusion of individuals of widely differing ideological molds soon split the reorganized Guomindang along factional lines. This division meant that the post-1927 GMD inherited two distinct approaches to society and two contradictory policies toward local elites. In order to get at the texture of party affairs in this formative period, it is necessary to examine factional infighting from 1924 to 1927 and consider the differing policies and attitudes toward local elites that the two factions in the Jiangsu GMD exhibited.

Guomindang Reorganization

In 1923 Sun Yat-sen, with the aid of Soviet advisor Michael Borodin and several GMD leaders, began considering a reorganization of the Guomindang on the Leninist model. The GMD's First National Congress met in Guangzhou (Canton) from January 20 to January 30, 1924, to debate and formalize the reorganization. The First National Congress adopted measures to broaden the social base of the party to include more peasants, workers, and youth. It also strengthened the party's central structure. The acceptance of Communists into the GMD, the adoption of a propaganda line that was militantly anti-imperialist and anti-warlord, and the establishment of a well-trained party army helped to reverse the party's previously dismal fortunes and attracted thousands of members.[1]

Soon after the Congress, the GMD Central Executive Committee (CEC) appointed Liu Yunzhao, Fan Xiongyi, Shen Jing, Chen Qubing, Zhang Shushi, Zhu Jixun, He Haiqiao, Qin Xiaolu, and Gu Ziyang to the Jiangsu Provincial Provisional Party Committee. The first meetings of the committee, held in the office of the Shanghai Executive Committee in Shanghai's French Concession, were poorly attended because college teaching duties prevented several members from being present. Zhu, Liu, and Shen had no other pressing matters to manage, so they were selected as a standing committee to handle daily party affairs.[2]

Zhu Jixun quickly emerged as one of the most active leaders in the reorganized GMD. He and close friend Hou Shaoqiu had entered the party in April 1923 after sending the Party General Affairs chairman an essay they had written "in support of GMD enthusiasm" and in which they had volunteered to "restore the party affairs of the GMD in Jiangsu." In response, the two received the introduction they needed to enter the party.[3] Zhu and Hou were both natives of Songjiang County near Shanghai and had studied together in the forestry department of Nanyang University.[4] Zhu's position as principal of Jingxian Girl's Middle School in Songjiang increased his status in the eyes of central GMD leaders and contributed to his success as a provincial party leader.[5] Zhu used the school as a cover for revolutionary activities. In addition, Zhu, Hou, and several other revolutionaries in Songjiang had earlier formed a group called the *Sanwu she* (literally, "three-five society") as a Marxist study society and revolutionary organization.[6]

Although Hou was a member of the Chinese Communist Party, Zhu's relations with the CCP are less clear.[7] The Songjiang *Sanwu she*'s Marxist ideological tone may be inferred from the accoutrements of its meeting hall. Hanging in the front of the room were three photographs: Marx in the middle, Lenin on the left, and Sun Yat-sen on the right.[8] Zhu's personal lifestyle reflected his avant-garde temperament; he cohabited with one of his female students, an enchanting beauty who was later immortalized in three of Mao Dun's novels.[9] The importance of the *Sanwu she* and other study societies in the genesis of the Jiangsu GMD is in accord with Stephen Averill's observation that study societies were stepping stones to formal political parties.[10]

Citing illness, Zhu withdrew from managing the school in the winter of 1923. He was in fact troubled by tuberculosis, which soon took his life, but his ailment did not dissuade him from making party-building his full-time job.[11] Seeking to expand the party and his own power base, he sent *Sanwu she* members and other acquaintances, Hou Shaoqiu being one of the most important of them, to surrounding counties to induct new people into the party and to establish new local GMD organizations. Several party branches in the Lower Yangzi core resulted from Zhu and Hou's work, including those in Kunshan, Jinshan, and Wu Counties. Both Zhu and Hou traveled extensively, speaking at party functions and fighting political battles within the GMD. In 1926 the GMD Second National Congress in Guangzhou rewarded Zhu for this work by electing him to the GMD Central Executive Committee.[12]

Gu Ziyang also played an important role in the newly reformed GMD. He had been a member of the GMD's revolutionary predecessor, the *Tongmenghui*. Born in 1875 and a native of Tongshan County (Xuzhou), Gu had received both an old-style and modern middle school education and had studied in Japan, where he first entered the revolutionary movement.[13] In 1912, immediately after the revolution overthrowing the Manchus, Gu had become a member of the Tongshan County Assembly and was active in the Guomindang branch in Xuzhou. After Yuan Shikai dissolved the county GMD, Gu taught in a local school and spread party propaganda. When Yuan announced his plan to make himself emperor, Gu participated in an unsuccessful military plot to oppose his control of the county. Gu later established and administered the Xuzhou Private Middle School and a newspaper, *Minsheng ribao* (People's Livelihood Daily), to disseminate party propaganda. By 1923 he had been appointed head of the GMD branch in Xuzhou, and he also assumed a leadership position in the provincial GMD headquarters.[14] Unlike most party members, as a former county assemblyman, he had once been part of the established power structure in his county; however, by the early 1920s he had not been among the power "in-group" in the county for several years. He was also much older than most members of the reorganized GMD.

After the reorganization, the Jiangsu Guomindang delegated much of the responsibility for party affairs in the North China zone to Gu. Since his school attracted students from several counties in northern Jiangsu,

Gu was able to spread his influence throughout the area. He introduced students and teachers into the GMD and sent them back to their home areas to start county party branches. He also traveled throughout northern Jiangsu, leaving in his wake a trail of new party organizations. In addition, Gu introduced some of his students to the GMD's Huangpu (Whampoa) Military Academy, and several of them graduated with Huangpu's first class.[15] In 1927 Gu would emerge as leader of one of the main factions in the Jiangsu party.

Factionalism

From 1924 to 1927 factionalism based primarily on differing attitudes toward Communism plagued Jiangsu's reorganized Guomindang. The left wing, led by Zhu Jixun and others, supported the GMD's alliance with the Chinese Communist Party and the acceptance of CCP members into the Guomindang, two fundamental elements of the party reorganization. GMD rightists were those who opposed Communism in general and, more specifically, decried dual party registration by Communists. However, ideological belief was only partially responsible for the rift in the party. The same cultural traits that caused local elites to divide along the fault lines of personal connections impelled factions within the GMD to recruit their members from factional leaders' and members' networks of personal connections, especially teacher-student and schoolmate connections. Thus, though GMD activists often vilified the established local elites, there were some ways in which the GMD counterelite resembled the very people they were attacking.

Zhu Jixun had a flair for factional infighting. In 1925 and 1926, when party rightists asserted that the GMD should not be divided into factions, Zhu, like other leftists and Communists, argued that only a leftist party could effect a true revolution because rightists feared "thorough" revolution.[16] From the beginning Zhu understood how to amass power in the reorganized GMD. Anticipating the election for the GMD Provincial Executive Committee that was to take place in 1925, Zhu and his subordinates organized county parties at a breakneck pace. While bringing individuals into the party, Zhu was building a network of patron-client ties. People entered the party only through introduction by two members, and a new member was likely to be somewhat beholden to his introducer, especially if that person helped to secure him a leadership position in a local party. This system of gaining membership in the party helped cultivate factionalism.

Although Zhu may have been the most effective factional leader in the Jiangsu GMD of this period, rightist Fan Xiongyi was probably the most intense. In the summer of 1923, Fan lived in Nanjing where, along with Zhang Shushi and about thirty others, he set up the People's Rule Study Society (*Minzhi xuehui*) at Jianye University. The membership of the society soon grew to over 160, and it was partly by virtue of this power base that Fan, Zhang, and another older and more prestigious member, Chen Qubing, were selected to be members of the Jiangsu Provincial Provisional Party Committee in 1924. Sun Yat-sen and the Jiangsu party committee asked Fan to set up a GMD organization for Nanjing. Fan obliged, but in contravention of official GMD policy, he instructed the Nanjing municipal party committee not to admit Communists "in order to prevent a disaster to the party in the future."[17] In response to this and other acts by Fan's group, the Jiangsu leftists—associates of Zhu Jixun—repeatedly advocated a stiffening of party discipline.[18]

Fan and some of the other members of the Jiangsu Provincial Provisional Party Committee felt that Zhu manipulated the GMD provincial party committee for the benefit of the Communist Party and himself. If so, Zhu must have been an expert at coalition politics, or he must have had winning ways, because according to rightist reckoning, he and Zhang Shushi were the only Communists on the committee.[19] Rightists charged that Zhu tried to have the committee headquarters moved permanently to his stronghold in Songjiang, despite that city's less-than-central location. After one trial meeting there, the headquarters returned to Shanghai. Later, Zhu convinced the committee to hire one of his protégés, a Communist *Sanwu she* member, as committee secretary. Reacting to Zhu's growing power, rightists Fan, Chen Qubing, and Shen Jing in mid-1924 persuaded the committee to apprise Sun Yat-sen of "Communist plots" to "destroy the GMD." They apparently did this in coordination with the GMD Central Supervisory Committee's mid-1924 effort to expel all Communists for their published intention to act as a "bloc within" the GMD rather than as individuals. Such a CCP strategy would have violated promises made by Communist leader Li Dazhao at the inception of the reorganization.[20]

Zhu exasperated and frightened the rightists by disobeying the provincial party committee. In contravention of committee decisions,

Zhu reportedly took larger monthly subsidies for his Songjiang GMD than were given to other county branches, an act for which he was severely beaten by Liu Yunzhao, a committee member whose penchant for fisticuffs was shared by Fan. Later, when the party center's finances became strained and its subsidies to the Jiangsu committee reduced, Zhu reportedly increased his own power and importance to the Jiangsu party by providing a subsidy from the *Sanwu she*. Predictably, the rightists criticized him not only for his earlier practice of taking money from the provincial GMD committee, but also for his later subsidies to it.[21]

By the time of the seventh meeting of the Jiangsu Provincial Provisional Party Committee, Zhu had fallen into deep disagreement with staunch anti-Communists Chen Qubing, Qin Xiaolu, and He Haiqiao. Thereafter, these three refused to attend meetings of the committee.[22] And later as others ceased attending, Zhu became, by default, the only active member of the standing committee. From this time forth, he treated the party as his personal property. He managed it without reference to most of the provincial committee members and worked closely only with Zhang Shushi, who was a Communist despite his earlier association with Fan Xiongyi, and was also one of the original provincial committee members. Zhu never called meetings of the full Jiangsu Provincial Provisional Party Committee and, therefore, had a free hand in running party affairs.[23]

Upset that Fan's right-wing Nanjing municipal GMD had not admitted CCP members into the party, Zhu ordered new elections for the Nanjing party committee. A complex dispute ensued between leftists and rightists in Nanjing that resulted in a bloody brawl between the two sides and, eventually, the expulsion of the rightists from the GMD by both the provincial committee that Zhu controlled and the central party headquarters in Guangzhou.[24] But Fan's Nanjing rightists refused to disband their Nanjing party organization, although neither Guangzhou nor the Jiangsu party committee recognized it. The rightist Nanjing municipal GMD, independent from Guangzhou by March 1925, claimed to have over two thousand members. Because Zhu's provincial party committee also established its own Nanjing municipal party headquarters, by mid-1925 Nanjing contained two hostile local GMD organizations, each contesting the other's legitimacy, and each heaping verbal and physical abuse on the other.[25] Thus, in Jiangsu some local GMD branches had split months before the Western Hills Conference ruptured the party on the national level.

Disturbed at Zhu's domination of the Jiangsu party committee, Fan Xiongyi convened a meeting of Jiangsu rightists, a gathering he styled the "Provincial Party Executive Committee Restoration Committee." Meeting first on June 3, 1925, with five of the original Jiangsu Provincial Provisional Party Committee members present, the conference resolved to move the provincial party headquarters to Nanjing, because the GMD in Nanjing enjoyed the protection of the warlord police and because that city was a rightist stronghold. The group also petitioned the party center in Guangzhou to expel Zhu Jixun from the party. The conference passed its resolutions on to the Shanghai Executive Committee (a creature of the GMD's central party headquarters in Guangzhou, but one that had been commandeered by anti-Communists), which forwarded the accusation against Zhu to the Guangzhou party center. Henceforth, Jiangsu had two provincial party headquarters—one in Shanghai headed by Zhu and his leftist associates and the other in Nanjing headed by Fan Xiongyi and his anti-Communist partisans.[26]

Although the Jiangsu Provincial Provisional Party Committee had delegated oversight of each section of Jiangsu to particular members of the provincial committee, Zhu disregarded the assignments, sending his protégés all over Jiangsu's Lower Yangzi core to build party branches and his own power base. By contrast, the anti-Communists were not nearly as active in recruiting party members. Thus, although rightists contended that Zhu manipulated the August 1925 election of the GMD provincial executive committee because that election produced a committee that was 80 or 90 percent Communist, it is clear that Zhu's leftist forces would have done very well in the elections owing solely to their activities in creating local political bases.[27] There can be no doubt of the vigor of the activity of the leftists. The minutes of the GMD's Organization Department for one three-month period in 1924 mention Zhu and his protégés more often than any other person or group.[28]

Jiangsu was not the only province in which tension between anti-Communists and those who favored the Communists' inclusion in the GMD had reached the boiling point by 1925, about the time that Sun Yat-sen died of cancer. In November 1925 a group of fourteen rightists from several provinces held a conference near the temporary resting place of Sun's body in the Western Hills of Beijing. Sitting as a rump conference of the Guomindang's Central Executive Committee, they in effect formed a new CEC. Claiming to be the Fourth Plenum of the CEC of the GMD, they passed formal resolutions impeaching left-leaning party Chairman Wang Jingwei, expelling the Communists from the GMD, and firing the party's Russian advisers.[29] This anti-Communist group, which came to be called the "Western Hills faction," decided to set up a new central party headquarters in Shanghai to oppose the increasingly Communist-dominated one in Guangzhou, which of course failed to execute the resolutions. The Western Hills organization was in fact only a slightly modified version of the Shanghai Executive Committee; it was even headquartered in the Shanghai Executive Committee's building at 44 Huanlong Road in Shanghai's foreign concession.[30]

Tension between rightists and leftists continued to increase throughout 1925 and 1926. Ugly scuffles and bloody, pitched battles between club-wielding forces of the two sides marred the March 1926 memorial services in Nanjing commemorating the anniversary of Sun Yat-sen's death.[31] In July 1926 the Guangzhou party center launched the Northern Expedition, a broad military campaign against the warlords who ruled most of China at the time. Since this campaign made it seem that the GMD was on the threshold of power, conflicts escalated between Jiangsu rightists and leftists who coveted leadership positions in the future government.

Like the Jiangsu party, the Guangzhou central party organization was split between those who favored Communist participation in the GMD and those who opposed it. During 1926 the conflict between those two groupings in Guangzhou deepened. In March 1926, Chiang Kai-shek, the superintendent of the Huangpu Military Academy, carried out a limited coup against the Communists in Guangzhou that deprived them of some of their leadership positions in the Guomindang and its mass organizations, and circumscribed the influence of Russian advisers to the party. By the end of 1926, however, the Communists had regained much of their strength.[32]

Because of the progress of the Northern Expedition, in late 1926 the Central Executive Committee of the GMD (in Guangzhou) tentatively decided to move its offices from Guangzhou to Wuhan. Chiang Kai-shek, the commander in chief of the GMD armies, became spatially separated from the party center because he was directing armies in the southeast. But this only partially explains the eventual split between Chiang and the party center that was being set up in Wuhan. The

Wuhan center supported the alliance with the CCP, while Chiang and his followers felt that the coup in Guangzhou had not solved the problem posed by Communist membership in the GMD. Chiang's associate, Chen Guofu, who had controlled the Organization Department of the party since the March coup, spent most of 1926 surreptitiously preparing for a decisive anti-Communist purge. In early 1927, Chiang and his followers assembled, first in Nanchang, Jiangxi, and then in Shanghai, and put their final touches on the plans for the purge. On March 28, several of the members of the Central Supervisory Committee of the former Guangzhou party center adopted a resolution calling for expulsion of all Communists from the GMD, citing a Communist plot to take over the party and the National Government in Wuhan.[33] This resolution gave Chiang a legalistic justification for the purge that he executed soon thereafter.

Having received reports of Chiang's plans to purge the Communists in Shanghai, Fan Xiongyi's Nanjing rightists took it upon themselves to purge the Communists and leftists in Nanjing. On April 9, 1927, three days before Chiang's bloody action in Shanghai, the rightists attacked and destroyed the leftists' Nanjing municipal party headquarters, their General Labor Union, and their provincial party headquarters, which had just moved from Shanghai to Nanjing. The rightist forces also arrested and executed many staff members and officials of the leftist headquarters. The next day when leftists complained to GMD army leaders, they were beaten by over two hundred club-swinging rightists. In this fight, thirty leftists and Communists were killed or injured, and those who survived either left Nanjing or went underground.[34]

In early April the leftist National Government in Wuhan unceremoniously "fired" Chiang Kai-shek from his position as commander in chief of the Northern Expeditionary armies, thereby ratifying earlier leftist denunciations of him.[35] The dismissal and the denunciations must have hardened Chiang's determination to carry through with the purge. Thus, on April 12, 1926, Chiang's weak military forces in Shanghai joined with several underworld gangs to disarm workers' organizations and kill hundreds of leftists and Communists. Within a week the purge had spread through southern Jiangsu and claimed the lives of hundreds more Communists.[36]

Following the purge, Chiang and his group established a new GMD central party headquarters and National Government in Nanjing in opposition to those in Wuhan. The Western Hills group also maintained its headquarters in Shanghai, so the GMD was temporarily divided into three antagonistic organizations. Although Chiang's group had broken with the Communists as the Western Hills group had long advocated, the purge did not immediately unify the Nanjing and Shanghai party centers. In fact, Chiang's group in Nanjing continued to scorn the Shanghai rightists for their earlier disloyalty to the Guangzhou center, an organization of which Chiang's group had been a part.

Clearly, the purge demonstrated that the 1924 reorganization of the party had not been tenable. In an effort to boost party membership and enthusiasm, Sun Yat-sen had chosen a strategy of inclusiveness, which doomed the GMD to divisive intraparty struggle. Old party leaders resented the sudden influx of radicalism and feared even more the young radicals' ambitions for leadership positions. Moreover, the ambitions of rightist leaders like Fan Xiongyi were considerable. The party failed to develop effective means for binding together its widely disparate elements. Nominally a Leninist-style, centralized, revolutionary organization, the GMD was actually built on networks of personal relationships, the stuff of which factions were made. But as we shall see, those networks were energized by ideological issues.

The Leftist Assault on Local Elites

The fragmentation of the Guomindang between 1924 and 1927, though based partly on the strength of personal relationships and the ferocity of the struggle for high political and social positions, was also to a considerable degree due to differing perspectives on political and social policy. The rightists were a complex group unanimous about almost nothing but their aversion to Communism. This antipathy was so intense that most rightists came to adopt a set of values consonant with that distaste. The leftists, who were adherents to the Guangzhou party headquarters and, outwardly at least, its alliance with the CCP, were an even more diverse group. Those loyal to Guangzhou included representatives of a wide spectrum of political belief, ranging from Communists to those plotting anti-Communist coups. The Guangzhou party apparatus and the leftist Jiangsu GMD, however, championed a perspective on social problems that was probably shared, in many respects, by the majority of party members. That perspective was roundly hostile to the existing order of local society and politics.

The January 1926 pronouncements of the Second National Congress, the supreme deliberative body of the left GMD, rang with the iconoclasm that had first attracted many radical intellectuals to the party. Congressional propaganda had nothing kind to say about contemporary Chinese social structure or incumbent power holders on the national or local levels. It directed the party-led peasant movement to "employ force to stop the monopolization of rural administration by local bullies and evil gentry," whom it described as the "countless bastard sons (*yunie*) of feudalism." It ordered the movement to "eliminate the warlords, compradores, and local bullies and evil gentry who stand in the way of peasant rights and benefits."[37] Existing chambers of commerce (or, at least, some of them) were characterized as organs manipulated by compradores and gentry. Those old chambers were to be reformed of "bad habits" and, more importantly, displaced by merchant associations composed of the middle and small merchants. Similarly, although merchant militia beyond the areas of GMD control were encouraged to resist taxes and oppose the warlords, the Congress left little doubt that there would be no place for them when the GMD came to power.[38] The meeting's criticism of "exorbitant taxes and miscellaneous levies" (*keshui zajuan*) and its advocacy of unification of tax collection authority in the hands of county governments was a broadside against the local elite-managed finance organs which had proliferated in the late Qing and early Republican periods. In fact, congressional propaganda, like other statements by leftist GMD organs, may be read as a sweeping indictment of "local self-government" and other government-sponsored organizations through which traditional elites exercised and bolstered their authority. At the same time, the party promised that it stood for "genuine" self-government and democracy.[39]

Although the Congress identified incumbent county- and township-level political elites as appropriate targets of invective and party pressure, it did not proclaim a generalized campaign against *economic elites*. In fact, it reassured merchants that the Guomindang's revolution was "for the mutual benefit of the various classes" and that merchants were considered an integral part of the citizenry. However, the Congress distinguished between two sorts of merchants: those who served the imperialists (i.e., "compradores") and those who did not. The revolution was to strip the former of their power, while the latter, identified as middle- and small-scale merchants, would gain through their control of new party-led merchant associations.[40]

Similarly, the Congress did not announce a sweeping campaign against landlords. In fact, even the Communist Party spoke in terms of revolutionary *alliance* with small and middle landlords, though the CCP advocated opposition to "reactionary," absentee, big landlords.[41] Nonetheless, some leftist GMD policies, if enacted, would have harmed the interests of landlords and certain other economic elites. For example, in October 1926, the Guangzhou central party headquarters and its provincial branches decided to push forward a 25 percent reduction in land rents and a loan interest ceiling of 20 percent per year.[42] Despite this, even in Guangdong Province, where party-led peasant associations were strongest, few real attempts were made to effect rent reductions until 1928.[43]

Although these pronouncements from on high should have suggested to local party branches and mass organizations a few guidelines for determining local revolutionary targets, Jiangsu's left GMD authorities usually spoke of their local enemies in hazy slogans and clichés. This may have been because, as Harold Isaacs has suggested, there was no broad agreement on how to define the rural targets of GMD policy.[44] Or it may have simply been a reflection of the sloppiness of some of the categories in Guangzhou's prescriptions. Jiangsu's leftist leader Zhang Shushi listed the enemies of the revolution with imprecision: "imperialists, Chauvinists (*Guojia zhuyi* [*pai*]), evil warlords, wicked bureaucrats, local bullies and evil gentry, academic cliques, the compradore class, opportunist elements, and all similar reactionary cliques."[45] Clearly, all of the terms applied to enemy elites were value-laden and did not delineate any particular socioeconomic classes as defined by Marxism or any other comprehensive system of social analysis. Most simply implied moral opprobrium, without indicating the system of morality from which the terms derived.

Although the Congress had obliquely fingered incumbent county- and township-level political elites as enemies of the revolution, local parties were largely on their own when it came to determining which individuals should be targets. A large segment of the modern, educated counterelite of which the party was comprised advocated thoroughgoing revolution.[46] Some leftists looked on the warlords and all who had power and privilege in the warlord era as enemies to be attacked—unless, of course, those older elites decided to throw in their lot with the left GMD. Presumably local factional alignments (preexisting networks of personal relations) played a role in determining whom party and mass organization leaders would choose to attack as "local bullies and evil gentry." The left GMD envisioned two methods of dealing with these enemies: before GMD governmental authority was established over an area, the GMD-led mass organizations were to direct attacks on the noxious elites; after the party-controlled government was formed, it was to use its administrative and judicial power in tandem with the mass organizations against these elites.

Despite the leftist GMD's statements of concern about oppression of peasants, it was more interested in the labor movement in Shanghai than in a peasant movement to free the surrounding countryside of undesirable elites. Perhaps this was a product of the urban bias of the Marxist ideology embraced by many of the leftists. Whatever the reasons, it was March 1926 before Jiangsu's provincial party headquarters had formally established a Peasant Department, which thereafter was active in only a few counties. At first crippled by a lack of cadres, party operatives attempted to use preexisting organizations like the Red Spears, the Big Sword Society, the Red Gang, the Green Gang, and Limen (literally, the "Righteous Sect," a semi-religious organization that forbade smoking and drinking) to fight the government and unpopular local enemies. This strategy of mobilizing already extant secret societies as elements of the peasant movement was more common in Jiangsu's North China zone than in the Lower Yangzi area, where the GMD peasant associations were more likely to be newly founded, party-spawned bodies, rather than warmed-over secret societies. In both zones, however, GMD agents attempted to take advantage of local peasant grievances in order to attract local residents into party-led organizations.[47]

The Jiangsu Peasant Department reported that until August 1926 it had advocated establishment of clubs, cooperatives, and academies for peasants, and only after that time had emphasized mass struggle in the form of "opposition movements" against enemy elites and oppressive conditions.[48] It may be true that before August the department did not press for vigorous struggle in all counties; for example, the leftist GMD's Kunshan County headquarters' peasant program was an innocuous combination of rural education, improvement of recreation, establishment of peasant associations to inculcate ideology, and opposition to high interest loans.[49] Even before August, however, some county party organizations attacked aspects of the existing land tenancy system and pressed opposition movements against locally targeted elites.

Peasant Movement Martyr Zhou Shuiping

The pioneer of the Jiangsu GMD's peasant movement and its most famous martyr was Zhou Shuiping, a native of Gushan, a market town in Jiangyin County in the Lower Yangzi core. After graduating from normal school in 1917, he traveled to Japan to begin his higher education. While there, Zhou became a political activist, participating in protests that were part of the surrounding May Fourth Movement and being jailed twice for his political exertions. After returning to China and settling in his hometown in 1919, he taught in a public school and founded a night school for common people (*pingmin*) where he "imparted scientific knowledge and progressive thought." Zhou seems to have been restless, though, and he soon bounced around from teaching post to teaching post, relocating first to the Xuzhou area (in the extreme north of Jiangsu), then to Chuansha (near Shanghai), and later to a site in Zhejiang province. While in Chuansha in 1924, he joined the GMD, with leftist Liu Yazi and Communist Hou Shaoqiu as his sponsors. The year 1925 found him teaching at a university in Shanghai, where under the radicalizing influence of that city, he joined the Communist Party.[50]

During his summer break in 1925, Zhou returned to his home area in Jiangyin County and began his brief but eventful career as a peasant organizer. Over the few months before his arrest in November, Zhou worked at a blinding pace. Together with a friend, he co-founded a study group called the Star Society (*Xing she*) and a journal known as *The Star's Rays* (*Xing guang*), which was packed with articles that promoted proletarian revolution, advocated the "liberation of peasants," and "lashed out at the crimes of local bullies and evil gentry."[51] At a press conference on October 3, 1925, he also announced the organization of the Tenant's Cooperative Self-Salvation Association (*Dianhu hezuo zijiuhui*), a peasant association that he would soon press into service in a rent resistance movement. Among other things, this organization demanded a 25 percent reduction in land rents. Taking advantage of the crowds that gathered at temple festivals in Jiangyin as well as two neighboring counties in early November 1925, Zhou spread propaganda tracts and made speeches advocating rent resistance.

His organization's pamphlets laid out a strategy for dealing with rent collectors who charged tenants excessive amounts. Peasants should, he said, meet together to achieve solidarity and send representatives to negotiate terms with the collectors. He further proposed that if the talks

The Early Period, 1924–1927 57

provided no satisfactory solution to the excessive rents, all tenants should withhold rent. His pamphlet even suggested reprisals against any tenant who broke ranks and paid rent when others had determined to withhold payment.[52]

Zhou did not, however, concentrate solely on the rent reduction campaign. He also aimed his seemingly limitless energies at challenging a local elite who managed a landed endowment fund called the Southeast Townships Study Society (*Dongnanxiang xueshe*). This organization held several thousand *mu* of older land, the income from which was earmarked to provide scholarships to students from disadvantaged families. For a decade or more, the Study Society manager had allegedly been underreporting the income of the endowment and pocketing the difference—the embezzled funds said to amount to over 10,000 *yuan*. Zhou fought the manager by organizing the Southeast Townships Study Society Property Cleanup Committee (*Qingli Dongnanxiang xueshe caichan weiyuanhui*) and spreading propaganda leaflets which explained the financial irregularities and pointed a finger at the manager.[53]

Kathryn Bernhardt aptly notes that the case of Zhou Shuiping illustrates the dangerous conditions under which Jiangsu peasant organizers operated prior to the arrival of GMD armies.[54] Zhou would soon lose his freedom, then his life, because of his revolutionary activities. In November, some thirty-three local elites, including most notably National Assemblyman Sha Bingyuan, presented a joint accusation of Zhou to the Jiangyin county government, accusing Zhou of "preaching Communism." Communist histories charge that county assemblyman Tang Guohua also bribed yamen runners to secure Zhou's arrest. Zhou was nabbed by the county government on November 18, 1925, though it took nearly two months for the government to decide what to do with him. Pleas of local landlords and assemblymen went out to warlord Sun Chuanfang to persuade him to order Zhou's execution. These elites cleverly included an implicit threat in their correspondence with Sun. They could not, they intoned, come across with the earlier-than-usual land tax payments that Sun had ordered because Zhou's rent resistance campaign had deprived them of rental income. Sun took the hint, and his command that Zhou be put to death was carried out on January 17, 1926. As a warning to other would-be agitators, local authorities publicly displayed Zhou's head for three days on a wall in front of the county government building.

Other Attacks on Local Elites

Despite the dangers of revolutionary activity in the mid-1920s, some other young activists pushed ahead with assaults on selected local elites. Even before early 1927, when a centrally organized GMD campaign against "local bullies and evil gentry" swept across the Lower Yangzi portion of the province, some Lower Yangzi core party branches were already pressing such movements on their own. For example, as early as 1925, Xia Lin, a CCP member and founder of the Danyang County GMD branch, engineered action against Hu Yinjie, a member of the provincial assembly and chair of the Danyang County Chamber of Commerce. The exact reasons for Xia's selection of Hu as his target are difficult to determine, though memoirs cite Hu's wealth—he had investments in several pawnshops, a silk shop, a biscuit baking concern, and a livestock sales business—as well as his "oppressiveness" and his many connections with powerful people.[55]

The local GMD may have chosen Hu for his propaganda value. A David-versus-Goliath contest always attracts attention, and as the David figure in this battle, the party was certain to engage the sympathies of a fair number of young intellectuals by virtue of its pluck and audaciousness. Whatever Xia's reasoning, he assembled a crowd of hoe- and rake-wielding peasants and down-and-out city dwellers at Hu's grand residence just outside the East Gate of the Danyang county seat. After whipping up the gathering with the chant "Down with local bully and evil gentry Hu Yinjie," Xia led the assemblage in pillaging and burning Hu's house. As a result of this mob action, Hu went into hiding for over a month. Surprisingly, in this case the Danyang party did not face the kind of reprisals that sometimes befell Jiangsu's political activists. Instead, the local government quietly helped rebuild Hu's house. Although the administrator of the school at which Xia taught issued a warning to him to refrain from political activities, it appears that he went right ahead with his revolutionary endeavors without losing his job.[56]

Other actions of the party in Danyang County illustrate the left GMD's strategy of creating, embellishing, and taking advantage of already existing local grievances and local "opposition movements." In 1924, marauding government troops had robbed a pawnshop in the town of Lücheng of a large sum of money. The pawnshop tried to recoup its losses by falsely reporting that clothes pawned by peasants had also been stolen; the shop then expropriated the pawned garments. A Lücheng

GMD member responded by organizing a pawner's association (*danghu lianhehui*) that directed a successful movement opposing the pawnshop's actions. In addition, a three-hundred member peasant advancement society (*nongmin cujinhui*) succeeding the pawner's movement continued to pit itself against persons (labeled by GMD sources as "local bullies and evil gentry") who had colluded with the pawnshop in its plot. Later, in the summer of 1926, the local party led another campaign; this time it chose as its target businessmen who had formed the Prosperous Farmer Pump Company (*Yunong hushui gongsi*). During a drought these entrepreneurs (whom the party dubbed "local bullies and evil gentry") had bought a mechanical irrigation pump and rented it out to peasants at rates the party deemed outrageous. Reacting to an announcement that the government would fine peasants not using the pump, the GMD-related Peasant Advancement Society urged peasants to form a cooperative to buy another pump. The cooperative was so successful in attracting peasant business and ruining the original company's business that concerned local elites set about convincing the warlord Sun Chuan-fang that the Peasant Advancement Society was "red." Sun eventually ordered the arrest of provincial GMD Peasant Department personnel, local peasant movement leaders were incarcerated, and the local Peasant Academy was closed.[57]

Although the GMD and its mass movement were prime movers in the Danyang pawner's campaign from its inception, in some other localities the party only slowly sensed the opportunities open to it. In Qingpu in early 1926 the GMD, hoping to make political hay, belatedly involved itself in a local dispute that had been raging for almost three years. In 1923 a group of landlords had established a land reclamation company that used its influence with the government to cheat farmers out of the land they had reclaimed from marshes. By paying the government a one *yuan* per *mu* fee, the company had established its title to the new farmland, which it proceeded to try to sell to the peasants who had developed the land. For several years the affected peasants had carried on a protest movement to contest the company and its practices. Only in February 1926 did the fifth ward of the county's GMD begin publicly to proclaim its support for the land reclaiming peasants. One of the novel ways the Qingpu leftist GMD rallied peasants to oppose the rural status quo was to put on dramatic performances crafted to spur peasants to heroic revolutionary acts and lead them to associate the GMD mass movement with their own concerns. One such theatrical performance was a play that Hou Shaoqiu had written about Zhou Shuiping, the most famous martyr of the Jiangsu GMD's peasant movement.[58]

Like the mass movements in Danyang and Qingpu, the Songjiang County peasant movement coalesced around opposition to a company and its owners. One of the party's targets was Zhang Baopei, described by one source as a member of the gentry and by another as "a great landlord." He had been arrested and incarcerated briefly in the 1910s for setting up his own private kangaroo court which he used on his tenants. After his release from jail, Zhang had studied law in Japan. Upon his return to China, he flourished financially by encouraging and handling litigation. He also held partial ownership in land reclamation companies in several counties, including the Huinong Company in Songjiang, which used questionable means to acquire peasants' lands. Reacting to Zhang's business methods, over one hundred peasants rallied and beat up the agent sent to collect rent on Zhang's land. Sensing an opportunity, in November 1926 the GMD's Peasant Department sent agents to Songjiang to capitalize on the incident; they were to organize village "peasant self-salvation societies" (*nongmin zijiuhui*), and bring peasants into the party.[59]

Here leftist GMD operatives employed a technique the CCP would use in the 1930s and 1940s to catalyze local revolutionary situations. Party agents orchestrated a "speak bitterness" session in which well-selected witnesses were urged to testify before a mass meeting about the ways in which a targeted individual had exploited them. On March 25, 1927, after the National Revolutionary Armies (NRA) had arrived in Songjiang and brought a new county government to power, 10,000 peasants gathered for a mass demonstration and assembly. The local GMD and its Punan Peasant Association secured the release of an old peasant surnamed Shen, who had been incarcerated for several years due to Zhang Baopei's prosecution of him for rent nonpayment. Shen's heart-rending testimony and accusation of Zhang whipped the crowd into a frenzy. In reaction to the call by the mass meeting's organizer to help those who owed rent to Zhang Baopei's Huinong Company, the crowd rampaged out of control. Though Zhang had fled beyond the reach of the throng to the foreign concession in Shanghai, the mob pillaged his house. Following the violence, the party closed the house and put it under police protection. It appears that the party, now in power, was horrified by the violence its peasant association had unleashed. After the robbing and burning of

Zhang's mansion, some of the party's leaders began to voice concern for order and the need to rely more on trials and administrative action to handle elites and less on opposition campaigns. However, there are some hints in the sources that this was a case of the party's right wing attempting to demobilize masses that had been activated by leftists.[60]

Despite attempts of some in Songjiang's GMD to tone down the anti-"local bully and evil gentry" movement, that movement continued for a few more weeks. Soon after the burning of Zhang Baopei's mansion, the Songjiang party leftists' campaign against selected local elites drew its first blood. Since most of the prominent pre-1927 county-level elites in Songjiang had taken to their heels to escape the clutches of the GMD activists, the radicals set their sights lower and began to struggle against smaller fry. One of the lesser targets who faced a mass struggle meeting was Qiu Yugu, who had at one time been head of the chamber of commerce in the market town of Yexie. A mob put a dunce cap on another Yexie elite, Gu Zifang, a landlord and moneylender, and paraded him through the streets to face mass humiliation. But the first Songjiang figure to lose his life in the anti-"bully" movement was Chen Jinju, a yamen runner, rent collector, and local tough. Party agents brought Chen before a mass trial in Xianglin (a market town) to be confronted with testimony from ten or so witnesses who recounted how Chen had raped their wives and relatives (causing the victims to commit suicide or become emotionally disturbed), cheated boatmen out of their cargoes, charged tenants fees over and above the legal land rents, and beaten people to death. Petty charges were mixed with the serious, as when one man blamed Chen for smashing a basketful of his watermelons. The party turned the sentencing of Chen over to the crowd, which soon fixed on the death penalty. As Chen grabbed for a bamboo carrying pole to defend himself, several persons in the throng proceeded to stone him to death. Since few, if any, other elites in Songjiang were executed during the anti-"bully" movement, some local residents later savored this one case of revolutionary justice in which a somewhat powerful person was destroyed. Memoirs recount that those who reveled in Chen's death coined the chant: "Chen Jinju, [your] blood debt is piled so high, even dogs won't eat your corpse!"[61]

A pattern developed in the peasant movement in Songjiang: party incitement of peasants through slogans against exploitation, followed by the peasants' violent direct action, followed again by GMD suppression.

On April 7, 1927, for example, a GMD ward-branch in Yexie called together several tens of thousands of peasants for a mass demonstration. GMD leaders roused peasants by calling for freedom, unity, and an end to oppression. During the ensuing march, conflict broke out with town police, injuring one policemen. When the mob confronted various rice dealers and demanded price controls, the merchants refused. The mob then destroyed rice shops and terrorized the merchants, compelling party and army action to restore order.[62]

In most counties the social strategy of leftist GMD leaders was similar to that in Songjiang and Danyang. That is, the party leaders chose a few individuals of wealth and power to serve as revolutionary targets. For example, in Suining County (North China zone) party leaders decided to target a couple of persons, whom they termed "the vilest great landlords," as objects of a "peaceful" rent reduction campaign. Party reports about these campaigns paint the local GMD in flattering revolutionary shades: the party branch was embroiled in a heroic struggle against exploitative landholding elites. However, other interpretations of the situation are possible. The Suining party was unusual in that it claimed to control quite a number of that county's militiamen. In fact, by late 1926 the party asserted that it had over 7,000 Suining militiamen under its control— probably an exaggeration.[63] But if the party quickly gained control over a sizable armed forces, it was most likely achieved by co-opting certain of the existing militia. In other words, it appears that the Suining party was being drawn into a factional fight between different groups of incumbent elites and certain militia leaders chose to ally themselves with the GMD against the handful of elites the party was attacking.

In several counties, local leftist GMD leaders spoke derisively of large landlords, usurers, and the prevailing tenancy system in general. Nonetheless, even while blasting "great landlords," many local party branches expressed the desire to ally with "upright gentry" and small landlords.[64] The leftist GMD in most areas of Jiangsu did not pursue a general assault against the whole of the landlord class or even the old examination degree-holding gentry. The Changshu County GMD, for example, attacked only two elites as "local bullies and evil gentry," and ran a successful campaign to break the grip of a third individual over the night soil business in the county seat. This night soil boss (*fenfei tou*, literally, "manure head") was a convenient target because his monopoly rights over night soil collection was unpopular with peasants in the surrounding countryside who had to pay a premium for fertilizer and were themselves prevented from collecting sewage directly.[65] The party chose its enemies according to its perception of their moral conduct and its judgment of their unpopularity. In some cases a party leader chose as allies those elites who were part of his own network of connections—friends, kin, teachers, and so forth—and chose as enemies those elites who were feuding competitors of his friends.[66]

In addition to espousing revolutionary mass action against selected local elites, the leftists assumed that when the warlords were overthrown and the GMD had established a new government, their new administrative authority would pursue and prosecute undesirable local elites. In early 1927 the Jiangsu leftist GMD drew up articles to govern such prosecutions. These draft laws on the prosecution of "evil gentry and rotten managers" specified a list of crimes for which local elites could be punished, including bribery, extortion, embezzlement of government funds, and swindling. The articles, however, left great latitude for official discretion in administering punishments. A number of offenses were not specified in any detail; individuals could be punished for "directly or indirectly harming the masses" or exhibiting "counterrevolutionary words or actions."[67] Despite the extreme vagueness of the strictures, the GMD leftists clearly believed that the post-revolutionary government should continue to identify certain local elites for punishment.

Many local branches of the left GMD considered elites in the self-government and government-sponsored organizations at the county and township levels to be among their most important enemies. Township managers had always been objects of party reproach, but as the National Revolutionary Armies approached Jiangsu, the province's leftist GMD leaders assailed them all the more. Strapped financially because of the war with GMD armies on the Jiangxi, Zhejiang, and Jiangsu fronts, Sun Chuanfang announced that county governments were immediately to contribute vast new amounts of money to his coffers. They obeyed. For example, the Dantu (Zhenjiang) County magistrate wrote to township managers in the county, telling them that within five days they were to borrow funds from the rich gentry of their area and send the entire amount to the county government.[68] A similar process occurred in other localities, while in some counties township managers helped the warlord government by levying in advance land taxes for several succeeding years. In response, the Jiangsu leftist headquarters on March 20, 1927, announced that it was investigating the "evil gentry" and "corrupt managers" (i.e., *xiangdong*) who were still providing public funds for warlord armies. The provincial GMD ordered local party organizations to collect evidence against these elites—the goal being to bring them to trial. In effect, the party was warning them that if they sent any more funds to Sun, their families' property would be confiscated.[69]

When GMD armies finally liberated areas in Jiangsu, local government officials and local political elites felt the effects of the party's hostility toward them. Anticipating harsh treatment, some escaped before the NRA occupied their area.[70] This sometimes left localities without any government. In most places the turnover was more orderly, with officials resigning after GMD armies had arrived.[71] The party, the NRA, and the provisional governments they established took over offices and funds smoothly over a period of days. In a few areas, however, the transition was not peaceful. In Jinshan County, for example, after taking over the government offices, a mob attacked party personnel.[72] Much of the violence and discord stemmed from competing desires of rightist and leftist party headquarters, the sometimes rightist NRA, and the usually leftist Political Department of the NRA to dominate local government appointments. In Wuxi County, party incitement against the township managers led to random mass attacks on them and their property.[73] In some other areas crowds attacked local government offices against the wishes of the local GMD.[74] And in at least one case, massed peasants demanded that the GMD's new government release a former township manager whom it had just arrested, demonstrating that whatever the GMD thought of these local figures, some of them maintained networks of supporters who did not think them "evil."[75]

One of the most common ways of handling former government officials and the heads of government-sponsored organizations was investigation, arrest, and prosecution—usually for embezzlement of public funds. Township managers often refused to turn over remaining public funds and documents. In fact, many had never kept good records in the first place. Committees for settlement of accounts set up by local party branches not infrequently recommended confiscation of township managers' property.[76] But in some cases the township managers did not fare badly at all. For example, in Wujin County, most of them won positions under the GMD regime as "township administrative affairs deputies" (*xiang zhengwu weiyuan*). While the name of the office they held was changed, it is likely that the functions and personnel remained the same.⁷⁷ Despite protests of local GMD branches, post-Northern Expeditionary local governments sometimes entrusted subcounty administration to the old township managers. In contrast, some localities saw all incumbent officeholders at the county and township levels turned out of office, at least for a time.⁷⁸

The Rightists

The Guomindang right wing, consistent with its hatred for anything that smacked of Communism, class struggle, or "disorder," had little use for the leftists' campaigns against local elites. The anti-Communist writings of Dai Jitao provided the theoretical underpinnings of the rightist Western Hills GMD, while the Sunist Study Society in central China (largely coterminous with the right GMD) further consolidated these views. By a selective culling of Sun Yat-sen's eclectic writings, GMD rightists built an edifice of solidly anti-Communist theory and policy that was at odds with the left GMD program.⁷⁹

The rightists most hated the Communists' advocacy of class struggle, and criticism of it appeared in almost every rightist publication. Taking a page from Confucian thought, Dai Jitao claimed that the foundation of Sun Yat-sen's character had been humanity and love (*ren'ai*) and that this had prevented Sun from accepting class struggle. Instead, Dai said, Sun had advocated a "revolution of the several classes united," including the ruling class after it was "enlightened." Dai apparently believed that even local elites closely identified with the warlords could be transformed into responsible citizens and leaders.⁸⁰ The rightists took this idea of "revolution of the several classes united" and transformed it into the slogan "revolution of all the people" (*quanmin geming*).⁸¹ Later this caused theoretical problems because it seemed to deny that there were any domestic enemies of the revolution.⁸²

The primary targets of revolution cited by the rightists were imperialists and warlords. This does not mean that they were satisfied with the existing social and economic order, but they tended to envision reform according to Sun's *Three People's Principles* and *Fundamentals of National Reconstruction* rather than social revolution. Changes in society were to be initiated gradually by the government and only after the political revolution against the warlords had succeeded. Most rightists only rarely mentioned exploitation and social enemies like "local bullies and evil gentry," and in their view only governmental action, both judicial and administrative, were to be used against enemy elites. It is unclear what standards the government was to use in cases of alleged oppression. The goal of the rightists was the eventual elimination of classes through continuous, gradual improvement of the lot of workers and peasants.[83]

Fearful of the prospect of social chaos, the rightist GMD decried riots and disorder fomented by Communist propaganda and incitement of the masses. Accordingly, the rightists' strategy for mass organizations differed sharply from that of the leftists. The rightist labor organizations, for example, were supposed to aid in the political revolution and increase harmony and unity between laborers and capitalists. They were to be, in essence, mutual cooperation societies.[84]

In its statements on the peasant movement, the Western Hills GMD gave recognition to the peasants' problems of "direct oppression and exploitation by warlords, officials, evil gentry, local bullies and some landlords" and "indirect encroachment by the imperialists." But unlike the Jiangsu GMD leftists, the right wing did not propose to use the peasant associations to combat oppressive elites. In fact, its leaders asserted that class struggle by peasants had eroded the good feelings between themselves and their social superiors and had hurt mutual enterprises. Henceforth, all peasant organizations were to be open to all peasants regardless of their wealth, and they were to direct their efforts toward agricultural improvement, rural education, and economic relief. After the victory of the GMD armies, peasant associations were to have the power of presenting petitions and accusations of exploitation to the government. Although many GMD peasant associations had encountered resistance from landlords, Zhejiangese Western Hills figure Shen Dingyi expressed confidence that "We can enlighten the landlords that peasant organizations should exist." He added, "At present we really are not striking down (*dadao*) landlords; we only advocate peasant organization and want to enlighten landlords."[85] As Jiangxi rightist Sun Jingya stated it, "This party . . . [advocates using] nationally stipulated policy to harmonize the interests of peasants and landlords."[86] In the view of the rightists, peasant organizations, rather than targeting objectionable local elites, were supposed to unite rural society in a quest for economic and social improvement.

The rightists' love of social harmony did not prevent them from embracing in theory Sun Yat-sen's "land to the tiller" slogan and program. Although their plan rested heavily on encouraging peasants to migrate to marginal areas to cultivate wasteland, it also included provisions for establishing the minimum "space" (i.e., land) necessary for a peasant family and spoke of providing low-interest loans that would enable peasants to purchase that minimum. Their propaganda did not mention the part of Sun's program which called for confiscation of landlord holdings not reported for tax purposes and forced purchase for lands whose value was underreported. On the whole, the rightists' land reform plan avoided anything that would, in their eyes, threaten social harmony and stability.[87]

Thus, the rightist GMD's approach to local elites was quite different than that of the leftists. While the leftists tried to attract a following by attacking local elites whom they believed to be unpopular, the rightist GMD feared the social chaos and conflict such assaults might create. Compared to the leftists' approach, rightist policies toward local elites could be called conciliatory. And it is not just at the level of pronouncements by high-level party bodies that one sees this difference. Out in the Jiangsu hinterland the contrast was even more pronounced. While one can find many instances of left-leaning party organizations launching mass campaigns against selected local elites, such actions by rightist GMD branches were nonexistent.

4

Jiangsu's Guomindang, 1927-1931: The Factional Background

In April of 1927 Jiangsu's Guomindang entered a new period in its troubled history. In important respects the situation looked hopeful for the party. The National Revolutionary Armies had cleared warlord troops from most of the province south of the Yangzi. On the county level, a plethora of governments were being appointed by the NRA, its Political Department, or the GMD itself. The purge of the Communists from party ranks was eradicating the main source of contention that had divided the GMD. Even so, continuing conflict and frustration marred provincial party affairs.

Within the purged party disagreement remained on many issues. New factions, based on networks of personal connections, were forming and competing for position and power within the regime's new governing apparatus. From 1927 on, factional divisions within the party were not based on the question of Communism. No longer was the party divided into one camp that favored Communist membership and one that opposed it. After the anti-Communist purge began, consensus quickly grew among Guomindang leaders that Communists should no longer be allowed to join the party. So the factionalism that raged within the party after mid-1927 had different foundations than the left-right division that had reigned since 1924.

This chapter dwells at length on the structure and clash of factions in the Jiangsu GMD after the Northern Expedition had brought the party to power in the province in 1927. At first glance it may strike some that such attention is misplaced, that the altercations between cliques were "full of sound and fury, signifying nothing." After all, since much of the scrapping concerned only the question of which group's people would hold what posts, why should it concern us? In the big picture of Republican China, did one person's—or one group's—control of an official chop really mean much? In fact, the factional story *is* important for a number of reasons. Not the least of these is that factional conflict was arguably the main mode of politics in Guomindang China. In the 1920s and 1930s, politicians could hardly function in the party or government at any level without navigating among the rocks and shoals of the cliques. The introduction of this book posed the question, "What animated GMD politics?" For a great many party members, the sort of factional competition that this chapter describes was front and center in their consciousness and motivations. Too few leadership posts on the local level were available for all members who thought they deserved them. Factional gamesmanship determined who would get a piece of the action along with the prestige and remuneration, modest though they were, of those local posts. It could be argued that for nearly every question about politics in Republican China, one needs to ask, "How does this relate to factionalism?" Serious observers of the Nanjing Decade cannot forget the fact that factional conflict had weighty consequences. Factional struggles on the central, provincial, and local levels meant that party leadership and structures on those strata changed repeatedly throughout the 1920s and 1930s.

As a result of the pervasive factional discord, the Guomindang was at times unable to act in a coordinated way on any issue. Fractious contention within the party affected the GMD's ability and inclination to respond either positively or punitively to particular social groups. Given this, it is no surprise that in the late 1920s the GMD handled local elites in a variety of ways. Although radicalism survived the 1927 purge of the Communists, and the party in a number of localities continued its assault on incumbent local elites and many of the institutions that they had controlled, the party in other places did no such thing. Because of lack of coordination, partly the result of factional disputes, a consistent approach was almost impossible. And if party and government contended and squabbled over policy toward local elites as well as other matters, one of the causes of this was that the party itself was split into factions. In some localities one faction was more strongly represented in the party branch leadership, while another was more firmly entrenched in local government organs. Factional clashing, therefore, not only harmed coordination within the party, but visited discord on the broader reaches of the regime.

The victory of one factional grouping, the Organization Clique, fundamentally transformed the party in Jiangsu. In 1930 and 1931, associates of the Organization Clique, acting in the name of the GMD

Central Organization Department, carried out a wholesale "rectification" of the provincial party and a large proportion of local party branches. The changes wrought by this factional takeover of Jiangsu's Guomindang were fundamental and sweeping. Until this time, young party radicals in many localities had continued to carry the day, pushing forward campaigns to remake local society and overturn incumbent elites. The rectification carried out by Organization Clique personnel largely ended the attacks on local elites and squelched the elements of radicalism that had survived the 1927 purge.

Factional Structures in Jiangsu

Many observers have pointed out that peasant societies have a tendency to split into factions at the village and higher levels.[1] We have already seen such a propensity to splinter into mutually hostile factions in the Jiangsu countryside prior to GMD rule. Not surprisingly, that situation continued after the GMD armies occupied the province. As one man described the situation in four counties in the North China zone:

> In recent years local factions and cliques have appeared to be rather well developed and so it is in the various counties in the district. The party headquarters, educational bodies, police, self-government organs, and mass organizations are all permeated with the demon of the cliques. Sometimes factions in the various domains will breathe with one breath [i.e., work together], while at other times they are all independent and will have nothing to do with each other. The struggles are very intense—the most serious involving armed demonstrations. If the opposition faction's principal leader does not have several muscle men following him around as bodyguards, he dares not act. When one day he has the power to mount the platform, then he will go in and out of the yamen, arguing cases and giving bribes, and he will cut a swath across the countryside and oppress the common people.[2]

Armed violence between local factions was probably more prevalent in Jiangsu's North China zone than in the Lower Yangzi area, but factionalism was a common feature in both areas.

Just as factions sometimes formed alliances across organizational boundaries, they also were linked together in nested, pyramidal structures that reached from the national to the provincial to the county level.

Andrew Nathan applies the term "complex faction" to these sorts of vertical chains of clientelist ties in which political actors at the top have as their clients leaders of secondary networks. In turn, the leaders of these secondary networks have ties with tertiary networks, and so forth.[3] One provincial party leader adamantly argued that the provincial party cliques were built on local cliques.[4] Any provincial leader attempting to secure a local base by recruiting a leader or member of an existing local faction, might instantly gain the following of that local clique, but would likely also earn the enmity of opposing cliques, thereby motivating them to ally with an opposition provincial-level faction.

In some cases, local cliques both inside and outside the party set up formal organizations to further their collective fortunes. Such bodies within the party were illegal and secret, and, therefore, not widely known unless they were discovered and their members prosecuted. Several members of the Kunshan County GMD who were linked with a provincial-level faction formed the *Weiguangshe* (literally, the "Concealed Brightness Society") in the late 1920s. In 1930, when their provincial patrons fell from power, nine *Weiguangshe* members were expelled from the party, nominally because of their membership in a "small organization" and their "reactionary propaganda."[5] Although these Kunshan clique leaders had gone too far by establishing a formal organization, hundreds of local clique leaders had similarly linked their fortunes to those of provincial cliques.

The Organization Clique (National Level)

One of the most powerful factions acting in national level GMD politics was the CC, or Organization Clique, as we shall call it to distinguish it from the provincial-level CC Clique, one of the several provincial-level branches of the Organization Clique in Jiangsu. Led by the brothers Chen Guofu and Chen Lifu, the Organization Clique was a network of personal relations based on the GMD Central Organization Department.[6]

Both Chen brothers, displaying the traditional propensity of Chinese to deny participation in factional politics, claimed that the Clique was merely a figment of the Communists' imagination.[7] In my interviews with former party leaders, those veteran GMD cadres preferred to allude to cliques as "groups" and denied that any formal organizations existed; nonetheless, they usually agreed that networks of personal relations and friendships did exist and were important in determining the course of party affairs. It is, however, possible that the Organization Clique had a formal organization, as outlined in some detail by Japanese intelligence officers in secret reports, but it would seem that the Organization Department itself should have been a more-than-adequate organizational backbone for the clique.[8]

The Chen brothers, like Chiang Kai-shek, were natives of Zhejiang. The brothers owed their close relationship with Chiang to their uncle, Chen Qimei, who was martyred in a revolutionary action against Yuan Shikai in 1916 and had long been Chiang's patron and virtual idol. In the early 1920s Chen Guofu had been involved with Chiang and several Shanghai capitalists in a stock and commodity exchange. After a brief stint in Shanghai recruiting students for the GMD's Huangpu Military Academy, Chen went to Guangzhou, where he acted as the assistant chairman of the party's Organization Department after Chiang's first anti-Communist coup on March 20, 1926. Although Chiang was the official chairman of the department, he entrusted most of the responsibilities to Chen. In this position Chen plotted the April 1927 purge.[9]

Chen Lifu had been studying at the University of Pittsburgh's School of Mining, but in the mid-1920s he returned to China and accepted a position in Guangzhou as Chiang's confidential secretary.[10] In 1928 he was appointed director of the Investigation Section of the Organization Department, which identified CCP members for elimination or expulsion from the GMD, and reportedly administered a "special affairs" (secret police) operation. Some have dubbed the Investigation Section—and the Central Statistical Bureau that it begot—the "nucleus" of the Organization Clique, because of its select membership and the power that its personnel files and "special affairs" activities engendered.[11] Similarly, only a few top Organization Clique leaders were members of the supersecret Blue and White Society (*Qingbaishe*) established in 1933.[12]

Andrew Nathan has suggested that Chinese cliques often used support structures to aid their pursuits financially or otherwise.[13] The Organization Department's considerable patronage meant that that body was the best support structure conceivable; the Standing Committee of the Central Executive Committee filled a great number of the party's appointive positions following recommendations of the Organization Department. The Central Party Affairs Academy (later the Central Political Academy) was also dominated by the Organization Clique, as were the Jiangsu Farmer's Bank and the Huai River Conservancy

Committee. Clique leaders used some of the abundant resources these organizations possessed to aid in building their personal followings.[14] Chen Guofu showed great generosity to certain promising young party members by helping them finish their schooling and aiding them in attaining positions of power and prestige, and his beneficence was mirrored by the personal loyalty that some of these protégés later showed him.[15] The Chens' lieutenants who held provincial party leadership positions also concentrated on recruiting young party members at the local level. When asked how Organization Clique associates polled more votes than some veteran party figures from other factional networks at provincial congresses, one former provincial figure replied that Organization Clique leaders actively campaigned among the youthful county party members and delegates. According to him, young people were easily flattered by the attention paid them by provincial party leaders.[16]

The Jiangsu government became one of the greatest bulwarks of the Organization Clique. Throughout the decade, some provincial government departments were headed by Organization stalwarts and people in some way tied to the Chens.[17] From 1930 to 1931, Ye Chucang was provincial governor. He was a senior member of the party, and his stature was such that he would not have been considered a factional subordinate of the Chens; nonetheless, he had good relations with the Chens.[18] In 1933, Chen Guofu himself assumed the post of provincial governor of Jiangsu. Chen's governorship opened a new source of patronage for the Organization group to dispense.

By advocating the modernization of China based on traditional Chinese values and culture, a few Organization Clique leaders at the central level went against the cultural iconoclasm which prevailed among Chinese intellectuals. Embracing a latter-day Confucianist "restoration of glory," these Clique leaders advocated fusing a renewed confidence in Chinese culture with the technical and material skills of Western science to bring about a "national renaissance." They advocated a "dialectical" melding of the cultures of East and West.[19] However, because this clique, like most other factions in the post-purge GMD, was built more on networks of personal connections than on ideology, one cannot assume that all party members or even the leadership associated with the Organization Clique shared this restorationist vision.

Provincial Factions

Far from being a unified entity, the national Organization Clique was split into several discrete factions in Jiangsu. At least four of the province's cliques—the CC, FF, Yang-Ma-Cao, and Central Party Affairs Academy Cliques—sported close ties with the Chen brothers and the Central Organization Department, and all were able to tap the resources of the support organizations of the Organization Clique.[20]

The provincial CC Clique was led by Li Shouyong, a native of Jiangsu's Yancheng County. While a student at Beijing University in the mid-1920s, Li had been a leader of the Sunist Practice Society (*Zhongshan zhuyi shijian she*), which was established after Sun Yat-sen's death in order to oppose the Western Hills Clique. Because of secrecy that had to be maintained at the time for members to avoid being nabbed by warlord police, other anti-Western Hills organizations formed, splitting Beijing University students into competing factions. In August 1929, Beijing's Practice Society disbanded under pressure from Chen Guofu, but Li had already used it as the nucleus for his Jiangsu CC Clique and recruited Jiangsu natives from its membership.[21] About 1930 Li Shouyong and another CC leader, Wang Baoxuan, went abroad to study, leaving the CC Clique's leadership in the hands of Qi Xiyong, who soon died, Zhou Shaocheng, and Zhou Jieren. In the mid-1930s Li joined a component of the Blue Shirt (*Lanyishe/Fuxingshe/Lixingshe*) complex of factions. This factional complex was composed of former students and teachers of the Huangpu Military Academy and is usually described as a bitter enemy of the Organization Clique.[22] Li took very few, if any, of his CC followers with him in this new departure.[23] The fact that the CC Clique survived Li's departure and that the group did not follow him to the Blue Shirt factional complex provides evidence that something more than dyadic relations were involved in factional construction. Contrary to Andrew Nathan's suggestion that "a faction cannot survive its leader," the CC Clique exhibited a group cohesion that outlasted its leader's clientelist ties.[24]

Another provincial group claiming strong ties with the Organization Clique was the FF Clique, the name of which derived from the English language moniker "Five Friends." The FF label was given by outsiders to a group of five young Jiangsu and Nanjing politicians who met (only twice, according to one source) in Nanjing in 1927 or 1928 for "friendly conversations" and, likely, discussion of party affairs.[25] The linchpin of the FF group was Ye Xiufeng, whose relationship with the Chen brothers derived from his years as classmate of Chen Lifu at the Pittsburgh School of Mining. Ye formally entered the GMD, with Chen Lifu acting as his sponsor, in an emotional ceremony on the day that the news of Sun Yat-sen's death reached Pittsburgh. Ye graduated in 1925, then returned to China. In 1927 Chen Guofu engineered Ye's appointment as a Jiangsu Provincial Party Purge Committee member. Sometime in the late 1920s Ye went to work in the powerful Investigation Section of the Central Organization Department, advancing to become its director briefly. In the 1930s Ye assumed duties in the Central Statistical Office, the secret police arm and nucleus of the Organization Clique, and he later became its head.[26] Although this should have given the FF group an inside track to appointments and use of the secret police, it is unclear whether the other provincial branches of the national Organization Clique were unfairly victimized.

Zhang Yuanyang headed yet another provincial grouping affiliated with the national-level Organization Clique: the Central Party Affairs Academy Clique (*Dangxiao pai*). The core activists of this loose faction were Central Party Affairs Academy graduates who had been appointed to local "directorate" committees in 1928 to register and screen party members. Although quite a number of local GMD cadres were connected with Zhang, this faction was less powerful than most other provincial factions.[27]

The Yang-Ma-Cao Clique was, on the other hand, a strong contender for power and position in the early 1930s. This provincial adjunct of the Organization Clique took its name from its three principal leaders: Yang Xingqin, Ma Yuanfang, and Cao Minghuan. Yang, a Central Organization Department insider, was sometimes said to have been this group's leader, though it is clear that Ma and Cao did not always see things that way—such as when all three competed against each other in Jiangsu Provincial Executive Committee elections in 1932. The meteoric ascendancy of this group in provincial party affairs in the early 1930s resulted from intervention by the Central Organization Department. That body engineered the appointment of the three to fill vacancies in the Rectification Committee, which controlled the Jiangsu GMD in 1930. Not surprisingly, many within Jiangsu party circles protested the appointments, dubbing the new group the "outsider faction" (*fei Jiangsu ren pai*), even though Ma was actually a Jiangsu native.[28]

Ranged against the many provincial arms of the Organization Clique was the so-called Anti-CC Clique (*Fan CC pai*), a coalition of local and provincial party leaders and members who were united against the incessant power hunger of the Organization Clique. Gu Ziyang, the northern Jiangsu GMD leader, was the patriarch of Anti-CC elements. He was popular with youth, and it is said that early every morning before he rose, protégés queued on benches in his antechamber, anxious to discuss party affairs with him.[29] Many youthful party members were radical in their political and social views, and, as one conservative CC leader put it, Gu was sometimes "irresponsible" in his choice of subordinates; indeed, on one occasion Gu felt compelled to ask the Central Executive Committee for punishment because he had helped someone who turned out to be Communist. One former GMD leader has suggested that were it not for this sort of "careless" patronage Gu should have been a member of the Central Executive Committee because of his age and long experience in building the party in Jiangsu. Another provincial leader stated in an interview that Gu was "somewhat leftist" in his policy orientation, but that person had difficulty identifying particular policies that Gu had advocated.[30]

Gu's personal connections on the national level are somewhat obscure, though he and several other Anti-CC leaders had ties to the Huangpu Clique, a loose assortment of military figures who had taught at or graduated from the Huangpu Military Academy.[31] In the 1920s Gu had recruited several prospective students for the Huangpu Academy. Later, some of those individuals and their friends in the Huangpu Clique occasionally aided Gu and the rest of the Anti-CC leaders.[32]

The Anti-CC Clique was a looser coalition than the CC or FF groups. Since it often sided with a wide variety of elements, including Wang Jingwei's "leftists," against the Organization group, its members were sometimes accused of being members of the outcast Reorganization Clique.[33] It is difficult to believe that the Anti-CC group had a strong ideological or programmatic commitment, because it included both Ge Jianshi, a former member of the right-wing Sunist Study Society, and Ni Bi, an insistent advocate of thoroughgoing social revolution.[34]

The Reorganization Clique (*Gaizu pai*) consisted of the followers of left-wing GMD leaders Wang Jingwei and Chen Gongbo. One of the leading lights of this group in Jiangsu was Teng Gu, a left-leaning litterateur and associate of Wang Jingwei.[35] Members of this faction tended to be more interested in sparking social revolution and creating and sustaining a mass base for the party than were those associated with the Organization Clique. Propagandists for this group advocated nurturing support for the party among peasants, workers, and small merchants by including them in party-led mass organizations which would fight for their interests. In general, although they disavowed class struggle—perhaps to defend themselves from the charge that they were Communists—some of them favored policies which had potential to engender social polarization: rent reduction, confiscation of the land of "large-scale landlords," overthrow of so-called "feudal powers" in rural China, and prevention of the development of rural capitalism.[36]

Until late 1929 the Reorganizationists and the Anti-CC Clique often worked together to oppose the Organization Clique. In fact, it is doubtful whether the two were completely separate entities until a Reorganizationist plot to overthrow the government in late 1929 both alienated the Anti-CC partisans and seriously damaged the future prospects of both factions.[37]

The Local Reaches of Factionalism

Guomindang factionalism reached down to the county level and below. In the counties, most political acts (and, of course, virtually all appointments) were part and parcel of factional conflict. However, the names given to the local factions were not always the same as those at the provincial level. For example, one memoir's author describes the split in the Siyang County GMD as being between the "Zhou" and "Chen" factions, two clique names not found in accounts of provincial politics. But it is clear that Zhou Huapeng, the leader of Siyang's Zhou Faction, was closely tied to the provincial FF Clique, while Chen Ruyi, the head of the county's so-called Chen Clique, was an associate of provincial CC leader Li Shouyong. Thus, two of the several provincial factions dominated politics in Siyang, even if their monikers were not usually invoked when referring to local political actors. Other provincial cliques were largely shut out of Siyang County.[38]

Local Elite Factions Beget Pi County GMD Factions. The rise of factionalism at the county level might appear to have been inevitable, given the way in which the provincial party was split. But the rise of GMD factions at the county level was rather complex, and the factors behind its genesis varied by locality. In at least one locality—and, perhaps, a few more—some of the GMD factions were lineal descendants of the cliques that local elites had formed prior to the rise of GMD rule in 1927. This, of course, means that such localities experienced no sharp rift between the party and incumbent local elites as a whole.

The Guomindang in Pi County (North China zone) was divided into the Number One, Number Two, and Number Three Factions (*Yi pai*, *Er pai*, and *San pai*). Of these three, the Number One and Number Two groupings first emerged in the period between 1911 and the 1927 Northern Expedition. Soon after the 1911 Revolution, Zhang Hongye became the leader of a circle of local leaders that styled itself as the local Guomindang, though no formal party organization seems to have existed in the county. This group competed for positions and power against a clique of local elites who identified themselves the Republican Party (*Gonghedang*)—but which may also have lacked a formal party structure. Zhang was a graduate of the Fourth Provincial Normal School in Nanjing, and by the early Republican era he had become the principal of the First Upper Elementary School in the Pi county seat and served as Pi County's education inspector. Although President Yuan Shikai had outlawed the Guomindang after the Second Revolution in 1913, Zhang's group enjoyed continuing clout on both the county and township levels in the early Republican period. One of its members was general manager (*zongdong*) of the Pi county seat, and another of Zhang's associates was manager of Guanhu, the largest city in the county. Therefore, during the pre-1927 era, the county magistrate had to consult with Zhang's people before he could hope to accomplish much of anything administratively. In the 1917 campaign, Zhang and another of his faction's members won election to posts as Pi County's provincial assemblymen.[39]

Thus, Zhang and his grouping had attained an enviable stature in Pi County politics by the early 1920s. When China's GMD was reorganized in early 1924, Zhang's local "Guomindang" seems to have remained outside of the new, centrally dictated party structure. One of Zhang's cohorts, fellow provincial assemblyman Feng Shaozhan, developed close ties with Communist Tan Pingshan, head of the GMD's Central Organization Department in the early- to mid-1920s, as well as with Zhang Shushi, a leader of the reorganized GMD's left wing. But there is no evidence that the party center controlled Zhang Hongye's grouping.[40]

By the late 1910s or early 1920s, Zhang had come to distrust the ambitions of one Wang Lantian, a member of Zhang's faction, and from those suspicions would grow a split in Zhang's grouping. Wang Lantian had earned a lower exam degree in the late Qing, but by the first decade of the twentieth century he had imbibed the thought of Sun Yat-sen and had come to favor revolution. Accordingly, he joined an anti-Qing army during the 1911 Revolution. After serving briefly as a bodyguard for Sun Yat-sen when that revolutionary icon was the Republic's provisional president, Wang returned to Pi County and accepted a teaching post at an upper elementary school there. In the late 1910s, Zhang watched with some trepidation as Wang and Zhou Xu, now the principal of the Pi County First Upper Elementary School, developed a large following among young intellectuals in the county. Zhang knew that being principal of that school was prestigious, and that the position could be a great launching pad for anyone seeking to challenge him for his post as assemblyman. Zhang had traveled that political road himself, and he was not inclined to allow Zhou or Wang to use their school ties to bring down either of the sitting provincial assemblymen.[41]

Thus, Zhang persuaded a student at Zhou's school to collect several classmates and lead them in a campaign to force the principal to quit his job. The student gathered a group of chums and invaded Zhou's office, shouting slogans, blowing whistles, and swinging clubs. Zhou, sensing that his situation at the school was now untenable, jumped out the window and vacated his post as principal. Wang, perceiving that the attack was as much aimed at him as Zhou, also left his job at the school. But if Zhang's goal was to eliminate Zhou and Wang as political rivals, he was to be disappointed. Before long, Wang had won appointment as principal of Pi County's new normal school, the county's only middle-level school. Zhang was even more troubled by Wang's new position than he had been about the prior post at the elementary school. Because a normal school trained future teachers and school administrators, Wang's new job would allow him over the next few years to spread his protégés all over Pi County in educational jobs, where they would use their prestige and followings to challenge Zhang. Thus Zhang, determined to use the same method to remove Wang that he had used to dispatch Zhou, sent a group of student toughs to thrash Wang. But Wang was out of his office when the ruffians arrived, and when he heard of the near-encounter with Zhang's students, he immediately responded by sending a group of his own student allies to attack one of Zhang's friends. Wang's student "enforcers" surrounded Zhang's friend in broad daylight on a city street and proceeded to daub him from head to toe with mud. Though this act of revenge by proxy may have been intended to demonstrate to Zhang that Wang would not run from a challenge, it ripped apart Wang's school. Before long, the normal school closed its doors because conflict between the two factions of students and teachers made teaching impossible.[42]

These two factions, Zhang's and Wang's, by the mid-1920s had thoroughly split the grouping that had started out in 1912 as the county "Guomindang." And when the Northern Expeditionary Armies reached Pi County in 1928 and the GMD provincial party committee began to organize a formal party branch for the county, that new body accepted members from both Zhang's and Wang's groups. From this time until 1938, when the county was lost to invading Japanese armies, Zhang's faction (the Number Two Faction) and Wang's faction (the Number One Faction) continued to feud and competed for control of the county's affairs. In the 1930s they were joined by a new group that was known as the Number Three faction.[43]

Thus, two of Pi County's GMD factions were outgrowths of conflict among established elites. This was, however, an exceptional situation; I have uncovered none others quite like it. In most localities there was a sharper divide between pre-Northern Expeditionary elites' cliques and the factions that formed within the GMD after the Northern Expedition. More typical was the situation found in Yancheng County, in which the GMD's post-1927 factions were different than those found among pre-1927 local elites, even though the older elites' factions came to exert some influence within the party by the late 1920s or early 1930s.[44]

Local Cliques in Other Counties. Not only were the party factions in most counties not rooted in pre-1927 cliques among local oligarchs, some did not appear until well after the new regime had established itself. For example, in Suining County the two Guomindang county cliques, the Bao and Xu Factions, first appeared in the early 1930s. One memoir explains the rise of these competing groups by totaling up the number of formal leadership positions in the party and comparing them to the number of ambitious and prominent GMD politicians; the latter were, the reminiscence avers, considerably more plentiful than the former. As the memoirist explains, while twelve or more Suining GMD members by experience and prominence were qualified to sit on the county executive committee and the supervisory committee, the executive committee could only have three to five members, and the supervisory committee could seat only one. Although in point of fact, the supervisory committee sometimes consisted of three members, the memoir writer's point is telling. Very soon in the party's development there were too few "goodies" to hand out, and too many members who had to share them. Similarly, there were too few positions such as county bureau heads, ward headmen, and school principals for the number of party members who felt themselves worthy of such posts. Since county governments sometimes appointed to plum positions persons who were not party members, the competition for nomination to the remaining slots was all the more brutal.[45]

That analysis does not explain, though, why the Bao-versus-Xu split did not occur prior to the early thirties. Perhaps the best explanation for the seeming unity before 1930 is that prior to that year the local party was under strong attack from the outside. During much of the period from 1927 through 1929 the Suining GMD was frequently under assault by the county government, pre-1927 local elites, Sword Society braves, and sometimes all three acting in concert. These harrowing conditions necessitated that party members temporarily set aside personal ambitions to gain the support of as many other GMD stalwarts as possible to insure survival. By 1930 the Suining political environment had stabilized. Many of the external threats had disappeared, making members less willing to hold in check their own aspirations for leadership positions.

Helen Chauncey has suggested that one of the chief fault lines in Jiangsu politics during the Nanjing Decade divided county-level politicians from subcounty (township- or ward-level) elites.[46] Although memoirs provide evidence that there were many localities in which county and township-level (or ward-level) party politicians were fairly well integrated, some party branches did experience county-township schisms. For example, from 1928 on, the Suqian GMD was fractured into a City Faction (*Cheng pai*) and a Township Faction (*Xiang pai*). This breach stemmed from the way reregistration of party members in 1928 was handled.

The party center appointed the committee that controlled the Jiangsu GMD through much of 1928, the Jiangsu Provincial Party Affairs Directorate. The provincial directorate named county-level directorate committees that supervised county party branches and screened and reregistered party members; these county directorates were supposed to exclude from the party Communists and others whose commitment to GMD party principles was suspect. The provincial directorate appointed a Suqian County Directorate that was overwhelmingly composed of members from Suqian's township-level municipalities. The registration that these township-based leaders supervised revoked the party cards of roughly two-thirds of the prior members of the Suqian GMD. A disproportionate percentage of those excluded as members were residents of the county seat, many of whom were longtime activists and pillars of the local GMD during the tough years when the party had been an underground revolutionary organization. Even though many of the city-based activists later regained entry to the Guomindang, they continued to nurse resentment against the township-level leaders who had so unceremoniously dumped them. Although it has been suggested that the GMD regime generally extended county-level authority at the expense of township- or ward-level elites and, thereby, fostered contentious relations with subcounty elites, throughout most of the Nanjing Decade township-based GMD leaders dominated Suqian politics.[47] Although at times a few City Faction figures acquired positions on the county party committee and in other arenas, there seems to be little question that the Township Faction (which was tied to Zhou Houjun, a key provincial FF Clique leader) took first place in Suqian politics.[48]

Only a few counties displayed this sort of estrangement between GMD leaders based in the county seat and those who hailed from subcounty-level communities. However, it was not unusual for a particular county faction dependably to garner most of its support from a predictable handful of market towns or wards. In elections for positions on county party executive committees, the ward-by-ward distribution of votes in some counties assumed a perennial this-side-of-the-county-versus-that-side pattern. For example, Funing County's GMD was sundered into a Dai Faction (*Dai pai*) and an Overthrow Dai Faction (*Dao Dai pai*), also known, respectively, as the Southwest Faction (*Xi'nan pai*) and the Northeast Faction (*Dongbei pai*). The leader of the Southwest Faction, Dai Jizhi, has been described as a slick politician from a well-heeled family who availed himself of the aid of "powerful elites" (*haoshen*) to establish his commanding position in the Funing GMD branch. Additionally, he used his office as head of the county party's Organization

Department to secure his mastery of the Funing party—to the point that people commonly spoke of the local party as being his "household" (*Dai jia dang*). Dai hailed from Goudun, a market town in the southern part of Funing, and he and his clique derived most of their support from party people hailing from towns in the southern and southwestern parts of the county, including Caoyan, Donggou, and Yilin. Zhou Zhongchen, the leader of the opposing Northeast Faction, sprang from "an upper gentry family" (*juren jiating*) which resided in the northeastern Funing market town of Dongkan. Zhou's clique consisted of GMD members primarily from market towns in Funing's northeastern and eastern reaches, most notably Dongkan, Caiqiao, Batan, and Chenyang.[49]

This kind of territorial basing for county factions was fairly common, judging from memoir accounts of factions elsewhere in the province. The fact that county factional leaders could frequently depend on their home ward for support might lead one to anticipate that a provincial factional leader could also expect his home county to align itself with him and his own clique. In fact, some provincial leaders did derive strength from their own county's GMD branch. For example, provincial CC Clique head Li Shouyong was from Yancheng County, a locality whose GMD branch was dominated by CC partisans through most of the Nanjing Decade, though this domain was hardly unchallenged by Anti-CC diehards. Li brought several Yancheng natives to work in the provincial party headquarters, helping to propel them to careers in party affairs at the provincial level. It is worth noting, though, that while Li abandoned his CC faction in the early thirties and became a Blue Shirt, his supporters in Yancheng remained tied to the provincial CC Clique.[50]

Some provincial faction leaders had a harder time maintaining their clique's unquestioned dominance in their home county. For example, although provincial Anti-CC head Gu Ziyang was from Tongshan, that county's GMD politicians were split into several groupings; two, the East and West Factions (*Dong pai* and *Xi pai*), were somewhat evenly matched, and one, the Third Faction, was a weaker clique of more recent vintage. Gu, like Li Shouyong, propelled a few of his Tongshan area friends into provincial party jobs.[51] He also helped to groom the leader of the county's East Faction, Zhu Limin, for power in the community by making him principal of Xuzhou Private Middle School, an institution which Gu had founded and managed for many years. Roughly commensurate in power to the East group was the West Faction, whose leader, Xu Ximing, used his position as Tongshan County Experimental Elementary School principal to hire many members of his clique as teachers. Associates of both the East and West Factions held important posts during the Nanjing Decade. East Faction member Lan Bohua was head of the Tongshan Chamber of Commerce until West Faction accusations of corruption dragged him down and brought about a West Faction takeover of that body. Others in the East Faction included the county's education association head, Liu Zihou, and the chairman of the county lawyers' association, Liu Chuanjing. Counterbalancing those prominent East Faction members, West Faction partisan Liu Tianzhan was, for a time, the head of the county office of education, and another West Faction ally, Sun Gong, controlled the General Labor Union. Provincial Anti-CC leader Gu Ziyang sometimes intervened to help Zhu Limin's East Faction, as in 1932 when Gu helped overturn the election of a county executive committee which had gone in favor of the West group. Despite Gu's support for the East camp, the West group seems to have been somewhat more successful in garnering positions of party leadership.[52]

But if Gu had difficulty in maintaining Anti-CC influence in his old stomping ground of Tongshan, provincial FF Clique leader Ye Xiufeng had an absolute devil of a time in his own hometown of Yangzhou. From 1927 until 1930, the CC Clique largely controlled the GMD for Jiangdu, the county in which the city of Yangzhou was located. In 1930 the provincial party headquarters sent out a rectification team to control the Jiangdu GMD and carry out a reregistration of members. The county rectification committee included one Yang-Ma-Cao, two CC, and two FF partisans. But the CC and FF stalwarts on the committee were not able to work together, and this gave Ling Shaozu, who was a provincial-level Anti-CC figure and also a Yangzhou native, an opening to construct an alliance between Anti-CC and Yang-Ma-Cao forces. Thus it was that by late 1930 or so, Ling's Anti-CC people were able to dominate the county—to the point that many of those who had been members of the previously ascendant CC group in the county changed their allegiance to Ling and his Anti-CC Clique. In short, the FF group was again nearly shut out of the party leadership on FF chieftain Ye Xiufeng's own home turf.[53]

Factional Tactics: Using Local Resources. Local factions employed a dazzling repertoire of tactics to expand their power and deflate the sails of their opponents. For purposes of analysis, one can distinguish between, on the one hand, tactics that entailed fostering and relying on local resources to enhance factional fortunes and, on the other hand, methods which involved seeking intervention by provincial or other outside authorities.

One of the strategies that involved reliance on local resources was to control strictly who could be a member of the party. A memoir from Jingjiang County testifies that it was difficult, if not impossible, for a person to join the party without support from either of the two factions in the Jingjiang GMD. The requirement that anyone joining the GMD be sponsored by two members meant that many ambitious young persons who believed that the road to public office ran straight through the local GMD branch were disappointed in their bids to join.[54] Furthermore, even after gaining entry to the party, a person could be thrown out in any of the several reregistrations that were designed by the center to expose and eliminate Communists and others "not faithful to party principles." Sometimes deputies sent out from the center had the gatekeeping responsibilities during these reregistrations, but often local factional personnel oversaw the screening. And even when a wholesale reregistration was not taking place, the county GMD's supervisory committee had the power to impeach members, with an eye toward expulsion. Thus a key tool to facilitate membership restriction rested in the hands of whatever faction controlled the committee. On the other hand, a faction could choose to boost its chances in the next election of party officers by emphasizing the recruitment of new members by its own agents out in the various wards of a county.

Like political machines in big American cities in the late nineteenth and early twentieth centuries, factions heavily relied on their patronage power to bolster their local following. Faction chiefs handed out whatever plums they could get for their members. Leaders who were school principals provided teaching jobs to members of their group. Sometimes the positions doled out were in county and subcounty government, while others were spots on public committees that exercised authority in the various administrative realms of education, water control, local defense, and so forth.[55]

Local factional wars went beyond competition for patronage, however. Faction captains wished to be able to shape the public's perception of events to justify their members' activities and to vilify their opponents. Therefore, factions attempted to control the media. Many of the local newspapers and journals published in Jiangsu were associated with one or another of the factions. For example, the Suqian County GMD branch's official organ, *Suqian minbao* (*Suqian Citizen's Report*), was managed by members of the county's Township Faction, the clique which held most of the positions on the county party committee. Sometime around 1932, City Faction stalwarts, hoping to gain favorable press coverage for their members' deeds and views, founded *Suqian ribao* (*Suqian Daily*), a paper with a circulation of about one thousand copies. Before long, the Township Faction began to feel that *Suqian minbao*, because it was the official paper of the entire local party, was insufficiently partisan in its support of Township Faction personnel. Therefore, Township Faction cadres founded a new paper, *Xin Su ribao* (*The New Suqian Daily*), which was more effusive in its Township Faction sentiments than was *Suqian minbao*. The way in which Suqian newspapers evinced their factional sponsorship can be seen in their coverage of a 1935 disaster in which an overloaded boat sank during a flood, killing over forty people. The Township Faction's *Xin Su ribao* blamed the tragedy on Liu Zisheng, a prominent City Faction member who was head of the ward that included the Suqian county seat. The newspaper charged that Liu's "leadership is typically weak, his investigation of matters is not vigorous, and his planning is incomplete." In general, the Township Faction critics charged that Liu's bungling had helped cause the mishap. The City Faction's paper, predictably, took a more generous view of Liu's conduct, essentially exonerating him of blame.[56] Such factionally biased shaping of public opinion was an important part of political gamesmanship in Jiangsu localities.

In addition to managing journalistic ventures, certain local faction leaders ran other sorts of businesses and used these companies as tools in factional battles. In Jingjiang, for example, leaders of the two local GMD cliques, the East Faction and the West Faction, founded competing bus companies as extensions of their political rivalry. The two sides regularly employed factional "disciples and hangers-on" to go into the streets and block the path of the competing company's coaches. Each side also deputized its minions to toss stones and bricks at the opposing faction's passing buses, giving the observer some insight into how important the health and well-being of the general public was in the eyes of factional potentates.[57]

Much of the thuggish brawn that Huang Zhian, Jingjiang's East Faction boss, could count on was provided by members of the local Green Gang (*Qing bang*). The leader of this group of gang members was Zhu Ji, a gruff and beefy man. As an elementary school student, Zhu had often sported a bloody nose and swollen face because of his penchant for brawling and bullying. Since 1927, through pluck, bravado, and political skills, Zhu had become the overlord of a faction within Jingjiang County's Green Gang. He had an uncanny ability to appeal both to local ne'er-do-wells who lived by their wits and fists, and to young men from wealthy families. He brought both sorts into his Green Gang fold. It was largely Zhu's Green Gang henchmen who lobbed the rocks that spoiled the West Faction's buses. Zhu also did other duties for Huang's East Faction, including denouncing the county magistrate, whom the East Faction wished to bring down, in front of a large public gathering. Huang, for his part, offered his help to Zhu when the offended magistrate arrested the Green Gang leader. Huang cranked up the East Faction's newspaper—which he himself edited—to expose the magistrate's "unfair" treatment of Zhu. Huang also financed and orchestrated litigation that brought about Zhu's release from jail. In short, the East Faction of Jiangjiang's GMD had a tacit alliance with Zhu's grouping in the Green Gang. Not to be outdone, Jingjiang's West Faction's chieftain, Sheng Xiru, developed his own link with Zhu's main rival in the Green Gang, Liu Shengping. Thus, the factionalism in Jingjiang's GMD was replicated within that county's Green Gang lodges.[58]

The hurling of stones at buses in Jingjiang was by no means the only example of violence associated with local GMD factionalism. We have already cited instances of factional leaders inciting students to beat up or intimidate school administrators and teachers. Clique masters also at times used hired thugs to scare off or, rarely, to kill an opponent. For example, Li Tongfu, the leader of Yancheng County's Anti-CC Clique, in 1930 hired a group of toughs, outfitted in uniforms replete with Napoleon hats, to rough up and generally terrorize a special deputy the provincial GMD headquarters had sent out to reorganize the local party. Li had correctly surmised that the provincial CC Clique had given this deputy the task of destroying all vestiges of Anti-CC power and ensuring unchallenged CC Clique supremacy in the county.[59]

Outside Intervention and Resources. Local factions, in their quest for stature and power, certainly did not rely solely on local resources. Accounts of local politics are replete with leaders' appeals, both successful and unsuccessful, to outside agents to persuade them to intervene on the local stage. These appeals took the form of joint petitions, accusations against local rivals, and face-to-face lobbying. The outside entities to which local factions looked for help included the local, provincial, and national governments (and their various bureaus); the provincial and central party headquarters (and their various departments); and the commanders of nearby army units.

The aura of legitimacy that higher-level organs could confer on local party leaders was a potent weapon. When upper-level party authorities sent out deputies or rectification teams, those agents were frequently able to boost the fortunes of local factions whose leaders they chose to confirm in power. This kind of action was common during the period of the provincial directorate (see Appendix I) and the provincial rectification committee (see the last section of this chapter). And agents of higher-level party organs could go a long way toward destroying a local faction's political standing, effectively delegitimizing that faction's leaders. Although in many cases outside interference in local politics came at the request of one or more local factions, higher authorities often intervened without prior entreaties by any local actors.

Of course, it was the desire to tap outside resources that caused local factions to align themselves with provincial party factions. A local party clique leader who had a tie with an upper-level clique leader had a much more realistic hope of calling upon outside resources to bolster his group's lot than one who did not. Although sometimes these ties were products of longtime prior association with a provincial clique leader, often they were simply a result of fortuitous, random choice by clique leaders at the provincial and county levels. No matter how the identification between a particular county-level faction and its corresponding provincial faction may have arisen, that tie was usually durable. Nonetheless, there were cases of county factional leaders shifting allegiance from one provincial faction to another and bringing all or part of their county clique with them. For example, by 1927 the Huai'an

County GMD was split into the North Township and West Township Factions (*Beixiang pai* and *Xixiang pai*), but the provincial factional bonds of a number of individuals in these groups did not endure throughout the Guomindang era. Although at the beginning of the Nanjing Decade the North Township Faction was allied with the Anti-CC Clique and the West Township group oriented itself toward the CC Clique, sometime in the early 1930s a large number of West Township Clique members switched their allegiance to the provincial FF Clique.[60] These shifts in provincial factional connections seem to have been precipitated both by personal enmities that had grown up within the West Township group and by the lure of resources the provincial FF group had to offer—resources that had gone unused in Huai'an until this time. After this reshaping of the county's factions, people stopped speaking of the North Township and West Township factions, but instead began referring to the CC, FF, and Anti-CC factions. Thus, as the logic of events worked out, the Huai'an County party's divisions (and labels) came to mimic more closely those on the provincial level.

The variety of provincial resources that local factions could use was limited only by the ingenuity of their political operatives and the tolerance of higher administrators for chaos on the local scene. In fact, there are signs that provincial authorities, when they felt that local factions' actions threatened paramount administrative objectives, denied those factions access to coveted resources. One memoir suggests, for example, that the regime restructured its Communist suppression apparatus to insulate it from local factions' influence. For a brief period in the early- to mid-1930s, the Communist suppression (*sufan*, literally, "suppression of counterrevolutionaries") system appointed someone in each of the various counties to serve as "commissioner for suppression of counterrevolutionaries" (*sufan zhuanyuan*). This commissioner was chosen from among county branch leaders, and his office was lodged in the county party headquarters. Often the people who were appointed to this post were also members of the county executive committee of the GMD, and as such, were already knitted into one local factional web or another. For example, Shi Yiqian, who was appointed Haimen's commissioner, was also a county executive committee member and a partisan of the county party's West Clique (*Xi pai*), a group which contended for power against Haimen's East Clique (*Dong pai*). To prevent local cliques from diverting the suppressive powers of these commissionerships into the arena of local political gamesmanship, the provincial authorities, presumably provincial governor Chen Guofu, abolished the posts. In place of the commissioners, the province established county special affairs offices that were directly controlled by the Special Affairs Office (*Tewu shi*) of the provincial party headquarters and by certain regional offices. This can be seen as a move toward bureaucratizing and centralizing the suppressive branches of the regime, though some might also view it as an administrative reorganization designed to ensure that Communist suppression mechanisms were firmly in the grip of Organization Clique personnel, who by that time largely controlled the provincial party apparatus.[61]

Provincial leaders' suspicions that party factions in the county arena were using the Communist suppression apparatus to savage factional opponents were not without foundation. One case of this sort occurred in Huai'an County, where a group of leaders connected with the provincial Anti-CC Clique were said to have framed as "Communist" a factional enemy, Liu Xifan, by printing up a stack of ersatz Communist propaganda, planting it in incriminating locations, and then escorting a contingent of garrison forces to the spot where they nabbed him. Although Liu faced a determined group of opponents, the courts ultimately freed him, and he continued to be an influential local party leader throughout the Nanjing Decade. However, a memoir argues that Niu Jianchu, a ringleader in the plot against Liu, finally got his way. During the Japanese occupation of the county, he managed to persuade the GMD's Special Affairs Office for Jiangsu to arrange Liu's assassination. Thus, although the province's leaders had taken measures to limit the ability of local politicians to use the special affairs apparatus in intra-GMD politics, some local politicos were little restrained.[62]

From Leftist Rebellion to Rectification

For nearly the first three years of the Nanjing Decade, Jiangsu's provincial-level factions battled. If the proponents and opponents of the national Organization Clique were not completely evenly matched, at least the players were of the same stature. This period from 1927 through late 1929 was punctuated by frequent changes in party structure and in the membership of committees that controlled the provincial and local parties, with most of those changes affecting the relative power of the various factions. After a brief, four-month period of dominance by the Western Hills Clique in late 1927, that group was virtually excluded from serious contention for power. So the main battle came to be one between the Organization group's branches (especially the CC and FF Cliques) on one side and the Anti-CC and Reorganization Cliques on the other—though the Organization Clique's branches by no means always saw eye to eye, especially on the question of appointments.

Those opposed to the Organization group were able to draw upon the vast network of protégés that Gu Ziyang, Ge Jianshi, and other Anti-CC leaders had built before the purge. Anti-CC leaders and Reorganizationists also rode a crest of social radicalism which continued to sweep the party at the local level. They encouraged radicalism through their rhetoric as well as their occasional protection of radicals from the clutches of central party headquarters.

The provincial appendages of the Organization group, by contrast, drew much of their strength from the intervention of the central party headquarters on their behalf. That help came in the form of (1) an indirect method of electing party committees, which gave the central headquarters considerable power over who would serve on GMD executive committees; (2) direct appointment of some provincial party committees by the central headquarters; and (3) prosecutions, reprimands, and expulsions from the party of certain opponents and competitors of the Organization Clique. Over time, Jiangsu's Organization Clique associates were able to build their own very substantial followings among the membership of the county party branches.[63]

The details of factional conflict between 1927 and 1929 need not detain us here (for a more detailed survey, see Appendix I), but suffice it to say that through 1929 the opponents of the Organization Clique—the Reorganization and Anti-CC Cliques—were doing reasonably well for themselves. In late 1929 they held, for example, four of nine positions on the provincial executive committee, and they were even more dominant on the county level. However, in late 1929 a shocking series of events ripped the party, and with these came a golden opportunity for Organization Clique partisans to increase their hold over the Jiangsu GMD and transform it.

In November 1929, Reorganization Clique adherents, irate at the party center's policies as well as its treatment of leftist leaders, carried out a series of military uprisings in Jiangsu designed to topple Chiang Kai-shek's Nanjing government. The revolt in Jiangsu was but a small part of a grandiose scheme by Reorganization leader Wang Jingwei to catapult himself into power by means of an ill-starred alliance with militarist Zhang Fakui against Chiang Kai-shek's allies in southern China. Jiangsu's Reorganizationists formed a Jiangsu Action Committee, which directed a series of poorly synchronized, badly conceived, short-lived putsches throughout Jiangsu. Though a primary objective of Jiangsu's rebels was to cut the Shanghai-Nanjing railway, their ragtag forces ranged as far north as Yancheng County.[64] Not having learned from Sun Yat-sen's unhappy experience with total dependence on warlord and secret society forces, the Reorganization Clique relied most heavily upon braves of the Big Sword Society in a few southern Jiangsu counties, a handful of mutinous National Army units, and some local elite-run militia.

The rebellion began in Liyang County on November 12, 1929, roughly a week ahead of schedule. The rebels jumped the gun because one of their ringleaders, Cai Hanyu, was already under pressure by provincial police organs. Cai, a squat, sallow-faced man of about forty, had capitalized upon the vast personal connections his position as head of Liyang's land tax office afforded, to make himself the commander of the rebel forces in the county. He was also leader of a number of local Big Sword Society lodges, enabling him to mobilize Liyang's Sword Societies.[65] Judging from accounts of Republican era Liyang, it was not too difficult to energize the lodges of the area's Sword Societies against the government. In the prior year alone, braves of the county's Sword Societies had risen against government authority no fewer than three times, and on at least two of those occasions they had briefly taken the county seat.[66]

Many, if not most, local lodges of the Sword Society in Liyang, as well as other places in the province, were said to have been founded by village headmen or other "prominent" local elites to combat banditry. In other words, the Swords were often, like local militia, instruments through which local elites exerted control over their bailiwicks.[67] In light of the leftists' calls for policies which would put pressure on local elites—including confiscating the lands of many—the Liyang Reorganizationists' willingness to ally with some elites against the government may seem initially perplexing. The alliance seems equally improbable owing to the secret societies' parochial concentration on local interests, a far cry from the leftists' boisterous nationalism and their vitriolic broadsides against a National Government they saw as insufficiently anti-imperialist. It might be tempting to posit that Liyang Reorganizationists lacked the insistent ideological edge that Reorganizationists elsewhere displayed.[68] However, it appears that Liyang Reorganizationists identified rather closely with the national- and provincial-level leadership of the Reorganization Clique.

Two Liyang Reorganizationist figures, Xu Wentian and Tang Guohua, are sometimes listed as key provincial Reorganizationist leaders. The Liyang Reorganizationist journal, *Liyang pinglun* (*The Liyang Critic*), seems to have mirrored the provincial Reorganizationist organ, *Jiangsu pinglun*, and was seen by Liyang intellectuals to be considerably more radical than the local GMD's official publications. Like the provincial Reorganizationist journal, *Liyang pinglun* regularly lambasted the GMD government and advocated fundamental and uncompromising reform of the "old society." *Liyang pinglun* especially concentrated on persuading the reading public of the nefariousness of a number of township-based elites who had dominated the county, including the county seat, for many years. A main target of the leftist journal in the months prior to the late-1929 uprising was Chen Xiekun, a former provincial assemblyman who was an associate of Shanghai gangster Huang Jinrong and controlled Liyang's native banks and silkworm cocoon dealers as well as several other businesses. Chen seems to have been the single most powerful incumbent elite in Liyang County. The Liyang Reorganizationists also led a campaign to destroy the religious idols in the Temple of the City God, a site that enjoyed the protection of the Liyang Chamber of Commerce.[69] All told, the Liyang leftists were very much an antiestablishment force in the late 1920s.

How then does one explain the alliance between Liyang Reorganizationists and the local elites who ran the Sword Societies? On the one hand, the late 1929 uprising coalition appears as a brief, ad hoc alliance between a party faction that perceived itself as being under attack by the party center and secret society leaders who did not concern themselves with (and may have been unaware of) the policy preferences of the Reorganizationists. The alliance must have been seen as tactical and temporary by both sides. The leaders of the Liyang Sword Societies may have had little connection with Chen Xiekun and his contingent of elites occupying center stage in Liyang politics. In other words, it may be that the Liyang Reorganizationists, who saw themselves as political outsiders, were allying with certain elites who also found themselves political outsiders. This could mean that the Liyang Reorganizationists were mixed up in a battle between Liyang's local elites.

Cai Hanyu, the leader of the Liyang Sword Societies, did not rely on Sword Society structures and sectarian ideology alone to raise his army. Reportedly he richened the pot with cash payments—ten *yuan*, the amount a skilled worker might earn in ten days—to any man who would join his band. Shanghai newspapers reported that an entity in Shanghai, presumably the Reorganizationists' national headquarters, had provided Cai with the several tens of thousands of *yuan* that he was distributing with such largess. The Reorganizationist cash contribution to the Swords might partially explain their leaders' motivation to ally with the Reorganizationists. With those funds, Cai and local Reorganization Clique leaders fashioned a force they dubbed the "Army for the Protection of the Party and Salvation of the Nation" (*Hudang jiuguo jun*). The phrase "Protect the Party and Save the Nation" was a favored slogan of the GMD leftists, who saw themselves as champions of democracy fighting against Chiang's personal dictatorship.[70] The Reorganizationists recruited part of this corps, which was decked out with boots and blue uniforms with green insignia, from unemployed Liyang natives and migrants from neighboring provinces, including soldiers who had deserted from a unit in Anhui. The bulk of the Reorganizationist units, however, were none other than the long-active lodges of the Big Sword Society, whose braves were numbered in the thousands.[71]

Several leaders of the uprising were Reorganizationist-leaning members of the Liyang GMD County Executive Committee and its standing committee. They performed most of their acts in the name of the party, as well as the Liyang Action Committee they had created, though they apparently took their orders from the Shanghai headquarters of the Jiangsu Action Committee, which upper-level Reorganizationists had formed.

The rebels succeeded in commandeering the government of Liyang County and the county seat itself for three days. The Sword Society troops were able to capture the county seat easily, in part because of the recent withdrawal of garrison forces from the city. Unfortunately for the rebels, Reorganizationist attempts to occupy the capitals of other nearby counties were checkmated by the quick transport of the GMD regime's police, army, and militia units from more remote locales. Due to the paucity of government forces in the immediate area, authorities had to call upon the aid of Provincial Police Academy cadets for help in suppressing the rebellion.[72] Liyang rebels never reached their objective, the Shanghai-Nanjing Railway and consequently did not succeed in cutting that line. Within less than a week, National Government forces had retaken the city, captured many of the Reorganization Clique leaders, reconstituted the county government, and dispersed the bulk of the rebel troops. The rebels in their haste to withdraw from the city had left a roster of their forces, together with documents outlining their next moves—items that government leaders found quite useful.[73]

A few disgruntled National Army commanders struck the next blows in this surreal insurrection more than a week after the Liyang coup had been suppressed. Major Peng Jianzhang, whose thousand-odd troops had just days ago put down the Liyang uprising, mutinied. His forces occupied the Wujin county seat and, in addition, immediately moved to take Yixing County.

Peng's mutiny, along with those of his commander, Wang Xizhai, and his colleague, Li Bingxin, were motivated in part by the government's six-month salary arrears, but probably more important were rumors of happenings in the Nanjing area. There, Battalion General Shi Yousan, who had recently mutinied against warlord Feng Yuxiang and whose troops were in the town of Pukou across the Yangzi from Nanjing, had declared he would support Wang Jingwei's Reorganization Clique rebellion.[74] The National Government sent loyal troops from Zhejiang and suppressed Peng's forces in short order. Shi soon lived up to his nickname "Triple-crosser Shi" by temporarily switching sides to the Nationalist Government.[75]

By late December 1929, roughly a month after the uprisings had begun in Jiangsu, not only had the disturbances been put down, but the left wing in Jiangsu had also been discredited. Nearly overnight, Reorganization Clique and Anti-CC leaders went from being powerful figures within the party to virtual pariahs—some of them went to jail, while a few others fled to the foreign concession in Shanghai.

Jiangsu's Commissioner of Civil Affairs, Miao Bin, in his zeal to make a name for himself by suppressing the revolt, subjected Anti-CC and Reorganizationist party leaders to a drubbing from which they never completely recovered.[76] Miao was, by most accounts, an arrogant and ambitious young man, and his name had become synonymous with corruption during his term as commissioner. Reportedly he brazenly sold positions over which he had the power of appointment, especially those as heads of county public security offices (*gong'an juzhang*) and as county magistrates. The Jiangsu GMD's First Provincial Congress impeached him for corruption and demanded his expulsion from the party. His vehement anti-Communist stand and love of martial virtues merged in his prolific writings, as well as in his participation in the Blue Shirts in the 1930s, and his defection to the Japanese puppet regimes in north and south China after 1937. Whatever his failings, he apparently enjoyed the trust of Chiang Kai-shek in the late 1920s through the mid-1930s and turned that relationship to his advantage.[77]

Angry at the Anti-CC role in pressing the corruption charges against him, in November 1929 Miao produced evidence that members of the Jiangsu GMD's provincial executive committee—Teng Gu (Reorganization Clique), Gu Ziyang (Anti-CC), Ge Jianshi (Anti-CC), Ni Bi (Anti-CC)—and many of their subordinates were involved in the Reorganizationist rebellion in southern Jiangsu. Claiming that Chiang had secretly ordered him to act, he arrested Gu, Ge, and Ni and the entire staff of the Propaganda and Training Departments of the provincial party. Supposed co-conspirators He Minhun and Teng Gu (who probably had been in on the Reorganizationist plot) escaped to the foreign concession in Shanghai. Underlining Miao's paranoia and megalomania, he even disarmed the bodyguards of the provincial governor, Niu Yongjian, and then placed the governor under house arrest. Niu was a conservative party elder, an intimate of Chiang Kai-shek, and a man utterly beyond reproach; he was most certainly not involved in any Reorganization Clique coup plot. Miao's precipitous action sent a shock wave through the GMD, and Hu Hanmin, the head of the Legislative Yuan, was said to be furious. Reportedly he exclaimed to Chiang that "if a Commissioner of Civil Affairs of a province can arrest the Provincial Governor, then you can arrest me!" (This was, of course, an apt prognostication by Hu, for Chiang did arrest him in 1931.) Hu later punished Miao by blocking his drive to become a CEC member.[78]

The central party headquarters sent Xiao Jishan, an Organization group associate, to investigate. Xiao released most of those arrested, but he did bind seven Anti-CC partisans over for trial, including Ni, Gu, and Ge. Anti-CC stalwart Ni Bi had convinced several generals with whom he had been associated at the Huangpu Academy to obtain the release of the seven under those officers' recognizance; nonetheless, the prisoners'

98   *Radicalism and Its Demise*

release came only after several months spent in custody.⁷⁹ One of those released early on, Ling Shaozu, a subordinate of Gu, Ni, and Ge, immediately went to his good friend Lin Biao, the Chief Justice of Jiangsu, to plead on behalf of his patrons.⁸⁰ Perhaps his efforts and Lin's own predisposition were both related to Lin's eventual ruling that Gu, Ni, and Ge were innocent; in reaching that verdict he implied that Miao had fabricated the evidence of their complicity in the uprising. Despite the apparently happy outcome for the Anti-CC leaders, the imbroglio had permanently transformed Jiangsu party affairs to their disadvantage and helped to end social radicalism in Jiangsu's GMD.

Rectification and Its Aftermath

In late 1929, after prodding by the Organization Department, the CEC's standing committee acted to repair the fractured Jiangsu party by dissolving the former provincial executive committee and appointing in its place a Jiangsu Provincial Party Affairs Rectification Committee (*Jiangsu sheng dangwu zhengli weiyuanhui*) that would manage the Jiangsu party until August 1931.⁸¹ This rectification period of over a year and a half was a significant turning point for the Jiangsu GMD. Unfortunately, however, reliable information on important aspects of party affairs during and after this period is rarer than that relating to earlier periods, due to increasingly strict censorship of newspapers and magazines.

Despite this caveat about the decreased coverage of party matters after early 1930, the rectification clearly strengthened the position of groups associated with the Organization Clique and seriously undermined the Anti-CC and Reorganization Cliques. All seven original members of the provincial rectification committee were members of the FF or CC factions or were otherwise associated with the central Organization Clique. Of the members, Ye Xiufeng was head of the FF group, Qi Xiyong was a provincial CC Clique leader, and Zhang Daofan was Ye's mentor in the Investigation Section of the Central Organization Department. Zhu Jianbai was one of CC leader Li Shouyong's oldest allies; they were from the same locality, and together they had attended Beijing University and worked in the *Zhongshan zhuyi shijian she*. Wu Baofeng had earlier been drafted by Chen Guofu to work in the Central Organization Department, and Zhang Yuanyang had graduated in the first class of the Central Party Affairs Academy, a school closely associated with the Chens.⁸² In a few months, a complex series of personnel changes within the provincial rectification committee essentially put it in the hands of the Yang-Ma-Cao Clique, a provincial branch of the Organization Clique. Whatever the permutations, all of the officials ever holding a place on the committee had ties with the Organization Clique.[83]

One of the provincial rectification committee's primary duties was to dissolve the previously elected county executive committees that had not scrupulously obeyed orders of the central headquarters or that had experienced internal or party-government disputes. In fact, some of the county executive committees were in disarray because members connected to the Reorganization and Anti-CC Cliques had fled when Miao Bin had arrested Gu Ziyang and the others.[84] The provincial rectification committee delegated county-level party affairs rectification committees in each of those localities to control the party branches. This occurred in roughly two-thirds of Jiangsu's sixty-one counties. One provincial party leader assured me that each county committee member had either previously been connected with the Organization Clique or thereafter maintained such an affiliation. This gave the Organization Clique an unprecedented grip on the Jiangsu GMD, although Organization leaders preferred to see it not as the victory of one clique, but as a strengthening of central authority over unruly local party branches.[85] The results of the 1931 elections by county party branches and mass organizations for the new National Assembly (*Guomin huiyi*) showed that the Organization group had quickly built local support throughout Jiangsu; that clique demonstrated remarkable vote-getting strength in nearly every county in the province, capturing three of five seats allotted to the party, the other two seats going to party elders Niu Yongjian and Di Ying. The group also did well in balloting by mass organizations, particularly educational associations, gaining at least four more seats and thereby shutting the Anti-CC Clique out of the National Assembly.[86]

The number of county party branches rocked by disputes may have decreased with the deputation of the rectification teams to the localities, as the Organization Clique muscled out opposing forces.[87] However, it is quite certain that factional disputes did not disappear.[88] And according to one provincial figure, the rectification did not completely destroy the local bases of the Anti-CC Clique.[89] When the Second Provincial Congress met in August 1931 to elect a new Jiangsu Provincial Executive Committee, it was clear that many county congresses had elected Anti-CC delegates to the meeting. But as a result of the selection by the

Central Organization Department and the CEC's standing committee from the slate the Congress had nominated, Gu Ziyang was the only Anti-CC member of the new seven-person provincial executive committee.[90] Although available information does not reveal which of the provincial branches of the national Organization Clique predominated on the committee, it is certain that nearly all of the members of the Third Jiangsu Provincial Executive Committee were connected with the Organization group.[91]

After the termination of the Jiangsu Rectification Committee and throughout the remainder of the Nanjing Decade, although some serious altercations jolted the provincial GMD headquarters, somewhat fewer county-level party disputes occurred than before the rectification.[92] The Organization Clique and the central party headquarters maintained their firm hold on the Jiangsu party through several techniques. For example, the party center scrapped the standard process for electing the provincial executive committee; the Third Provincial Congress in late 1932 was the last such gathering to elect provincial leaders. Such congresses were supposed to meet every year, but for the next five years the central party headquarters and the Central Organization Department arranged and rearranged the provincial party organization and appointed its leaders without any vote by county party representatives.[93]

The Fourth Jiangsu Provincial Executive Committee, nominated by the Third Provincial Congress and appointed by the party center in 1932, was also heavily balanced in favor of the FF and CC groups, with only one of seven (Ling Shaozu) having Anti-CC connections.[94] Even so, the committee was torn by conflict when it attempted to meet—perhaps because of discord between FF and CC elements. Therefore, the central party headquarters decided to eliminate the committee system and, according to Gu Ziyang, "try a system of dictatorship."[95] Each member of the committee was appointed "director" (*zhidaoyuan*) for a group of county parties over which he was to be the authority; the provincial committee apparently no longer met as a body while the system was in effect from April 1934.[96] The party center then appointed Li Jingzhai to oversee and coordinate the direction of the provincial party as a whole. Gu Ziyang praised Li's work, saying that Jiangsu party affairs began to improve markedly, something that is surprising considering that Gu was Anti-CC and Li must have been appointed on the advice of the Organization Department. Li soon resigned, however, and the Organization Department tried another system to oversee Jiangsu's GMD.[97]

The party center attempted to increase its hold on local branches with a scheme adopted at a February 1935 meeting. This system bypassed the provincial party completely by placing all directors of multi-county "areas" (*qu*) directly under the center's control. It became illegal for county party branches to communicate with the provincial party headquarters without sending the same correspondence to the center. Also, the multi-county *qu* offices were enlarged and their functions increased.[98] The system operated in this manner until August, when it was merged with a restored provincial committee system. Then in January 1936 the provincial committee was abolished, and the center again sent out a group of special deputies, the vast majority of whom were connected with the Organization Clique, to control the party.[99]

The entire series of upheavals in the Jiangsu GMD from late 1929 through 1931—from the Reorganizationist uprising to the bold aggrandizement by the Organization Clique—does not conform closely to some of the patterns that Andrew Nathan has posited for Chinese factions or factions in general. Nathan writes of a "code of civility" that "circumscribes the nature of factional conflict." He argues that factions "seldom kill, jail, or confiscate the property of their opponents" and that "factional systems require punctiliously polite face-to-face conduct between politicians." According to this prescription, factions employ "comic-opera" politics of bribery and character assassination rather than violence and force. They avoid all-or-nothing struggles to eliminate their factional rivals.[100] In fact, as we have seen, the Reorganizationists did turn to armed force in late 1929 in an effort to overturn Chiang Kai-shek and the factional complexes attached to him. The Organization Clique took advantage of the situation to make sure that Anti-CC Clique leaders stayed in jail for many weeks. Throughout 1930 the provincial branches of the Organization Clique pursued a party rectification that sought to eliminate the power bases of the Anti-CC Clique. This looks a good deal like an all-or-nothing struggle.[101]

From the advent of rectification until the 1937 Japanese invasion the Jiangsu GMD was virtually the private preserve of the central party headquarters and its alter ego, the Organization Clique. By boosting the Organization Clique and its various provincial-level components, the party center pursued a factional solution to the problem of factionalism.

It is understandable why the center felt continued factional conflict was undesirable. Party spokesmen of all stripes denounced factionalism as the source of many of the GMD's difficulties. The factional battles had a debilitating effect on the party because they directed much energy into nonproductive pursuits. The lists of county party committee members from 1929 and 1934 reveal that in most counties almost none of the local party heads kept their positions for five years.[102] Nearly all of this widespread and disruptive turnover in personnel arose from factional warfare. Even had the party center not decided to scotch the mass organizations, it is doubtful that the party could have led an effective mass movement. As a report on the Funing County party testifies, the recurring shifts in local party leadership seriously damaged the climate for pushing the mass movement forward.[103]

The tightening grip of the central party headquarters and the Organization group on the Jiangsu GMD altered the nature of that formerly revolutionary organization. The center's increasingly heavy hand tended to stifle initiative in local parties. Local and provincial party branches became relatively unimportant in the policy-making process. Under central guidance, the GMD became a meek, quiet, and unassertive adjunct of the government. And, as is documented in a later chapter, the center's increased control over local GMD branches produced a significant easing of tension between local party branches and the established local elites.

5

JIANGSU'S GUOMINDANG, 1927-1929: PARTY-ELITE RELATIONS

Historians have long recognized that Chiang Kai-shek's anti-Communist purge in April 1927 marked a crucial turning point in the history of the Guomindang. It answered with finality some very basic questions about the direction of the party. Most importantly, the purge guaranteed that the Chinese Communists would not be able to usurp and maintain control of the Guomindang, something which had not been a foregone conclusion in the months and years before the purge. In addition, the violence of the purge drove many young activists from the GMD and dampened the enthusiasm of many who remained in its ranks.

Despite the very real significance of the purge, it would be easy to exaggerate its importance, as some have. The purge did not end the efforts of many members to press forward social revolution on the local level. Thousands of young revolutionaries survived within the Guomindang and continued to set the tone for party affairs. For many months following the April 1927 purge, Jiangsu was still beset by the kind of ferment typical of revolutions in progress. Although Chiang Kai-shek and his followers established in Nanjing a National Government and a central party headquarters, both of which sought to reestablish order and tranquility, a great number of party members still believed that social revolution was necessary. The central party headquarters had only a weak grip on local partisans, and in many counties, cabals of young GMD firebrands set about to remake society.

Many local Guomindang branches continued the prepurge leftists' policy of targeting certain local elites for punishment. However, the Nanjing party center and certain other party members were ambivalent about this punitive program. The high priority given to purging the Communists initially blunted any GMD campaign against "local bullies and evil gentry." Despite this, many local party branches, encouraged by the provincial headquarters, eventually investigated and pressed for prosecution of certain nonparty elites. In quite a few localities this generated or exacerbated conflict between party and government, since county governments were often more closely interconnected with the local power structures than were the party branches.

The Purge: Local Elites' Revenge

The anti-Communist purge was a crucial struggle that thoroughly absorbed the energies of the leaders of the Nanjing party center and the provincial party headquarters. The purge itself reflected the weak position in which Chiang Kai-shek and the other anti-Communists found themselves. Their backs were against the wall; they were deprived of many important party positions; and lacking a large base of support in the local parties, the purge leaders did not have the power to oversee and guide political life in the far-flung cities and countryside of Jiangsu. During the first few weeks of the purge, moreover, as terror and confusion reigned supreme, communication between the provincial and local party headquarters was disrupted or completely cut off.[1] All these factors together created a situation that some local elites, previously under pressure from the new and rising GMD counterelite, were quick to exploit. Another advantage was afforded local elites who wished to punish GMD activists when the Nanjing party center disarmed and dissolved the worker and peasant organizations that had been established and led by the left GMD.[2] Thus, local party branches lost the support of those bodies, which might have tipped the local balance of power in their favor and against preexisting elites.

At a May 1927 meeting of the Jiangsu party committee, provincial government member Niu Yongjian described the situation in Jiangsu as "very complex." He warned that in some areas the CCP had even taken control of the purge. In such cases CCP members within the Guomindang had prevented non-Communists from entering the local GMD and slapped those would-be members with the charge of "outside interference" when they attempted to purge the Communists. Niu also reported that "common opportunist elements" were acting in the name of the party,[3] but failed to explain that many of the nonparty elements attempting to tamper with the party were local elites charged by GMD activists with being "local bullies and evil gentry."[4]

In some areas, nonparty elites voluntarily effected the purge themselves by assaulting local party headquarters with armed bands. Chiang Kai-shek himself had carried out the purge in Shanghai with the aid of the leaders of nonparty secret societies, most particularly the Green Gang. In Songjiang County the calls by Chiang and the Central Supervisory Committee for a party purge evoked an eager response from at least some local elites. On April 18, 1927, Zhang Zhi (a shop owner the party labeled an "evil gentry"), Zhang Baopei (a prominent entrepreneur and owner of a land reclamation company who had earlier been attacked by the party), and others led over one hundred armed followers in destroying the county party headquarters. In the process, they burst into houses and shops, and, claiming that they were conducting searches, seized property and wrecked one party member's store. They also kidnapped over twenty people. Not surprisingly, they falsely accused many of being Communists.[5]

Emboldened by their coup, these forces fanned out and attacked party headquarters in surrounding towns and villages. The party headquarters for the first and second precincts of the second ward reported that on April 19 an "evil gentry" named Ni Bingruo led some twenty local followers in demolishing the local party headquarters.[6] Likewise, more than ten assailants—the newspaper called them "bullies" (*dipi*)—armed with Mauser firearms overran a precinct party headquarters in Sijing on April 22.[7] The sixth ward branch met a similar fate.[8] Obviously the party was under assault by powerful local enemies who were coordinating their moves across the entire county.

The situation in Jinshan County was similar to that in Songjiang, except in Jinshan the elites attacking the leftist GMD acted even before the formal announcement of the purge. At least four distinct, yet complementary, dynamics converged to bring about this early, violent purge of the Jinshan County party branch. The first of these four was the competition between old elites and the new GMD counterelites. Shanghai newspapers reported that the problem had begun when the local GMD refused to allow pre-1927 county elites to enter the party after the Northern Expeditionary Armies had liberated Jinshan. The county's left-wing GMD party branch office had long been headquartered in the market town of Zhangyan, while the warlord-era county government had been located in Zhujing. The Political Department of the First Division of the First Army, preferring that government and party be headquartered in the same town, suggested that due to the presence of old county elites in Zhujing, the government should be moved to Zhangyan. The department also granted the county party the right to appoint governmental personnel. Pursuant to this, a county party congress selected left-leaning party member Mo Baichou as Jinshan magistrate. When Mo went to Zhujing on March 28, 1927 to gather the warlord-era government files and the county government seal for the move to Zhangyan, local inhabitants turned in three persons to be jailed as "local bullies and evil gentry."[9]

The competing elites based in Zhujing, however, were not willing to stand by while the GMD displaced and prosecuted them. In the evening a crowd of several hundred gathered, presumably at the instigation of Zhujing-based elites. Taking advantage of the disturbance, the three men incarcerated as "local bullies" escaped, taking the government files with them. Newspaper accounts dubbed the mob leaders "local bullies and evil gentry," and reported that they directed their followers to beat many people and kidnap more than twenty party members.[10]

But beyond the pattern of "old elites versus new" noted in the Shanghai newspapers, three other dynamics were at work in this case. First, the conflict in Jinshan was energized by a left-versus-right split in the county GMD branch, and second, it was related to local township-versus-county competition. Memoir literature reveals that the county GMD had for years been divided into left and right wings. The left wing had been based in Zhangyan. Under the leadership of Communist Li Yi'e, the left-wing GMD county branch had flourished, especially in the townships in the county's southern part. But right-wing GMD members had dominated the party in the area of the county seat, Zhujing, in the northern section of the county. The suspicion that factionalism based on local chauvinism was one of the forces motivating the conflict is borne out by the slogans shouted by the crowd that ransacked the leftist GMD's new county government: "Down with the men from Zhangyan; support Zhujing men." The third factor in the civic struggle was the uncoordinated political dabblings of the political departments of various GMD army units. Just as the left-wing county GMD branch enjoyed the support of the Political Department of the First Division of the NRA, the right-wing party branch relied on another NRA force, the Political Department of the Twenty-sixth Army. The latter had authorized the right wing's establishment of its own county government in the old county seat, just as the former unit had legitimized the left-wing GMD's new government. Thus, in Jinshan several different dynamics converged in the left-right strife.[11]

In some localities, the purge had such a permanent chilling effect on party branches that they never again displayed social radicalism or launched attacks on local elites. Such a case was Lishe, a market town of 3,600 people situated in the southwest part of Wuxi County. The city of Wuxi was a major revolutionary center (the site of one of the Communist Autumn Harvest Uprisings), so it is no surprise that Lishe was greatly affected by the Northern Expedition and its attendant revolutionary upsurge. Over a hundred peasants took part in the 1927 movement to "strike down the local bullies," which was led by local GMD members. According to a journalist who wrote about the events years later, this burst of intimidation persuaded many big landlords who depended heavily on income from usury to move from the danger of the countryside to the protecting arms of the city.[12]

The 1927 purge suddenly reversed the local power lineup, however, and relieved much of the pressure on Lishe's elites. The local GMD was gutted; ninety-four out of approximately one hundred members reportedly left the party or were expelled, and those who later returned to the town were dispirited and spent. So effective was a long-powerful local lineage in reestablishing its domination of the town that by 1932, landlords from the Xue lineage again controlled most of the formal organizations and arbitrated the affairs of the market town, just as they had before the Northern Expedition. For example, the town office (*zhen gongsuo*) was manned by a headman, two vice-headman, and five inspectors (*jiandu*), all Xue landlords. A similar situation prevailed in the local GMD headquarters, the merchant militia, and the village agricultural association (*cun nonghui*).[13]

It is no accident that these examples of local elites taking advantage of the purge to batter the party come from the Lower Yangzi area. In April 1927 the GMD's National Revolutionary Armies had not yet pushed into the North China area of the province. Party headquarters there were still underground, and their leadership and membership were still largely secret. Anyone who had wanted to clobber the local GMD partisans there might have been hard-pressed to locate them. Further, while the CCP and Zhu Jixun's radical friends from Songjiang had been instrumental in developing the GMD in the Lower Yangzi, especially in the core, they had been far less important in Guomindang growth in the North China area. It is quite possible that many of the party branches in the Lower Yangzi core were more insistently radical and had already made more enemies among local elites than their northern counterparts.

The Provincial Party's Counterattack, 1927–1929

Despite the reprieve the purge granted incumbent elites from party pressure in some localities, a considerable element within the GMD continued to push for retribution against certain powerful local personages. Indeed, the official duties of the Nanjing-appointed purge organs, such as the Jiangsu Provincial Purge Committee, were expulsion of the Communists *and* elimination of "local bullies and evil gentry." Some provincial leaders were concerned about reports from local cadres that "evil powers" were using the purge to harass local parties and expand their grip over the countryside. At the same time, the central party headquarters vacillated on the proper approach to and definition of enemy local elites.

The Jiangsu Special Committee, the provincial GMD's supreme organ at the time, on May 12, 1927, sent all county magistrates in Jiangsu an order that had the mien of a propaganda diatribe, especially since it was printed in full in Shanghai newspapers. The statement intoned that "local bullies and evil gentry" were "relics of feudal society" that, like "imperialism, warlords, and the comprador class," were "objects of this revolution." It charged that these malevolent elites "manipulate political and economic power, settle matters by the use of force, and exploit peasants and workers." The committee declared that in the liberated areas these sorts of elites "must be eliminated without exception." It argued that

> according to numerous cables from comrades of various counties, . . . ever since the beginning of the purge movement, local bullies and evil gentry have thought that the elements in this party that are eliminating the Communists are, likewise, abandoning the policies on peasants and workers. Therefore, the evil bullies and gentry have seized the opportunity to rise up . . . and seek revenge.[14]

The committee claimed that those "vile" local powers were branding as Communist anyone who "aids peasants and workers." The statement then equated the Communists and the "evil" local elites, saying that both cheated the masses. At the end of this proclamation, the committee ordered the county magistrates to prohibit nonparty elites and administrative personnel from "taking it upon themselves to purge the party" and oppressing GMD members.[15]

Shortly after the above declaration was published, the party center dismissed the Jiangsu Special Committee, charging that body with "vainly spouting empty words inciting disturbances."[16] The committee's declaration was a more detailed and venomous denunciation of "local bullies and evil gentry" than the central headquarters was itself issuing, and earlier campaigns against local elites had occasioned violent clashes. Moreover, some central leaders were not certain that administrative and nonparty personnel should not, when necessary, aid in executing the purge. At the time of the Jiangsu Special Committee's statement Chiang Kai-shek argued that many spouting the slogan "down with local bullies and evil gentry" were radicals pushing forward unwanted peasant or labor disturbances, or were themselves "bullies" and "bad gentry."[17] In fact, Chiang was in a sense right; there were indeed cases of one elite faction enlisting the party in that faction's fight with another clique of local elites.[18]

After this, the reorganized Jiangsu Special Committee treated the issue of "local bullies and evil gentry" more circumspectly, but it did not entirely abandon the idea of attacking some local elites. The new committee avoided further conflict with the party center by refraining from detailed public pronouncements on its policy toward local elites. Nonetheless, in July the committee appointed a group to draft articles governing the investigation and accusation of "local bullies and evil gentry."[19] The provincial committee in charge of the purge also continued to affirm the necessity of eliminating these noxious elites, classing them with "Communists, . . . corrupt officials, reactionary elements, and rotten, evil (*fuhua ehua*) elements," and citing the party center's orders for their banishment.[20]

Jiangsu Special Committee member Ge Jianshi, speaking at the inauguration of the provincial purge committee, stated the importance of concentrating on the "chronic illness" that the "rotten elements" (i.e., "local bullies") constituted, as well as on the "urgent illness" that was the CCP. Ge reported, "Some people say that now the GMD's road is too narrow. On one side is the CCP, on the other are the local bullies, evil gentry, and corrupt officials, and both sides are attacking us." Ge expressed confidence, however, that this slim path between extremes was the "proper" and "glorious" one for the party.[21]

Perhaps confused about the party center's grounds for dismissing the earlier Jiangsu Special Committee and perplexed about the reconstituted committee's policy on handling local elites, the Jiangyin County GMD petitioned the provincial committee to explain in detail how the local party should defend itself and its territory from "the rottenness of local bullies and evil gentry." In response the Jiangsu Special Committee sent the Jiangyin party branch a letter and a deputy to "guide them."[22] It may be that the committee chose this private way to explain its policy to avoid forewarning opposing local elites of party tactics. But the secrecy might also have been intended to forestall widespread riots against local elites or the distrust of a cautious central party headquarters that either a public excoriation of local elites or detailed exposition of party policy toward them might have provoked.

In July 1927 the Jiangsu Special Committee presented a joint party-government conference with its views on handling established local elites. It recommended replacing the old offices of township manager and municipal township manager with a new system of village self-rule. It also asked that the old county education associations (*jiaoyu hui*) dominated by nonparty elites be eliminated in favor of the GMD's own education associations (*jiaoyu xiehui*). And although Helen Chauncey has pointed out that the Jiangsu GMD ultimately did not succeed in supplanting the old education associations, at least at this early date the intention to do so was made known.[23] Beyond the matter of education associations, the Jiangsu Special Committee upheld the party's power to identify "local bullies and evil gentry" for prosecution and to participate in the confiscation of their properties.[24]

Like the GMD rightists before the purge, the leadership of the provincial party headquarters preferred government prosecution of targeted local elites to direct action by mobs or individuals. But like the prepurge leftists, the provincial party committees and many local party branches exhibited far more interest in rooting out incumbent elites than prepurge rightists had. With the possible exception of the short-lived, Western Hills-dominated Jiangsu Provincial Provisional Executive Committee, which lasted from October through December of 1927, all of the provincial party committees that succeeded the Jiangsu Special Committee until late 1929 continued to support action against local elite targets. Ni Bi, a prominent Anti-CC member of the directorate, the provincial committee that succeeded the Special Committee, vehemently spelled out the need for elimination of "local bullies and evil gentry." He raised the specter of great landlords and the rich who had become "local hegemons and kings." They constituted, he said, "the fundamental obstacle to the effectuation of democracy (*minzhi*)." Indeed, he believed that they were only one manifestation of Jiangsu's "feudal society" and that the society itself needed to be drastically transformed by the party. In addition to using force to eliminate the "feudal powers," therefore, the party was to use education to combat the prevailing feudal, familial, clannish, passive, and Confucian thought.[25]

Who Were the Attackers?

The many local GMD members who shared Ni Bi's view that Jiangsu's prevailing local power structures were "feudal" (read "vile"), and who participated in attacks on persons in those local systems did not fit one mold. Yet one can observe some commonalities in their backgrounds and the underpinnings of their actions against local elites. The animus which many party members harbored against incumbent elites stemmed, in part, from the educational and generational gulf between the two groupings. Although the purge had jettisoned a large number of GMD members, the overall educational and age characteristics of the Jiangsu GMD had not been fundamentally altered. A majority of the members still boasted a modern education at or above the middle school level. A 1929 survey revealed that nearly 67 percent of Jiangsu GMD members were under the age of thirty.[26] These young members with modern educational backgrounds were a part of the May Fourth generation, or were its immediate successors.[27]

Part of the guiding spirit of the May Fourth Movement had been opposition to warlords, and quite a few of these young party members believed that many, if not most, incumbent elites had been the allies and tools of the warlords. Furthermore, the New Culture Movement—the intellectual side of May Fourth—registered a vociferous reaction against traditional Chinese culture. Beginning in the second decade of the twentieth century, a growing number of Chinese youths with modern educations learned to despise not only Confucian thought, which they deemed moribund, but also the existing political and social systems, which they charged were excrescences of that debilitating "feudal" tradition.

In reality, local elites were a mixed lot. By no means were all of them devoted either to Confucianism or the existing social and political order in all of its particulars. Many were reformists in their own right. Mary Rankin has observed that since the late Qing, "a culture of elite civic participation was developing, with an agenda that was not always the same as that of government officials."[28] However, many incumbent elites tended not to share the New Culture generation's desire for wholesale rejection of the Chinese past. And most local elites could not sympathize with visions of radical change that might threaten their own power and position. The modern, middle-level schools which GMD members had attended had largely been founded and nurtured by prominent local individuals. But even in the 1910s and 1920s, when GMD members and future GMD members had been attending those schools, some of the locally powerful founders of the schools were angered and frightened by the mental distance between the students and themselves. The students' iconoclasm and their tendency to participate in strikes and other sorts of unrest was unsettling to some of the schools' founders.[29] The opposing groupings—incumbent elites and GMD counterelites—thus displayed somewhat differing mentalities. This reality, plus the young GMD radicals' desire for position, created a formula for conflict between GMD organizations and established elites.

At least some of the radicalism displayed by the Guomindang, even after the purge, came from continuing Communist domination of some GMD branches. The April 1927 purge had not dislodged all Communists from the party, and they remained in leading positions in a few county GMD branches for many months after the CCP Central Committee had ceased advising its operatives to maintain a "united front" with GMD elements.[30] For example, in 1927 and early 1928, Communist Party member Shen Yi was also a member of the Taixing County GMD committee. Shen organized a peasant association which launched a campaign to resist taxes, rent, and debt payment, thereby incurring the wrath of the local government and certain local elites.[31] In a similar vein, a memoir by a former Communist activist in Lianshui suggests that in the late 1920s that county's antisuperstition movement and the campaign against merchants who sold Japanese-made goods were led by an underground CCP branch. Some of the Lianshui CCP members who were also operatives in the Guomindang used the GMD as an organizing frame for their agitation.[32]

Lenore Barkan has documented the case of Rugao, where Communists actually controlled the GMD's county purge committee, which had been set up in April 1927 to weed out Communists. Rugao Communists continued to exert partial control over the county GMD through February 1928. During this period the local GMD engineered public campaigns and prosecutions against several local elites. In a number of other counties, Communists survived the April purge and continued to exert their influence either in leadership positions in the local GMD or in GMD-led mass organizations. Information exists on such cases in counties from the Lower Yangzi area—Wujin, Yangzhou, Dongtai, Yixing, and Qidong—as well as a few counties in the North China zone—Lianshui, Shuyang, and Ganyu. The Communists in these counties' GMD organizations worked under a variety of conditions. These circumstances ranged from those of the Communists in Rugao, who for a number of months enjoyed actual ruling authority and seemed not to have hidden their membership in the Communist Party, to the more common situation of party-straddlers who hid their Communist connections to preserve their lives and freedom.[33]

Yet, even if Communists participated in and led some of the anti-elite actions so pervasive in Jiangsu in the late 1920s, there is no reason to assume that they were behind all or even most such assaults. The vast majority of county Guomindang branches that displayed a radical complexion probably did so without significant Communist participation or prodding. Communists were simply too rare after the purge to have been a serious factor in most county Guomindang branches. And even in Rugao, some of the ringleaders in the assaults on local elites were non-Communists.[34]

Many of those activists in the Jiangsu GMD who sought confrontation with preexisting elites must have identified, at least to some degree, with Wang Jingwei, the kingpin of the Guomindang left wing. Widespread sympathy for Wang within the Jiangsu party was demonstrated by the GMD Provincial Congress's adoption of a resolution asking him to return to China to assume a leadership position—at the very time in 1929 when Chiang Kai-shek and his followers were doing everything possible to ensure that Wang was excluded from power.[35]

The Jiangsu leftists' urge to confront and overturn many established local elites, not to mention the social and economic institutions that sustained them, was clearly expressed in a book published in 1929 by the editors of *The Jiangsu Critic*, a Reorganization Clique journal. The texture of the Reorganization Clique's rhetoric may be surmised from this book, *The ABC's of the Left Wing of the Guomindang* (*Zhongguo Guomindang zuopai ABC*).[36] Leftist advocacy centered around calls for reinstatement and reinvigoration of the party's mass movement, which the central party apparatus repeatedly moved to halt in the late 1920s. In the eyes of some leftists, worker and peasant associations were supposed to replace gentry and other elites as intermediaries between the government and the people. The *Critic*'s leftist editors envisioned a massive assault on the power and interests of most incumbent elites. Those persons who controlled local chambers of commerce and militia, as well as people who had held office in the local self-government apparatus were characterized as "local bullies and evil gentry" who should be toppled. Mass organizations and government were to work together to expropriate the land of the "great" landlords, reduce land rents, distribute idle lands to the poor and unemployed, raise worker wages, shorten the workday to eight hours, abolish the contract (gang) labor system, establish credit institutions which would eliminate high interest on loans, and pursue a host of other policies which would clash with the interests of many existing local political and economic elites. And even the leftists' stated goal of reducing local taxes, which might have been cheered by certain local elites, struck at the interests of those elites active in the local self-government system.[37]

However, Reorganizationists were not the only elements in the party interested in radically restructuring society. Some of the chief leaders of the Anti-CC Clique—for example, Ni Bi—seem to have shared much of the perspective of the Reorganizationists.[38] And, although the Organization Clique eventually put a lid on most radicalism in the party, certain individuals associated with even that group wanted to transform society in ways at odds with the interests of some local elites.[39] For example, Li Shouyong, leader of the CC Clique, a provincial adjunct of the national Organization Clique, wrote angrily of gentry and "local bullies" who had been prosecuted by "brave comrades," but who managed to gain release from jail or get away with light sentences. He blamed local government for protecting abusive elites, including powerful local figures who had established anti-GMD organizations. Li wrote of the party's need to "break through" the environment created by "counter-revolutionary powers," and he looked forward to the time when the party could effectively eliminate the clout of "local bullies." However, in the meantime, he warned that the strength of "local bullies" and other "counter-revolutionary powers" in Jiangsu was so formidable as to raise questions about the wisdom of running campaigns against them. Without proper planning and organization, local party branches pushing such movements were doomed. Thus, Li counseled that in addition to embracing the longer-range goal of breaking out of a situation circumscribed by local elites' power, the party had to, for the time being, learn to "deal with" (*yingfu*) that situation. He explained that while he was not advocating surrender to nonparty elites, it was important for activists to recognize that the "raging tide of the revolution" sometimes rises and sometimes falls. To act unrealistically during a revolutionary low tide would guarantee that the party would slam into a wall and ultimately fail. Thus, Li advised caution, steadfastness of purpose, and careful preparation as important ingredients in action against nonparty elites.[40]

The Party Center Tries to Assert Control

Eventually, agitation within the party against local elites convinced the party center that it needed some method for evaluating charges against particular individuals. In August 1927, the center established a system of temporary special courts (*tezhong xingshi fating*) and promulgated "Articles on the Punishment of Local Bullies and Evil Gentry" to handle the prosecution of local elites.[41] GMD central authorities had grave misgivings about campaigns of mass incitement against local elites, and the establishment of the special courts appears to have been an attempt to take the power of revolutionary retribution and social refashioning out of the hands of mass rallies and Jacobin cabals. The regulations governing the courts granted procedural protection to those accused of being "local bullies and evil gentry"; if an accusation was ruled to be false, the accuser was to be punished. No mass accusations were to be honored.[42] This relieved much of the pressure on local elites, since few peasants were foolhardy enough to brave the elites' revenge and potential punishment by a court in order to accuse even elites who directly oppressed them.

The central authorities' step-by-step squelching of the party-led mass movement was even more of a boon to the interests of established elites. During the purge that began in April 1927, peasant and labor organizations faced suppression. That, however, was not the final curtain for the mass movement. The Guomindang's Jiangsu Special Committee soon established preparatory committees for provincial peasant and labor organizations, which in turn appointed similar committees on the county level. Although in name they were merely "preparatory committees," they seem to have acted as actual mass organizations. Some of these preparatory committees, along with other surviving county peasant associations, spearheaded rent reduction campaigns and demanded the abolition of the perennial rent-prompting stations that were set up by county governments and police in the Lower Yangzi core to help landlords collect rents from recalcitrant tenants. Certain other county preparatory committees identified "local bullies and evil gentry" for prosecution. Some of these embryonic mass organizations fomented rent resistance riots, and, in fact, the peasant organizations for Yixing and Wuxi counties were enlisted in localized revolts that were part of the CCP's Autumn Harvest Uprisings.[43]

In January 1928, Chiang Kai-shek's Nanjing party center again tried to take control of the situation and deal with the Communist threat by calling a "temporary" halt to the mass movement. It ordered that the peasant and worker associations be disbanded and that the movement undergo a period of rectification. Many party members were disturbed at the suspension. Some advocated prompt resumption of local mass movements, fearing that otherwise the party would separate itself from the masses. Others argued that local party branches, stripped of peasant and labor organizations and the muscle they could provide, were easy targets for wrathful "local bullies and evil gentry." In quite a number of localities the mass organizations continued their work surreptitiously, leading the party center to begin its two-year fulmination against local disobedience of its orders.[44]

Eventually, in late 1928, the party center authorized the formation of provincial mass movement rectification committees that were to spawn similar county-level committees. Some of the resultant peasant association rectification committees were enterprising enough to press for measures such as land tax remission, which would have been advantageous to small landholders, tenants, and landlords alike.[45] Most "rectified" mass organizations, however, were timid, inactive, and superfluous. Any momentum the mass movement had previously built up was destroyed. Throughout the remainder of the Nanjing Decade, the party center or centrally appointed provincial leadership repeatedly stepped in to reorganize the mass organizations and sap whatever vitality had survived the early 1928 suspension. Even the center's own spokesmen had to admit in 1932 that the mass organizations after 1928 were lethargic (*huan*). One of the center's agents blamed this ennui within the reorganized mass organizations on their preoccupation with "abstract economic and moral questions." But at the root of the problem, as he only implied, were the frequent reorganizations of the movement, and the party's heavy-handed domination of it. Party bureaucrats filled so many of the leadership positions in the mass organizations that, as the spokesman observed, the party was leading "a peasant movement of nonpeasants, and a labor movement of nonlaborers . . . ."[46]

Clearly local elites had little to fear from mass organizations after the party center had repeatedly worked its will on them. Although the party continued to call them mass organizations, it was transforming them into vocational associations to propagate technology, support credit cooperatives, and ameliorate class conflict. Some labor unions continued to fight for higher wages and better working conditions, but the peasant associations were almost universally dormant and concentrated on issues that were of no interest to peasants. Furthermore, the center's stipulation that the peasant associations be open to "anyone with a direct interest in agriculture . . ." raised the likelihood that they would be dominated by landlords, rich peasants, and other propertied interests.[47] So, despite the fact that authorities at the central level temporarily instituted special courts to prosecute "local bullies and evil gentry," it gave substantial relief to the interests of established local elites on certain other counts.

An Insistent GMD Harries Elites, 1927–1929

It would be late 1929 or early 1930 before the party center would be able virtually to eradicate radicalism in local party branches. In the mean time, the fervor with which many young GMD activists assaulted preexisting institutions and elites shocked some observers, Chinese and foreign alike. Most of the members of local party organizations were more radical and outspoken in their hatred of a wide array of established local elites than were central party and government leaders. Determined to remake China in a single stroke, some of these young politicians alienated local residents—both elites and non-elites—with their sometimes naive attacks on everything deemed old, "feudal," or "reactionary."

One of the best examples of a locality that witnessed a party offensive against a broad range of political elites at both the county and township levels is Donghai County in Jiangsu's North China zone. A correspondent of the *North China Herald*, presumably an Englishman, wrote a series of critical and detailed articles documenting the GMD takeover and administration of Haizhou, the county seat, in 1928 and 1929. Though Western and anti-GMD biases were manifested in these writings, the reports were largely consistent with some Chinese accounts. Although the reporter felt that the members of the Donghai party branch were less radical than many of their contemporaries, he called the rule of the local GMD "tyranny" and "government by children," and recounted the many excesses of its members. Citing party moderates' revulsion at the acts of the party, he reported:

> So great is the prestige of the Dang [party] that a mere servant employed on their [sic] premises becomes an important personage. A secretary, a mere child in his teens, can write letters of accusation against citizens formerly prominent, stamp them with the Dang seal and send them to the Hsien Chang [county magistrate] for action. So far as can be learned of the policy and practice of the Hsien yamen on receipt of such an accusation it immediately sends out and arrests the accused and claps him into the gaol. Proofs may be lacking but this is a small matter to this so-called court of justice. A man in gaol is a sure source of revenue and there he lies being constantly called upon for "expenses." There is no recourse but flight and as soon as any man gets wind of any proceedings being instituted against him he drops everything and runs as fast and as far as he can. Whatever property he may possess runs a fine chance of immediate confiscation.[48]

In Haizhou the new GMD counterelite was clearly in conflict with many, if not most of those who had previously enjoyed power and prestige. The correspondent wrote that the "well-to-do Chinese" were fleeing GMD rule. He stated that "prominent Chinese friends" who had become exiles complained that "life is unendurable in Haichow now . . . ," though he noted that there were few if any executions of local elites in Haizhou. When he "asked about numerous friends, the answer . . . [was]

always, 'He too has had to run away.'" He reported that the several township and subtownship managers were among the first of the local elites overturned and swept away by the party.⁴⁹ This was a common pattern; township managers were objects of attack in many other localities as well. The chairman and the secretary of the county chamber of commerce, judged by the correspondent to be "able businessmen," were exiled. The reporter despaired that it seemed the GMD activists' "plan . . . [was] to destroy everything not of their making."⁵⁰

The *Herald* correspondent noted that the party's confiscations of the property of local elites had started with the seizure of holdings belonging to "an ex-official . . . of large abilities . . .[who] had turned to his own profit and amassed great wealth." The party reportedly sent the victim to Nanjing in chains. Discovering that this action met with popular acclaim and that confiscation was an easy source of booty, the local party determined to press "a general campaign against the wealthy . . . regardless of whether they were good or bad." According to the reporter, "At one time last year it was said that there was hardly one man left in Haichow and vicinity who could be called prominent." The journalist also detailed the case of his

> old friend Mr. Yang Five, long known for his genial disposition and harmlessness, [who] learned one day to his amazement that charges were being instigated against him for having "built roads in the time of General Bei Bao-san [*sic*]." As such could not be denied he fled for his life and remained away nearly a year until it became evident that there were no charges against him that were worthy of death, exile, or confiscation. Although returned, he rarely ventured forth from his own door.⁵¹

Although the Haizhou party found confiscated urban properties easy and profitable to administer, large rural holdings presented unexpected difficulties. Like much of the North China zone, Donghai County was a sharecropping area in which landlords traditionally provided seeds, fertilizer, tools, and draft animals to their tenants. The price of these items, together with the trouble and expense of collecting the harvested grain from scores of tenants who cultivated many small parcels of land scattered over a wide area, presented a problem for the party. Lacking the finances for such outlays, the new GMD managers attempted to collect the landlord's share without furnishing the requisite capital. Tenants understandably resisted GMD efforts to collect the landlord's share of the crop on the grounds that the party had violated the terms of the peasants' unwritten contract. The reporter noted that one large estate that "ordinarily yielded about $5,000 a year to its owner . . . yielded nothing at all" under GMD management. Rather than aiding the tenants and gaining their allegiance, GMD administration required that they "find ready money for taxes, seeds, animals, fertilizers, etc., to which they gave no concern before—and they have not the ready cash."[52]

Summarizing one of his articles, the correspondent derided rule by the Haizhou GMD: "To the best class of people it is a terror. To the middle classes an abomination [sic]. The coolie class has reaped some benefits more apparent than real. The military are [sic] openly hostile to it."[53] Reversing the common pattern of rural propertied elites moving to the security of urban areas because of disturbances, wealthy city dwellers were said to be retreating from GMD-ruled Haizhou to their rural estates. This probably indicates, despite the previous references to confiscation of some large landed estates, that the fury of the party seldom touched elites in communities in Donghai County that were at the bottom of the scale of central places, such as villages and minor market towns. The party was primarily an urban force and was represented badly or not at all in most areas outside county seats and major market towns. The *Herald* correspondent argued that the recent trend of nonbandits owning fine Mauser pistols was increasing rural security; a Mauser was becoming "by far the most coveted possession in North Kiangsu." Also contributing to the security of elites in the countryside was an increase in the fortification of certain large villages. Reportedly, "[many] small villages . . .[were] abandoned and merged into larger ones with guntowers on the outskirts."[54] Whatever the contributing factors, in Haizhou a fair portion of the elite population was attempting to escape from the GMD-ruled city.

A memoir by a left-leaning leader of the Donghai GMD written decades after the events of the late 1920s adds texture to the picture painted by the *Herald* correspondent. It verifies parts of that account and also presents a different perspective. Predictably, the most salient dissimilarity in viewpoint is that the memoirist celebrates, rather than lambastes, the Donghai party branch's radicalism and speaks approvingly of party actions against incumbent elites. He defends the confiscation of property of "warlords" and punishment meted out to persons charged as "local bullies and evil gentry" by contending that the expropriated wealth underwrote loans to Haizhou's poor, thereby "remedying the difficulty of their lives" and helping to fund their small businesses. He does not indicate whether the loans were given out at low or no interest, but since the loans were limited to five *yuan* per household, one must surmise that they could not have greatly improved the lot of the poor.[55]

The memoirist treats one aspect of the Donghai GMD's campaign to reshape society that the *Herald* ignored: the women's movement. In his view the GMD's women's movement played an important role in "liberating the thought of" people in the county. Feng Jufen, a young woman who was sixteen or seventeen at the time of the Northern Expedition, was a key organizer of the county's women's movement. According to the memoir, Feng emphasized the goal of gender equality, the unbinding of women's feet, and the bobbing of women's hair. Although she concentrated some of her effort on mobilizing female students in the local schools, she also went out into some market towns and villages to spread her message. This led to conflict with Wang Changhao, a landlord from Juntuncun who publicly denounced the women's movement and used bombast and threats to dissuade women from unbinding their feet. In reaction, Feng made Wang the object of public ridicule. She and her lieutenants in the women's movement dragged him before a mass demonstration, where the crowd chanted a humiliating jingle: "Wang Changhao is quite ludicrous. He talks tough, but will be hanged. The crowd in the streets roars with laughter!" Although I have found no evidence that a hanging took place, the leaders of the GMD-led women's movement in the county did move to counteract and destroy any prestige and power enjoyed by elites who opposed the movement's agenda.[56]

Merchant protests against their treatment by the party eventually prompted the provincial government to send the magistrates of two neighboring counties to sort out the shrill charges and countercharges emanating from Donghai County. The resulting investigative report both verifies the general picture drawn by the *Herald* and adds important dimensions. Much like the *Herald's* reporter, the inspectors observed that Donghai's politics had become polarized between a "New Faction," comprised of the young activists of the GMD, whom these inspectors contemptuously referred to as "novices," and an "Old Faction" comprised of "wealthy and distinguished merchants."[57] However, unlike the *Herald* correspondent, the inspectors noted that the county government was beginning to side with local elites and to withdraw its support from the local party branch. Further, the inspectors argued that the party's mass organizations, especially its labor union—which had so far avoided disbandment—spearheaded the struggles against local elites.

According to the investigators, the county party branch had angered hundreds of local merchants by attacking Liu Zhendian, the longtime vice-chair of the county's chamber of commerce. GMD leaders accused Liu of being an "evil gentry," and persuaded the Political Training Bureau head of a nearby GMD army unit to arrest him. In reaction, hundreds of local merchants rose to Liu's defense. Yang Tongshou, a merchant from the market town of Xinpu, collected the chops of over four hundred merchants on a petition to the county magistrate, asking him to secure Liu's release. Though in this instance the magistrate initially demurred, he eventually became more sympathetic to local merchants' desires. The party's action against Liu drove a wedge between the local GMD branch and many Donghai merchants that would divide the two sides for many months.[58]

Leaders of the Donghai GMD's General Labor Union led several of the assaults on politically active local merchant leaders and their interests. Union leader Gu Nancun enraged Donghai shop owners by forcing them and their employees to enter his union and then squeezing them for high union dues. Further, Gu and his followers blocked Merchant Association leader Wang Ziyun's transport of a large shipment of beans from Donghai, ostensibly out of fear that he was supplying Japanese armies at Ji'nan (Tsinan) and because he had hired nonunion transport workers. By no means a mere gentlemanly disagreement, this incident escalated as both sides resorted to armed force—union pickets kidnapping Wang's brother and Wang striking back by engineering Gu's arrest at the hands of local police and merchant militia.[59]

By this time the county magistrate was on the merchants' side. He sent the fifty police and merchant militiamen who rescued Wang's brother and arrested Gu. The county's general labor union reacted by calling a meeting to consider ways to oppose the magistrate. The magistrate immediately arrested twenty more union representatives, though he soon released all but the five ringleaders of the attacks on Wang. Over the protests of many county party spokesmen, the magistrate bound General Labor Union leader Gu over for trial on charges of "unauthorized private arrest" of Wang's brother.[60] Donghai County had started down a road that many other Jiangsu counties would travel—the twisted path of party-government tension and disputes.

Certain features of Donghai politics were replicated in numerous localities in the province: growing government links with a group of local elites, escalating party-government fights, and mass organizations temporarily evading the party center's attempts to reign them in. And although the actions of the Donghai GMD were clearly intended to reshape society rapidly, some of the clashes between that county's party branch and incumbent elites seem more like pitched battles for power and control over resources than arguments over how radically society should be restructured; both the former and the latter patterns were evident elsewhere in the province. But although the tendency of the Donghai party and mass organizations to alienate many local elites was typical of situations in a number of other counties, it was atypical in that this conflict became so severe and counterproductive that the provincial GMD headquarters eventually felt the need to expel the Donghai leaders from the party for "oppressing merchants."[61]

Except in the handful of cases in which overt violence broke out between local party organizations and persons they charged with being "local bullies and evil gentry," Chinese sources on other localities give less detailed treatment to party-elite relations than the Donghai sources. They do, however, provide enough information to flesh out the picture of such relations.

The GMD in Ganyu County, which adjoined Donghai County, focused much of its energies on attacking and prosecuting one local elite, Wang Zuoliang, together with a few individuals who were close to him. Wang had been county magistrate for over a decade and a half, something of a record of longevity in such a post. He had created a local political machine and had, consequently, become quite wealthy. Because the Northern Expedition arrived late in Ganyu and the county GMD was formed late in the game, Wang's machine managed to ride out most of 1927 without incident. However, in late 1927 political activist Zhang Jingtong returned to Ganyu from Nanjing and started to build a local GMD branch. By hiding his Communist membership, Zhang had earlier served as a clerk in the provincial headquarters of the GMD. In late 1927 this Nationalist *cum* Communist, together with Chen Jianbo, a left-wing GMD adherent, began to build an anti-Wang alliance that included people from various social strata, and even a few "old bureaucrats." In early 1928 the anti-Wang group approached Li Mingyang, the commander of a GMD army unit based in Haizhou, and proposed that he help overthrow Wang's machine. Li's unit swept into Ganyu, arrested the old magistrate and a number of government functionaries and local elites, and transferred them to Nanjing to be tried by the special court system. Wang was found guilty and sentenced to life imprisonment, and the government ordered his property confiscated. The local GMD used Wang's expropriated moveable property to set up a welfare office (*jiuji yuan*), and that office drew up plans to distribute his 4,000-odd *mu* among landless peasants who were to be given the land gratis. However, the land redistribution plan was never carried out, perhaps because of Zhang's untimely death due to natural causes.[62]

Just as in Haizhou, the move in Ganyu against entrenched magistrate Wang Zuoliang was but a part of the radicals' larger attempt to remake society. The attack on Wang was accompanied by the establishment of a general labor union, a peasant association, a women's association, a merchant association (for small merchants), and an association for the "promotion of commoners' education" (*pingmin jiaoyu cujinhui*). The local GMD branch, in addition to its attack on Wang, pressed an anti-superstition campaign and an anti-footbinding movement. The party's actions affected more than just those elites it directly assaulted or prosecuted; some elites who were not arrested immediately fled the county to avoid trouble. For example, Zhu Shoushi, a *juren* degree holder and one-time member of the provincial assembly, took refuge in Shanghai for half a year because party leaders had named him as a "local bully" who needed to be overthrown; after returning to Ganyu, it is said that he became a recluse—seldom leaving his house for fear of running into trouble with the new regime.[63]

Some county parties could not generate enough power to confront and control local nonparty elites. For example, a Jiading County party and mass movement leader, Zhang Laifang, committed suicide in 1928, leaving a note which spoke of his despair that the county party and its peasant movement were being irreparably harmed by the CCP on one hand and "local bullies and evil gentry" on the other. The Jiading party had earlier aroused the ire of certain Jiading elites by executing one who had disrupted the Northern Expedition, and the GMD's county peasant association preparatory committee had alienated landlords by launching a rent reduction campaign.[64] But while Zhang Laifang may have felt that the Jiading party branch was too weak to do its job, some county GMD organizations exhibited compelling power in their own localities—so much so that the provincial party reprimanded a leader of the Wuxi County party for strutting about with armed police patrols, arresting people.[65]

A Summary Execution in Feng County, Or Taking a Satrap by Stealth

Though a party branch's perception of its own weakness might at times prevent it from taking on powerful enemies, attacks on incumbent elites did not always stem from the local GMD's confidence in its own power. One especially well-documented execution of a local elite in Feng County was a desperate act of the new GMD regime, carried out in order to alter the configuration of local power in its favor.

Feng County was located in the extreme northwest tip of Jiangsu's North China zone. In 1927 it had been captured by the GMD's Northern Expeditionary Armies, only to be lost to counterattacking warlord forces, and subsequently retaken. The Northern Expedition's shifting front line meant that GMD administrators were operating in an atmosphere of uncertainty and high risk.

For at least a decade, elites in Feng had been split into two factions. The leader of the Northern Faction (*Bei pai* or *Bei dang*), Sun Jishi, was a lower gentry (*xiucai*) who had been elected to the provincial assembly in the early Republican period. His considerable wealth came from the prominent Taiyuangong Piece Goods and General Store that his family owned, as well as the family's part ownership of several other shops. In the early Republic, Sun had parlayed that wealth into appointment as head of the county's chamber of commerce. By the 1920s he also controlled a large proportion of the militia forces in the county—all told, several hundred guns.[66] Competing with Sun's Northern Faction in local politics was the notably weaker Southern Faction; most of the members of the latter were educators, and a few had been *Tongmenghui* partisans. Memoirs describe the Southern Faction as more progressive and more interested in reform than Sun's Northern Faction. The two groupings competed in many arenas, including local schools, resulting in frequent student unrest. In chapter 4 we saw that Pi County elites used students over whom they had influence to cause trouble in schools administered by their factional opponents. The story in Feng County is strikingly similar. In one case in 1920 a group of students at an upper elementary school, acting at the instigation of Southern Faction mentors, beat up the school's principal, a Northern Faction associate.[67]

Despite such petty challenges, Sun's faction clearly enjoyed ascendancy in the county's politics through the 1920s until the advancing Northern Expeditionary Armies caused warlord forces to withdraw from the area in early 1927. Fearing loss of power with the militarists' withdrawal, Sun first fled behind northern warlord lines to Tianjin, but he soon decided to take the chance of traveling to Nanjing in hopes of using connections there to protect his position. Although when he arrived in the GMD capital, he managed to get an appointment with Niu Yongjian, who at the time was the GMD regime's commissioner of civil affairs for Jiangsu, Sun soon found himself under arrest. The exact reasons behind his incarceration by Nanjing police are unclear, but his detention probably stemmed from suspicions of his ties with Sun Chuanfang's warlord forces—at a time when the northern front was far from secure. Sun Jishi languished in jail for several months, while a nephew tried to use his former classmate ties with a number of Huangpu Military Academy graduates to gain Sun's release. A bribe given to a military justice finally gained Sun's release, yet Sun did not immediately return to Feng, but instead ran to the cover of warlord protection in Tianjin.[68]

In November of 1927, warlord forces withdrew from the Feng area north to Shandong, and GMD military authorities appointed an acting magistrate for the county. This official, finding anarchy in the county, invited Sun Jishi back to organize militia forces to pacify the area. So Sun reentered the county's political scene and quickly took control of it.[69]

But within weeks, the provincial government appointed a new magistrate, Wang Gongyu, who would soon checkmate Sun. Wang understood the alignment of political power in Feng quite well, having several months earlier been sent as a GMD special deputy to oversee the county's party branch. Immediately upon his return to Feng, Wang must have been struck by Sun's local might. Sun styled himself "the commander" (*zong tuanzhang*) and controlled several local armed forces. As head of the county chamber of commerce, Sun controlled the merchant militia, which was led by his nephew. He could also rely on the county's peace preservation corps (*bao'an dui*), since its commander was his old Northern Faction buddy, Liu Yanxiang. And although militia leaders in outlying areas of the county were not united, they had a healthy respect for Sun's power, and Sun could expect many of them to side with him in a pinch.[70]

Magistrate Wang, who commanded only a few reliable policemen, understood his precarious position. He began his term in office by accommodating Sun and showing deference to him. He heaped rewards on Sun for successes Sun claimed to have achieved while fighting bandits, and he compensated Sun for injuries the local satrap asserted had been incurred in those fights, even though Wang knew there had been no fights. Wang even provided ammunition to Sun's troops when requested. As for the many aspirants whom Sun recommended for government offices, Wang duly appointed many, though he postponed action on some appointments that he thought would be harmful. All in all, Wang's goal seems to have been to lull Sun into a false sense of security by making concessions to him.[71]

Some accounts of these events underscore Magistrate Wang's political isolation as he sat in the shadow of Feng County's strongman, secretly planning to eliminate him. However, there may have been a tacit alliance between Wang and the Southern Faction, the local elite clique that had long competed with Sun's grouping. A key figure in the Southern clique was former provincial assemblyman Dong Hancha, who had earned a lower exam degree in the late Qing era. Dong aided Wang by dispatching to the special court in Nanjing—the body that handled indictments of persons charged as "local bullies"—a detailed complaint about Sun. Happily for Magistrate Wang, the provincial government ordered Sun's execution.[72]

Wang, armed with this authorization which he kept secret, invited Sun to his office to "discuss a financial difficulty." Sun, suspecting nothing, went directly to the magistrate's office, accompanied by only one of his factotums. Magistrate Wang confronted Sun with the provincial order to execute him, and immediately had a bodyguard take the strongman out to the nearby courtyard and shoot him.[73] It appears that the provincial government had decided to execute Sun, both because of his ties to warlord Sun Chuanfang's forces and because he had escaped from his Nanjing prison cell.

Without delay, Wang moved to exert control over the armed forces Sun had commanded. Some of them willingly shifted their loyalty to Wang's government, though others slipped out of the city and attempted, unsuccessfully as it turned out, to patch together a militia coalition to attack the county seat in revenge for Sun's killing.[74] Wang proceeded further to establish his authority by confiscating the property of Li Houji, a Feng County native who had been a warlord in Fujian Province in the 1910s and early 1920s. Li owned extensive landholdings in both Feng and Tongshan counties, as well as an oil milling operation, and a few shops and pubs. Li had not been resident in Feng for years, and to get at his property, Wang had also to face off against another military man who had long defended Li Houji's interests in Feng County. Wang and the county GMD branch took this local militarist's property.[75] From this time forth, the power of Feng County's Northern Faction was no more.

With these audacious strokes, Wang established the new GMD regime's authority, enabling him to accomplish a good deal in the three years that he served as Feng county magistrate. Longtime Feng residents credit him with having dealt effectively with local banditry, solved an endemic water control problem on the border with Shandong province, and eliminated a number of corrupt practices of the local government.[76]

Was Wang's attack on the Northern Faction of local elites merely a means to establish his power in the county or was it part of a sweeping refashioning of local society? Certainly it was the former, but Wang's administration also embraced some modest measures of social refashioning. For example, Wang cooperated with the head of the local GMD branch in pressing forward an antisuperstition campaign, the crowning achievement of which was to transform the Temple of the City God into a Mass Education Institute.[77]

Articles on Prosecuting "Local Bullies"

Although a few party branches called together mass meetings to confront directly certain elites, and in rare cases the Nationalist Government or army leaders summarily executed a local elite, most local party organizations contented themselves with investigating and accusing a select handful of local elites. The party usually left their arrest, trial, and punishment to the government and the system of special courts. Often county party branches, lacking the cooperation of county governments, petitioned the provincial party headquarters to investigate and prosecute individuals they saw as "local bullies and evil gentry." The provincial headquarters usually acceded to such requests by sending deputies to investigate and recommend for or against prosecution. If action seemed warranted, the provincial party branch turned the case over to the provincial government for prosecution.[78] The government balked at prosecuting some cases, prompting the provincial party in July 1927 to call for the government to "honor the party's opinion . . ." and "forthrightly punish . . . any local bully or evil gentry the provincial party has accused."[79] It is likely, however, that the party was able to significantly affect the outcome of cases in the special courts.

As with the leftists before the Northern Expedition reached Jiangsu, the party's criteria for identifying a person as a "local bully" or "evil gentry" were vague. Central party and government authorities had provided an operating code—a guide for party action—in the form of the "Articles on the Punishment of Local Bullies and Evil Gentry" that governed prosecutions in the special courts. But, these articles list a remarkably disparate assortment of acts that could mark a person as a "local bully" to be punished. These crimes included:

> [1] using military force to oppress commoners and causing injury . . . disablement . . . [or] death . . . ; [2] bullying orphans and the weak or using violence to compel marriages . . . ; [3] on the basis of property relations, depriving others of their personal freedoms . . . ; [4] usury . . . ; [5] establishing or giving protection to opium dens or houses of gambling . . . ; [6] swindling money by instigating and handling litigation . . . ; [7] extorting officials into taking or not taking a certain course of action . . . ; [8] bullying and stirring up a mob to obstruct either local public interests or reconstruction projects . . . ; [9] fabricating evidence and directing worthless people to harm good people . . . ; [10] compelling people to harm good people . . . ; [11] compelling people to buy or sell property . . . ; and [12] misusing public money while holding public office or using any pretext to embezzle money.[80]

Despite the hydra-headed quality of this benchmark "definition" of "local bullies and evil gentry," one thread runs throughout: abuse of power or economic position. Clearly, the party leadership visualized "local bullies" as powerful persons, in other words, local elites—but only an immoral subset of them.

The articles gave little clue as to how many local elites should be prosecuted or in what strata or type of local leadership they were most likely to be located. There are certainly no signs in these articles that central authorities were prescribing an across-the-board attack on incumbent local elites. But local party branches, which had to fill in the gaps in the operating code, enjoyed great leeway in pursuing specific cases. Some of the listed offenses, like "bullying to obstruct public interests," were elastic enough as to provide a hunting license to anyone who wished to see elites who were his competitors behind bars. For radicals who longed to sweep away most of the preexisting powerholders, the articles provided a broad broom. The opportunistic nature of party actions against local elites is illustrated by the pointed admonition that one party deputy delivered to assembled Liuhe County township managers and other local leaders in 1927: "[Those] . . . local bullies and evil gentry who . . . accept party domination will be allowed to reform themselves, but if they enter the party and harm party affairs, then party power absolutely will not tolerate them."[81] But regardless of such warnings, longtime local political elites were entering and taking control of some local parties, thereby forestalling their community GMD branch's drive against incumbents. There were also many reports of *foiled* attempts of so-called "local bullies" to manipulate local parties through ingress, bribery, or intimidation.[82]

Many of the party assaults on local elites were natural outgrowths of the social radicalism that lived on in the GMD well after the purge. In fact, we have already seen that in a few counties Communists not only survived the purge but continued to work within the Guomindang, contributing to the party's radical coloration in those localities. Even in those many instances in which social radicalism propelled the drive against certain local elites, other factors often came into play. For example, it might be tempting to posit that the anti-"bully" campaign led by the Rugao County GMD, which we know to have been controlled by the CCP for many months after the purge, was simply an across-the-board social revolution fueled by radicalism. Yet, many prominent elites escaped attack, so some manner of selection must have been employed. Certainly social radicalism stimulated by Communist leadership was a key factor that motivated the Rugao party to lodge charges against some of the individuals, but it does not account for the far-from-radical government's continuing prosecution and punishment of some of them months after the Communists had been pushed out of the party. Lenore Barkan has suggested that the Rugao county government, which was never Communist, was motivated by financial considerations. In short, it wanted the elites' confiscated properties. She may well be correct in her surmise that the rationale behind the county government's selective punishment of particular members of the local elite in Rugao was to "punish those who resisted in some way the government's efforts to collect funds."[83]

The "Bullies" in GMD Eyes

More important to local politics than the center's code defining "local bullies" was the manner in which the local party branches chose to apply it. Local party branches contained members of many stripes, ranging from radicals who saw virtually all incumbent power holders and wealthy persons as revolutionary targets, to those who had little or no interest in campaigns against local elites. Along these lines, one member of the county purge committee in Fengxian County (Lower Yangzi core) discounted the need for an anti-"bully" campaign by announcing that his county had no "local bullies or evil gentry."[84] Radicalism, though common, was by no means universal in Jiangsu's GMD.

Still, a high percentage of Jiangsu's county GMD branches launched assaults of one kind or another on persons they called "local bullies and evil gentry." In fact, we have reports of actions taken or contemplated against, all told, hundreds of individuals.[85] But who were these persons the local GMD leaders and activists sought to topple? Sadly, the vast majority of the reports do not provide enough information on the social, economic, and political background of those under attack to allow us to determine this with precision. And for most localities such biographical data is woefully lacking. Thus, I rely on the relative handful of cases for which I have such data.

All of those charged as "local bullies and evil gentry" for whom background information is available were local elites.[86] But what kinds of elites were they, and from what level of local society did they come? The answer is that no stratum or type of local elite seems to have enjoyed immunity from such charges.

A few members of the upper crust of pre-Northern Expeditionary leaders—those who also played roles in provincial politics—found themselves under suspicion. For example, the Funing County GMD branch engineered the prosecution of the brothers Chen Boming and Chen Yaxuan, both of whom had been Funing representatives in the provincial assembly before 1927. These two, who were also local militia trainers, in 1928 faced charges as "local bullies and evil gentry" because, according to party sources, they had served as advisers to warlord Zhang Zongchang, "secretly stocked munitions," and provided aid to a "bandit." The special court in Nanjing found the Chens guilty of some of the charges lodged against them, and they were sentenced to fourteen years in prison. All told, the county GMD branch formally charged over thirty of Funing's local elites with being "bullies," and over twenty of the accused received sentences of varying severity. Local GMD activists were incensed a few months later when Miao Bin, provincial commissioner of civil affairs, released the Chens—the sort of act that led some party members to charge that Miao was in league with the "local bullies" of Jiangsu. The truth is, such "reversal of verdicts" by Miao, other authorities, and the judicial system in general were rather common.[87]

By no means were the Chens of Funing the only former provincial assembly members who were prosecuted as "local bullies" by the GMD regime. Guanyun County's former provincial assembly representative, Ge Jincheng, faced prosecution for "colluding with warlords, manipulating affairs in the locality, and instigating litigation."[88] We have already noted the case of a provincial assemblyman from Feng County who was under attack by the party. It is, of course, impossible to evaluate the truth or falsity of the charges against these persons. However, it seems probable that the crucial element that marked these men for party struggle was not so much their status as former provincial assembly representatives, but rather their support, suspected or real, for "the enemy" in the ongoing war against the northern warlords. I have found no evidence of a generalized, province-wide attack on former provincial assemblymen.[89] It is probably no accident, however, that all of these cases are from the North China portion of the province. Throughout 1927 the front shifted back and forth across the two-thirds of the province north of the Yangzi, making elite "collaboration with the enemy" a salient worry for the party. Former provincial assemblymen, because of their presumed personal acquaintance with Jiangsu's former military rulers, were natural objects of scrutiny.

But it was not just former provincial assembly members who stood charged with abetting warlords. Some purely county-level elites faced the same charge. For example, in late 1927 the Dongtai County GMD inveighed against the chair and vice-chair of the county assembly, charging that they had cabled Sun Chuanfang's army to request reinstatement of one of Dongtai's warlord-era magistrates. If the party's evidence is to be believed, a wide spectrum of county elites, including leaders of the county executive council, the agricultural assembly, the public property office, and the education association, as well as a person identified only as "a member of the local gentry," were implicated in the plot. Although the local GMD called its evidence against these persons "ironclad proof" that they were "local bullies and evil gentry," read from another perspective the documentation evokes sympathy for them. The GMD-appointed magistrate had fled when the front shifted southward, leaving Dongtai essentially ungoverned. Thus, the cables these beleaguered elites sent to Sun's army come across as plaintive pleas for somebody to establish a degree of order.[90]

Lenore Barkan argues that in Rugao *only* subcounty personnel were successfully prosecuted and punished under the label "local bullies and evil gentry."[91] If true, this was likely a function of county elites' residual power—their strong networks of political connections and, perhaps, their ability to buy off potential accusers and prosecutors. It is clear, though, that in a number of other areas, selected county-level elites did face prosecution as local bullies. In no sense did county elites enjoy immunity from such action, as we have seen in the fairly detailed accounts from Feng and Shuyang counties. But, in fact, there was not always a clear distinction between county and township elites; some leaders operated on both levels. For example, county assemblymen who were elected, one per township, sometimes resided and exercised power in the township seat.

Wuxi County's Pu Rongqian was both a county and a township elite, having been both a county assembly member and a township manager. In 1928 two persons complained to the county GMD that Pu was a "local bully." They argued that he (1) unlawfully involved himself in litigation, (2) falsely accused others of piracy in order to extort money from them, (3) compelled persons to divorce in order to profit by arranging a new marriage for the woman, (4) collected a local faction around himself, (5) accepted bribes, and (6) embezzled. After investigating the charges, a provincial party agent who supervised the Wuxi GMD asked the county office of public security to arrest Pu. Although police organs often balked at such party requests, Pu soon found himself in jail.[92]

Unlike Pu, most township elites had not held office at the county level. This does not mean, however, that they did not have important ties beyond the township seat. Chambers of commerce and other bodies in market towns were commonly offshoots of similar organs in the county seat. And some township elites owned property and had connections not only outside their township, but also outside their own county. Not surprisingly, some of these peripatetic township elites had gained enemies from beyond the township borders. One such former township manager, Yao Heling from Luhe township in Taicang County, was pummeled from both sides of the Taicang-Changshu county line with charges that he was a "local bully and evil gentry." The specific charges against Yao were similar to those faced by many other subcounty elites: (1) extorting funds, (2) using terror tactics to cheat money from one of his land tenants, (3) swindling persons by means of litigation, (4) compelling divorce in order to profit as a matchmaker, (5) embezzling public funds, and (6) committing fraud. Although the Shanghai Local Court eventually absolved Yao of most of the charges because of a legal technicality, he was sentenced to eight months imprisonment for embezzling government funds.[93] A memoir suggests how important the Taicang GMD leaders believed the action against Yao to be. In the latter several months of 1927 two different groups of individuals had been appointed by higher party organs as Taicang's party committee. Thus, both the county provisional committee and the county special committee claimed to be the authoritative party committee for Taicang's GMD. But although the two bodies could agree on almost nothing, and they were embroiled in constant disputes, the *one* item of work on which they cooperated and which they saw to completion was the investigation and prosecution of Yao.[94]

It was not just warlord-era township elites that felt the party's wrath. Sometimes township heads appointed by the GMD regime's own local magistrates came under party fire as "bullies."[95] This kind of assault on sitting government and subgovernment officials precipitated larger party-government disputes that rocked many localities.[96]

In many counties, townships had long been further subdivided into precincts (*tu*), each headed by a precinct manager (*tudong* or *dibao*). Like elites at higher levels of the hierarchy of central places, some precinct managers confronted charges that they were "local bullies and evil gentry." One such case, that of forty year-old precinct manager Yu Yichen of Wuxi County, illustrates a factor which affected the party's selection of elites to prosecute as "local bullies": local elite factionalism. One of the men who accused Yu before the party and government was widely known as his long-time enemy, making this litigation just one chapter in a long-running vendetta between these two elites.⁹⁷ Yu languished in jail for several weeks in late 1927 and early 1928 while the county magistrate, who bemoaned a "lack of precedents for prosecutions of local bullies and evil gentry," deliberated. In January 1928 the magistrate turned the matter over to the Suzhou Local Court, but available information does not describe the outcome of the case.

In mid-1929 Shanghai County witnessed another case of this sort. A precinct manager brought charges against a former township assistant manager (*xiangzuo*) before the county GMD and county office of public security. After investigation, the party upheld the charges that the township officer was a "litigation rascal and a local bully and evil gentry . . . in conspiracy with other dubious characters." Public security officers arrested the suspect.⁹⁸ Both party and government were weapons that local elites, depending on their connections, could use against factional opponents.

While many of the elites under GMD assault or prosecution as "local bullies and evil gentry" were leaders of assemblies, professional associations, or township governing organs, some were players in and masters of more private networks of power. For example, the Kunshan County party charged rent collector Wu Shaoxi as a "local bully," alleging that Wu "relied on armed force . . . to collect rent illegally beyond the contracted amount."⁹⁹ Of all those charged as "bullies" on whom I have information, Wu comes closest to being a nonelite. However, he would have been seen as powerful in a village context even though his power was probably exercised in a smaller arena than that of assemblymen or managers at the township or county level.

The Shuyang Massacre:
Factionalism and Radicalism Combined

Despite the very real role of leftists in a considerable proportion of the attacks on incumbent elites, party conflict with those elites was not always simply the product of pronounced social radicalism on the part of the local GMD branch. In some localities such disputes arose from the co-optation of a party branch by one or more competing factions among established local elites. Some of the accusations before the special courts had been lodged by members of one elite faction against members of another, something akin to what we have already seen in the Feng County case cited above. But local elite factionalism and social radicalism were not necessarily mutually exclusive entities; unlike oil and water, they could be mixed together in a complex and potentially explosive brew. Thus when radicals in the Shuyang County GMD branch were drawn deeply into an already long-running war between elite factions in 1927 and early 1928, it led to armed conflict that destroyed the county party branch. This incident, Shuyang's "January 6 Massacre," is one of the most thoroughly discussed local political events of the Nanjing Decade in Jiangsu.[100]

Two factions of Shuyang elites had competed for ascendancy in the early Republican period. The more dominant of the two cliques, the East Faction (*Dong dang*), a part of which hostile chroniclers later derisively dubbed the "Eight Local Bullies" (*Ba tulie*), is depicted by the Shuyang gazetteer as having consisted primarily of landlords and old gentry. Its leader was Cheng Zhaoshi, the scion of a family that owned a large chain of dry goods stores, an oil mill, a brewery, pawnshops, various other types of shops, commercial properties that were rented to other shop owners, and vast landholdings. It is said that he personally owned some 40,000 *mu* of land, which was rented out to hundreds of tenants. Cheng was so clearly the towering figure in his clique that it was often just called the "Cheng Clique."[101] At the beginning of the Republican era, Cheng had won election to the provincial assembly, and after that had moved up to the National Assembly. He was, likewise, head of the county chamber of commerce; one source intones that this position was his by hereditary right due to his family's towering stature in the county's economy. This local strongman had cultivated close relations with Bai Baoshan, the militarist who held the position of regional commander for the Haizhou area and who dominated much of northern Jiangsu in the 1920s. This tie had allowed Cheng to threaten local administrators and secure their obedience; Cheng was known to have accused as "bandits" persons who crossed him, and Bai's forces obliged him by executing them. Bai, for his part, could depend on Cheng to compel selected Shuyang merchants to come up with forced contributions to support Bai's forces.[102] Cheng held sway over the commanders of all three units of the county police force, and directly controlled the county's merchant militia. Beyond that, far and away most of the township and subtownship managers were Cheng's men. Memoirs hostile to Cheng argue that he used the force at his disposal brutally. They cite two cases in which he had soldiers kill landlords who had caused problems for him. They also charge that in

1926 his forces not only killed the leaders of a large bandit gang whom his agents had persuaded to surrender by offering complete amnesty, but also carried out a methodical week-long orgy of beheadings, slaughtering several hundred rank-and-file members of the gang.[103]

Despite his influence in all of the arenas cited above, Cheng's relations with educational circles and, in general, with persons who had attained a modern education were, at best, strained. The clique that opposed Cheng's group was known as the West Faction (*Xi dang*) or the Zhou Faction, named after its most prominent member. It drew most of its members from the modern educators and the modern educated, though it also included a very few older scholars, township managers, and militia leaders. Sources frequently paint Zhou's faction as the more reformist of the two local cliques. Cheng had alienated the small modern-educated cohort in the county by supporting President Yuan Shikai's ill-fated attempt to make himself emperor. It is said that Cheng had even fingered anti-Yuan dissidents in Shuyang, some of whom were subsequently executed by military authorities. Educational circles believed that through the years, Cheng had constrained education expenditures in the county and had misdirected funds earmarked for instruction. Fearing independent local schools as a platform for criticizing him, and perhaps recognizing the founders of these institutions as his enemies, Cheng and his cronies had, over the years, done all they could to prevent the opening of some schools and had created special hardships for them after they had commenced operations. Since Cheng largely controlled local politics and had close relations with regional and local military powers, educators blamed him for the behavior of militarists who arbitrarily billeted troops in school buildings for indeterminate periods of time and allowed soldiers to vandalize, and in some cases, virtually destroy the edifices. Cheng was, as memoirists suggest with understatement, no scholar—a fact that did not engender respect for him among educators. It was, therefore, probably not love of learning that led Cheng in the early 1920s to attempt to get himself elected head of the county education association. Some seventy-odd educators of the West Faction furiously organized and lobbied authorities on both the provincial and county levels to prevent Cheng from attaining either this or any other position in education.[104]

The leading light in the anti-Cheng faction was Zhou Xiaoshi. Zhou was from a wealthy landlord family that owned more than 10,000 *mu* of land. Zhou's father, a holder of a Qing-era lower exam degree, had studied law in the early Republican era and while practicing as an attorney had established a reputation as a reformer. Zhou Xiaoshi himself had graduated from the Third Provincial Agricultural Middle School in Qingjiang, and in the 1920s he ran his own transportation company. Through this venture Zhou was trying to live up to his father's dream that he would, like the famous Nantong reformer, Zhang Jian, contribute to China's national strength through local economic development projects. Zhou was a talented public speaker, having made a name for himself among those with modern educations by winning one speaking contest on the subject of "scientific democracy" and another competition conducted in English. After graduation, local educators from the West Faction had persuaded him to run for Shuyang's seat in the provincial assembly, a race which he won. In 1920, soon after winning the seat, Zhou announced the formation of a county self-government association, which he intended to use to consolidate the anti-Cheng forces. But as he and a colleague were out walking down the street the afternoon before the inaugural meeting was to be held, a group of local toughs surrounded the two, thrashed them, and proceeded to plaster them with night soil. Although the assault had been witnessed by a large crowd, Zhou found the county magistrate uninterested in investigating, since the incident had likely transpired at the behest of Cheng's forces. Such was the precarious, unprotected situation of the outgroup West Faction for many of the years prior to the Northern Expedition, even though one of its members held a seat in the provincial assembly. The self-government association meeting was never held, Zhou's clique having found that it could not operate in an open, public manner.[105]

Available sources depict Zhou and many, though by no means all, of the people around him as "progressives" and "reformers"—members of the May Fourth generation. Quite a few of them were teachers, especially in upper-primary schools, and many of these opponents of Cheng's Faction had participated in study societies (*dushu hui*) formed in the wake of the May Fourth Incident. Their gatherings had entailed discussions of science, democracy, imperialism, and what many of them saw as the "feudalism" of Cheng's group. Some of them were involved in the publication of a journal, *Shu sheng* (*The Voice of Shuyang*), in which local authors ventilated their critiques of local society and its leadership. Not surprisingly, Cheng's forces shut down this periodical after the publication of only a few issues.[106]

With the approach of the GMD's Northern Expeditionary Armies in 1927, Zhou saw an opportunity to use against his old nemesis, Cheng, the campaign against "local bullies and evil gentry" that was sweeping the province. At age thirty-two, Zhou was relatively young, considering his local prestige, and because his political base included many modern educated intellectuals, it is not surprising that he had friends in the embryonic local GMD branch. One of them was Xie Lunxian, a teacher in Shuyang and a leading light among the county's radical intellectuals. Xie was a former schoolmate of Zhou's and a longtime friend of Zhou's family. Like three or four other well-known teachers in the county, Xie had nurtured the political consciousness of a number of his students through his teaching, by lending copies of *New Youth* and other journals, by participating in reading and study groups, and by helping in the publication of the local radical journal, *Shu sheng*. Around April of 1927, Xie had moved to Wuhan, the location of the GMD party center recognized by the party's left wing; unlike Chiang Kai-shek's Nanjing party center, the Wuhan center had not yet broken with the Communists. However, when the Wuhan center also purged the Communists in mid-1927, Xie, a Communist as well as a member of the GMD, fled back to Shuyang, where he went to live with Zhou. Two considerations that attracted Xie to Zhou's mansion were friendship and Xie's need for protection against both Cheng's forces and those of the GMD right wing, which Zhou's local power might provide. But another factor that brought the two together was the shared desire to topple Cheng Zhaoshi in an anti-"local bully" campaign. Xie, who was secretary of the GMD's Shuyang County Provisional Executive Committee, Zhou, and other members of the county GMD committee, as well as a few of their protégés began to lay the groundwork for a movement to overthrow Cheng and his henchmen.[107]

Was this campaign to depose Cheng merely another chapter in the East Faction-versus-West Faction feud that had been going on for years? One memoirist, looking back at this political contest in which he and his friends had participated, insists that the group that lived and plotted at Zhou's house "was not [just] the old West faction springing to life again, but instead this was revolution." As he put it, "Many of the feudal bullies and evil gentry from among the old colleagues [of the West Faction] refused the request to take part; instead, they only responded the moment that Cheng was actually attacked, and they did so then only to protect their own skins."[108] However, at least one important West Faction elite besides Zhou took part in the scheme to oust Cheng's local regime: Wang Xianghe, the township manager for the county's sixth municipal township.[109] In fact, Zhou's ability to call upon the aid of persons such as Wang, who had his own armed force, must have been one of the attractions that had led young GMD radicals to ally with Zhou in the first place. Not only did Wang have his own small armed force, but he expanded it and gave its members additional training to support the anticipated anti-Cheng actions of the group that had formed at Zhou's house. Further, Zhou raised and drilled his own militia, recruited from neighboring peasant communities. It was this sort of muscle, as well as Zhou's prestige, that the young radicals wished to borrow to tackle Cheng, establish GMD power in the county, and remake local society.

From April 1927 through the end of the year, the Northern Expedition's battle lines had repeatedly shifted, causing this North China zone county to change hands several times. In late 1927 the GMD forces took what turned out to be ultimate control of the locality, and a GMD unit commander appointed Shan Xintian acting county magistrate. Zhou and his allies on the county GMD committee immediately approached Shan and discussed with him how best to go about arresting Cheng and his closest lieutenants. After Shan and the radicals agreed on how to attack the local potentate, Zhou and his associate Wang Xianghe's armed forces, some 300 strong, escorted Shan into the county seat to protect him from Cheng's men. But within a couple of days Cheng had bought the acting magistrate off, both by a cash payment and a promise that the chamber of commerce would come up with funds that the GMD army was demanding of Shan. In return, a grateful Shan not only apprised Cheng of the local party branch's plan to arrest and prosecute him, but in other ways began to assume the role of a cog in Cheng's machine.[110]

At this vexing moment Zhou and the county GMD radicals were suddenly cheered by the arrival of a new magistrate who had been appointed by the provincial government to replace acting magistrate Shan. But unfortunately for the radicals, Shan was unwilling to turn over the county government to the newcomer. Predictably, the radicals and Zhou, together with a deputy sent by the provincial party headquarters, quickly developed a plan to seat the new magistrate in his office and begin the anti-"local bully" campaign against Cheng. On January 5 the

GMD plotters managed to slip into the county government building and take custody of the recalcitrant magistrate Shan, his chop, and the files.[111]

But calamity ensued on January 6, 1928, as Cheng counterattacked. For several hours Cheng's police forces tried to shoot their way into the building where Zhou and the GMD's provisional executive committee were holding Shan, the acting magistrate. Soon Cheng's forces were augmented by a unit of the Twenty-sixth National Revolutionary Army, which had appointed Shan originally. The Twenty-sixth was a GMD force in name, but it was actually composed of units from warlord Sun Chuanfang's army that had turned coat and joined the GMD side in the midst of the Northern Expedition. Thus, just as Zhou had succeeded in getting the GMD's provisional executive committee to help attack Cheng's interests, Cheng managed to get a local unit of what was supposedly the GMD's army to do his bidding and assault the local GMD branch itself. Additionally, Cheng enjoyed the support of one member of the previous GMD county committee (the county special committee). So in Shuyang, as in a number of other counties, the line between local elites and the Guomindang was not hard and fast.[112]

With the intervention of the army in the shootout, Zhou and the local GMD found themselves outgunned and outmanned. After the firefight had gone on for several hours, Zhou decided to surrender, both because of his concern for the lives of the several students who were in the headquarters under attack and because he trusted the army commander's guarantee of the personal safety of all. But Cheng's men shot and killed Zhou almost as soon as they had him in custody, and before long they had also executed Wang, the township manager who had provided muscle for Zhou. Some, though it is unclear how many, of Zhou's peasant militiamen were injured, and some buildings suffered considerable damage. Cheng's men mopped up, arresting others tied to Zhou.[113]

Most of the GMD leaders who had sided with Zhou found themselves in prison for over a month, charged with having led a Communist riot. In fact, Xie Lunxian was the only Communist among the leaders of the movement against Cheng's faction. Most of the rest were merely left-wing GMD members, and some were not members of any party. So the antiestablishment hues of this group can hardly be said to have flowed only from Communist domination of the local GMD branch. But, in this immediate post-purge period, Cheng like many other local elites found that he had only to make the charge that particular individuals were Communist in order to dispose of them.[114]

Although Cheng, the leader of the victorious local clique, may have thought that his position was now secure, by May he found that he was again the target of an anti-"local bully" campaign Vanquished clique-leader Zhou's power reached beyond the grave as his family, as well as another "prominent, wealthy" rural landowner Geng Xuannian, and others, successfully pushed prosecutions of most of Cheng's group through the special court in Nanjing. Cheng himself fled to avoid prosecution, and his considerable properties were soon seized by the county government. The special court meted out stiff penalties to eight of Cheng's cronies, five of whom received death sentences. Eventually, however, all eight gained their freedom because the special court system was eliminated. After five years of litigation in the regular courts, seven gained acquittal because of "lack of evidence," and, another, whom the court judged guilty of murder, was released because he had already been in jail longer than the allotted three years for his crime.[115] As for Cheng's property, after four years of litigation the Cheng family obtained a court judgment that returned all their property, over the objections of the provincial party branch.[116] Just as the Shuyang case illustrates that the GMD was sometimes dragged into feuds between factions of incumbent local elites, it also exemplifies another reality: although many dozens of local elites across the province faced confiscation of their properties in 1927 and 1928, a sizable proportion of those properties were returned to their owners in the early 1930s.

The GMD and Merchants

This study has already examined cases of tension between local GMD branches and key local businessmen—even one case in 1928 in which a merchant in Feng County was executed as a "local bully and evil gentry."[117] That tension was nothing new. Even before the Northern Expedition the party had eyed the chambers of commerce with suspicion, seeing them as part of the local ruling establishment under the warlords. Although some chambers of commerce in the Lower Yangzi zone had participated in an anti-Sun Chuanfang "local autonomy movement" in 1926 and 1927, few chamber leaders were enthusiastic GMD partisans.[118] In fact, after the victory of the Northern Expeditionary forces some former county chamber of commerce leaders protested GMD rule by retiring, shutting themselves off from the world, and refusing all offices offered by the government.[119]

Despite the tensions between the GMD and many merchants, the party was not without friends in merchant circles. In fact, over 11 percent of party members in Jiangsu were merchants by occupation.[120] Soon after the reorganization the party had included merchant organizations, along with those of workers, peasants, students, and women, as an integral part of its mass movement. Before the Northern Expedition the GMD Central Executive Committee had established a party Merchant Department to recruit wealthy merchants and small shopkeepers alike to the revolution. Some businessmen had found common cause with the party as it proclaimed its fight against "international capitalism and its running dog warlords."[121] From 1925 through 1926 the party had set up many merchant associations (*shangmin xiehui*) in Guangdong, and the CEC had established the Merchant Movement Academy (*Shangmin yundong jiangxisuo*) that graduated twenty-eight students in its first class. After graduation the academy's students went on to positions of responsibility in the local merchant associations.[122]

The GMD's Second National Congress in early 1926 had predicated policy dealing with the business community on the premise that there were two kinds of merchants: those who would profit from imperialism and those who stood to lose from it. The first grouping was to be carefully monitored, while the second was to be encouraged to participate in the revolution. Businessmen who colluded with imperialists were to be denied some citizenship rights, including eligibility to hold public office. In addition, they were to be constrained from spreading "traitorous propaganda." The party's suspicion of "traitor-merchants" in part originated in the uprising of merchant militia in Guangdong Province in 1924, which Chiang Kai-shek had quashed only with difficulty. But the Congress's lack of faith in a sizeable proportion of merchants was also a natural result of CCP and leftist control. Distrust of merchant militia was evident in the Congress's ruling that no new merchant-controlled armed forces could be established in areas under GMD control; the party promised to provide security for merchants so their militia would not be needed. In areas not yet under party control, the local party headquarters were supposed to transform all merchant militia into "genuine weapons of the small merchants" to insure that those local armed forces were not "capitalist instruments for oppressing the masses."[123]

It was early 1926 before Jiangsu's left GMD established its Merchant Department, at about the same time that the province's Western Hills GMD took shape, replete with its own Merchant Department. Apparently, however, neither faction did much serious organizational work among merchants.[124] In October 1927, after the Northern Expedition had brought GMD rule to much of Jiangsu, the Merchant Department could muster a list of only twenty-one counties or municipalities in the province in which GMD-led merchant associations had been organized, and there is no reason to believe that these organs were yet very active.[125]

After the GMD swept to power in 1927, some local party branches fostered the growth of party-sponsored merchant associations that stood in opposition to the preexisting chambers of commerce. Many party leaders distrusted the old chambers and wished to abolish them. By the same token, the leaders of some of the old chambers sought to get rid of the new party-established merchant associations which were trying to supplant the chambers. In Yancheng County, for example, where the party fostered the establishment of the Yancheng Merchant Association, the leader of the Yancheng chamber, Huang Lisan, battled against the new body. He had no desire to see the position of the organization he had led for almost a decade be usurped by the upstart body, and he caused as much trouble for the competing institution as he could. One memoir suggests that he delegated to a friend the task of getting involved in the merchant association and preventing its smooth operation and development. In this case, the old chamber leader seems to have been successful, since the party's merchant association disappeared after a little over a year of conflict with the chamber of commerce.[126]

As might be expected, throughout the province the party and government sometimes called on the GMD's merchant associations for support. For example, the Jiangsu Provincial Merchant Association was enlisted into the campaign to establish a provincial farmer's bank—long a party goal.[127] But these associations were not mere cheerleaders for government or party policies. Although references in the media to the merchant associations' policy positions were rare, in a rather high proportion of the occasions for which such information is available, the associations were at odds with government tax agencies. For example, the head of the Yixing County Merchant Association had opposed the government's establishment of a new county office to collect revenue stamp taxes and was suspected of having incited the five or six hundred persons who vandalized the new stamp bureau.[128] In Wuxi the county merchant association chose a less impetuous course by agreeing to a compromise formula that slashed a posted increase in the revenue stamp tax by 80 percent. The association assented to this increase, however, only after protracted argument with the representatives of the tax office.[129] Even when not openly clashing with duly legislated tax policy, merchant groups often sought special exemptions, as in the case of the Suzhou Merchant Association, which petitioned the government for remission of a special levy against landlords of two months rent to provision the Northern Expeditionary armies.[130]

Much of the merchants' animus against rising taxes under the Nationalist Government was probably transferred to the party, even though some county branches fought against higher taxes for merchants.[131] Like Chiang Kai-shek, many merchants looked on the county party branches as sources of social instability and disorder. To be sure, the GMD's anti-Communist purge had brought cheer to some merchants in Shanghai and other cities in the Lower Yangzi core because it decreased, if not eliminated, the need to deal with aggressive, CCP-led unions and strikes. And Chiang had a few friends among the upper ranks of Shanghai merchants from his days in the Shanghai commodities market, such as Yu Xiaqing, who had been instrumental in the purge efforts. Chiang also maintained ties with a few important bankers in Shanghai, though his terror tactics to force merchant contributions probably estranged many.[132]

In times of nationwide anti-Japanese campaigns in the early part of the Nanjing Decade, tension in Jiangsu between the party and those merchants who dealt in Japanese-made goods escalated sharply. The April 1928 Ji'nan Incident, in which Japanese blocked the route of Northern Expeditionary armies, produced one such campaign, while the Japanese invasion of Manchuria and the Shanghai area in 1931 and 1932 stimulated another. However, anti-Japanese activities continued with lessened intensity even without the impetus of fresh acts of Japanese aggression. In many counties in Jiangsu, local party leaders supported organizations advocating boycotts of Japanese goods, sometimes incurring violent attacks by the merchants of such items. This kind of local party participation in the anti-Japanese campaigns at the time of the Ji'nan crisis ran counter to the policy of the party center and the National Government, both of which sought to contain the tension between China and Japan.¹³³

One encounter between a local GMD branch supporting anti-Japanese agitation and local merchants which attracted a good deal of attention occurred in October 1928 in Wujin County. There the county's anti-Japanese association (*fanri hui*) had confiscated a large quantity of incoming Japanese-made wares. The goods' owners, later labeled "traitor-merchants" by the party, plotted to recoup their losses and claim revenge. They somehow influenced the head of the investigation department of the GMD-led anti-Japanese association to affix to their cargoes the association's seal authorizing release of the impounded Japanese-manufactured goods. The county party's mass training committee investigated the case, and a deputy of the provincial mass training committee prohibited redemption of the merchandise. In reaction, angry merchants gathered several hundred paid toughs wielding clubs, knives, and bricks in the vicinity of the county office of public security and the post office in which the confiscated goods were stored. They sent some of the rioters to recover the Japanese wares and others to thrash the offending party officers. These merchants were reportedly emboldened in their actions because they had escaped punishment earlier in the year for violent attacks on students interfering with a shipment of Japanese candy at the time of the Ji'nan Incident. Partly as a result of the half-hearted defense of party officers by the county office of public security, the mob beat and severely injured over ten of them. Reportedly the merchants' shouts, "Down with the county party branch and the Guomindang which oppresses merchants!" filled the air.¹³⁴ Although the government soon brought the situation under control, later riots in Wujin by persons the party labeled "traitor-merchants" claimed at least one life.¹³⁵

The Wujin case illustrates not only the common close relationship between local GMD branches and anti-Japanese associations, but also indicates that not all merchants enjoyed the same relationship with the party. Whereas the "traitor-merchants" who dealt in Japanese goods and attacked party leaders were outright enemies, the party continued amicable communication with other merchants through their chambers of commerce and party-led merchant associations.¹³⁶

By 1929 the anti-Japanese associations in Jiangsu had been reorganized as National Salvation Societies, but they continued to manage the anti-

Japanese boycotts with the aid of some local GMD branches. As before, ill will, riots, and other disturbances plagued party relations with merchants who sold Japanese goods. In some instances the Wujin pattern was reversed, with the National Salvation Society beating merchant representatives, as in a case in Nantong County. It appears that in this case, as in some others, the National Salvation Society indiscriminately impounded both foreign- and Chinese-made goods.[137]

Merchants were by not always cowed into submission by the party and government, nor did they consistently lack the organizational strength to protect their interests. For example, when the Wuxi GMD's National Salvation Society had two express company managers arrested, other merchants reacted by instigating a plan whereby escalating numbers of merchants were to go to the county government to obtain the release of their friends; first six were to go, and if they failed, then twelve and later twenty-four would go to plead, until finally all one thousand of the merchants of Japanese goods in the county were to pack the yamen. The plot proved unnecessary, however, because the government—perhaps having heard of the plan released the two managers.[138]

The frequency with which local merchants and their agents assaulted opponents—at times with impunity—belies the argument sometimes made that they were powerless against the party or government. Dissatisfied merchants also exerted muscle by executing general strikes and lockouts, as they did in Huaiyin County in 1931 when the National Salvation Society and the Boy Scouts tried to enforce a boycott of Japanese goods. The merchants' clout was underlined by the Huaiyin magistrate's observation that the strike had effectively halted business in the city and was beginning to affect public security, partly because those who had worked in the shops were without income.[139] Some county parties apparently respected merchant power so much that they limited anti-Japanese activities. A few county party headquarters were damaged by mobs of middle-school students dissatisfied with the meekness of the local party's anti-Japanese actions.[140] There were also charges in Jiangyin County that the local GMD branch there had accepted bribes from merchants of Japanese goods in return for allowing those business owners to move their goods.[141]

Merchants of Japanese goods were not the only segment of the business community sometimes in the party's disfavor. Rice dealers in particular were often viewed with distrust, especially during periods of sharply rising prices. Some local party branches set up special offices and committees to monitor staple prices.[142] Others petitioned county governments to stabilize or reduce rice prices, to prohibit speculation, and to enforce an embargo on shipment of grain out of the county.[143] This is one matter on which local governments and party branches frequently concurred, because they knew that spiraling staple prices and food shortages constituted a menace to public peace, a fact brought home in the early 1930s by rice riots and robberies of granaries and storehouses.[144] In a similar vein, some local parties were also suspicious of cocoon merchants and asked county governments to stop those dealers' manipulation of cocoon prices.[145]

All told, the balance sheet of party-merchant relations in the late 1920s is complex. The radical tone of party rhetoric, together with rising taxes, party-led campaigns of direct action against sellers of Japanese goods, and the GMD's attempts to displace the old chambers of commerce, drove a wedge between many merchants and the party. The discord that these factors provoked was probably more significant than the Guomindang's efforts to forge ties with a fraction of the commercial class via the party-led merchant associations. Yet the GMD had not given up on the mercantile class, and the party did manage to establish and maintain some links to business circles through those associations.

The GMD's Antisuperstition Campaign

The social composition of the Guomindang counterelite in Jiangsu entailed certain consequences. As college and middle school teachers and students (and, by the late 1920s, recent graduates), most GMD members had imbibed fully the cultural iconoclasm and scientistic ethos of the New Culture Movement.[146] A high proportion saw need for social revolution or reform, and many felt that eradication of superstition was prerequisite to a new social order. In fact, in 1924 some GMD recruits responded to a query on their social attitudes with a simple formula: "Eradicate superstition."[147]

In contrast to these GMD members, a fair number of the established, nonparty elites had not received modern secondary or higher-level schooling.[148] Therefore, it is not surprising that some of them did not share the insistently scientific and antireligious bias displayed by many party members. In Qing and early Republican times, local elites had publicly demonstrated their leadership by subsidizing or collecting contributions to underwrite local religious processions, festivals, and dramatic performances, the ideological content of which were amalgams of elements from Buddhist, Confucian, and other mythic traditions, some of them local in origin. The cultural nexus that underpinned local elite prestige and authority included religious institutions and concepts. To be sure, in the late Qing and early Republic a variety of forces had begun the process of desacralizing local elite authority. The Qing government was under pressure from Western countries that sought to protect Chinese Christians from having to pay local tax levies to support local cultic festivals and theatrical performances of a non-Christian religious nature. The Qing authorities responded to Western governments' concerns by outlawing religious levies. Further secularization of local leadership came with reform programs in the 1890s through the 1910s that began the process of converting local religious properties to secular, especially educational, uses. Nonetheless, in the 1920s some local elites still rooted their prestige in a cultural framework that included religious institutions and rites.[149] The difference in mentality between these powerful local residents and GMD counterelites must have contributed to recurrent tension and conflict between them.

The Northern Expedition of 1926 through 1928 presented the GMD counterelite with an opportunity to put its beliefs into action. Taking advantage of the absence or weakness of warlord and local elite forces, these men and women laid waste to scores of temples and shrines. For example, in 1927 the Baoshan County Guomindang led a mob in wrecking the Temple of the City God.[150] Moreover, the movement to eradicate superstition continued after the pacification of Jiangsu and the 1927 party purge.

Prasenjit Duara has argued that "the discourse of modernism" and "scientism" employed by young intellectuals and the state in early twentieth century China was embedded in the larger political situation at the time. Thus, Jiangsu's antisuperstition campaign was not merely a matter of young, modern intellectuals putting their rationalistic beliefs into action. The antisuperstition rhetoric and deeds of GMD activists in the late 1920s had an instrumental aspect. Duara sees the local party activists' antisuperstition campaigns in the late 1920s as part of a "desperate rearguard battle" to revive GMD leftists' control over local politics, control they were losing to central party and government authorities. The "discourse of modernism" was used as banner to legitimize local party operatives' play for power; the "superstition" label they attached to certain local institutions, practices, and individuals was a tarbrush brandished to delegitimize their competitors.[151]

Throughout the Nanjing Decade, local religion and superstition posed knotty problems in elite relations. though those problems did abate somewhat in the latter part of the decade. Local Guomindang organizations, composed primarily of modern-educated intellectuals, occasionally pressed antisuperstition campaigns with a vigor that invited the opposition of certain local elites. Sometimes the familiar practice of expropriating local temples and temple properties to aid public schools or other public organs provided the spark for local elite opposition to party or government, while on other occasions, idol-smashing forays by party members and students provoked mass mobilization against the party, government, and schools.

Even when not provoked on religious grounds, local elites who for whatever reason were alienated from the new political order had only a limited number of ideologies to choose from in mobilizing opposition to the government or party; thus defense of local religion provided a supporting pretext, and, sometimes, ideology for the elites' mass mobilization of peasants against the GMD and its government.

The Yancheng Massacre

The October 8, 1928 Yancheng Massacre received more attention on the provincial level than countless other religion-related altercations, but is illustrative of a pattern of party and middle school involvement common to many other religion-related incidents in Jiangsu. Somewhat less typical is the rather narrow group of local elites that reacted harshly to the local party branch's antisuperstition campaign. But though the role of the Yancheng county government and magistrate in this incident was unusually evil from a party standpoint, there is much in this case that is typical not only of the alignment of forces in religious disputes but also of the fractious relationship between party and government in many counties.

Yancheng, a populous county in the North China region of the province, had a relatively low tenancy rate and a highly developed, rich peasant economy; it also supported a sizable religion-related economic sector. Fifty-six percent of the Yancheng GMD members were teachers or students, 17 percent were college-educated, and all told, 76 percent had attained an upper middle-school education. Approximately two-thirds of the party members were between twenty and thirty years of age.[152]

For some time the Yancheng GMD, along with the county office of education, the county office of public security, and local schools had been advocating the destruction of the idols in the Temple of the City God, arguing that "simple folk" were wasting too much money on worshipping and maintaining these idols and that superstitious beliefs engendered incalculable social evils. On October 4, 1928, the seed planted by party propaganda bore fruit. The local GMD called together a rally of about one thousand people to demand abrogation of the unequal treaties. Afterwards, when parading past the Temple of the City God, some people in the crowd suddenly shouted for destruction of the temple idols and establishment of a "People's Recreation Hall." In less than an hour all the religious images had been broken or removed. The next day the county party called a meeting of all administrative organs and professional organizations in the county to organize a People's Recreation Hall Preparation Committee to collect funds for the conversion of the temple. The meeting delegated the office of education to manage the new facility.[153]

But the head priest, surnamed Pan, whose yearly income from the temple had amounted to several thousand dollars, was extremely bitter. Similarly, the attack on the temple raised a red flag for Wang Yuzi, the manager of the temple maintenance committee (*sasao hui*, literally, "committee for sprinkling water and sweeping the floor"). Although Wang was judicial clerk of the county, a post that did not bring with it a munificent salary, he had been able over the years to become rather wealthy, most notably coming to own a general store and pickle shop. For years, say memoir sources, Wang had been skimming large sums of money from the contributions and levies that had been collected for temple festivals and upkeep. Critics also charge that Wang was corrupt in discharging his official duties. The GMD attack on the Temple of the City God raised Wang's fears that the party would soon demand the temple's ledgers and figure out its finances. He knew that he stood a good chance of being charged with malfeasance. To cover up his misdeeds, he and Pan plotted with magistrate Li Yicheng and Public Security Corps commander Jin Pinsan to burn down the temple, so he could claim that his records had been destroyed in the fire. Magistrate Li was willing to cooperate with Wang because Li wanted revenge against the local GMD, which had accused him of maladministration and corruption; he aimed to blame the fire on the party. These conspirators apparently included in their cabal several minor county government functionaries.

On the night of October 8, someone acting at the behest of these plotters spread oil in the temple and set fire to its main hall. Almost immediately people gathered around the burning building, and demonstrators who had been instructed by Li, Pan, and the others started beating gongs and shouting the slogans, "Protect County Magistrate Li! Down with the county party, the office of education, and schools of foreign studies (*yangxue tang*)." Magistrate Li and Public Security Corps head Jin suddenly appeared at the site of the fire and declared that the party was responsible for the building's destruction. Li and Jin melodramatically implored heaven and knocked their heads on the ground, pretending to be shocked by the crime. Then several minor officials led rioters in destroying the county party headquarters, the office of education, and various elementary and middle schools in Yancheng. "If the county magistrate allows the destruction of the party headquarters," shouted county judicial secretary Wang Bingheng, "no one need shrink from the task!" In a five-hour rampage, the party headquarters was completely sacked, many people were injured, and some disappeared. Many private residences were also destroyed. But the most serious incident—and the one that made the case a "massacre" and a *cause célèbre* in party circles—was the mob's immolation of middle school student Wang Changjiang.

Although the rioters paraded back and forth in front of the county government building and office of public security, Li and Jin took no action to obstruct them. Nearly every public bureau, except the county government itself and two other offices that had not participated in accusations of Li, was destroyed. The terror continued the next day as rioters carried on "investigations" of party members. GMD staff members and many governmental employees fled Yancheng and cabled the provincial party for help. In Nanjing students and party members staged mass rallies calling for the execution of Li and demanding better protection for party members. The case attracted the attention of the provincial government and was often referred to when the party discussed policy toward religion and superstition.

In some counties GMD antisuperstition campaigns elicited explosive antiparty reactions by a wide variety of local elites, but in this instance in

Yancheng the individuals who linked up with disgruntled government officials to attack the party were mainly local leaders who were active in temple affairs and had directly borne the brunt of the antisuperstition campaign. Prior to GMD rule, local politicians from two factions, the Central Clique (*Zhongyang dang*) and the Southwest Clique (*Xi'nan dang*), had dominated administrative and educational affairs in the Yancheng county seat and surrounding townships. Those elites, who had administered the schools, the local tax and finance offices, professional associations, local assemblies, and township management offices prior to the GMD's arrival, seem not to have taken part in the Yancheng Massacre. Instead, according to local memoirs, elites belonging to the Central and Southwest Cliques laid low, withdrawing from local political affairs during the first year or so of GMD rule, in hopes of avoiding prosecution as "local bullies and evil gentry." That approach was not altogether successful, however, since some leaders of both cliques found themselves on the receiving end of a party-led anti-"local bully" campaign.[154]

Although during the Nanjing Decade neither clique of local elites would ever regain the level of prestige and power it had enjoyed before the Northern Expedition, after the first couple of years of GMD rule the Southwest Clique experienced something of a comeback. It eventually gained control of the county's opium suppression committee and the Local Defense Office (*Baoweituan bangongting*). By the early 1930s the GMD government had also entrusted to Southwest Clique leaders the compilation of the county gazetteer—a real coup that put a powerful propaganda tool in their hands. Southwest Clique members may have steered clear of the Yancheng Massacre because they perceived that their group's fortunes were already on the mend. They may also have felt that Li Yicheng's frontal assault on the party stood little chance of success in the long run. Finally, since Southwest Clique leaders had been instrumental in the founding and administering of many of Yancheng's modern schools, they were probably just as troubled by the attacks on modern schools as GMD members were.[155]

The reasons for the Central Clique sitting on the sidelines while Magistrate Li Yicheng attacked the party are less clear. In many respects this group had been more dominant in Yancheng county and township administration before the Northern Expedition than had the Southwest group. But after the GMD regime gained control, the Central Clique was not able to perpetuate its power. There is no question that the Central

Clique was disgruntled at its treatment by the GMD regime. In fact, several members of this group participated in the late 1929 uprising of the Reorganization Clique against the regime. Despite this, the Central Clique chose not take part in the anti-GMD rioting that was the Yancheng Massacre. Like their counterparts in the Southwest Clique, some Central Clique members had played important roles in the establishment of modern educational institutions, probably dissuading at least some of them from participating in the massacre, which was partly directed against modern schools.[156] Possibly the Clique's leaders reasoned that no local uprising without very substantial support from outside the county stood any chance of overthrowing the GMD regime and restoring the Central group's fortunes. But whatever the reasons, neither major faction of Yancheng's local elites participated as a bloc in the 1928 anti-party riot.

The Antisuperstition Movement in Other Counties

Some local parties that led antisuperstition movements recognized the potential that assaults on local religion created for elite and mass opposition and took measures to minimize such reactions. For example, the Feng County party and government decided not to involve police and other armed forces in their attacks on local temples because they feared that local elites and rural masses might consider participation of armed forces a provocation. This strategy seems to have been effective, since conflict was avoided.[157]

In some cases the suppression of local religion worked in concert with other issues to induce opposition to the party and government by coalitions of local elites, including some Qing-era degree holders, monks, secret society leaders, businessmen, and others. In the period from 1927 to 1930, a series of prolonged uprisings of the Small Sword Society (*Xiaodao hui*) ebbed and flowed across several counties in Jiangsu's North China zone. The rebels destroyed local GMD headquarters and schools in Suqian, Funing, and Pi counties, and their power also extended to Suining and Tongshan counties. Several provocations together precipitated these Sword Society rebellions. These ranged from the party's antisuperstition campaign to the government's policy of sending teams of student surveyors to check land deeds, a particularly sensitive subject in Jiangsu's North China zone, where many large landowners had occupied the ancient bed of the Yellow River without proper title to the land.[158]

The best documented of the Sword Society uprisings occurred in Suqian County in the first half of 1929. The Suqian GMD had been refashioning local society into what it saw as a more "modern" order, and it was doing so forcefully enough to cause a foreign correspondent to report that it had "been all winter carrying things with a high hand."[159] Besides leading an antisuperstition campaign that ransacked the Dongyue Temple and converted it into a public lecture hall, the party (or the local government) had arrested the powerful monk Huimen on suspicion of being involved in banditry. Rumors were rife that the government was set to confiscate Huimen's Wuhuading Temple, which together with its affiliated temples and shrines reportedly owned more than 100,000 *mu* of land.[160]

The party, in cooperation with local educators, also spearheaded a campaign to persuade—and if that was not enough, then to force—people to abandon the old lunar calendar in favor of the solar "national calendar." Suppression of the lunar calendar was an emotional issue, and at least a few journalists saw it as the main cause of the disturbances in Suqian.[161] For young GMD radicals the new national calendar was a visible symbol that a new order was in the making, but certain local elites saw the old calendar as a practical necessity. Religious elites made much of their money selling paraphernalia for use in religious celebrations and festivals, most of which were governed by the old calendar. In addition, many economic elites benefited from the venerable custom of paying off all debts at the New Year, a folkway they feared might disappear with the old calendar. Furthermore, the new calendar seemed genuinely unpopular among the general populace, which had little to gain from the prohibition of festivals and holidays like the Spring Festival that they had welcomed as punctuation of their hard and austere lives.[162] The Suqian local government supported the party's social refashioning by prohibiting religious festivals, superstitious practices, sales of lanterns for festivals, use of the old calendar, gambling, and opium smoking.[163]

The competition in Suqian was, however, not merely between old and new practices. It was, in part, a scrap between the new GMD counter-elite and some of the old elites who were being displaced by the party's power. The county party had charged at least seven, and possibly more, elites as "local bullies and evil gentry" and had ordered their arrest. According to Shanghai newspapers, the Sword Society braves who were arrayed against the party and government in Suqian County were in large part tenant farmers on land owned by these elites. Friends, underlings, and allies of the arrested leaders energized the lodges of the Small Sword Society to gain those elites' freedom and secure their property, some of which had already been confiscated by the government.[164] No doubt this mobilization of the Small Sword Society against the GMD was facilitated by a campaign the local party had earlier pushed, calling on people to "strike down the Small Sword Society."[165]

Journalists reported that the monks of the Jile Temple and its affiliated shrines, Suqian's wealthiest temple complex, financed and provisioned the Sword Society uprising. In fact, monks led many of the braves' local units. However, the overall commander of the Sword forces was said by one source to be a fifty-year-old lower gentry from Suqian surnamed Zhang. At least one journalist argued that the county chamber of commerce was also providing funds to the insurrectionists. He noted that a number of the braves were tenants on land owned by Xi Yutang, the head of the Suqian Chamber of Commerce, implying that Xi had been involved in mobilizing the Swords against the party.[166] Another investigator argued that the boycott of Japanese goods which the local party branch had led angered some merchants, and he implicated these merchants in the Sword Society affair.[167] It may, therefore, have been more than a coincidence that no businesses seem to have been attacked or disrupted by braves. However, it is not possible to determine whether chamber leaders had helped stimulate the uprising through proffered funds or whether their alleged support was merely an example of the common practice of buying protection from a potentially harmful force. Chinese businessmen had grown accustomed to giving provisions to rampaging warlord troops to persuade them not to harm local businesses. In fact, the Suqian Chamber also ended up funding the military units mobilized to defend the city from the Swords.[168]

Many of the accounts of the uprising of the Sword Society in Suqian portray it as a Luddite attempt by "ignorant conservatives" (*shoujiu wushizhe*) to roll back the clock and strike down anything new and foreign, like modern education. Although party propaganda and journalists depicted many of the monks, Sword Society leaders, and braves who stood opposed to the GMD in Suqian as antimodern troglodytes, some of the enemies of the local party seem to fit easily into Joseph Esherick's category of "urban reformist elites." Two of the persons the party charged as "local bullies and evil gentry," Zhang Ziqin and Liu Menghou, had been eminent local educational reformers. Though both had earned lower examination degrees during the Qing era, they had also both acquired modern education in Japan. Both had been *Tongmenghui* members, and both had spent considerable time in cosmopolitan Shanghai--Zhang, editing journals and writing revolutionary novels, and Liu acting as a lawyer. Both played important roles in the establishment and administration of modern middle schools in Suqian.[169] Thus, they stand as proof that while many of the Suqian party's enemies saw themselves as warriors against modern education, not all did. Whatever pitted these two against the local party—perhaps the pre-1927 factional alignments or the GMD's desire to "partify education" (*danghua jiaoyu*)—can only be a matter of conjecture. For some reason, in early 1929 Zhang and Liu lost their positions as middle school principals, a turn of affairs that could not have caused them to celebrate the new order in the county.[170]

The Sword Society attack on the county's party branch and modern education system began on February 13, 1929. The society's braves broke into the party headquarters, kidnapped eight party leaders, and wrecked the building. The braves attacked middle schools in the county as well as Suqian's Sun Yat-sen University. They kidnapped several educators and students, including a number of women with bobbed hair, a "modern" affectation that some said maddened the braves and led them to presume the women were of easy virtue. All told, the rebels seized over twenty persons. The Sword braves ransacked the homes of party leaders and educators and destroyed the telegraph office. Police stood by doing nothing for hours, and they offered very little resistance for days; Sword Society forces had virtually a free hand, leading some to speculate that certain county security forces had ties with the rioters.[171] For several days, thousands of Sword Society members armed with rifles and swords demonstrated, shouting anti-GMD slogans, mainly in areas outside the county seat.

After hours of skirmishes, the Suqian magistrate ordered the city gates closed, while county forces took potshots at braves outside the city wall. Sword leaders communicated their demands, most of which were unacceptable to the government. These included: (1) abolishing the county GMD branch; (2) releasing those individuals arrested as "local bullies and evil gentry"; (3) abolishing the "schools of foreign learning" (i.e., modern schools); (4) prohibiting title transfer of the property of temples and shrines; (5) ending prohibitions on opium use, gambling, and prostitution; and (6) allowing customary religious processions and festivals.[172] Although

Sword Society braves rioted a second time, they released all but one of the kidnapped persons within a few days.[173] Not surprisingly, however, several educators and party leaders slipped out of the county to safer climes and did not return for months. The magistrate alternately negotiated with Sword representatives and sent security forces on forays to burn villages and temples. The unrest simmered for weeks, but seems to have died down by mid-year, as a relief committee organized by the government and the chamber of commerce helped rebuild peasant houses that government troops had burned in their "pacification" sweeps.

The local party was duly chastened after this cataclysm. By mid-1929, local government and community leaders were beginning to agree that the party had to be restrained in the future. Nonetheless, the Suqian case provides a graphic demonstration of the whirlwind that GMD branches could reap when they attacked local religious beliefs, institutions, and elites. It was not the party's treatment of religion alone that energized those who opposed the GMD, but the antisuperstition campaign was uppermost in the minds of many who participated in the attacks on the party in Suqian.

At the same time, elites and would-be elites demonstrated a great deal of opportunism. Persons who had either enjoyed power in the past or hoped to exercise it in the future saw that the new regime was taking a public relations beating because of its attacks on local religion. These ambitious individuals decided to take advantage of the situation, regardless of their own feelings about religion. Even the Communist Party, not known for spirited defense of local religion, got into the act. Early on in the Suqian Swords' agitation, the Suqian CCP, which was at the time an organization in hiding, decided to try to use the Sword Society's power to occupy the county. CCP leaders developed ties with Liu Shirong, one of the county's key Sword Society chieftains, in hopes of gaining some control over the growing anti-GMD movement. The Communists recast the peasant associations they controlled in one part of the county into lodges of the Small Sword Society, and eighteen Communist cadres assumed the roles of Sword Society masters (*shifu*) of those lodges. The Communist units played a part in one of the Swords' attacks on the city, but in the end it became clear that leaders of the Sword Society and the CCP could not cooperate, and their alliance fell apart.[174]

Religious Leaders as Elites

The above discussion of religion-related altercations indicates that under certain circumstances people not normally counted as social and political elites were able to assume such status. Religious professionals, a grouping not usually considered to hold elite status in pre-Republican society, demonstrated the ability to mobilize and lead mass actions, to negotiate with governmental officials, and to exert pressure on decision-making organs. In the Yancheng Massacre, the monk named Pan displayed attributes that might qualify him as a political and social elite: he had power and moved in concert with other local leaders as an equal. Similarly, the most powerful Suqian monks worked hand-in-hand with other local elites disgruntled with GMD rule.

Perhaps the most bizarre example of religious professionals and para-professionals functioning as political and social elites occurred in Gaoyou County. On February 27, 1931, old women who served in temples and convents (*daopo*) incited mass opposition to the local party's attack on religion. Two members of the Gaoyou GMD Standing Committee, Huang Songtao and Huang Renyan, had earlier led personnel from several local organizations in destroying the idols in the Temple of the City God. In retaliation, the *daopo* led hundreds of people in wrecking the county party headquarters and the homes of the two offending party leaders and, as a pressure tactic, forced businesses and newspapers in the county to close. They then called upon fellow *daopo* of neighboring counties for support until over a thousand of the women joined the demonstration, carrying flags, shouting slogans, and collecting contributions from households in the county. The county magistrate investigated the situation at the temple, talked with several of the women, and agreed to negotiate with their representatives. The *daopo* apparently succeeded in forcing the GMD to allow restoration of the Temple of the City God and to abandon the party's plan to convert that building into a Sun Yat-sen shrine (*Zhongshan si*).[175]

The Government's Concern for Order

Concern for maintenance of order and prevention of elite and mass opposition caused the government to pursue a more cautious policy toward religion than did the party. This divergence between the stances of government and party on religion persisted from 1927 to about 1929, when the party rectification drastically changed the nature of politics in

Jiangsu's GMD. The provincial government's concern for order was the primary motivation behind its objection to confiscation of temple property by local government organs.[176] The government's position not only countered that of many local party branches, but also that of administrators at Central University, which managed public education in Jiangsu until 1930.[177] Since the university advocated using confiscated temple property to fund local education, county offices of education needed little prodding to occupy temple property. In some counties, such expropriated temple wealth constituted nearly all of the local education office's assets.[178] And local party bureaus, whose leadership often overlapped with that of local educational institutions, usually sided with the offices of education.[179] Besides pitting governments against educational organs, temple confiscation was a factor in Jiangsu's common government-party disputes.

The provincial government's policy regarding the GMD's idol-smashing forays vacillated, but, in general, the government was less enthusiastic than the party about pressing the antisuperstition movement.[180] Many county governments took seriously the provincial order to protect temple property, thus bringing party branches into conflict with local governments.[181]

However, the provincial government's concern for maintaining order caused it by the mid-1930s to pass laws restricting local religious expression. That is, the government prohibited religious festivals, reasoning that this would simplify the job of preserving order, since without festivals bandits would not have crowds to rob and stir up into uncontrollable mobs.[182] In several cases, however, the prohibition backfired and county governments faced mass opposition from the peasantry and local elites who demanded that their festivals be permitted. In one case, an angry, threatening mob surrounded a county government building after a magistrate announced that a new law would forbid a forthcoming local festival; the magistrate was apparently saved only by his radio transmitter, which allowed him to contact the provincial government and request troops.[183] In another case in Songjiang County, after the magistrate sent police to close a temple and confiscate religious paraphernalia to forestall celebration of a customary religious festival, local protesters broke into the temple at night and worshipped. Reports that members of a certain Xia family, mounted in sedan chairs, took part in the unauthorized festival suggest participation of local elites in this action.[184]

The reluctance of the provincial government to use force to support violent attacks on temples became more apparent in late 1933 when Chen Guofu became provincial governor. Chen felt that eradication of peasant superstition would take a long time and that only education, example, and moral influence could effectively change peasant beliefs. He advocated flexibility when dealing with religious festivals and felt that, "If monks can raise funds to build temples, why cannot principals raise money to build schools?"[185] There is also evidence that by 1935 the organ responsible for administration of education in Jiangsu had modified its position on the use of temple property to aid local education, from advocating outright confiscation to proposing sharing of temple buildings by worshippers and students.[186] Chen Guofu indicated in his memoirs that one of his main administrative goals was to win the allegiance of Jiangsu's nonparty elites.[187]

Modern Schools and Intellectuals' Alienation
From the General Populace

Y. C. Wang has pointed out that the Western-style, modern education attained by a majority of the GMD counterelite was poor preparation for dealing with the problems of rural China.[188] Wang holds that modern education separated treaty-port intellectuals from the villages, though he writes primarily of spatial separation. One cross-cultural study, however, has argued that even though persons with modern education may continue to live in a rural community and "receive a traditional authority and respect," they also "belong to an educated commercial world."[189] In other words, modern education can put a person out of sync with the community of his or her birth.

Thomas Curran has highlighted features of Republican-era modern schools (both upper-primary and middle-level) that alienated those institutions, and by extension their students and teachers, from the largely peasant society in which they were situated. Unlike the traditional primary-level schools (*sishu*) and the old academies, the new schools frequently hired outsiders to the community as teachers. Society traditionally enjoined respect for teachers, but these did not fit the culturally accepted mold. Most of them were young, in a society that put a premium on seniority. Their "alien (urban) habits" grated on rural sensibilities.[190] Many of these instructors forged close friendships with students, unlike *sishu* and academy teachers who had commonly appeared as remote, and therefore, somewhat awe-inspiring social superiors. Traditional school teachers, often natives of the community they served, were known quantities; their credentials, frequently traditional exam degrees, were comprehensible and respected. In general, teachers in the modern schools were not as highly regarded as their traditional counterparts.[191]

Teachers in the new schools based their instruction on a Western curricular model, and they often slavishly followed that model without regard for village tastes or needs. Peasants were perplexed by classes that involved students in organized singing, game playing, and athletics. It was unclear to parents how these activities would prepare students for productive lives in their communities or for degrees and positions of social prestige. Modern middle schools sometimes included instruction in international law, national economics, and civics, the value of which, Curran argues, "was often quite beyond the comprehension of rural Chinese who might expect never to travel more than 5 or 10 miles from home."[192]

Aside from the unfamiliar nature of the curriculum, the teaching methods used in modern schools seemed odd. Farmers accustomed to classes devoted to recitation found that students in the new schools spent much time taking part in group discussions and listening to teachers' lectures. Curran suggests that many local people "felt alienated by the similarity of this latter style of teaching to Christian church services."[193]

The cost of modern schools exacerbated the farmers' suspicions of them, as well as of their teachers. Tuition, fees, and room and board costs meant that the new schools were dispensing largely elitist education for the children of the wealthy. Taxes levied by the county governments to pay for modern schools created resentment, particularly because farmers could not afford to send their children to be educated in the county seats, where many of the new secondary schools tended to be located. Even the modern primary schools, which charged lower fees than middle schools and were often located out in the villages, presented problems for farmers. Unlike the old *sishu*, which often charged fees according to the parents' ability to pay, the new schools had set prices. And while the *sishu* had sometimes accepted agricultural products as partial payment of fees, the modern schools demanded cash. Moreover, the old-style schools permitted students to study at their own pace and to drop out temporarily in order to help with farm work. The new schools were not nearly as flexible, herding students into grade-levels with curricula that students could not miss without jeopardizing their continued schooling.

Even when a farmer gave up the labor of his sons and paid the price to send them to the modern schools, he was often rewarded by having to watch them imbibe foreign (that is, "Western") values that separated them from their village and set their hopes on careers that would take them away from their community.[194]

The modern intellectuals' psychological separation from the village was, perhaps, most visible in the scientific ethos that many of those young people adopted. It was this mentality that resulted in religious confrontations such as one that occurred in 1929 in Rugao County. Because of prolonged drought there, two villagers went to see a village elementary school principal to ask him to hold public prayers for rain. As luck would have it, he was gone. In the principal's absence, some teachers declared that they were there to teach, not pray. Angered by news of this rebuff, a crowd gathered, injured one teacher, and threatened the principal's life. Such were the consequences of failing to live up to the traditionally conceived responsibilities of elites in Rugao.[195] In the eyes of some of the Rugao villagers, the teachers seemed like immoral individuals, since they refused to protect the community against the vagaries of weather by intervening with the spirits and Heaven. Likewise, GMD leaders throughout the province who risked endangering the community by attacking its spiritual battlements, the altars of the temples of earth and the temples of the city god, must have seemed to some people antisocial and irresponsible. In many cases, a subset of nonparty elites gladly grabbed the opportunity the GMD antisuperstition campaign presented to play the role of protector of community interests.

It is not easy to assess the overall importance of religious policy in determining the relationships between party, government, and society in Jiangsu during the period in question. Certainly the party's antisuperstition policies did not cause serious problems in every cranny of every county at all times; we have records of but a few dozen such occurrences of unrest. But the cases of open conflict are likely the tip of the iceberg; other instances of religious persecution may have caused resentment and passive resistance that went unrecorded. It seems indisputable that the party's orientation toward religion was one of several factors dividing the GMD and at least some nonparty elites. The GMD, in return for its alienation of these elites as well as a substantial portion of the masses, received precious little advantage. And the GMD could ill afford alienating anyone unnecessarily.

Party-Government Relations

For many years, historians of Republican China considered relations between the party and government in the Nanjing Decade to have been so close and amicable that those chroniclers tended to use the terms synonymously. However, Noel Miner has suggested that party and government were often at loggerheads, both on the provincial and local levels, a finding that is entirely consistent with the situation in Jiangsu, at least before 1930.[196] We have already seen the conflict between the provincial party branch and the Miao Bin-dominated government that led to the arrest of several provincial GMD leaders in 1929.

Certainly one bone of contention at the local level was the meager funding that local governments provided GMD branches. Local party branches depended on subsidies from county governments, but those finances were not always forthcoming, and the local party leaders often complained about the amount.[197] Local parties, because of their poor funding from county governments, could offer only the most modest of salaries to county party leaders and operatives, trifling sums that stood in sharp contrast to the much larger monthly pay for county governments' top officers. A memoir recalls that while county executive committee members in one Lower Yangzi locality received just forty or fifty *yuan* a month and persons holding the rank of clerk (*ganshi*) in the party earned only between twenty and twenty-eight *yuan* a month, a county magistrate's pay was 300 *yuan* a month. And even the heads of the various county bureaus and police officials at the county level received higher salaries than top party leaders. Party leaders generally came from somewhat more modest economic backgrounds than did government officials, a reality that may well have increased their resentment of those officials. Add to this the fact that party leaders were mostly local people, while the largest proportion of government officials were from outside the county, and one can easily see that there was ample fuel for party-government conflict.[198]

Aside from these socioeconomic factors in the party-government discord, the one-party state suffered from systemic dysfunction. David Tsai has analyzed the inability of the party and government to develop a satisfactory arrangement to delineate and regulate their respective functions and powers. Although the slogan "party rule" (*yi dang zhi guo*) was often bandied about during the Nanjing Decade, there was no real agreement on what the phrase meant. Tsai traces shifts in Sun Yat-sen's own conception of party rule from "direct rule" by top party members to "rule by party principles," and finally to rule by the party organization "with the government taking orders from the party."[199] The GMD experience with parallel party and governmental structures in the Guangzhou base area produced no reliable precedent to govern party-government relations after the Northern Expedition reached Jiangsu. Tsai notes that provincial government leaders usually did not hold concurrent leadership positions in the party; except in a handful of cases, the same held true at the county level.[200] Laws dealing with local governance "failed altogether to acknowledge the party's role . . ." or "mention the relationship between government and party."[201]

Many GMD and government leaders favored a strictly defined "functional separation" between party and government. For example, Hu Hanmin, head of the Legislative Yuan, "contended that the Party had delegated the task of governing to the government while retaining the responsibility of educating, leading, and training the masses in carrying out local self-government."[202]

In mid-1927 the GMD's Central Political Committee accepted a proposal by Chen Guofu that it hoped would prevent future party-government disputes. This regulation stated that county party organizations had both "supervisory power" over county governments and the "responsibility" of making suggestions to them. It warned, however, that the local party could not compel government action. The county government was responsible for giving financial and other support to the party, but was not supposed to "interfere in party affairs." To prevent direct action in disputes, county party branches were to place total reliance on upper-level organs. A county party branch was to submit any matter of contention between itself and the county government to the provincial party authorities. The provincial party would then take up the issue with the provincial government. County governments were, likewise, to present their grievances to the provincial government for solution on the provincial level. Except in cases of disputes, county parties were to control all mass organizations.[203] Significantly, these new regulations effectively rebuffed those who felt that the party should be the supreme arbiter of local affairs.

The rather clumsy regulations boiled down to the oft-repeated slogan: "The government is not to interfere in party affairs; the party is not to interfere in administration."[204] For several years many provincial and local party leaders did not accept this injunction, which seemed to be a shocking denial of party power. By barring local parties from a more authoritative role in policy formation than mere "suggestion," the stipulations rendered pitifully hollow the frequently intoned phrases about the party's guidance of the masses, the revolution, and the government. The awkward formula also failed to avert further party-government disputes.

Provincial Governor Ye Chucang in 1930 postulated that the chief cause of disputes between the provincial party and government lay in those two institutions' tendency to protect their own subordinates. The supervisory function of local parties dictated that they lodge accusations against county magistrates, heads of the county offices of public security, or other corrupt local officials. The provincial government then commonly refused to dismiss the impeached official and, thereby, incurred party wrath. Ye believed that prompt and efficient investigation and prosecution of corrupt officials by the provincial government could prevent such disputes. It appears that he favored relieving the local party branches even of their watchdog role and preferred that the government be trusted to purge itself of corruption.[205]

Although the party's function of overseeing government to weed out corruption and incompetence was a factor in much of the tension between party and government, factionalism internal to the party itself was occasionally behind the problem. For example, the Pi County GMD branch was split into several groupings, the two strongest being the Number One and Number Two Factions. The Number Two group held the largest proportion of leadership positions in the county party branch, while people associated with the Number One Faction predominated in the county and ward government offices. Thus, tension and strife between party and government leaders in Pi was, in part, a function of the two factions' attempts to increase their influence and reach.[206]

Moreover, Jiangsu's county party branches' and governments' differing approaches to and connections with local elites were frequently at the root of party-government discord. In some cases, the county party branch and the local government cultivated ties with opposing factions of local elites, leading to party-government conflict. This chapter has already examined the case of Shuyang County in early 1928, in which the county party branch and the county government's forces ended up in a pitched battle because of their links with two mutually hostile elite factions that were largely external to the party.

County governmental officials were more often deeply enmeshed in webs of mutually supportive transactions with local elites than were local party organizations, leaders, and memberships. Although there were instances, like that in Shuyang in 1928, in which local parties had close ties with a faction of incumbent elites, it appears to have been more common for local GMD branches to begin the Nanjing Decade as outsiders in conflict with the incumbent insiders. Even in Shuyang, the GMD was allied with the less established of the two local elite factions. The outsiders, the GMD counterelite, frequently resented the degree to which incumbent elites were able to influence the new, GMD-supervised local governments after the Northern Expedition.

For example, provincial party leader (and Anti-CC Faction leader) Ni Bi in 1928 contended that the "manipulation and destruction of local politics in some counties by local bullies and evil gentry . . . is a fact that cannot be covered up." He argued that government-party conflict stemmed from the insistent efforts of party members to apply party principles and from the reluctance of government officials to accept those principles. Ni averred that the financial demands of the Northern Expedition had caused county governments to align themselves with local gentry; in response to provincial demands for bond sales to support the war effort, county governments had importuned the gentry to buy large amounts of bonds. The gentry, in turn, forced the bonds on the peasantry. Ni indignantly added:

> [These] gentry then used this pretext to curry favor with the government . . . [which they used as a] baleful shield to maintain their position. Consequently, the noxious power of common local bullies and evil gentry not only has not been extirpated . . . [by] the great tide of the revolution, but to the contrary, it has daily been strengthened. This is a most distressing phenomenon.[207]

Ni went on to outline a common and "mutually profitable" system of relationships that, he said, concentrated the "power of life and death, security and danger" in the hands of a few "local bullies and evil gentry." "[Because] the local bullies and evil gentry want to take the law into their own hands, they must collude with the [county] office of public security," which controls the police, and that office in turn "curries favor with the county magistrate." The crucial cement that maintained this nexus of government-elite relations was bribery. Ni repeated a popular joke to the effect that, considering the paltry budgets allotted to the county offices of public security, it was fortunate they were able to attract bribes, otherwise they would not have enough cash to operate at all. He related that many county magistrates made no effort to alleviate corrupt practices because they feared offending local elites who could obstruct administration. Ni observed sarcastically that when corrupt local officials left office, "local bullies and evil gentry" often burst forth with litanies of praise for them and petitioned the provincial government for their reinstatement.[208]

Ni also contended that party-government enmity was the product of a profound generation gap between old county magistrates (many of whom had been members of the *Tongmenghui*) and more youthful party members. These older officials characterized the party members as "reckless . . . children" and, according to Ni, wrongly labeled "Communist" and arrested any youth whose thought was "a bit radical." Ni critically likened the government's unrelenting suppression of Communists to the former Qing government's repressive campaigns against the GMD's revolutionary precursors. He claimed that many upright youth had abandoned careers in government because they had seen first hand the corruption and collusion with "local bullies."[209] However, it should be noted that other observers believe that new government employees were easily seduced into the government's system of corruption and collusion.[210]

It was not just relatively radical GMD spokesmen like Ni Bi who felt that "radical party versus local elite-sheltering county government" was a most common pattern. During the last three months of 1927, the Jiangsu GMD's highest deliberative council was the Jiangsu Provincial Provisional Executive Committee, a body controlled by the right-wing Western Hills faction of the party. The provincial Organization Department, at that time a creature of that committee, made it clear that it opposed campaigns against local elites, but it also noted that many local party branches were pushing such crusades forward on their own. An investigative report issued by the Organization Department in November 1927 argued that conflicts between local party branches and administrative organs were common south of the Yangzi, owing partly to party zeal in prosecuting "local bullies and evil gentry," and the administrative organs' opposition to such action. The resulting clashes between party and government sometimes led to government arrests of party workers.

The same report held that north of the Yangzi, however, party and government worked closely in prosecution of "local bullies and evil gentry," with the party taking the responsibility to investigate and bring charges and the county office of public security arresting and holding the offenders. Since the report was a product of the provincial GMD during the brief period when it was dominated by Western Hills partisans, people generally unenthusiastic about campaigns against local elites, the document characterized this party-government cooperation against powerful local individuals as "collusion" and indicated that party and government officers in such cases extorted graft through out-of-court settlements.[211]

The report is undoubtedly correct in suggesting that in some counties the party's anti-"local bully" campaigns led to conflict with local governments, whereas in other counties governments and party branches acted jointly in that sort of political movement. And there is a certain logic that might predict differentiation between north and south in the province along the lines described by the Organization Department's analysis. Communists and those close to them had built far more of the GMD branches in the Lower Yangzi region than they had in the North China zone. That fact might lead one to expect a more radical GMD in the Lower Yangzi zone than in the north. That same element—the greater role of Communists in the shaping of the Guomindang in the southern part of the province—might also have led to greater conflict between local government and party branches there than in the north. Local governments were supposed to be vigilant against Communists. County government efforts to root out the remaining Communists in the GMD in the Lower Yangzi core were certain to stir up a hornet's nest of protest from those county party branches as party members were arrested and prosecuted, and as party-led labor and peasant movements were shut down or hindered by Communist-hunting local governments.

Still, it is not clear that the regional distribution of the two patterns necessarily followed the overly simplistic north-south dispersion model that the Organization Department document posits. Contrary to the prediction of the model, there were cases north of the Yangzi in which party and government conflicted over anti-"local bully" campaigns, and there were also cases of county governments south of the river cooperating with local party branches in the prosecution of selected local elites. In fact, on the basis of available media reports of individual party-government conflicts, I cannot verify any systematic relationship between macroregion and such disputes.

One reality that clearly does emerge from study of party-government discord and its connection to the campaigns against "local bullies and evil gentry" is that local party branches tended to be more radical than local governments. In many cases local party branches sought to push forward crusades against "local bullies," but the county government dragged its feet. There were not, though, any cases in which local governments were more interested in targeting and attacking local elites as "local bullies" than were local party branches.

Collision in Taixing County

Confounding the Organization Department's statement that party-government conflict over the issue of handling local elites was found only south of the Yangzi, one of the most widely known cases of this phenomenon occurred in Taixing County. This notorious clash, which included a pitched gun battle between a local party branch and the local government, arose from tensions that came to a head in June 1927.

As GMD-related sources recounted the incident, the problems began when the provincial party committee sent special deputy Li Yafei to Taixing to organize a county party headquarters. Li and another GMD leader, Shen Yi, enraged a number of powerful persons in the area by leading the GMD's Taixing County Peasant Association Preparatory Committee and local tenant farmers in a campaign for "rent avoidance and debt nonpayment." In fact, this was but a continuation of a campaign that had begun early in the 1920s. Li, Shen, and their followers pressed their "rent reduction and debt nonpayment" themes at a June 29, 1927 mass meeting of several thousand persons, primarily peasants. This assemblage, meeting in the Taixing county seat, also called for the prosecution of at least four individuals as "evil gentry." To be sure, a couple of right-wing members of the local GMD had earlier argued in a party gathering against the idea of an anti-"bullies" campaign, but they had lost on the issue and stormed out in a huff. These rightists' lack of influence on the policies of the radical county GMD branch is not surprising, considering that they continued to maintain their own separate GMD county branch, denying the legitimacy of the left-leaning county GMD organization, even though it had been recognized by provincial party headquarters.[212]

Although sources do not reveal the precise background of most of those whom the June 29 mass meeting charged as "evil gentry," Li described them as "famous persons of very substantial power from my township."[213] The party-led attacks on the tenancy system and on selected local elites precipitated serious conflict between Li's county party headquarters preparatory office and Lu Wenfeng, the head of the county office of public security, whom the mass meeting had charged with criminal conduct. In fact, a day before the mass meeting, the county GMD had impeached Lu for embezzling government funds, accepting bribes, and oppressing people.

Lu, a former Taixing County Assembly member, was the leader of anti-GMD forces in the county, and arguably the most powerful individual in the government. Memoir literature states that Lu had gained his position as head of the Taixing Office of Public Security by disbursing 800 *yuan* to grease the palms of GMD military officers who could influence the appointment. However, since records of bribes are seldom kept, one might well wonder at the fortuitous inside knowledge of the source.[214]

A local party leader's recapitulation of the events in Taixing inveighed that "the old powers (*jiu shili*) . . . unanimously conspired" to punish the party for its policies and, especially, its attacks on the alleged "local bullies."[215] Carrying out this resolve, Lu Wenfeng joined with a police official and another person identified by a hostile source only as "Tiger Zhu" (Zhu Laohu) to lead a band of over one hundred police and other persons (dubbed "bullies and hoodlums" [*dipi liumang*] by the source) in action against the local GMD branch. On the evening of June 30 this crew made its way to the Temple of the City God where Party Special Deputy Li Yafei was speaking and beat him so severely that he lost one eye and nearly bled to death. The assailants also robbed and destroyed the county party headquarters and jailed Li and over twenty party leaders in the office of public security.[216]

Reacting to the unexpected turn of events, Shen Yi, vice-chairman of the Taixing Peasant Association Preparatory Committee, rallied thousands of peasants in surrounding villages to march on the city and demand Li's release. Many of the city's leaders held that Li and Shen were Communists, and therefore the rumors of Shen's peasant advance on the city had a frightening revolutionary appearance. Although some reports suggested that Lu and his group had manufactured the "red scare" by pasting up Communist slogans around the city, in fact, Shen Yi, but not Li Yafei, did eventually turn out to be a Communist Party member and was executed as such in 1928.[217]

One somewhat atypical aspect of the Taixing incident is that the county magistrate seems to have been rather powerless and peripheral to the events that were transpiring. This man, Weng Hanzhong, had only arrived in the county in June, and seems not to have found the locality's levers of power. Lu Wenfeng, the head of the county office of public security, actually controlled the local government, and he clearly ran roughshod over the new county magistrate's prerogatives. When Weng first arrived in Taixing, the county GMD branch wined and dined the new magistrate in a formal welcoming ceremony and quickly persuaded him to go along with the party campaign against Lu and his allies. On June 29, just after the party had lodged its accusations against Lu, Weng ordered that Lu be fired and arrested. However, Weng soon succumbed to a concerted campaign of pressure from Lu's local allies, and he seems to have cooperated, perhaps not entirely willingly, with Lu's forces in defending the city against the onslaught of Shen Yi's massed peasants.[218] To beat off the "Communist attack," the county magistrate closed the city gate to the advancing peasants. When they tried to assault the wall and enter the city, Lu and the magistrate's forces fired on them, killing at least seven and wounding several more.

Angry Taixing GMD members flooded the provincial party headquarters with denunciations of the actions of "local bully and evil gentry Lu Wenfeng" and requests for the release of Li and the others. Not to be outdone, Lu and his cohorts cabled He Yingqin, provincial commissioner of military affairs, to ask for troops to aid in suppressing the "Communist attacks." The magistrate and the Taixing Chamber of Commerce also cabled military commanders in neighboring counties for aid against the "bandits."[219]

Provincial leaders had difficulty sorting out the conflicting reports, and by July 8 one Shanghai newspaper concluded that the disturbance was not a Communist uprising, but rather a fight between two local factions over which would control the office of public security.[220] This newspaper's report raises the question of whether the Taixing convulsion was just another case of two old factions of local elites using the GMD and its government as weapons in their battle with each other. While there seems to be little question that Lu and his group were backed by the chamber of commerce and many persons of considerable local power, it is not so clear that Li Yafei, Shen Yi and other local GMD leaders were doing the bidding of another local elite faction. Although one memoirist indicates that Shen had displayed a talent for forging ties with certain local gentry and even winning some over to the GMD, there is no sign that the local GMD's movement against Lu and his associates was urged on it by a group of local elites or that Shen or Li received advice from such a group.[221] In other words, this case is best understood not as simply one more contest between old elites, but rather as an instance in which a radical and assertive GMD party branch and its peasant movement confronted entrenched elites tied to the county government, especially its office of public security.

In the wake of the attack by the Taixing government's security organs on the local party and its leaders, the provincial party committee (the Jiangsu Provincial Special Committee) held an emergency meeting on July 4, 1927 to discuss the problem. It decided that if those responsible for attacking the local party were not punished, party affairs would become "impossible to manage," and that "public peace . . . would be difficult to maintain." Reacting to the requests for protection for the Taixing party branch, the provincial committee sent representatives to investigate and ordered that Lu and his co-conspirators be arrested and sent to the provincial government "to uphold party power." To prevent the execution of party deputy Li Yafei, it also told the Taixing magistrate and the head of the office of public security not to act until the provincial deputies had arrived to manage the affair. The provincial GMD asked the provincial government to send troops to control the situation and protect Li and the county GMD.[222]

The provincial government did take custody of Li and other Taixing party leaders who had been arrested. It was mid-August before the provincial government finally released Li, but by that time party members all over Jiangsu had seized upon the Taixing case to demand adequate protection for party members from local governments that, they said, were allied with "local bullies and evil gentry." At a meeting of the GMD Central Executive Committee, Jiangsu Special Committee members Ge Jianshi and Xu Enceng reported that "recently the special deputies for several counties . . . have been arrested by the local military and police." Citing the Taixing instance and another in Wuxi in which "local bullies and evil gentry colluded with the county government and office of public security," the Jiangsu representatives asked the party center to devise a method to prevent such occurrences in the future. The CEC responded by "ordering" the National Government and Chiang Kai-shek to issue a general order to all military organs that no party staff members were to be punished or arrested without prior approval of a superior party headquarters.[223] This order had no noticeable effect, however, because local parties continued to be confronted with hostile governments possessing the military and police powers that the party lacked.

The Taixing fracas illustrates one salient feature of party-government conflict: because the county governments and their offices of public security controlled local police and military forces, they usually came out on top in any dispute with the defenseless local party branches, at least temporarily, although the provincial party sometimes stepped in after the fact to protect the local party. (The Taixing case is atypical in that the Taixing county government actually seems to have acted as a subordinate partner to the county office of public security.) There were, however, a few cases in which county party branches were accused of riding roughshod over local governments in contravention of the Central Political Committee's prohibition of party interference in administration.[224] But those incidents were rare, and the Taixing case became a rallying cry for party workers demanding better protection and bolstered party power.

The Kunshan GMD's Nemesis: Magistrate Qiu Fu

The Taixing altercation was only the most renowned incident of its kind. The Organization Department of the provincial party headquarters during the period of the Directorate (see Appendix 1) cited other cases in Yancheng, Wujin, Lianshui, and Huai'an counties in which government officers sided with "local bullies" and pro-Japanese merchants to attack the county party. And these instances, far from being exceptional, were broadly representative of scores of others revealing similar power relationships.[225]

In some counties, outright warfare between party and government was a temporary phenomenon that grew out of antagonism between the local party branch and a particular magistrate. Magistrates frequently stayed in office only a few weeks or months, and when the magistrate whom the local party found offensive moved on, party-government relations were often patched up. Such was the case in the Lower Yangzi core's Kunshan County.

In March 1927 the Political Department of the Twenty-sixth Corps of the GMD army installed as Kunshan magistrate Qiu Fu, a nephew of martyred revolutionary Qiu Jin, and it threw out the county and subcounty governmental officers the local party branches had appointed. After this inauspicious beginning of Qiu Fu's term in office, the county GMD found Qiu generally unwilling to cooperate on any matter. Soon the party began to charge Qiu with corruption. And when the anti-Communist purge began on April 12, Qiu Fu, with the help of the local police and a number of local elites, began the process of rounding up, arresting, and charging party leaders as Communists. Party leaders saw this not just as weeding out Communists, but as an all-out assault on the GMD.

Although a number of GMD leaders, fearing for their lives, fled the county, before long some of them were deputized by the Political Department of the Twenty-first Division of the GMD army to reconstitute the county party. County party leaders came to look upon the Twenty-first as a bulwark and protector against the Twenty-sixth Corps and its creature, Magistrate Qiu Fu. Very quickly the newly reorganized local party found itself involved in an anti-"local bully" campaign that the Twenty-first Division's Political Department had launched. Peasants had lodged complaints about a certain subcounty elite, Lu Donghao, and Twenty-first Division soldiers immediately arrested the man, interrogated him, and then handed him over to a "provisional court" set up by the county party branch and its peasant association. This court consisted of one representative of the county party, a middle school student who represented the students' association, and a principal of a girls' elementary school who represented the women's association. The party representative dominated this group, ruling that the death penalty was inappropriate for this case, since Lu was really a small fry compared to the county elites who had earlier aided Qiu Fu in attacking the party. This court sentenced Lu to life in prison, though the party representative wrote in his memoirs that he knew that in the unsettled political environment at the time, this was really an empty sentence; Lu would soon find a way out of jail. In fact, within days Magistrate Qiu Fu set Lu free, which only exacerbated tension between the local party and government that was still simmering because Qiu retained custody of a number of key party leaders he had arrested during the purge. Party leaders raged that Qiu was himself a "local bully and evil gentry" who was protecting other bullies. Provincial party and Reorganization Clique leader Teng Gu echoed local GMD sentiments when he lambasted Qiu for "ingratiating himself with local bullies and evil gentry, while progressively humiliating and assaulting the party."[226]

To get rid of Magistrate Qiu, Kunshan County party leaders knew that they could not rely on their own power. They developed a strategy that used both their good relations with the commander of the Twenty-first Division, Chen Cheng, and the connections with the Central Organization Department enjoyed by Wu Baofeng, a Kunshan GMD leader. The Kunshan party leaders persuaded the Political Department of the Twenty-first Division to name Wu as Qiu's successor as magistrate and hoped that Wu's personal ties with Chen Guofu, head of the GMD's Central Organization Department, would offer some protection for him against Qiu and the Twenty-sixth Corps. After installation of Wu as magistrate, Qiu left Kunshan, but he remained close-by in Taicang and kept an eye on developments from that vantage point, hoping for an opportunity to reclaim his power in Kunshan. Wu Baofeng did not disappoint the GMD leaders that had nominated him; he quickly determined that two key party leaders who had been arrested in the purge were not Communists and ordered their release. But Wu's days as magistrate were to be few. Almost immediately after he assumed the post, the Twenty-first Division, which had been the local party's prop, left the Kunshan area, removing the protection that force had provided for the new magistrate and for the group then running the Kunshan GMD. Only days after Wu had become magistrate, former magistrate Qiu Fu swept back into town, backed by soldiers of the Twenty-sixth Corps and local elites with whom he had maintained contact. Qiu's allies surrounded the county government office, then proceeded to arrest Wu and the handful of GMD leaders who were in his office at the time and to take possession of the magistrate's seal. So Qiu reigned again as magistrate, and once more the county GMD fell into disarray as many of its leaders fled to safer locales. Within days, Chen Guofu used his influence to get Wu out of jail, and before three weeks had passed since Qiu Fu's reinstatement as magistrate, the provincial government had appointed a new county magistrate. Qiu left Kunshan with the remainder of the county treasury in hand, thus proving the county GMD's charges that he was corrupt.[227]

When the two-month-long skirmish between Magistrate Qiu and the Kunshan GMD was over, the Kunshan GMD badly needed to rebuild. One could question how well the party refashioned itself, since it was ripped by factional strife through 1930. But it does appear that a more productive party-government relationship flourished during that period. Qiu's successors as magistrate seem to been more willing to consult with the GMD than Qiu had been. The records of party conferences suggest that while tension between party and government in the county persisted, there was more business-like give and take between the two institutions than there had been under Qiu's administration. A fair number of the measures the county party proposed to the Kunshan county government in 1928 through early 1929 concerned the question of which subcounty functionaries and rent collectors should be prosecuted as "local bullies and evil gentry." It appears the government prosecuted some of the people the party fingered, though the local GMD complained when the government released one of them. Until the Kunshan party underwent "rectification" in the early 1930s, its left-leaning leaders continued to criticize local government for its subservience to "feudal" pre-Northern Expedition elites, claiming that 70 to 80 percent of the county's townships were still under the disguised control of township managers from before the Northern Expedition. Party spokesmen also argued that the government had yet to accomplish any significant transformation of the county for the better.[228]

However, tension between the Kunshan party and government after the departure of Qiu Fu from the scene through mid-1929, when the quality of available information on this problem declines, stayed within bounds. No longer did party or government frequently resort to violence against each other. Government representatives attended certain party functions and sometimes responded to party queries. Thus, party-government warfare in Kunshan was a temporary phenomenon that disappeared as soon as a controversial personality departed and once army interference in local administration vanished.[229]

Magistrate Versus Party in Suining

Although the party-government battles in Taixing and Kunshan occurred in 1927, such problems were not seen only in that first year of the Nanjing regime. Similar blowups continued at least through 1929, though at a lessening pace. A 1929 fight between Suining county's magistrate Li Zifeng and the local GMD branch illustrates the way the campaign against "local bullies and evil gentry" could aggravate tension between party and government.

To understand what kindled the 1929 party-government firestorm in Suining requires some knowledge of the county's politics in the 1910s and 1920s. Immediately after the 1911 Revolution the local Guomindang briefly appeared to be strong, holding over two-thirds of the seats in the county assembly. But as Yuan Shikai moved to quell Guomindang strength throughout China in 1913 and the succeeding years, Suining Guomindang leaders largely lost their power in the county. Many members left the Guomindang, while a few continued to resist Yuan, dodging police whenever possible. A group of local elites attached themselves to Yuan Shikai's banner and formed the local Republican Party with Yuan's financial support. The Guomindang's early electoral success in the county faded as the 1910s and 1920s wore on. Memoirs hostile to Suining's Republican Party elites charge that those oligarchs flourished in the elections for provincial and national assemblies by various means, including having substitutes vote in place of qualified voters, switching ballots after they had been marked, and disbursing money and other gifts to buy votes. One of the most colorful means used to intimidate voters was to ensconce twenty or thirty local toughs, known as the "diluted shit brigade" (*boshi tuan*), outside the polling place. This band's job was to sling a watery night soil mixture on all Guomindang voters as they entered or exited the hall. Republican Party leaders, a large proportion of whom belonged to four prominent and wealthy extended families, came to occupy virtually all elective assembly positions in Suining as well as the non-elective county and township offices.[230]

Xia Zicheng, a Suining Republican Party kingpin who was elected as a National Assemblyman, owned some 5000 *mu* of land, as did both of his brothers, who were also noted Suining politicians. Xia Zicheng, while not fabulously wealthy compared with some other Suining Republican Party leaders, was so widely acknowledged as the head of that group of oligarchs that people referred to him as "the little mastermind" (*xiao zhuge*). Memoirs record that he was so dominant that only local administrative plans that he authored could be enacted. Newly appointed magistrates knew that upon arrival in Suining to take up their office, they needed first to pay their respects to Xia, and they also carefully heeded his advice on appointments to county and township positions.[231]

Memoir accounts give the impression that for some time Xia acted almost as a local dictator. His imperious behavior may have contributed to the split that appeared among Suining Republican Party elites by the

1920s. By that time, Suining Republican oligarchs on occasion found themselves divided into two factions, with Xia leading the Xia Faction and Wang Yushu, who like Xia had been a national assemblyman, heading the Wang Faction. But when the local Republicans faced outside threats, they were often able to act together. Thus, most accounts of Suining politics refer to the two Republican factions as one, and sometimes those accounts call this grouping of local leaders the Wang-Xia Faction, or, more pejoratively, the "Local Bully Faction."[232]

In June of 1927 the Northern Expedition's armies reached Suining. The Republican Party oligarchs, fearing for their futures, quickly set up their own Guomindang branch in the hope that the new regime would accept them into its ruling structure. However, the provincial party rejected their Johnny-come-lately GMD branch, and instead embraced as the core of the county's GMD a group of Suining intellectuals that had been working as an underground, revolutionary organization since 1924 under the supervision of the reorganized GMD center in Guangzhou. The GMD army and Jiangsu's GMD authorities began organizing a local government for Suining, but before that new regime had been consolidated, an advance by Sun Chuanfang's warlord forces caused the Northern Expeditionary army to withdraw southward in late July of 1927. Most of the local GMD's personnel, lacking protection, followed the army, clearing the slate for a return of Suining's Republican Party elites. The longtime Suining oligarchs searched for the few GMD people remaining in the county; although they found none, a bandit group with which the oligarchs had some connections killed the wife of one GMD leader.[233]

By early 1928 a new advance northward by GMD armies allowed reconstitution of the Suining GMD and the local government that was, for a while, to be its creature. For a brief time the GMD did not harass the old elites, who quietly retired to their estates in nearby market towns and rural areas.[234]

The provincial government named as Suining County magistrate Yao Erjue, an intellectual who had been a key leader of the local GMD in its underground years in the mid-1920s. Yao's first moves as magistrate, although not especially radical by some measures, did establish him as a force for change. He encouraged the women's association of the GMD to attack the practice of footbinding. And though people in the county seat had long ago abandoned the queue (the hairstyle the Qing dynasty had forced on Chinese men), many males in the more remote towns and villages of the county still wore it. As a sign that the revolution had finally arrived in force, Yao sent out soldiers to clip the remaining pigtails. The new local authorities also accommodated an antisuperstition movement pressed by Suining teachers and students, turning some of the newly abandoned temples into schoolhouses, and transforming the Temple of the City God into the county party headquarters. Although the provincewide anti-Communist purge had begun in April 1927, as late as mid-1928 Magistrate Yao was still turning a blind eye to Communists in Suining, appointing many of them to educational posts. Because of Yao's conduct, Suining's CCP was able for a time to operate largely in the open. In addition, Yao led the Public Security Corps on several forays out of the county seat to take inventory of and confiscate the properties of a number of persons charged as "local bullies." During one of these trips, the head of the county's office of public security grabbed one of the accused elites, bound him with leather straps, and flogged him with a horsewhip.[235]

The partisans of Suining's Republican Party did not wait long to begin their counterattack against the GMD onslaught. The Suining GMD did not enjoy the unanimous support of intellectuals with a middle-level education. For years, a portion of this social grouping had attached itself to the Republican Party. Memoirs hostile to the Republican Party charge that these pro-Republican intellectuals, anxious to gain and keep jobs that kept them away from manual labor, were seduced by the patronage system that Republican Party leaders had controlled before 1927. It is possible, however, that some of these intellectuals who leaned toward the Republican Party did so for the same mixture of reasons that led other intellectuals to the GMD: beliefs, family connections, influence by teachers and peers, and so forth. Whatever their reasons for embracing the Republican group's side, some of these intellectuals participated in an ideological counterattack on the GMD. They came up with and circulated a little ditty based on the "Three Character Classic," lampooning the GMD's Magistrate Yao Erjue and criticizing some of his public works projects. "Yao Erjue," it ran, "is quite detestable. He rips down the outer battlements of the city walls. He builds johnny houses. He snips little pigtails. He frees big feet."[236]

More important than this whispering campaign of insults and calumny directed at Magistrate Yao, the old elites are said to have bribed Jiangsu's notoriously corrupt commissioner of civil affairs, Miao Bin, to persuade him to fire Magistrate Yao and replace him with someone more amenable to the interests of the old Republican Party leaders. In April of 1929, Miao appointed Li Zifeng to be Suining's magistrate and Meng Guangtai as the new head of the office of public security. Memoirs charge that Republican Party leaders greased the palms of the two new officeholders to gain their favor. Whether these allegations of bribery are true or not, Li and Meng did help restore the fortunes of the old Republican Party men in Suining.[237]

After arrival in Suining, Magistrate Li Zifeng quickly began an all-out offensive against the local GMD and other local residents who had been instrumental in the campaign against the Republican Party elites. He and public security head Meng collected a band of county policemen and local militia and headed for the residence of Gao Juemin, the former head of the office of public security who had earlier horsewhipped one Republican charged as a "local bully." Magistrate Li's force nabbed Gao and beat him to death on the spot, also killing three other persons. Soon thereafter, when Gao's relatives brought suit against Li to make him account for his part in Gao Juemin's murder, Li clapped those family members in jail. Li also began arresting the staff and other members of the local GMD, charging them with being Communists. Many party members fled, while others remained in the county, operating the GMD branch as an underground organization. Li tried to complete his ouster of the local GMD by firing persons who had gained administrative positions under local Guomindang champion Yao Erjue and replacing them with his own appointees, many of them coming from Republican Party ranks. Li also looked the other way when Guo Yin'gao, a local elite who had earlier led the resistance to the GMD regime's measures to examine land titles, allied with the Sword Society in a neighboring county to drive the GMD out of his part of Suining.[238]

Magistrate Li's first attacks on the party came in April 1929, but it was not until September of that year that outraged Suining GMD members finally secured Li's dismissal from office and his arrest. Thus, for nearly half a year the Suining GMD had suffered under a reign of terror as severe as it or any Jiangsu county party branch had faced under warlord rule. But unlike during the warlord era, the Suining party could now appeal to provincial and central party and government leaders for intervention. Suining GMD members sent a barrage of petitions to upper-level organs calling for those authorities to support the local party branch and deal severely with Li. As luck would have it, Zhang Minquan, a Suining GMD leader who had earlier fled to the provincial capital, Zhenjiang, bumped into the rogue magistrate on a Zhenjiang street. Zhang immediately grabbed Li and dragged him to the provincial GMD headquarters. The provincial party cabled the center for an on-the-spot judgment on how to deal with the controversy. The party center soon replied with an order dismissing both Li and public security head Meng from office and binding them over for further action. At the same time, though, the party center also threw the local party a curve ball, dissolving the Suining GMD's executive committee and appointing in its place a rectification committee to manage the branch temporarily, citing the Suining party's lack of diligence in rooting out Communists. Nevertheless, the Suining Republican Party elites were now out of power and, for the most part, would remain so for the balance of the Nanjing Decade. Although the Suining Guomindang was soon split into two factions, for the remainder of the decade it enjoyed influence over local administrative and educational appointments in a way somewhat akin to that exercised by the Republican Party before the Northern Expedition. Even so, at least one local elite associated with the Republicans was named an elementary school principal by a GMD leader in 1935, so the eclipse of their power was not total.[239]

The three explosions of party-government discord that the latter part of this chapter has described were not at all unique. Other cases of violence between party and government occurred, but multitudes of other instances of tension and strife never reached the stage of outright bloodshed. This party-government disharmony irritated central party and National Government leaders who were committed to political centralization and national unification. By the same token, leaders at the center were troubled by the autonomy local party branches had displayed throughout the late 1920s. And the center had on many occasions displayed misgivings about the radicalism with which local GMD activists had been churning society. Likewise, the center was dismayed about factional division and wrangling within the party. Therefore, it is not surprising that certain national GMD leaders devised a plan they hoped would alleviate all of these problems. Their plan, a party rectification movement, did not ultimately succeed in meeting all of its goals. Party factional contention and bickering, for example, continued during and after rectification. But rectification would reshape party-government relations, just as it struck a blow against the autonomy and radicalism of local party branches. It also helped put an end to local party branches' campaigns against local elites.

6

THE PARTY'S REVERSE COURSE DURING AND AFTER RECTIFICATION, 1930–1931

If the purge had cooled the GMD's social revolutionary ardor, the central party headquarters' rectification of the Jiangsu party—beginning officially in December 1929 though most of it took place in 1930 and 1931—brought about a second cooling, perhaps more profound than the first. The party's central leaders had long been concerned that local party actions directed against "local bullies and evil gentry" threatened social order and hindered the government's efforts at construction and social stabilization. The enhanced degree of control that the rectification granted to the center and its agents gave them means to squelch most of the radicalism still lurking in the local party branches.

The Center Takes Over and Radicalism Recedes

The party rectification presented a golden opportunity for the central party headquarters (and more specifically the Organization Clique, the factional embodiment of the Organization Department) to remake local GMD branches in its own image. The rectification was, in essence, a takeover of the provincial party headquarters by centrally-appointed Organization Clique partisans and similar personnel turnovers on the local level. After the rectification, even some of the leaders of the provincial Anti-CC Clique began to work more closely with the Organization Clique's leader, Chen Guofu. But it was not just in Jiangsu that the party center succeeded in steamrolling provincial and local GMD branches. For example, Noel Miner has observed that about the same time rectification of the Jiangsu party was taking place, the party center and the Zhejiang government were forcing the Zhejiang GMD to shift its attention from rent reduction campaigns to activities the center saw as noncontroversial, such as spreading pro-government propaganda and promoting education.[1] Thus, the rectification of Jiangsu's Guomindang was just one rather significant incarnation of the center's nationwide campaign to reign in local branches after the Organization Clique had ensured its hold on the party's central apparatus by defeating the leftists at the 1929 Third National Congress.

The center's deepening imprint on Jiangsu's party affairs in 1930 and 1931 can be seen in the pages of *Jiangsu dangwu zhoukan*, the official organ of the Jiangsu Provincial Party Affairs Rectification Committee. The committee ostentatiously displayed its fidelity to the will of the central party headquarters, devoting pages of its journal to the center's pronouncements and views.[2] Minutes of the provincial party committee and its various departments showed them to be absorbed with determining the center's will, and the provincial Organization Department, especially, seems to have acted as an extension of the Central Organization Department.[3] In short, the provincial rectification committee appears to have concentrated more on ascertaining, fulfilling, and propagating the dictates of the central party headquarters than did previous provincial party committees.[4] Moreover, spokespersons for the provincial rectification committee prescribed that county committees too should act primarily as conduits for the center's edicts.[5]

Since 1927, central party leaders had expressed misgivings about attacks on local elites and the disorders that had grown out of the movement to prosecute and destroy "local bullies and evil gentry." In the early 1930s, the party center was more adamant than ever that such campaigns must cease, and the provincial rectification committee's main journal helped to apprise local party leaders of the center's concerns on that score. On the pages of the journal, the Central Executive Committee pointedly critiqued local cadres' involvement in such agitation. The CEC charged that a common "mistake" of local cadres was they

> do not understand Sun Yat-sen's teaching about the brotherhood of man, and instead take destruction as their goal, even to the point of copying the Communists' techniques of using the masses as a tool. . . . [Cadres often wrongly spout] empty talk of striking down local bullies and evil gentry, while in fact, they . . . [are] used by those vile elites.[6]

Apparently, most of the new personnel, who by dint of the rectification gained key posts in the Jiangsu party, accepted the center's view that attacks on local elites were harmful. Such assaults by local

GMD branches virtually disappeared from view with the advent of rectification. A comparison of reports on party activities, proclamations, and demands before and after the rectification began reveals marked changes in the party's relationship with society. While before rectification, local and provincial party pronouncements and accusations against persons branded as "local bullies and evil gentry" were fairly common, after the onset of rectification, even that deprecating term was largely dropped from party parlance.[7] In fact, the party turned inward. Organizational, financial, and personnel problems dominated party meetings. After rectification's onset, GMD branches rarely advocated or considered the sorts of attacks that radicals had previously been pressing.[8]

In some areas the rectification not only ended Guomindang attacks on local elites, but also presaged actual amity between the party and local elites. For example, in 1935, a multicounty administrative inspection team found that in Xiao County "the local gentry, party personnel, and county governmental offices have become as one . . . like a family." The report stated that the party, government, and local gentry were "able to confer on all matters," and that after such parlays had determined a particular course of action, it "could be thoroughly implemented." This situation contrasted with the *immobilisme* experienced where elites, government, and party were in conflict. Underscoring the party's conciliatory social and political approach in the postrectification era, the report's authors argued that the human energy available in the localities was limited, so it was necessary to channel everyone's power in the same direction and avoid dispersion of efforts. Repudiating the party's earlier campaigns to "strike down local bullies and evil gentry," the authors held that "you strike me down, and I strike you down" was a perfect formula for mutual dissipation of power on both sides of the fight, destroying any hope for constructive work on the problems facing Chinese society.[9] Of course, these authors had a different conception of what constituted society's real problems than had the earlier party radicals. The postrectification line touting conciliation with old nonparty elites was light years from the attitude expressed in 1929 by some local party leaders who claimed that they had "never heard of an incorrupt or revolutionary gentry."[10] It is worth noting, however, that the inspection team presumed that party-elite relations in certain other localities continued to be more tense than those in Xiao.

The Xiao County example illustrates another feature of the rectified party: it was less frequently embroiled in serious disputes with the government than before rectification. One reason for this was that rectification swept many radicals out of power at the provincial and county levels. Those radicals had often attacked local government personnel, seeing them as part of the corrupt local establishment that needed to be overturned if China was to be remade from the stump up. Many stability-minded local governments had looked askance at party radicals who ran mass campaigns that were hard to control. Thus the removal of radicals from party leadership positions eliminated an important source of contention between party and government.

The party center had long held that party-government disputes meant suicide for the GMD.[11] Accordingly, the provincial rectification committee made it more difficult for county party branches to attack local governments, and it made those local parties subordinate, in many respects, to local governments. For example, the provincial rectification committee's representatives to a party-government conference apparently acceded to a ruling that when county parties disagreed with county governments, they could not publish their opinions without prior approval by the provincial party; this reduced the ability of the local party branches to rally public and party opinion against the government.[12] The provincial party committee also narrowly defined the role of county parties by preventing them from establishing committees to handle properties confiscated from undesirable elites on the grounds that this was an administrative function that was properly the responsibility of government.[13] The committee similarly promulgated a directive barring county party branches from recommending candidates for government and educational posts, though this edict seems not to have been effective in ending party patronage power.[14] More significantly, the provincial rectification committee disbanded all county party executive committees involved in disputes, including those with governments, and appointed rectification committees in their place. This must have displaced many of the GMD leaders who had been active in monitoring local governments.[15] And rather than automatically siding with county branches in their disputes with local governments, the provincial rectification committee sent joint party-government teams to investigate each case.[16]

Although the number of party-government disputes decreased with the advent of rectification, those conflicts by no means disappeared.[17] A few county party branches still lodged accusations against their county magistrate or the head of the office of public security. And the provincial rectification committee did intervene on very rare occasions to support county party branches in disputes.[18]

Decline in Party Power

Some observers recall that by the latter part of the Nanjing Decade the party, at both the provincial and local levels, had declined in power relative to the government. One memoir suggests that this evisceration of the party came about because Chen Guofu became provincial governor in 1933, and he "laid particular stress on administration" rather than party affairs. As a result, the memoir argues, "party affairs . . . [came to be] . . . an empty name," as individual local party leaders scrambled to garner official posts and "aggrandize themselves."[19] In fact, the corporate power of the GMD at the local level had slipped by the end of the Nanjing Decade, but that downturn had begun some years before Chen became governor.

Although county Guomindang branches were often weak and vulnerable even in the late 1920s, they weakened even further during the rectification period. By and large, Jiangsu's local Guomindang branches were relegated to an auxiliary role in politics and frequently excluded from the process of policy formation. Provincial rectification committee operatives lambasted party branches for the role that they had played before 1930. For example, party spokesperson Pan Juemin charged that local party branches had arrogated to themselves a "special position" separate from both the government and the masses. Local parties had accepted requests, demands, and complaints from individuals and organizations, then pressured local governments to comply with the party's judgment on these matters. Pan asserted that this process made policy discussion take on a spirit akin to litigation, since party initiatives often started with someone's "accusation" against the government. Such accusations, Pan contended, fostered mass suspicion of the government. Pan laid out in stark terms the new role prescribed for county GMD branches. County parties were not to interfere in administrative matters— that was the government's realm. Rather than soliciting the opinions of the masses and foisting them on the local government, county parties were to concentrate on ascertaining the center's position on important matters and then to make sure that subcounty branches followed those rulings and orders.[20]

Provincial and central authorities now made it clear that local GMD organizations were to act as helpmates to local governments. A party-government conference determined that the party would disseminate whatever propaganda the provincial government deemed necessary. In essence, this reduced the party to a propaganda arm of the government, a gross violation of the principle of party rule and leadership of the revolution.[21] The party was to facilitate local governments' efforts by teaching the masses the reasons behind government policies. The Central Executive Committee argued that local party branches could in this way help discharge the government's "tutelage" responsibility. The CEC specifically called on local parties to disseminate propaganda explaining why the government was (1) inspecting households to bring household registrations up to date, (2) establishing new government organs, (3) enacting the "land value tax," (4) building new roads, (5) reclaiming wasteland, and (6) founding new schools. The CEC also instructed local party people to be good soldiers, doing social service in local parks, schools, mass education institutes, exhibitions, and militia.[22]

Although provincial and central party leaders sometimes, in an aside, referred to the party's supervisory role over government, by and large that notion of the local parties' duties and powers receded into the background. When certain local branches, refusing to recognize the new dispensation, continued to attempt to affect policy in their localities and to oversee local administration, they were reprimanded by the provincial rectification committee. For example, the Liuhe GMD Party Congress faced rebuke by the provincial party apparatus for having passed a bill of suggestions relating to county governance. The bill included a recommendation as to who should be appointed the next county magistrate, the nomination of education personnel, and a proposal that would have enabled the local party to assume greater control over the subcounty self-government system than it had enjoyed in the past. The provincial rectification committee dismissed these proposals out of hand, asserting that the Liuhe party's petitions constituted interference in administration.[23] The provincial committee repeatedly returned to the theme that the local party branches' proper role did not include administrative matters.

The party rectification raises rather perplexing questions about the motivation of Organization Clique leaders. These men derived the greatest part of their power and prestige from their commanding positions at the head of the party's Organization Department. And yet they presided over a rectification process that reduced the influence and strength of their power base, the party and its many local branches, vis-à-vis the government and rendered the GMD nearly irrelevant to policy formation in the province. Indeed, Chen Guofu himself had initiated the process of weakening party influence in 1928 when he proposed the regulations that effectively barred local parties from "interfering" in administration.[24] This ironic turn of events can be explained by recalling the unflinching loyalty of Organization Clique leaders to Chiang Kai-shek. They were apparently anxious to please him by eliminating the political threat and danger of social disruption that left-leaning activists and localistic county parties posed. Although the power of central Organization Clique leaders emanated in part from their control of the party, and they thereby stood to lose influence and prestige with a drop in party power, they held their posts at the Chiang's pleasure.[25] And Chiang wanted an Organization Department staff that could deftly manipulate the party and wring out all traces of radicalism. The only way to control the party at the provincial and local levels was to emasculate it.

That answer, taken by itself, might seem to imply that the Chen brothers did not share Chiang's distaste for mass agitation, social confrontation, and local party autonomy. There is, in fact, no evidence to suggest such a parting of views. Rather, Chen Guofu revealed a strong preference for a top-down, bureaucratic approach to society.[26] Guided and nurtured by the Chens, the Central Party Affairs Academy took as its mission the training of operatives who could act as efficient and loyal cogs in such a bureaucratic machine.[27] Although Chen Guofu had argued in favor of a party-led mass movement, it was to be tightly controlled from above.[28] Thus, there is no reason to suspect that the Chens had serious misgivings about destroying local party autonomy and squelching local activists' power to affect policy. Because the Chen brothers wielded a great deal of clout in the central political arena, they could be content with a political process that concentrated most decision making in that arena.

However, not all cadres associated with the Organization Clique, even those at the provincial level, were pleased with the results of the rectification. A few months after the rectification was over, Zhou Houjun, a leader in the provincial FF Clique, an affiliate of the national-level Organization Clique, expressed his dissatisfaction with the state of the party. Most notably, he decried the party's weakness vis-à-vis the government, and he charged that due to the party's decrepitude the revolution was at a low ebb. To be sure, some things he called for were in tune with policies of the rectification era. For example, he championed centralized control within the party, including an end to elections of party executive committees.[29] However, Zhou found fault with the political ways of the newly "rectified" party and saw its strength as inadequate. Too often it compromised with imperialists and with "feudal powers," a shorthand for non-GMD local elites, or at least a subset of them. Zhou advocated a new movement to root out "the traitorous among the despotic gentry, landlords, compradores, bureaucrats, politicians, literati (*shidafu*) and warlords." To strengthen the party so it could stand up to the "feudal powers," he called for its militarization. The National Revolutionary Armies, he said, had not really served as the party's army. The party needed its own armed force with which to flatten its enemies. Moreover, he longed for a party dictatorship which would exert its will to "train the government," screen and weed out unfit government officials, transform Chinese society for the good, and protect those citizens who could not protect themselves. In short, the meek, retiring, and exhausted GMD that emerged from the rectification did not suit Zhou, and it is possible that it did not please other Organization Clique associates. However, what was done was done. Although the Guomindang was reorganized several times in the decade's remaining years, the party never achieved the revival of which Zhou spoke so longingly.[30]

A Weakened Party and Commercial Organizations

Despite the Chen brothers' obvious power at the central level, they did not get their way on all issues before the CEC and the National Government. Joseph Fewsmith has noted that in June of 1929 the CEC explicitly withheld authority from the Organization Department to supervise mass organizations, instead turning over sole responsibility for those bodies to the Training Department.[31] Later in 1929 the National Government clipped party power by enacting a new set of laws governing chambers of commerce and other occupational groups. These statutes took away from the party its authority to supervise commercial associations and handed that power and responsibility to the government.

These laws spelled an end to the party-supervised merchant associations that had been sprouting up in most counties in the late 1920s, often in opposition to the old chambers of commerce, which were largely controlled by the largest-scale merchants in the counties. The party had touted the merchant associations as vehicles which would enable small merchants to overcome oppression suffered at the hands of compradors, imperialists, and warlords and which would aid in reaching the GMD's revolutionary goals. Under the new laws, however, all large and small merchants' enterprises were to be banded together into "trade associations" (*tongye gonghui*) organized according to the type of commercial activity in which they engaged. In other words, firms involved in one type of business endeavor (for example, bean curd producers) were to come together under government oversight to form their own association. That trade association would then choose a representative who would meet with representatives of other trade associations to elect members of the executive committee of the county chamber of commerce. One list includes names of over 130 different types of trade associations formed and subsumed under the reorganized chambers.[32]

The prescribed reorganization of commercial groups took place in many Jiangsu counties during 1929, 1930, and 1931, though some county party organizations were loath to give up their accustomed prerogative of steering commercial associations. The Tongshan County Party Rectification Committee, for example, attempted to perpetuate its hold on commercial organizations by quickly recasting that county's merchant association into a chamber of commerce organized according to the new law's dictates. Only after completing the task of building the new county chamber out of the old party-led merchant association did the local party order the disbandment of the old chamber, thus shutting the older body's personnel out of the new organization's leadership. But the old chamber's elites were not to be thrust aside so easily. They appealed to the Jiangsu Provincial Amalgamated Chambers of Commerce, an alliance made up of representatives of many of the old chambers in the province. Together, the old Tongshan Chamber of Commerce and the provincial organization successfully lobbied the National Government, which soon produced an edict ordering the Tongshan party to stop exceeding its authority and cleared the way for the old chamber's people to be included in the new county chamber of commerce. Similar controversies raged in Shuyang and Yancheng counties, capped by similar denouements.[33]

But even if the new laws on commercial organizations seemed stacked against local parties and their authority, some GMD branches were still able to salvage a bit of influence over commercial organizations. In Tongshan, despite the eventual inclusion of old chamber members in the new chamber, the person who was elected to chair its executive committee was none other than the party member who had been head of the earlier GMD-led merchant association.[34]

In Wuxi too, the county GMD parlayed personal politics into influence within the newly reorganized chamber, though the road to that connection was rocky. In the late 1920s the Wuxi party had tried in vain to start a genuinely party-led merchant organization. Soon after GMD armies arrived in Wuxi the old chamber of commerce was disbanded and replaced by the county merchant association, which was nominally party supervised. The leader of the new body was Qian Sunqing, a man who even before 1927 had been one of the county's most politically active local elites. He had at various times served as county assembly representative, provincial assembly representative, head of the county education association, manager of the public property office for both the city and the county, chair of the county education association, and township manager for the area that included the Wuxi county seat. Beyond this, Qian had served in county government and had been principal of Gongyi Middle School. This educational institution was founded and funded by the Rong family, which had extensive financial interests in Wuxi and Shanghai, most notably cotton and flour mills. Qian's relations with Rong Desheng and Rong Zongjing gave him strong backing for his political activities. Thus, Qian had his own bases of power independent of the party, and he was hardly a pliable tool of the new GMD regime, despite his position in the merchant association. In 1927 he had issued statements in the name of the Wuxi Merchant Association, calling upon the GMD government to withdraw its arrest warrant for local industrialist Rong Zongjing, who had angered Chiang Kai-shek by not providing promised funds to the Generalissimo's army. Although some members of the executive committee of the merchant association harshly questioned Qian for releasing this and other statements not authorized by the committee as a whole, Qian had shown that he was able to use the supposedly party-led merchant association to criticize actions of the GMD regime. There is really no evidence that the local GMD called the shots when Qian acted.[35]

In 1929 the Wuxi Merchant Association was closed down, and a new chamber of commerce, organized according to the dictates of the

1929 national law on trade associations, took its place. The party could not have been pleased when Qian won the top leadership spot in this new organization. Moreover, though the party had long advocated merchant organizations that gave greater voice to small and medium-scale merchants than to the owners of the largest concerns in the county, this new organization was clearly even easier for Wuxi's big businesses to control than had been the prior merchant association. Both the Rong and Xue families, which owned the largest industrial concerns in Wuxi, were well represented on the new body. The party, on the other hand, had a hard time establishing hegemony over the organization. The laws that provided the framework for the new chambers did not provide for local party branches continuing to "guide" chambers, but that did not prevent Wuxi's county GMD from trying. In early 1931 the county party branch appointed one of its executive committee members to serve as director of the chamber. At first it might have appeared that Qian had no good way to prevent this director's unwelcome intrusion into chamber affairs, but he found one. He simply closed down most chamber activities, giving the party representative next to nothing to supervise. In a few months the party retreated, ending the position of the director, who by this time must have been thoroughly bored with his duties.[36]

Even so, relations between the local GMD and leading merchants in the Wuxi chamber remained hostile until 1932, when a personal connection was struck between chamber head Qian and party member Li Tiping. In 1931 Li had been sent by the local GMD to teach "party morals" (*dang yi*) at the middle school where Qian was principal, and the two men before long became friends. Soon Qian hired Li to work as an assistant in the Wuxi County Public Property Office, which Qian controlled. Li quickly established warm relations with several other key figures in the county's merchant community and became a pivotal link between the party and commercial circles. One memoir suggests that from the time Li began to act as go-between for the local party branch, the government, and the chamber, relations between key merchants and the regime were smoothed considerably. In 1936 when labor unrest hit the Shenxin cotton mills owned by the Rongs, Li was especially helpful in inspiring cooperation between the regime and local businessmen as they handled that crisis.[37]

So, regardless of the increasingly meager statutorily defined party role in the 1930s, some local GMD branches pushed at the limits of their prescribed duties and powers. In at least one locality, Qidong, the leaders of the county party even went so far as to push a land reform program aimed at transferring ownership of much landlord-owned land in the county into the hands of tenants. (See Appendix 3 for more information on this case.) The Qidong situation was exceptional, however, in the radicalism displayed by Qidong party members long after the rectification. For the most part, the rectification had wrung the radicalism out of the party in Jiangsu. Local party branches had been weaned from using their earlier tactics of frontal assaults on persons of established wealth and power. Most local party branches' exertions of influence were restricted to channels that the center prescribed. During and after rectification, the party in Jiangsu was relegated to a position subordinate to local government. In this auxiliary role, it aided in the spread of propaganda, cooperatives, and mass education. The local parties also assumed a supporting role in enacting the government's "local self-government" program, in censoring leftist publications, and, in some areas, even in the training of militia.[38]

Residual GMD Role in Appointments

If rectification meant a virtual end to local party branches' influence on policy formation, it did not make the GMD powerless in all respects. At least in the realm of appointments to local self-government bodies, educational administrations, and certain other county and subcounty posts, local party branches still had clout. What this meant was that in many cases factions within county parties used their muscle to get posts for their members. For example, Chu Shuxin, who served as a ward head (*quzhang*) in Jingjiang County from 1929 through 1937, recounts that the two factions in that county's GMD used their influence to secure appointments for their members as ward heads and township heads (*xiangzhang*).[39] He recalls that whenever he was supposed to appoint new township heads, his residence was besieged by people attempting to curry favor. As he puts it, those aspirants to township posts who did not brandish letters of introduction from local elites (*difang shili*), proudly displayed the name cards of leaders of one of the two local GMD factions to impress and put pressure on him. Although Chu contends that he ignored this blatant importuning and chose the best persons for the openings, his account leaves little doubt that local GMD faction leaders had much say over who held local positions of authority. That influence by no means died with party rectification.⁴⁰ Memoirs from Tongshan County indicate that there too county GMD factions retained a great deal of influence over local appointments after rectification. In that county, which included the city of Xuzhou (North China zone), three local GMD factions competed for positions. During the 1930s, none of the three cliques enjoyed a long-term hold on all of the posts; instead, the plum positions were spread out among associates of the three groups. Choice slots held by members of the three factions included chairman of the chamber of commerce, head of the county office of education, head of the county agricultural assembly, and many others. ⁴¹

Other Factors in Deradicalization of the GMD

Although the rectification of the provincial Guomindang was the primary reason why the campaign against "local bullies and evil gentry" withered and most other sorts of radical advocacy within the party disappeared, other factors also contributed to the change. It could be argued that the passage of time itself promoted an end to attacks on older elites. The party's assaults on local elites might logically be expected to decline in number after local parties had already struck out at and punished the most obvious targets. For example, in some localities the party had already struggled against—and sent to Nanjing in chains—those local pre-1927 leaders who had conspicuously offered aid to Sun Chuanfang's armies. No new targets of this sort were likely to be discovered. And as the GMD regime itself became "the establishment," it might reasonably have become less zealous in routing out establishment figures. In fact, it was not just the case that far fewer elites faced GMD-led assaults by the early 1930s, but many who had been attacked early on were now released and their properties restored.

The Deradicalization of the GMD Leftists

Although the provincial party affairs rectification committee's meticulous program of weeding out leftists from local parties was the main cause of GMD de-radicalization, a secondary factor was ideological change among leftists themselves. Studies of the left-leaning Reorganization Clique demonstrate that from 1928, national-level Reorganizationist leaders gradually altered their ideological stance in ways that watered down their radicalism. In 1928, when Chen Gongbo was the primary leftist spokesman after Wang Jingwei had temporarily retired to Europe, the left had embraced the idea that the revolution should be "anti-imperialist, anti-feudal, and non-capitalist."[42] The leftists' theme of antifeudalism targeted the big landlords, whom leftists sometimes equated with "local bullies and bad gentry," and "warlord bureaucrats" as social entities that stood in the way of revolution and, thus, had to be toppled.[43] Chen advocated "land equalization," that is, land redistribution, and restriction of capitalism; he also thought that the state should own and manage most large enterprises and should control foreign trade.[44] Virtually all leftists called for a vibrant worker and peasant movement and firm party control over the government and the military.

But by March 1929 Wang Jingwei's influence on leftist thought began to overshadow that of Chen Gongbo, and Wang's call for "democracy" gradually displaced in leftist journals the ideological program of broad socioeconomic revolution that Chen Gongbo had envisioned. By 1930 Reorganizationist leaders had largely jettisoned their earlier ideology to solidify Wang Jingwei's alliance with the warlord Yan Xishan against Chiang Kai-shek.[45] "Democracy" was almost the only remaining leftist theme in 1931, as Wang Jingwei and other key Reorganizationists at the national level assumed prominent roles in the "Extraordinary Conference," a cobbled-together coalition of southern warlords, Western Hills rightists, Reorganizationists, and assorted party elders. Wang Jingwei abandoned even the "democracy" motif when he formed a political alliance with Chiang Kai-shek in January 1932, and agreed to assume the chairmanship of the Executive Yuan in Chiang's National Government. Clearly, the left's ideology had been abandoned by its leaders, especially Wang, for reasons of political expediency.[46] Thus, the overall de-radicalization of the Jiangsu GMD was, in part, a symptom of the dulling of the left's own ideological edge.

CCP Failure in Jiangsu

Yet another factor in the deradicalization of the province's Guomindang was the increasingly tenuous position of the Chinese Communist Party in Jiangsu. Early in the Nanjing Decade, even after the purge, some Communists remained active within the GMD in a number of localities and contributed to the social revolutionary ardor exhibited by some local GMD branches. However, as the GMD regime gradually improved its ability to suppress Communism in Jiangsu, this leftist "leavening" in the party was eventually reduced, contributing to GMD deradicalization.

Lacking reliable year-by-year statistics on Communist Party membership in Jiangsu, one must rely on indirect means of mapping the faltering health of the Communist movement there. One method, imperfect to be sure, is to chart the number of revolutionary activities planned and carried out by the CCP in Jiangsu year by year that are listed in a chronology edited by the CCP's Jiangsu Provincial Party History Committee. Such an analysis of trends in CCP history suggests a high level of CCP activity through 1930. Then in 1931 and 1932 the reports of CCP revolutionary actions decline by about one-quarter. In 1933, reported Communist activity falls almost to half of the level of the previous year, and it is cut in half again in 1934. With some year-by-year variations, the frequency of Communist activity recounted in the chronology remains near this low level through 1937.[47] Another measure of the troubles facing the Communist Party in Jiangsu can be found in memoir accounts of the history of CCP county branches. These historical sketches for a large number of counties indicate that by the early- to mid-1930s the local CCP branches had either ceased revolutionary activities or drastically cut back on them.[48]

Memoirs and other writings reveal that one of the main factors behind the precipitous slide in CCP fortunes was an avalanche of defections to the Guomindang side. In many Jiangsu localities throughout the province, turncoat Communist cadres informed on their former comrades, enabling the GMD regime to arrest large numbers of remaining CCP members. In this period, Guomindang intelligence forces were able to destroy many county CCP branches. Memoirs suggest that the dramatic increase in defections of key Communist operatives was due in part to beefed up GMD intelligence (*tewu*, literally, "special affairs") organizations, which had learned techniques to persuade CCP cadres to inform on other Communists. Laws passed in the early 1930s offering favorable treatment to Communists who turned themselves in to GMD authorities are also cited in the memoirs as a factor in defections.[49]

The intelligence organs most active in Jiangsu emanated from the Organization Department of the central party headquarters. Chen Guofu, at Chiang Kai-shek's behest, had established the Investigation Section of the Central Organization Department soon after the purge "to monitor and suppress [C]ommunist activities."[50] By the early thirties, that section had grown in size and sophistication, gradually even establishing bureaus in certain Jiangsu counties to oversee multicounty districts.[51] To some degree, the bolstered ability of the Organization Department's "special affairs" arm stemmed from its employment of a swelling team of former Communist cadres who had switched allegiance. These former Communists provided intelligence on the identity of members and leaders of the underground Communist movement. Additionally, at least one captured Communist who had been trained in the Soviet Union by the Soviet secret police, the Cheka, passed on what he had learned about intelligence techniques.[52] All told, turncoat agents did incalculable damage to the Communist Party in Jiangsu.

At the same time, part of the GMD regime's growing success at Communist suppression in Jiangsu in the early 1930s was a function of long-standing shortcomings in Communist strategy and coordination. The emphasis that the CCP had placed on local uprisings—CCP policy directives often called them "riots"—through at least the late 1920s, brought with it no lasting territorial stronghold, since GMD armed forces were usually able to recapture within hours or days any market town taken by CCP forces. And although in 1930 CCP corps in Rugao, Taixing, and other nearby counties attempted to carve out a stable, defended area governed by a CCP-controlled "soviet," this effort was an improbable enterprise from the start; if necessary, Chiang Kai-shek would certainly have employed GMD army forces to prevent the consolidation of a CCP-led state so close to his own political and resource base, the Shanghai-Nanjing corridor. As events developed, Chiang did not have to send any of the main body of his forces to face the Fourteenth Army, the CCP's military organization in the Rugao-Taixing area. Instead, in 1930 that CCP army met its end at the hands of a local elite-managed militia which the GMD regime had been fostering in the area since the late 1920s to meet the CCP threat. This militia was probably helped in its work by the multicounty coordination of security units upon which the GMD regime had embarked by early 1930. Factional strife within the CCP also contributed to the defeat of the Rugao-Taixing insurgency. As the CCP center began to impose its will and its leadership personnel upon the heretofore relatively autonomous local CCP units, some of the displaced local Communist bosses defected to the GMD side, encouraged by the GMD's offer of leadership positions in its own security apparatus.[53] The result was that the GMD's security forces were quickly able to destroy the Fourteenth Army and decimate CCP army leadership ranks in several of the counties.

If the GMD regime was now using a carrot-and-stick approach to suppressing Communism, it was the carrot that was relatively new in the game, though not completely unprecedented.[54] The institutional face of the policy to persuade Communists to abandon their party and ideology and to offer their services to the GMD regime was the Reeducation Institute (*Fanxing yuan*, literally, "institute for reflection and self-examination"), founded in 1931 to administer the ideological remolding of captured and surrendered Communists. This bureau was formally part of the judicial apparatus, but the Investigation Section of the Organization Department had by 1932 taken it over in all but outward appearance. The section's personnel had replaced the judicial system's appointees in many management positions of the Reeducation Institute, and the section had successfully asserted its right to place in the institute's holding cells inmates whom the section had detained without any court's ruling.[55]

The Jiangsu Reeducation Institute, located in Suzhou, was to some degree modeled after the first such organ, which had been established in Hunan in 1930. The Jiangsu institute's inmates included (1) persons who at one time had been Communists and whom security organs believed had not completely rejected Marxism-Leninism and the CCP; (2) individuals whom security officers believed to be Communist Party members, but who steadfastly refused to admit that they were; and (3) people whose thought was leftist, thereby leading security personnel to suspect that they were Communists. Reeducation Institute functionaries divided the inmates according to their educational background and employed different "reeducation" techniques, depending on whether internees were illiterate, had only attended elementary school, had graduated from a middle-level school, or had a college education. For prisoners with the lowest cultural attainment, manual labor was part of the regimen, while university graduates were put through classes and individual tutorials. The captive students received a steady diet of preachment and other inducements to get them to adopt the regime's ideological standpoint. They were pressed to embrace the idea of a "revolution of the entire people," and to reject proletarian revolution. Reeducation Institute operatives further "trained" inmates on the need to "reconcile the classes" and to "stand resolutely against class struggle." The institute also taught its prisoners to "use [Sun Yat-sen's] Three People's Principles to oppose Communism."[56]

Inmates faced concerted psychological pressure, including death threats. "Training personnel" regularly administered tests to the detainees to determine how their thought remolding was progressing. And even when inmates graduated from the Reeducation Institute with certificates that proclaimed that they were now "permitted to carry out . . . [their] own self-renewal," in reality the released prisoners remained under the scrutiny of the investigation section for three years. They were assigned to "self-renewal training groups," which held meetings that former inmates were to attend once a week. The released prisoners were also required to provide weekly reports to section personnel, listing where they had gone during the week, persons with whom they had contact, and any questionable activities of which they had knowledge. The Organization Department's secret police were often detailed to check up on released persons to make sure that their self-reporting was complete and accurate. Indeed, some who had seemingly surrendered their will to the GMD became active Communists again upon gaining their freedom and were subsequently killed by GMD security forces once their double game was uncovered.[57]

It is not entirely clear how effective the Reeducation Institute regimen was in transforming Communists into supporters or at least tolerators of the GMD regime. Some accounts depict the institute's methods and instructional materials as ludicrous. For example, one person who spent many months in the Suzhou Reeducation Institute lampoons the readings he was required to study. He reports that he looked upon the book *Weisheng lun* (*On Vitalism*) by Chen Lifu, which was part of the reeducation center's curriculum, as a laughable and unsatisfactory attempt to refute Marxist historical materialism.[58] It is possible that many others shared his view of this and other parts of the "ideological remolding" regimen, although there are no reliable figures from which the success of the Reeducation Institute can be judged.

Yet it seems beyond dispute that the CCP was in serious trouble in Jiangsu by the early- to mid-1930s. A primary factor in that reversal of fortune was clearly the significant numbers of people who had been key Communist cadres and were now informing on their former comrades. Also important in this equation was the increasing effectiveness of the Organization Department's intelligence service. Two localities that illustrate these phenomena are Tongshan County, which includes the major North China zone city of Xuzhou, and Nantong County in the Lower Yangzi core. Both of these areas had vibrant and active Communist movements until the early 1930s. Memoirs provide detailed descriptions of the harm that defectors visited upon the CCP in both of these localities. In both cases, traitors provided the evidence which allowed the GMD's security services to bring to a virtual halt effective Communist activity until the beginning of the war with Japan in 1937.[59] The Communist movements in many other counties all across Jiangsu were similarly stymied by defections and mass arrests.[60]

The decline in CCP fortunes meant that Communists hidden away within the ranks of the GMD were less a factor in the latter half of the Nanjing Decade than they had been earlier. The deradicalization of the Guomindang, mostly a result of the provincial GMD's rectification program, was helped along in some small measure by the destruction of the Jiangsu CCP.

7

Perspectives

The Guomindang's anti-"local bully" crusade began when the party was still a largely underground, revolutionary organization allied with the Communist Party. The movement was an expression of the cultural iconoclasm and the deep social and political dissatisfactions of the predominantly middle school- and normal school-educated intellectuals, whom the GMD was trying to forge into a revolutionary force. As the GMD armies' victories in the Northern Expedition led to the establishment of new local Nationalist governments, the anti-bully campaign proved a useful tool in establishing Guomindang power. Entrenched local elites were not going to cede their positions and authority to the Guomindang unless they were pressured to do so. In some localities the party attacked and prosecuted leaders of powerful local factions, thus clearing the political stage for party personnel to step into public leadership roles. In fact, in some communities incumbent elites were so alarmed by what they had heard about party-led campaigns against "local bullies and evil gentry" that they voluntarily withdrew from public affairs. Campaigns against selected local elites did not occur in all localities in Jiangsu, but they were a riveting and pervasive feature of Jiangsu politics in the early part of the Nanjing Decade. To be sure, in certain areas the post-1927 movement to attack or arrest certain elites as undesirables was energized in part by concerns other than the urge drastically to refashion society. In a few cases local elite factions hijacked a campaign and redirected its fury against competing elite factions. But by and large, the movement may be seen as an expression of residual radicalism that survived within the GMD after the purge.

While it is easy to see that the anti-"local bully" campaigns helped to establish GMD authority in various locales at the outset of the Nanjing Decade, the sum effect of the movement on the regime's ongoing efforts to modernize the country over the long term is, at best, debatable. Some elites whom the regime incarcerated or frightened into withdrawal from public roles had themselves been leaders of modernization efforts in their communities. Certain of these vilified elites were entrepreneurs whose expertise and capital might profitably have been mobilized by the new regime. Perhaps, however, it is to be expected that those party members who were most anxious to transform society quickly and fundamentally should seek to make examples of leaders from the previous era. And if only a fraction of the charges lodged against those elites deemed "feudal" by party radicals were true, some of these older leaders were responsible for much Chinese suffering.

There had never been unanimity within the GMD regime about the wisdom of the attacks on local elites. In fact, some local governments appointed by the regime had early on developed ties with certain powerful incumbent elites to insure the continuity of revenue collections and government bond purchases by the wealthy. Many party-government disputes resulted from local parties and governments not seeing eye-to-eye on the question of whether the party should press campaigns against wealthy and powerful local residents. The party center, too, had serious misgivings about campaigns to identify and attack persons as "local bullies," and it sought to reign in such activity by local party branches.

By the early 1930s the center had things its way. The regime had largely turned its back on campaigns against "local bullies and evil gentry," and this about-face signified both the defeat of the leftists within the party and the victory of a top-down, bureaucratic approach to governance. There is growing evidence, however, that many local elites discovered as little to like about the centralizing, bureaucratizing thrust spearheaded by the government as they had found in the anti-"local bully" campaigns the party had led. The Nationalist Government is, for the most part, beyond the scope of this study, but previous works suggest that some of the provincial government's policies were designed to wrest control of certain local institutions from the hands of local elites and to make those bodies subject to provincial control.

Not surprisingly, the government's drive for dominion over local organizations was met with disapprobation by many local elites. For example, many local educational leaders protested and resisted the regime's attempts to expand its oversight of local educational institutions, to appoint those entities' administrators, and to prescribe their programs.[1] Similarly, government attempts to systematize and tighten its sway over local finance challenged local elites' ascendancy in that important sphere.[2]

To be sure, the government at both the provincial and local levels was not utterly impervious to local elite influence, and in some contexts the government relied on local elite organizational efforts to supplement its often inadequate efforts to control and modernize China. In a number of circumstances the government had to compromise with the interests of local elites.[3] Most importantly, though, by the 1930s the government was setting the tone for regime-elite relations, and the party, especially on the local scene, had faded into the background.

Of the Nationalist regime's major constituent parts (the army, the government and the party) this study has only considered at length what happened to the party. At a glance, it might seem to some that things were going rather well for the party in Jiangsu by the early thirties. The Guomindang's intelligence organs were beginning to have considerable success at hunting down and eliminating Communists, and no other similarly large and organized entity that could challenge the GMD was on the horizon. The party was, in a limited sense, more tightly organized than it had been before the rectification of 1930 through 1931. Local party branches were no longer openly contesting the center's wisdom on all manner of issues, as they had been in the earliest years of the Nanjing Decade. By the same token, the Communist Party no longer controlled local GMD branches, as it had before the 1927 purge.

And yet, time would demonstrate shortcomings in the approach the GMD had adopted with the center's rectification of the provincial party organization in 1930 and 1931. The removal of the provincial and local party branches from most policy debates meant that most of the energies of party cadres were devoted to personnel questions, to the problem of who would get what posts. Although factional battles over the matter of appointments had been common before the rectification, not very much other than this sort of bickering was left to provincial and local party leaders after the center had worked its will on the Jiangsu GMD. Factional warfare occupied center stage in local and provincial politics, just as it did at the national level.

The party, as it settled into the role of an increasingly irrelevant cheerleader for the government, was losing the abilities that one would expect of a party in a one-party, authoritarian state, most notably the capacity to mobilize people and resources. The leftists (Reorganizationists and other radicals) had advocated vigorous, autonomous mass organizations as a means to ensure thorough revolutionary transformation of society and to prevent the party from becoming isolated from the masses. During the period of the party rectification, the center defeated the Reorganization Clique and imposed an approach to party affairs that on the one hand did not place great emphasis on the mass organizations and, on the other, imposed tight controls on them. It should come as no surprise, then, that studies of China's experience during the war with Japan find the Guomindang to have been sadly unprepared to lead in the total mobilization of the country.[4]

To deal effectively with the Japanese challenge, China needed to transform itself into a strong, cohesive nation-state based on an iron citizen-state bond. But having turned aside the concept of mass organizations responsive to the needs and pleas of peasants, workers, and others, the party contributed little to the strengthening of the ligaments between the people and the regime. After the rectification period began, the party offered some support to the government's bureaucratization effort, an endeavor that embodied the regime's hopes for gaining greater purchase on the lives and resources in the province. But at the end of the Nanjing Decade, China remained a rather weak garrison state, so much so that one 1936 Jiangsu government publication admitted with shocking candor that "it is an undeniable fact that [our control of] the localities depends on suppression (*zhenya*) by the armed forces."[5]

When those armed forces and the Nanjing government's bureaucracy were hammered by the Japanese invasion in 1937, the party could not give much help in reintegrating and solidifying the regime. The GMD continued during the war against Japan to operate in Jiangsu without an effective mass movement. Although the regime, the central apparatus of which had retreated to western China, developed connections with local guerrilla and other units that formed behind Japanese lines and attempted to lead them in action against the occupying armies (as well as against Communist-controlled detachments), the GMD found it impossible to impose unified control over such a disparate collection of autonomous armed forces.[6] A vigorous party that had at its disposal a large and committed phalanx of mass organizations might have been able to apply enough coordinated pressure on the elites who managed the detachments to keep them in line. But in the absence of such discipline, some units began to collaborate with the Japanese.[7]

Similarly, the GMD's timid and lackadaisical approach to mass organization left a vacuum in the countryside that the CCP would later fill during the period of the war with Japan and the civil war which followed. The wartime strategy of the Communists in Jiangsu during the war had at least some outward similarity to that of the GMD, in that it entailed a certain amount of reliance on local elites. Communist Party organizers in central China developed ties with selected local elites in order to gain entry into communities. While under the protection of these elites, the Communists developed mass organizations which ultimately organized the mass base right out from under those elites. These mass organizations then served to provide a resource base for Communist-led military operations and for the building of Communist-supervised governing structures.[8] GMD leaders, however, had not learned how to use mass organizations to leverage their position vis-à-vis the elites who commanded and controlled the so-called GMD guerrilla units.

Guomindang politicians after the Nanjing Decade continued to concentrate on factional infighting, much as they had during the late 1920s and early 1930s.[9] Lloyd Eastman, in his account of the period after the onset of war through the Communists' victory in 1949, argues that factionalism contributed to the internal decay of the regime and its ultimate defeat at the hands of the Communists. As politicians fought for power and position, using factions as their vehicles, they "lost sight of the larger purposes of government."[10] It is clear from the history of factionalism in Jiangsu that the processes that Eastman notes in the late 1940s were already well advanced by the early 1930s in this key province. It seems indisputable that factional battles were a major determinant of the political landscape in Jiangsu throughout the Republican era.

APPENDICES

1. THE EVOLUTION OF FACTIONAL CONFLICT, 1927–1929

Jiangsu Special Committee

After the Central Supervisory Committee decided to purge the Communists from the party in 1927, Chiang Kai-shek's Central Party Headquarters in Nanjing appointed the Jiangsu Provincial Special Committee (JSC) to lead the Jiangsu GMD, while the Central Party Purge Committee appointed a Jiangsu Provincial Party Purge Committee to direct the purge. Chen Guofu's influence on appointments to the provincial purge committee is obvious, since at least four of the ten members were adjuncts of the embryonic Organization Clique (including CC leader Li Shouyong and several FF partisans), although only one of the members of the JSC (Zhou Jieren) is known to have had connections with the Organization Clique.[1] The Nanjing GMD center also reorganized the Nanjing Municipal Party Headquarters, jettisoning the old one dominated by the Western Hills group. These new headquarters for Nanjing municipality (of which FF partisan Jin Hesheng and Chen Guofu associate Wu Yicang were members) and Jiangsu began to expel scores of Western Hills adherents from the party and arrested some of them. In reaction, Nanjing Western Hills leaders established a small organization called the Loyal Comrades' Club (*Zhongshi tongzhi julebu*) and cabled Chiang Kai-shek, the National Government in Nanjing, and the Central Party Headquarters, charging that the new Jiangsu and Nanjing party committees were Communist-dominated, apparently feeling that anyone who opposed the Western Hills group had to be Communist inspired. They also cabled Shanghai newspapers decrying the reorganization of the Nanjing municipal headquarters and warning that Communists were now slipping into the GMD.[2]

The newly appointed JSC soon faced criticism within the party that it was too radical and should be dismissed. Bowing to this pressure, probably quite willingly, the CEC dismissed the JSC less than a month after establishing it, charging that it had "vainly spouted empty words inciting disturbances."[3] The CEC then appointed a new nine-person JSC that included at least three who would be linked with the Organization Clique. Among these were Li Shouyong (CC leader) and Ye Xiufeng (FF leader). Anti-CC leader Gu Ziyang was dropped from the list.[4]

Since nearly all party records had been lost in the purge, one of the main tasks of the JSC was to manage a party reregistration.[5] The committee was also supposed to set up county parties where they had not previously existed. To do this, it sent to each county special deputies to investigate the local situation and choose five or six local party members to serve as a county special committee, which would manage local party affairs until the election of a county executive committee. The process provided much grist for the factional mill as provincial leaders recommended their local followers for the position of special deputy and thereby sought to extend their local bases. Since the special deputies had an extraordinary writ of authority to "guide" local party affairs, one can imagine their ability to expand personal followings. But some revealed considerable lack of tact in the process. For example, GMD members in Jiangyin County cabled the JSC in exasperation, inquiring whether Jiangyin's special deputy was a loyal GMD member. They argued that he neither "knows the party doctrine" nor "understands the limits of power." He had been in Jiangyin only a few days, they said, but "he does what he pleases; his measures are opportunist." Reportedly following him to Jiangyin was a coterie of "several tens of people who yen to become officials together, and who are colluding with several old schoolmates to monopolize" the party.[6]

The process of clique formation is even more obvious in accounts of Jiangsu Provincial Purge Committee meetings, where Organization group influence was strong. This committee appointed purge committees on the county level to identify and direct action against CCP members and "local bullies and evil gentry." Each of the county committee members were recommended to the provincial committee by one or more of the provincial purge committee's members. Provincial leaders apparently used this patronage system to reward their friends and create larger personal followings.[7] However, provincial clique lines had not yet completely hardened at this point, and members of what would emerge as separate cliques sometimes jointly introduced members.[8]

Jiangsu Provincial Provisional Executive Committee

On July 15, 1927, Wang Jingwei's Wuhan party center formally resolved to banish the CCP and thereby removed the fundamental difference between the Nanjing center and itself. This created a flurry of talk within both camps of reuniting the party. Affiliates of the Western Hills central headquarters in Shanghai became the strongest advocates of party reunification, probably because they felt that they were being shabbily treated by the Nanjing center and hoped that reunification would redistribute power in their favor.[9]

In late May, Chiang Kai-shek indicated his desire for reconciliation with the Shanghai rightist center by advocating that the Nanjing center accept some of the Western Hills partisans into the party because of their "revolutionary" nature.[10] Chiang also facilitated a reunification with the Wuhan center by resigning his post as commander in chief on August 13. Wuhan's partisans had so hated Chiang that they would not have considered reunion with the Nanjing center while he controlled it. The primary cause for Chiang's resignation, however, was his loss of political clout due to a series of military reverses.[11] Still, Chiang's resignation sent a shock wave through the party and led to rumors and fears of local disturbances.[12]

A series of talks between Nanjing, Wuhan, and Shanghai representatives produced a Central Special Committee (*Zhongyang tebie weiyuanhui*; CSC) to replace the CEC and the Central Supervisory Committee of the GMD. In theory the CSC was a coalition of equal numbers from all three organizations—a leadership equation that grossly overrepresented the Western Hills group, which could claim significant support in only a small number of localities. Moreover, soon many Wuhan and Nanjing partisans became convinced that the Western Hills group, in alliance with the Guangxi Military Clique, had completely usurped the CSC and the National Government. Therefore, by the beginning of November, Wang Jingwei and several politicians from the former Wuhan center met in Guangzhou and called for disbanding the CSC and for preparatory meetings so that a Fourth Plenum of the Second CEC could meet.[13]

In mid-October the CSC disbanded the JSC and appointed in its place as the supreme organ of the Jiangsu party the Jiangsu Provincial Provisional Executive Committee (*Jiangsu sheng linshi zhixing weiyuanhui*; JPEC).[14] At least seven out of eleven of the JPEC members had been affiliated with the Western Hills group, the Sunist Study Society, or the Guangxi Military Clique.[15] (Provincial CC Clique leader Li Shouyong was appointed to the committee but refused to serve.)[16] This gave the Western Hills group a clear majority on the JPEC and provided it with what appeared to be the power to transform the Jiangsu party into a Western Hills preserve.

In early November 1927, the JPEC began attempting to spread its influence to local party organizations by eliminating the county special committees and appointing in their place county provisional executive committees appointed by the JPEC. In some counties the situation was confused by the existence of two or more county party headquarters, all formed by and owing allegiance to different party centers or other organs like the Political Department of the army; the "coalition" JPEC was supposed to unify these local parties. Some of the county special committees willingly turned over their files and offices to the county provisional executive committees.[17]

The JPEC, however, like the CSC, which had appointed it, found that its power was quite limited and that it was resisted at every turn by opponents to the Western Hills group. In many areas, county special committees refused to disband and turn over their parties to the newly appointed county provisional executive committees. In Kunshan County, the county special committee rejected the county provisional executive committee as "unlawful." Negotiating the turnover with the secretary of the provisional executive committee, special committee representative Li Ziyi procrastinated, noting that the political situation was "unclear." He refused to set a date for the turnover. Thus barred from the party office building, the provisional executive committee contented itself with makeshift offices in a local inn.[18]

From the inception of the CSC, that body met opposition from many quarters. Soon after it was formed, the Hangzhou *Republican Daily News* (*Minguo ribao*), an official organ of the Zhejiang GMD, printed a joint communiqué by the GMD headquarters for Jiangsu and Zhejiang provinces and Nanjing municipality vociferously opposing the CSC.[19] And, immediately after the formation of the CSC, the Jiangsu and Nanjing Special Committees issued a statement welcoming "cooperation" and "unity" of the Nanjing and Wuhan party centers and pointedly omitting any such welcome for members of the Shanghai center of the Western Hills group. The notice also named policies the

Nanjing and Wuhan centers agreed on, including—ominously for the CSC—the "elimination of opportunist, rotten (*fuhua*) elements."[20] Weeks before, the JSC had denounced calls by the Shanghai Western Hills party center for union with the Nanjing center and labeled them an "insult to the Nanjing center."[21] The Jiangsu Peasant Association Preparatory Committee (*Jiangsu sheng nongmin xiehui choubei hui*), which had been formed by the JSC, continued in this vein by resisting the JPEC, refusing to turn over its materials and offices to a JPEC-appointed committee, and attempting to rally county peasant association preparatory committees to oppose the JPEC and CSC.[22]

The period of the CSC and the JPEC was a formative one for the Organization Clique. After the retirement of Chiang Kai-shek and before his trip to Japan, he withdrew briefly to Shanghai to meet with a wide assortment of GMD politicians (many of whom also resigned in sympathy) to plot his restoration as *the* leader of the party, army, and government. According to one source, he entrusted the leadership of a large number of provincial and local party leaders to Chen Guofu and appointed Zhu Shaoliang to direct the activities of a sizable contingent of former Huangpu Military Academy students. The group led by Chen, which is said originally to have been composed of around thirty members and eventually expanded to over one hundred, was known to outsiders as the "Central Club" (*Zhongyang julebu*).[23] Jiangsu's FF Clique leader Ye Xiufeng participated in the movement in Shanghai to overthrow the CSC, as did provincial CC Clique leader Li Shouyong.[24] Li mentions briefly traveling to Shanghai and gathering together leaders of seventeen municipal and provincial parties, but it is not clear whether he is referring to the so-called Central Club.[25] It is indisputable that a large number of Chen Guofu's associates gathered in Shanghai to plan and execute anti-CSC activities.

The most valuable and effective anti-CSC work was done by Chen's confreres in Nanjing. There, officials and students of the Central Party Affairs Academy, many of whom were connected with Chen, created a movement to restore Chiang and overthrow the CSC. On November 22, 1927, they precipitated the so-called "November 22 Massacre" (*Yiyi erer can'an*) in which soldiers or police controlled by the CSC and Guangxi Military Clique fired on a crowd of students, killing one academy student and three other persons. The incident became the *cause célèbre* that brought down the CSC.[26]

Many local party organizations seized upon the incident as an excuse to flagellate the CSC.[27] Nantong County's first ward party headquarters fired off cables (1) asking that a fourth plenum of the Central Executive Committee be held to supersede the CSC, (2) urging the National Government to investigate the massacre, (3) denouncing the CSC, claiming it was "manipulated by the Western Hills Conference Faction," and (4) advocating ejection of the "bogus revolutionary elements of the Western Hills Conference Faction" of the party. The county special committee also refused to transfer its authority to the county provisional executive committee appointed by the CSC's provincial arm, the JPEC.[28] In Songjiang County a similar situation developed. Only there, the first ward GMD's assembly boasted the support of many mass organizations and individuals—including a peasant association preparatory committee, several unions, a teachers' organization, some schools, army officers, and members of the county office of public security—in presenting the same sort of anti-CSC demands.[29]

In some counties this opposition to the CSC and the JPEC was prompted by the so-called Central Club in Shanghai. Jiangsu party leaders in the Central Club urged their local protégés to bring pressure on the CSC. For example, one of the ringleaders of the anti-CSC work in Jiangdu County (Yangzhou) was Zhou Houjun, a cadre of Ye Xiufeng's FF group. In late December Zhou and other members of the Jiangdu County Special Committee, saying they had received an order from the JSC (perhaps unofficially rejuvenated by Organization group affiliates to combat the CSC), told party and mass organizations not to turn their offices over to the county provisional executive committee. The CSC opponents then disrupted the inauguration of the Jiangdu County Provisional Executive Committee, ringing bells and shouting "Down with the Western Hills Conference Faction!" and "Down with the Imperialist Faction!" They proceeded to "arrest" three of the members of the new provisional executive committee.[30]

The widespread belief that the CSC leaders had ordered the November 22 massacre finally brought down the already weak CSC on December 28, 1927.[31] In place of the CSC, the old Nanjing central organization was reestablished to manage the party until the Central Executive Committee could meet in early 1928. The new party center then appointed Li Shouyong (CC), Ye Xiufeng (FF), and Qi Xiyong (CC) as the Jiangsu Party Affairs Maintenance Committee, which in turn dispatched county restored special committees (*huifu tebie weiyuanhui*) to the various counties in the province.³²

In some cases these county restored special committees met opposition from the existing county provisional executive committees, which rallied in Wuxi in late January 1928, to devise a plan to preserve their power and position. This conference of Western Hills-oriented county representatives declared that it would be "unreasonable" (*buheli*) and "impossible" to disband the county provisional executive committees, and that instead of restoring special committees, the center should establish "provisional special committees," presumably composed of members of both the county-level provisional executive and special committees. Participants in the conference were particularly irate that in making selections for the county committees the new party center had shut out Western Hills affiliates.³³ However, this gathering and its sympathizers were powerless to stop the rising tide of anti-Western Hills developments. From this time forward the Western Hills group was not a serious factor in Jiangsu politics.

Jiangsu Party Affairs Directorate

In February 1928, the Fourth Plenum of the Second CEC finally met to normalize party affairs after the demise of the extra-legal CSC and to chastise Wang Jingwei and his supporters for their alleged role in the abortive CCP-led Guangzhou Uprising of late 1927. After the meeting of the CEC, central party headquarters appointed "directorates" (*zhidao weiyuanhui*) to the various provinces to take the place of their previous provincial party leadership. The center appointed Leng Xin (Huangpu Clique connections), Li Shouyong (CC), Di Ying, Wang Baoxuan (CC), Teng Gu (Reorganization), Ye Chucang (senior figure, with some Organization Clique connections), Gu Ziyang (Anti-CC), Feng Ti (Huangpu connections), and Ni Bi (Anti-CC) as the Jiangsu Provincial Party Affairs Directorate.³⁴ It is not entirely clear why this centrally appointed committee contained so many members who were not intimately connected with the Central Organization Department; only Li, Wang, and Ye had such connections, though Di Ying's connections are unknown. It may be that the Standing Committee of the CEC overruled the Organization Department's candidates for the Jiangsu Directorate, or the department may have decided that it needed the good will and support of Gu Ziyang and his Huangpu-connected cohorts. One commentator simply observes that at the very beginning of the Nanjing Decade Chen Guofu was "generous" to other factions, though that soon changed.[35] It is also possible that Chen Guofu considered Gu to be in the Organization camp; after all, Gu had aided Chen in recruiting the first Huangpu class.[36] Considering that the CEC had just roundly rebuked Wang Jingwei, it is even more difficult to understand the inclusion of Teng Gu, a leftist and a friend of Wang. Perhaps the Organization Department did not yet have a firm fix on Teng's connections.[37]

The Anti-CC group did very well for itself throughout the period of the Directorate and appropriated for its personnel the positions of chairman of the provincial Organization Department (Ni Bi), and chairman of the Training Department (Gu Ziyang). Heading the Standing Committee of the Mass Movement Training Committee was Teng Gu, a left-wing Reorganizationist who often allied with the Anti-CC Clique. The Standing Committee of the Directorate was composed of Wang Baoxuan (CC), Ni Bi (Anti-CC), and Ye Chucang, a senior figure who was supposed to act as liaison with the central headquarters and oversee the Directorate, but who often did not attend meetings because of other duties.[38] All told, the Anti-CC group and its allies in the Reorganization Clique were in a pretty good position during the period of the Directorate, but so too was the CC component of the Organization Clique. During this period Li Shouyong, the provincial CC leader, like Anti-CC and Reorganization leaders, was establishing many of his protégés in leadership positions out in the county party branches, thus making himself a power to be reckoned with. There are even signs that the Chen brothers may have begun to worry that this provincial adjunct of their Organization Clique was getting too big to control; this may have led to their sending him abroad to study in 1929.[39]

The Directorate performed the tasks that the Jiangsu Special Committee had been executing before it had been so rudely interrupted by the CSC: selectively registering party members, appointing county party committees, and preparing for and guiding the county party congresses that would choose the delegates to Jiangsu's First Provincial Congress (which would play a part in picking delegates to the all-important Third National Congress that would rebuke leftist leader Wang Jingwei and clip his wings).

The Directorate's selection of members of the county party affairs directorates was by written and oral examination, though the provincial

Organization and Training Departments were allowed considerable power in the process.[40] Just as many of those chosen were aligned with Li's CC Clique, many also had marked leftist tendencies and supported the Anti-CC and Reorganization Cliques. Their "leftism" was evidenced in many ways, including their excoriations of the party center and the proposals they put forth that gave considerable aid and comfort to Wang Jingwei (e.g., some of their proposals called for party democratization, elimination of Chiang Kai-shek's post of commander in chief, and the return of Wang to his former position of party leadership).[41] When the party center revealed its plan to overcome the considerable electoral strength of the leftists in local party branches by directly appointing half of all delegates to the GMD's Third National Congress, many of Jiangsu's county delegates resigned en masse, calling for direct election of the delegates and prompt convocation of the Congress. These actions reveal the local delegates' leftist inclinations, since it was generally agreed at the time that direct election would aid Wang, and the center's repeated postponements of the Congress would allow time for Chen Guofu and the Central Organization Department to orchestrate the Congress behind the scenes.[42]

Eventually the delegates to the Jiangsu's GMD Provincial Congress and the provincial delegates to the Third National Congress were selected by the *jiabei quanding* system, by which the lower-level congress chose twice the number of delegates allotted it, and then the upper-level party committee selected the proper number of delegates from that slate of nominees. This process produced a Jiangsu Provincial Party Congress that defies easy factional characterization. Among other things the Congress, meeting in February 1929, adopted resolutions asking Wang Jingwei to return to the country—something certainly not consonant with the hope of the Central Organization Department. The Congress also chose a slate of delegates that consisted overwhelmingly of Organization group personnel.[43]

The First Provincial Congress, like both of the succeeding ones, was a freewheeling, circus-like scene of factional strife and contention, putting to rest the notion that party congresses in a Leninist-style organization are humdrum affairs in which all is preordained and carefully orchestrated. The Congress attacked several high officials in Jiangsu's government, including the commissioner of civil affairs, Miao Bin, who enjoyed the protection of military leader He Yingqin and Chiang Kai-shek; the commissioner of finance, Zhang Shouyong, who had ties to minister of finance, T. V. Soong, who had his own national-level faction;

and chief educational administrator Zhang Naiyan, a nephew of Zhang Jingjiang, a veteran politician.[44] The major Jiangsu party factions—the Organization Clique affiliates, the Anti-CC group, and the Reorganizationist Clique—certainly were not harmed by these impeachments.[45]

Jiangsu Provincial Executive Committee

The Standing Committee of the CEC, selecting from the nominees put forward by the Jiangsu GMD's First Provincial Congress, appointed five Organization Clique associates, three Anti-CC members, and one Reorganizationist to the Second Jiangsu Provincial Executive Committee. Four of the five Organization Clique associates on the committee were members of the provincial CC Clique. The period when this committee was active—most of 1929—represents the high tide of CC Clique power in Jiangsu; by 1930 other provincial cliques associated with the central Organization Clique would elbow the CC Clique aside.[46]

If 1929 was the high point for the CC Clique, Anti-CC people would also later look back to this time as a peak period of their own influence at the provincial level. The three Anti-CC members usually voted as a bloc with the Reorganization Clique member, and Ye Chucang was often absent, thereby giving the Anti-CC forces half the votes on the committee. It is somewhat unclear why the Provincial Congress and the CEC had produced a provincial executive committee so different in factional makeup from the slate of delegates that they had sent to the Third National Congress. Whereas only two of the nine Jiangsu delegates attending the National Congress were Anti-CC or Reorganizationist partisans, four of the nine members of the executive committee were.[47] Records of Provincial Congress's votes for the delegates to the National Congress indicate that the CEC's standing committee manipulated selections by by-passing the highest vote-getters at the Provincial Congress in favor of Organization Clique cadres, but that does not explain why the standing committee did not do likewise in choosing the provincial executive committee.[48] Perhaps compromise and horse trading were responsible; the Organization Department and Chiang Kai-shek placed a high priority on controlling the National Congress in the face of Wang Jingwei's opposition, so they may have traded seats on the provincial executive committee for delegates to the National Congress.

Just as perplexing is the manner in which the provincial executive committee divided its responsibilities and offices among its members. It voted Ye Chucang (with ties to the Organization group), Zhou Jieren (CC), and Qi Xiyong (CC) to its standing committee, while making Gu Ziyang (Anti-CC) head of the provincial Organization Department; Teng Gu (Reorganization) was designated head of the Propaganda Department; and Zhu Jianbai (CC), Ni Bi (Anti-CC), and Gu (Anti-CC) were picked to serve as the Mass Training Committee. This division of duties created a potentially unstable and unworkable situation in which the most important department heads, figures in the Anti-CC group, could easily be blocked in any action by an Organization group-controlled standing committee.[49]

Factional bickering soon immobilized the provincial party, and in June 1929 the Anti-CC and Reorganizationist members of the executive committee (Gu, Ni, Ge Jianshi, Teng, and three alternate members) resigned en masse. Gu later cited "lack of unanimity," "conflicting opinions," and "difficulties in work" as the reasons for the resignations.[50] It is likely that the factional incompatibility between the major departmental chairmen and the standing committee was partially responsible for the discord. A few days earlier the provincial Organization Department, which was controlled by the Anti-CC Clique, had announced a plan whereby it claimed sole authority in "guiding" county party organs, and, especially, their congresses.[51] This could have been unsettling to the Organization Clique-controlled standing committee, which had an interest in local party congresses and, particularly, their elections of local party officials and delegates to the provincial congresses. Moreover, the standing committee had concurrent powers and prerogatives to oversee and supervise Jiangsu party affairs.

The central party headquarters refused to accept the Anti-CC leaders' resignations and sent Dai Jitao to meet with the provincial executive committee to resolve the conflict. Since Dai was acting as the Central Organization Department's emissary, he not surprisingly redistributed committee responsibilities in favor of the CC group. Afterward he lectured the committee on the necessity of mutual cooperation. The restructured provincial executive committee removed the crucial post of head of the provincial Organization Department from Gu and gave it to CC partisan Qi Xiyong; Gu was made chair of the Training Department—a demotion. Ge Jianshi, an Anti-CC member, was appointed chair of the Propaganda Department. The former Propaganda head, Teng Gu, a left-leaning artist who had ties with both the Anti-CC group and the Reorganizationist Clique, was appointed to the standing committee, where his votes could be overridden by the three other members—Wang Baoxuan (CC) and two other persons linked with the Organization factional network.[52] The stalemate thereby had been resolved largely in favor of the CC Clique and its central-level sponsors.

Although this turn of events was quite negative from the perspective of the Anti-CC and Reorganization groups, those factions still retained considerable power in the Jiangsu GMD. But in November of 1929 a failed uprising by the Anti-CC group's Reorganizationist allies would permanently undercut the Anti-CC group's position and guarantee that the Organization group and its provincial allies would hold the preponderance of power for the balance of the Nanjing Decade. By late November, Gu Ziyang and several of this Anti-CC cohorts were cooling their heels in jail, while Organization-related groups assumed complete control of the provincial party. Indeed, those opposed to the Organization group would eventually look back at 1927 through 1929 as a "golden age" in which they enjoyed a great deal of authority.

2. Factional Affiliations of Selected Provincial-level Personnel[1]

CC Clique (a component of the national Organization Clique)
  Li Shouyong[2], Wang Baoxuan[2], Qi Xiyong[2], Zhou Jieren[2], Zhu Jianbai[2], Zhou Shaocheng[2], Wu Baojin[2], Chen Kanghe[2], Chen Sibai[3], He Xuyou[4], Zhao Yuzheng[5]

FF Clique (a component of the national Organization Clique)
  Ye Xiufeng[2], Zhou Houjun[2], Qiu Youzhen[2], Zhang Renjie (Zhang Gongren)[2], Zhou Fengjing[4], Pan Guojun[4], Niu Changyao[4], Zhou Huapeng[5], Huang Renyan[5], Zhang Xiaoyou[5]

Yang-Ma-Cao Clique (a component of the national Organization Clique)
  Yang Xingqin[4], Ma Yuanfang (Ma Yinbing)[4], Cao Minghuan[4], Xie Dengyu[4], Chen Zhongming[4], Wang Shan[4]

Political Academy Clique (a component of the national Organization Clique)
  Zhang Yuanyang[6], Yu Huaizhong[5], Cheng Ruyuan[5], Sun Dachen[5]

Anti-CC Clique
  Gu Ziyang[2], Ni Bi[2], Ge Jianshi[2] (prior to 1927 a member of the Western Hills Clique), Duan Muzhen[2], Ling Shaozu[2], Gu Xiping[4], Qi Shuzu[4] (also seen as part of the Reorganization Clique), Liang Cunren[5], Liu Chengrui[5], Cao Binggan[5]

Reorganization Clique
  Teng Gu[7], Lu Yinquan[6], Zhang Shishi[6], Luo Jigang[6], Xu Wentian[4], Qi Shuzu[5] (also part of the Anti-CC Clique), Lu Dun[5], Teng Yangzhi[5], Yang Fang[8]

Western Hills Clique
  Ge Jianshi[3] (after the 1927 purge, a member of the Anti-CC Clique), Fan Xiongyi[9], Yang Sili[9], Shen Susheng[9], Gao Yuesheng[9], Song Zhenlun[9], Tang Qiyu[9], Chen Qubing[9], He Haiqiao[9], Liu Yunzhao[10], Feng Shiqi[10]

3. The Qidong Land Reform Movement

There is a prominent exception to the general pattern of post-rectification local party torpor and disinterest in challenging local elites and their interests. The Qidong County GMD seems to have retained much of its radical character, even after rectification. This is largely a result of the fact that a couple of radical, but influential, party members managed to get themselves appointed to the Qidong County GMD's Rectification Committee. One of the two, Zhou Ruqian, had been appointed by the provincial party headquarters because he was an associate of Zhou Shaocheng, a key leader of Jiangsu's CC Clique. At the same time, Zhou Ruqian maintained close relations with important Communist leaders in Qidong county. In 1929 he cooperated with Qidong Communist leaders in supporting peasant rent resistance in one of the county's townships, and it is said that while he was a member of the local rectification committee he buried in the local party archives all of the center's directives ordering effective anti-Communist action. In short, he offered protection to local Communist leaders when he could.[1] His case demonstrates that, although Organization Clique leaders had succeeded in putting a lid on the radicalism, independence, and activism of most GMD branches, not all members of the Organization Clique network were uninterested in fundamental socioeconomic change.

After the local GMD's rectification, Zhou, together with a few leftists and Communists who had gone through the rectification unscathed, put together a land reform plan and attempted to get it approved by the provincial government. This original plan was based on the fact that Qidong had a permanent tenancy system, in which landlords owned the "subsoil rights" to the land and tenants owned "surface rights."[2] Tenants' ownership of surface rights to a plot of land guaranteed their permanent right to rent the land at stable rent levels—unless they came to owe more rent than the surface rights were worth, in which case they could be evicted by the landlord. For the past hundred years or more, the market price of tenants' surface rights had risen so dramatically that, according to memoirs, Qidong tenants' surface rights were selling for nine times the price of landlords' subsoil rights. Accordingly, the original land reform plan that Zhou and some Communist representatives constructed called for division of all tenanted lands, with nine parts of the land going to the tenants, and one part going to landlords, a partition formula supposedly based on the capital that the two sides had invested in the land.[3]

It was soon clear that this first plan had no chance of being adopted, so Zhou and his allies in the local GMD, together with the county's peasant association and education association, devised a new land reform scheme in 1936 and urged the provincial government to adopt it. Zhou argued that the proposed reform was designed to end landlord-tenant disputes and implied that it would increase the harmony between Qidong and neighboring Chongming County, and it would "restore villages." Thus, he justified it in language similar to that used by Organization Clique leaders, who often spoke on the themes of social harmony and "restoration."[4] No doubt, Zhou hoped through such rhetoric to get the Organization Clique leaders' support for the plan.

In fact, since this new plan called for government confiscation only of land held by landlords who resided in neighboring Chongming county, Zhou might appear more as a champion of local interests than a social radical; in fact, he was both. A unique local situation existed whereby roughly 80 percent of all the land in Qidong was owned by Chongming landlords.[5] After confiscation of the Chongming owners' lands, the government was to compensate the landlords with bonds to be paid off with interest over a period of six years with rent forwarded by former tenants. At the end of six years the land was to become the property of the former tenants, who were to begin to pay land tax.

After receiving a draft of Zhou's plan, the Jiangsu Land Administration Bureau asked its Qidong branch to investigate the local situation and report back. In reaction, Liu Xiuqing, the head of the Qidong Land Administration Bureau, came out with a more elaborate version of the plan. Liu, who was a graduate of the Central Political Academy's land administration division, submitted the revised version to the provincial bureau, which registered its approval and sent it to the provincial government committee for final approval. A cryptically positive response by the government to the proposal so thrilled the local GMD branch and its allies that they began to rally peasants to their cause, telling them to stop rent payments. The party then started to implement the program without specific provincial government approval, though it seems soon to have abandoned that impetuous course.

In fact, it appears that the provincial government had not yet made up its mind about the program. Throughout August 1936, various branches of the government gave conflicting signals. One of the more discouraging statements, which came from the Jiangsu Commissions on Civil Affairs and Finance read:

> . . .[The] sale of land is a matter of individual freedom and should not therefore be restricted to the boundary of the district [county]. Should such a step be taken, the chances are that the tenants all over the province will demand the adoption of the same program. This will not only invite an unending confusion but will surely bring about undesirable effects on the collection of land tax as well. At present when the problem of equalizing land ownership has not yet been solved, it seems too early to adopt a system whereby the land is to be owned by its cultivator. In view of this the petition should be considered at some later time.[6]

On August 29, 1936, the provincial government ordered consultations among representatives of party, government, and all interested organizations in both affected counties. Not surprisingly, this loosed a virtual frenzy of lobbying by opponents of the plan. Chongming landlords had established a landlord's association, replete with legal counsel, to defend their interests. Each member paid a fee which went to a war chest for litigation, lobbying, and, perhaps, bribes to thwart the reforms. The association sent six representatives to lobby provincial party and government leaders and dispatched others to talk with the head of the multicounty supervisory inspectorate (*ducha zhuanyuan*) that included Chongming. The association also rallied members of Chongming's native place associations (*tongxianghui*), especially those in Shanghai and Nanjing. Chongming natives in high positions in the government and party were enlisted in the cause. The landlords' partisans also published their views in local and provincial newspapers and journals, vigorously opposing the proposed land reform, and claiming that local GMD leaders were advocating "invidious communism."

It is not difficult to understand the landlords' hatred of the scheme; in financial terms it amounted to confiscation without adequate compensation. The suggested bond interest level was 6 percent a year, far below the common interest rates for loans in the countryside. Moreover, these bonds, which were to be paid back over six years, would have provided only a tiny fraction of the income that rent on the land would have produced over a lifetime of ownership.

Not to be outdone, the plan's supporters set up their own organization to lobby and disseminate propaganda. They marshaled to their side forty-three township peasant associations, which issued a statement of support. Local women held incense-burning public prayer vigils in support of the reformers.[7]

Besides the Qidong County leaders, it appears that few in Jiangsu's GMD supported the proposal.[8] Journals and magazines in Jiangsu detailed the arguments against it. The proposal, they said, distorted Sun Yat-sen's ideas on land reform, was confiscatory, and was shot through with local bias. Opponents argued that the program violated several principles of existing land laws and contravened the decisions of the GMD's Third National Congress, which had postponed land reform until productivity had increased enough to allow for sustenance of "self-tilling peasants." In addition, critics said that a new class of landlords would emerge from the program, and therefore no permanent advantage would be gained.[9]

The controversy dragged on through early 1937 with no final decision by the provincial government. The landlords and their allies in the government and the provincial party had at least delayed the program for many months. Unfortunately, it is not possible to determine with certainty whether the government ever approved the plan before the Japanese invasion of 1937 made the question moot. Decades after these events, Chen Guofu, who had been the provincial governor at the time that the proposal had been tendered, hinted that he had favored the program and that it had originated with the provincial government. He claimed that the government finally passed the measure, but that the Japanese invasion postponed its implementation. Chen's disciple Xiao Zheng writes that the plan was enacted in two year's time with the help of students of the Central Political Academy. But the veracity of both of these accounts is in doubt. There is no evidence in contemporary sources to back the claim that the provincial government ever approved the plan, and there is ample memoir testimony from other quarters that the reform scheme was blocked by a provincial government more conservative than the local GMD leaders who had conceived the plan. Moreover, the memoirs indicate that the provincial party headquarters in 1937 or 1938 revoked the party memberships of the Qidong GMD leaders who were behind the land reform plan.[10] In short, while the Qidong GMD was exceptional in its persistent agitation against landlord interests, it was apparently unsuccessful in that advocacy.

NOTES

Abbreviations

GMDA   Guomindang Archives, Taibei
NTHA   Number Two Historical Archives, Nanjing

Notes to Chapter 1

[1] Ni Bi, "Duiyu Jiangsu ge xian zhengzhi de ganxiang he xiwang" (Opinions and hopes with regard to the politics of various Jiangsu counties), *Jiangsu xunkan* 2 (September 11, 1928): 12.

[2] There are a few historians who have written about the radicalism that survived within the GMD after the purge. See, for example, Patrick Cavendish, "The 'New China' of the Kuomintang," in *Modern China's Search for a Political Form*, ed. Jack Grey (London: Oxford University Press, 1969), 138–86; So Wai-chor, *The Kuomintang Left in the National Revolution, 1924–1931* (Hong Kong: Oxford University Press, 1991).

[3] Kenneth Jowitt, *The Leninist Response to National Dependency* (Berkeley: Institute of International Relations, University of California, 1978), 1–33. Gunnar Myrdal has argued that the high degree of social and economic stratification in some parts of Asia has, in itself, impeded industrialization; see his *Asian Drama: An Inquiry Into the Poverty of Nations,* abridged by Seth S. King (New York: Pantheon, 1971), 97–109, 147–48. Some analysts have claimed that a key prerequisite to modernization of any country is the creation of a new elite with an ethos and skills suited to leadership in an era of mass politics and industrialization. For example, see I. Robert Sinai, *The Challenge of Modernization: The West's Impact on the Non-Western World* (New York: W. W. Norton and Co. Inc., 1964), 217.

[4] See, for example, Philip A. Kuhn, *Rebellion and Its Enemies in Late Imperial China* (Cambridge, Mass.: Harvard University Press, 1970), 225; Gilbert Rozman, ed., *The Modernization of China* (New York: The Free Press, 1981), 295–99. Yung Teh-chow, *Social Mobility in China: Status Careers Among the Gentry in a Chinese Community* (New York: Atherton Press, 1966) paints an ugly picture of local elites—he calls them "gentry"—in a locality in Yunnan. Ichiko Chuzo

downplays the patriotism and political consciousness of provincial and local elites and emphasizes their conservative nature in "The Role of the Gentry: An Hypothesis," in Mary Clabaugh Wright, ed., *China in Revolution: The First Phase, 1900–1913* (New Haven: Yale University Press, 1968), 311–12.

[5] Lloyd E. Eastman, *The Abortive Revolution: China Under Nationalist Rule, 1927–1937* (Cambridge, Mass.: Harvard University Press, 1974), 241–43, 286; Lloyd E. Eastman, "New Insights into the Nature of the Nationalist Regime," *Republican China* 9.2 (February 1984): 8–18. See also Philip A. Kuhn, "Local Self-Government Under the Republic: Problems of Control, Autonomy, and Mobilization," in *Conflict and Control in Late Imperial China*, ed. Frederic Wakeman, Jr. and Carolyn Grant (Berkeley: University of California Press, 1975), 294–95. For a more detailed survey of the historiography of the GMD regime's social relations—at least up to 1979, see Bradley Kent Geisert, "Power and Society: The Kuomintang and Local Elites in Kiangsu Province, China, 1924–1937" (Ph.D. diss., University of Virginia, 1979), 1–8. A more recent work that describes tension between the Nationalist regime and local elites is Helen Chauncey's *Schoolhouse Politicians: Locality and State During the Chinese Republic* (Honolulu: University of Hawaii Press, 1992). At one time I argued that because of a considerable number of documented cases in which entities outside the GMD regime were able to influence decision making, we ought to consider applying a pluralist model to Nationalist China (Bradley K. Geisert, "Toward a Pluralist Model of KMT Rule," *Chinese Republican Studies Newsletter* 11.2 [February 1982]: 1–10). I have decided, however, that because the term "pluralism" carries with it too many connotations of democracy, it might mislead some readers. Zhang Yimin argues that the conflict that Eastman sees between the rural landlord class and the GMD regime was temporary; he believes that the relations between the GMD regime (1927–1937) and "landlord gentry" changed over time. He characterizes the shift by repeating Mao's phrase "unity—struggle—unity." In his view, at the time of the purge the local elites and the GMD authorities were unified by their desire to purge the Communists. Soon thereafter the centralizing thrust that Eastman spotlighted created tension and conflict between the GMD regime and landlord elites. This was followed, Zhang believes, by a reevaluation of policy by the GMD and a recasting of measures and methods to rebuild unity between the regime and elites. See Zhang Yimin, "1927–1937: Nanjing Guomindang zhengquan yu Jiang Zhe dizhu haoshen" (The Nanjing Nationalist Party regime and the powerful landlord gentry of Jiangsu and Zhejiang, 1927–1937), *Dang'an yu lishi* (February 1989): 56–62.

[6] Prasenjit Duara, *Culture, Power and the State: Rural North China, 1900–1942* (Stanford: Stanford University Press, 1988).

[7] Prasenjit Duara, in his *Rescuing History From the Nation: Questioning Narratives of Modern China* (Chicago: University of Chicago Press, 1995), treats the

antisuperstition movement in a unique and insightful way. Another historian who has paid attention to the religious leadership roles of Chinese elites is Roger Thompson. See his "Cultural Imperialism and the Modernizing State: Reviewing Rural China, 1861–1911," unpublished paper prepared for annual meeting of the Association for Asian Studies, March 1998, Washington, D. C.

[8] William T. Rowe, "The Problem of 'Civil Society' in Late Imperial China," *Modern China* 19.2 (April 1993): 148. Works that follow this line include William T. Rowe, *Hankow: Commerce and Society in a Chinese City, 1796–1889* (Stanford: Stanford University Press, 1984); David Strand, *Rickshaw Beijing: City People and Politics in the 1920s* (Berkeley: University of California Press, 1989); and Mary Backus Rankin, *Elite Activism and Political Transformation in China: Zhejiang Province, 1865–1911* (Stanford: Stanford University Press, 1986).

[9] Rankin, *Elite Activism*, 24. Rankin has more recently stated that local elites "were not autonomous, but nevertheless enjoyed sometimes considerable latitude within culturally and politically constructed boundaries and derived part of their power from local societies or groups." See Mary Backus Rankin, "State and Society in Early Republican Politics, 1912–18," *China Quarterly* 150 (June 1997): 271.

[10] For a criticism of scholarship positing the existence of a civil society/public sphere in China, see Frederic Wakeman, Jr., "The Civil Society and Public Sphere Debate: Western Reflections on Chinese Political Culture," *Modern China* 19.2 (April 1993): 108–138. This article is part of a symposium on "public sphere/civil society" in China that fills an entire issue of *Modern China*. Taken together, the articles in the symposium demonstrate that quite a number of different definitions of both "public sphere" and, especially, "civil society" are employed by those writing about China, not to mention the many others who have used the terms in other contexts. Particularly influential in shaping use of the terms has been the work of Jürgen Habermas, though many Western thinkers (Locke, Hobbes, Hegel, Tocqueville, and Thomas Paine) all used the term "civil society" in their own ways. Both "public sphere" and "civil society," in fact, are used as shorthand for a cacophony of viewpoints and concepts, making interchange on this issue area, at best, very complex.

One of the China scholars known for her part in discussion of these concepts strongly advised me not to allow myself to be dragged into the civil society/public sphere debate—an area of inquiry that she characterizes as somewhat played out and overdone. Following her advice, I do not make this debate a centerpiece in this study, though in this note I do consider what my findings might mean in the light of the public sphere concept.

Definitional problems associated with the term "public sphere" are considerable. Many scholars base their work on Jürgen Habermas's writings; see especially his *The Structural Transformation of the Public Sphere: An Inquiry into a*

Category of Bourgeois Society, trans. Thomas Burger (Cambridge, Mass.: The MIT Press, 1989). Philip Huang has called attention to the fact that Habermas has used "public sphere" in two different senses, but in the passages that Huang cites, Habermas actually speaks of three (and also invokes yet another type of public entity that he does not dub a "public sphere"). One of Habermas's three versions of "public sphere" refers to a realm that arose (along with capitalism and the bourgeoisie) in England in the late 1600s and in France in the 1700s. This realm, the bourgeois, liberal public sphere, stood outside an earlier type of public arena that Habermas evokes. (He calls this fourth entity "representative publicness," a term he applies to some of the publicly visible ritualistic roles of the territorial lords in late medieval Europe.) The bourgeois, liberal public sphere, which in part grew out of the private sphere, was centered on rational discourse. Habermas draws his definition of the bourgeois public sphere so narrowly that he sees this entity as having died out in Europe and America in the nineteenth century with the advent of mass politics, propaganda, and eventually, the social welfare state. Habermas speaks of a second kind of public sphere, a plebeian public sphere, which grew up in the context of the bourgeois public sphere. This second variety of public sphere, though still "oriented toward the intentions of the bourgeois public sphere," took as its subject the uneducated masses. This second species of public sphere was represented by some of the organizational forms that appeared in the Robespierrean phase of the French Revolution, the Chartist Movement, and the anarchist workers' movement. Habermas also mentions a third sort of public sphere, something he calls "the plebiscitary-acclamatory form of regimented public sphere characterizing dictatorships in highly developed industrialized societies" (Philip C.C. Huang, "'Public Sphere'/'Civil Society' in China?: The Third Realm between State and Society," *Modern China* 19.2 [April 1993]: 216–17). Huang conflates the latter two versions. Also see Habermas, *The Structural Transformation*, xvii–xix. These three quite different, though somewhat vague, formulations are sometimes conflated or abandoned in discussions of the public sphere in China. Habermas further complicates the picture by distinguishing between "political public sphere," "literary public sphere," and "representative public sphere," three variants I will ignore here.

In fact, Rankin and Rowe did their early work without reference to Habermas's definitions, having been led to the concepts by the fact that the Chinese had used the term "public" to refer to an arena between the government's bureaucratic and the "private" realms. Not surprisingly then, their works use somewhat different working definitions of public sphere than Habermas. Neither of them put the emphasis on "rationality" of discourse in the sphere that Habermas's first definition would seem to demand. Moreover, Rankin's public sphere, though importantly related to the bourgeoisie, is not so thoroughly bourgeois as that of Habermas's first definition. Thus, Rowe's and

Rankin's working definitions of public sphere, though closer to Habermas's first definition than to his second or third, vary from it in important ways.

"Civil society" is a concept even more devoid of common definitional understanding than "public sphere." For many observers, the hallmark of civil society is the existence of "voluntary associations unconnected to and unsponsored by the state" (R. Keith Schoppa, "Contours of Revolutionary Change in a Chinese County, 1900–1950," *Journal of Asian Studies* 51.4 [November 1992]: 778). For others the issue is not lack of *any connection* of "civil society" to the state, but rather "autonomy" from the state, while others posit civil society to be "relatively autonomous." Still others insist that civil society "partakes of both [state and society], and faces and constantly interacts with both." Some treat the whole matter of any sort of autonomy of organizations as irrelevant. See Heath B. Chamberlain, "On the Search for Civil Society in China," *Modern China* 19.2 (April 1993): 202–207; and Heath B. Chamberlain, "Review Essay: Civil Society With Chinese Characteristics," *The China Journal* 39 (January 1998): 76–78. In fact, some see the form and relation to government of formal organizations as irrelevant to the issue of civil society, instead focusing on the rise of *guanxi* (networks of personal connections) as a type of civil society (Mayfair Mei-hui Yang, *Gifts, Favors, and Banquets: The Art of Social Relationships in China* [Ithaca: Cornell University Press, 1994]). Certain others who downplay the definitional importance of organizations' relations to the state argue that what is important is civility or lack of it in relations among individuals within organizations. In this formulation, it is the "relative freedom of group members," rather than the organizations' "relative autonomy from the state" that is important in identifying civil society. And to some scholars the mere fact that individuals in a society embrace a critical perspective on the state is enough to signify the rise of a civil society. Finally, certain commentators have argued against the use of the term "civil society" on the grounds that it is distortive to apply to China a term derived from Western European experience (Chamberlain, "Review Essay," 74–80).

Study of the Nationalist Party does not fit easily or neatly into the scholarly conversation about whether or not there was a public sphere in Republican China, and if so, what that sphere looked like. Some might choose, for example, to see the party as but a part of the state during the Nanjing Decade. In party mythology and sloganeering, the government was a creature of the party and was to do its bidding. This would seem to situate the party in the commanding heights of the state, rather than as part of a "public sphere" that was separate from the state. The rhetoric of party leaders that spoke in terms of "awakening" the masses to the party's vision suggested a top-down imposition of views rather than a free exchange of ideas—a rational dialogue, in the sense that Habermas invoked in his first definition of public sphere. In reality, in the 1930s local party branches became more like underlings of the government than directors of it, but either way the party would seem to have been a component of the state.

From another perspective, however, the party could be seen as a part of the public sphere, at least in the 1920s. In Jiangsu the reorganized GMD started as a nongovernmental organization—something clearly outside of the state. The Chinese Nationalist Party, as it took shape in the early to mid-1920s, provided a frame through which individuals other than established elites acted with considerable autonomy to explore what the demands of patriotism might be, to advocate radical change, to pursue leadership ambitions, and to attack pretty much whomever they saw fit to overthrow. To be sure, the propaganda work of the party and the electoral contests within the party in no way resembled the rational discourse that Habermas associates with the concept of "public sphere." See Craig Calhoun, "Introduction: Habermas and the Public Sphere," in Craig Calhoun, ed., *Habermas and the Public Sphere* (Cambridge, Mass.: The MIT Press 1992, 1994), 9. It is, of course, questionable whether the public sphere at any time or place ever embodied the rationality that Habermas associates with the concept.

The autonomy from the state that the party enjoyed in the period before the Northern Expedition came in large part from the fact that it operated outside of the law. It was a revolutionary organization. Prior to 1927 the GMD in Jiangsu was not licensed by the state, unlike the entities managed by established elites. It was not the case, of course, that the warlord-era state willingly granted political space to the GMD, or that a broad citizenry or powerfully organized interests forced the state to concede political space to the party. To some extent, the GMD in Jiangsu before 1927 occupied the same space in which rebel movements and secret societies had operated for centuries; the party existed underground, in the cracks between the points of government control. Nonetheless, local party activists became accustomed to acting in a rather freewheeling fashion.

After the GMD in Jiangsu became the adjunct of the government in a one-party state in 1927, many party activists continued to act autonomously, as if the party was an organization situated in the public sphere, as if it should, by all rights, not be closely controlled by central organs of the state. The theme of "democracy" that the GMD left wing touted, at the behest of Wang Jingwei, in the late 1920s bespeaks the concern of young GMD radicals that local party activists should enjoy autonomy. Wang held that Chiang Kai-shek's Nanjing regime had trampled on rights—that party rule, properly understood, would not restrict peoples' rights, but instead would augment them (So Wai-chor, *The Kuomintang Left*, 113). Wang wrote that mass organizations should enjoy independence and that the party should not coerce them to follow party dictates. Similarly, he argued that those highest in the party hierarchy should listen to local party leaders, and those local leaders should be free to press their case. However, Wang upheld the principle of "democratic centralism" and held that lower party levels should obey when those at the upper levels had reached a decision. Exactly how large a public sphere he and his minions would have left free for autonomous action had they controlled the state and central party is in the final analysis unclear. Wang saw the need for the party to "guide the people" and control "feudal elements" as it implemented local self-government. Despite his stated desire to limit party power, it is not so clear how Wang would have reacted if the party's bestowal of greater rights to the people had failed to elicit increasing measures of support from the people as he anticipated it would (So Wai-chor, *The Kuomintang Left*, 112–17). In other words, just as Chiang's Nationalist regime stood in the way of the emergence of a strong and vibrant "public sphere" in China, it is debatable how much public space Chiang's competitors for power might have been willing to concede for autonomous action and free interchange of ideas.

[11] Bryna Goodman, *Native Place, City, and Nation: Regional Networks and Identities in Shanghai, 1853–1937* (Berkeley: University of California Press, 1995), 204.

[12] This is not to say that the party is totally ignored by recent works. For example, David Strand pays some attention to the party, though it is hardly at the center of his vision. Christian Henriot also treats the Nationalist Party; see his *Shanghai, 1927–1937: Municipal Power, Locality, and Modernization*, trans. Noël Castelino (Berkeley: University of California Press, 1993).

[13] One recent study which does sometimes treat local and provincial factionalism, though it mainly deals with central-level politics is: Guo Xuyin, ed., *Guomindang paixi douzheng shi* (Shanghai: Renmin chuban she, 1992). An interesting article on local GMD factionalism, specifically describing Jiangxi's AB Clique, is Stephen C. Averill, "The Origins of the Futian Incident," in Tony Saich and Hans van de Ven, eds., *New Perspectives on the Chinese Communist Revolution* (Armonk, N.Y.: M. E. Sharpe, 1995), 79-115. Diana Lary has written of a provincial military clique in her *Region and Nation: The Kwangsi Clique in Chinese Politics, 1925-1937* (Cambridge: Cambridge University Press, 1974).

It has been argued by some social scientists that the term "clique" should be distinguished from "faction." F. G. Bailey has argued that cliques are "proto-factions," groups that are not necessarily political, but have "near horizons, are personalized, and covert." They embrace a "standard of morality and mutual forbearance" within the group. And though they "are not in combat with other groups such as factions, they are readily suspected by others of conspiracy." According to Bailey, if a clique takes political action, it is only for defensive purposes--to withdraw from a situation--rather than "to manipulate the world." If a clique does engage in political action in some way that goes beyond the defensive, it becomes a faction. See F. G. Bailey, "The Definition of Factionalism," in M. Silverman and R. F. Salisbury, eds., *A House Divided?: Anthropological*

Studies of Factionalism (Newfoundland, Canada: Institute of Social and Economic Research, Memorial University of Newfoundland, University of Toronto Press, 1977), 32. However, this definition for "clique" seems hazy at best. It seems to create a distinction without much of a difference. For example, should a clientelist network that is at four or five identifiable moments involved in political conflict be considered a "faction" at those moments, and a "clique" during the intervals in between those times of political conflict? Or is a grouping forever to be considered a faction because it participates just once in political conflict? And what exactly is "political conflict?" Is networking that enhances the prestige and influence of a person such that he is looked up to as an arbiter—someone who can solve everyday disputes—to be considered the action of a faction or a clique? What if the network builder is in quiet competition with the builder of another *guanxi* network? What if the network builders never compete for formal political office? Is this informal competition to be considered politics? Since most who study Nationalist China even append the word "clique" to the names of some of the GMD "factions," I will follow suit and use the two terms interchangeably. The metaphysical subtleties of the definitional distinction between "faction" and "clique" are, I believe, not useful; they require a certain obliviousness to the complexity of the real world.

[14] Henriot, *Shanghai, 1927–1937*, 3.

[15] John Lossing Buck, *Land Utilization in China* (Nanking: University of Nanking, 1937; New York: Paragon Book Reprint Corp., 1964), 67–68.

[16] Probably the most well-known work that focuses on the CCP in its secure base at Yan'an is Mark Selden, *The Yenan Way in Revolutionary China* (Cambridge, Mass.: Harvard University Press, 1971). Of course, Jiangsu was by no means completely secure, as demonstrated by the 1932 Japanese invasion in the Shanghai area. Although after about 1930, Communists did not pose a serious threat in the province, prior to that time GMD authorities faced an aggressive CCP movement centered in the area of Taixing and Rugao. The late 1920s also saw sporadic Communist uprisings in other Jiangsu counties, especially in the south. For information on the CCP in Jiangsu, see Lenore Barkan, "Nationalists, Communists, and Rural Leaders: Political Dynamics in a Chinese County, 1927–1937" (Ph.D. diss., University of Washington, 1983), especially 460–527.

[17] A well-informed discussion of these various terms, as well as the concept of Subei persons as an ethnic group, can be found in Emily Honig, *Creating Chinese Ethnicity: Subei People in Shanghai, 1850–1980* (New Haven: Yale University Press, 1992), 18–35.

[18] I follow G. William Skinner's definition of the Lower Yangzi and North China regions, which he delineated according to river valleys, with the North China region consisting of the watersheds of the Yellow and Huai Rivers; see his "Regional Urbanization in Nineteenth-Century China," in G. William Skinner,

ed., *The City in Late Imperial China* (Stanford: Stanford University Press, 1977), 210–20.

To define this urbanized and commercialized core area, I have relied heavily upon population density data for Jiangsu's *xian* supplied in Zhao Ruheng, *Jiangsu shengjian* (Shanghai: Xin Zhongguo jianguo xueshe, 1935), vol. 1, *zhang* 1, 28–36. While it would be better to use statistics on urban dwellers as a percentage of the population, we have no such figures that seem even marginally reliable. Both Skinner and Keith Schoppa have argued that population density figures may be used as an indicator, however imperfect, of degrees of urbanization and commercialization. Schoppa believes, however, that population density by itself is not an adequate determinant of core status. See R. Keith Schoppa, *Chinese Elites and Political Change: Zhejiang Province in the Early Twentieth Century* (Cambridge, Mass.: Harvard University Press, 1982), 17, 208; Skinner, "Regional Urbanization," 216; G. William Skinner, "Cities and the Hierarchy of Local Systems," in *The City in Late Imperial China*, ed. G. William Skinner (Stanford: Stanford University Press, 1977), 282-86.

[19] In the case of Baoshan, the most urbanized sector of the *xian* had been annexed into Shanghai municipality; thus Baoshan's relatively lower population density figures are, arguably, a result of gerrymandering; see Li Changfu, *Fen sheng dizhi: Jiangsu* (Shanghai: Zhonghua shuju youxian gongsi, 1936), 305–6. Although Chuansha city was not particularly big, many of its elites had originally made their fortunes in commerce and industry in Shanghai. Since my focus is on elites, it seems appropriate to consider Chuansha as a part of Shanghai's core.

In short, the *xian* is a less-than-perfect unit of statistical analysis. Yixing, the only county included in the core that is not in Shanghai's "nearby hinterland," would have made the list of core *xian* by virtue of its population density had it not been for the mountains in the southern part of the county. I include it in the core because the habitable parts of the county were densely populated, and descriptive sources indicate it was rather well developed. (Data on the habitable flatlands in each county are found in Zhao Ruheng, *Jiangsu shengjian*, vol. 1, *zhang* 1, 22–27. On Yixing's commercial and educational development, see Li Changfu, *Fen sheng dizhi*, 287–90.)

The northern delta of the Yangzi provides further evidence of the problem posed by using the county as the unit of analysis. Kathy Walker has recently observed that only some of the southern parts of Nantong County constituted the core area of the cotton textile industry centered in Nantong. Large portions of the counties in the northern delta that I include in the Lower Yangzi core were, she argues, economically peripheral. She observes that Chongming had "no modern nor native banks," Haimen boasted only "one small native bank . . . in 1920," and Rugao was part of the agricultural periphery of Nantong city. So some of the counties that I place in the Lower Yangzi core included large areas which displayed little if any industrialization or growth of commercial institutions. Nonetheless, Walker does posit that during the late Qing and early Republican eras, the influence of "international, comprador, and local urban-based capital" were powerful enough in the northern delta to provide a frame in which agriculture was drastically restructured to the disadvantage of peasant farmers. See Kathy Le Mons Walker, *Chinese Modernity and the Peasant Path: Semicolonialism in the Northern Yangzi Delta* (Stanford: Stanford University Press, 1999), 125–27, 203.

No scheme for dividing the province is perfect. Perhaps the greatest shortcoming of my depiction of the urbanized and commercialized core is that it fails adequately to take account of Nanjing. When this city became the Nationalists' capital in 1927, it was already a huge, if somewhat sleepy, metropolis with a population of around 370,000. (On the status of Nanjing on the eve of and during the Nanjing Decade, see Maryruth Coleman, "Municipal Politics in Nationalist China: Nanjing, 1927–1937" [Ph.D. diss, Harvard University, 1984].) It is, therefore, somewhat misleading to exclude that city from the core. One way to have handled this problem would have been to merge the figures for Nanjing and Jiangning County (which envelops it), thereby making Jiangning a part of the core. This would, however, have made the core less comprehensible to the reader because it would not have been contiguous. Another way to solve this problem would have been to follow G. William Skinner's map of the Lower Yangzi core and include virtually the entire southern third of Jiangsu in that core area (Skinner, "Regional Urbanization," 214–15). However, that would entail inclusion of some of Jiangsu's most sparsely populated and least urbanized large *xian* (in southwestern Jiangsu), most notably Lishui and Jurong. Available population density figures and other information do not justify inclusion of southwestern Jiangsu in the Lower Yangzi core. In conversations with me, Randy Stross has forcefully and persuasively made the case that southwestern Jiangsu was a backwater. The information in Li Changfu's gazetteer as well as other sources back up this impression. For more on the backwardness of Jiangsu's southwest, see Randy Stross, "A Hard Row to Hoe: The Political Economy of Chinese Agriculture in Western Jiangsu, 1911–1937" (Ph.D. diss., Stanford University, 1982).

Population density is not a completely reliable indicator of urbanization. (It measures, among other things, the labor intensiveness of agriculture.) Another shortcoming of population density as an index of urbanization is best demonstrated by the comparative rankings of Wu and Rugao *xian*. Whereas the population density figures would suggest that Rugao was more urbanized than Wu (Suzhou), we know that that was not the case. In fact, Lenore Barkan has described Rugao as a "backwater relatively isolated from the large cities of China," while Wu was one of the most commercialized and urbanized *xian* in

Jiangsu (Barkan, "Nationalists, Communists," 52). Although I have included Rugao in the core, I consider it, like several *xian* at the outer reaches of the core, to have just barely met the standards for inclusion. (One source which argues that business was "rather prosperous" in some parts of Rugao is Li Changfu, *Fen sheng dizhi*, 342.) Population density figures for Wu *xian* were skewed because so much of the *xian* was covered by water. When correction is made for this, Wu again assumes its place near the top rank. (For figures on habitable land, see Zhao Ruheng, *Jiangsu shengjian*, vol. 1, *zhang* 1, 22–27.)

[20] A considerable amount of information is, of course, available on Jiangning County, because it surrounded the Nationalists' capital, Nanjing. However, in the early 1930s when Jiangning became an experimental (and virtually autonomous) *xian*, Jiangsu's government and party lost authority over it. Therefore, policies pursued there cannot be considered to illustrate the policy and strategy of the Jiangsu government or party. Furthermore, the bulk of the available information on Jiangning relates to the period after that county had gained its autonomy from the provincial government.

[21] Skinner, "Regional Urbanization," 243–47.

[22] On the relative paucity of commerce and urbanization in northern Jiangsu, see Wu Shoupeng, "Xu Hai ge shu" (The various parts of the Hsu-Hai district), in Feng Hefa, ed., *Zhongguo nongcun jingji ziliao* (Shanghai: Liming shuju, 1935), 331–61, esp. 335–39. This general situation is confirmed by Li Changfu, though he does not paint quite as bleak a picture. (Li Changfu, *Fen sheng dizhi*, 154–66).

[23] Although there are many variations of the proverb, one of the most common versions is *shang you tiantang, xia you Su-Hang* (above there is heaven, here below there is the Suzhou-Hangzhou area).

[24] For information on crops grown in particular zones of the province, see Li Changfu, *Fen sheng*, 125–44; see also *China Industrial Handbooks: Kiangsu: First Series of the Reports by the National Industrial Investigation*, compiled by the Bureau of Foreign Trade, Ministry of Industry (1933; reprint, Taipei: Ch'eng Wen Publishing Co., 1973); Zhao Ruheng, *Jiangsu shengjian*; and Buck, *Land Utilization*.

[25] They were Shanghai, Suzhou, Wuxi, Zhenjiang, Changshu, Songjiang, Wujin, Haimen, Nantong, Yangzhou, and Rugao; see George B. Cressey, *Land of the 500 Million: A Geography of China* (New York: McGraw-Hill Book Co., Inc., 1955), 196–97.

[26] Information about a variety of commercial concerns abounds in *China Industrial Handbooks: Kiangsu*.

[27] For other examples, see the biographies of Zhang Wenming and Zhang Qingping in *Chuansha xianzhi* (1936) 10.16: esp. 19b, 21b, 28a.

[28] For information on gentry-merchants in the southern portion of the Lower Yangzi core, see Schoppa, *Chinese Elites and Political Change*, 59–62.

[29] Feng Hefa, ed., *Zhongguo nongcun jingji lun* (Shanghai: Liming shudian, 1936), 225–26; see also Robert Ash, *Land Tenure in Pre-Revolutionary China: Kiangsu Province in the 1920s and 1930s* (London: Contemporary China Institute, School of Oriental and African Studies, University of London, 1976), 9–11.

[30] On silting of the canal and its effect on industry and commerce, see Feng Hefa, ed. *Zhongguo nongcun jingji ziliao* (Shanghai: Liming shuju, 1935), 338.

[31] For information on railroads, highways, and waterways throughout the province, see *China Industrial Handbooks: Kiangsu*, 965–1026. However, this book is not always frank about the navigability problems of the waterways it describes.

[32] Buck, *Land Utilization*, 65–72.

[33] Elizabeth J. Perry, *Rebels and Revolutionaries in North China, 1845–1945* (Stanford: Stanford University Press, 1980), especially 40–95.

[34] Wang Yijin, "Zhongguo jindai renkou yidong zhi jingji de yanjiu" (Research on the economics of Chinese migration in the modern era), *Zhongguo jingji* 4.5 (May 1937): 5 (nonconsecutive pagination).

[35] Ash, *Land Tenure*, 9–11; Feng Hefa, *Zhongguo nongcun jingji lun*, 225–26.

[36] See Wu Shoupeng, in Feng Hefa, *Zhongguo nongcun jingji ziliao*, 331–61.

[37] Perry, *Rebels and Revolutionaries*; Skinner, "Regional Urbanization."

Notes to Chapter 2

[1] Joseph W. Esherick, *Reform and Revolution in China: The 1911 Revolution in Hunan and Hubei* (Berkeley: University of California Press, 1976), 66–142. Esherick argues that the "subordinate reformist elite" was not as effective or sweeping in its efforts as the urban reformist elite in the provincial or prefectural capitals.

[2] In Jiangsu such reformist activities seem to have been strongest in the counties of the Lower Yangzi core. For examples, see *Chuansha xian zhi*, 19:5–39. See also Mary Backus Rankin, "Local Reform Currents in Chekiang Before 1900," in *Reform in Nineteenth-Century China*, ed. Paul A. Cohen and John E. Schrecker (Cambridge, Mass.: Harvard University, East Asian Center, 1976), 221–30; Schoppa, *Chinese Elites and Political Change*, 4.

[3] See Wang Shuhuai, *Zhongguo xiandaihua de quyou yanjiu: Jiangsu sheng, 1860–1916* (Taibei: Zhongyang yanjiuyuan jindai shi yanjiusuo, 1984), 212–14; Amy Fei-man Ma, "Local Self-Government and the Local Populace in Chuansha, 1911," *Select Papers From the Center for Far Eastern Studies* 1 (1975–1976): 47–84;

Young-tsu Wong, "Popular Unrest and the 1911 Revolution in Jiangsu," *Modern China* 3.3 (July 1977): 321–42; Roxann Prazniak, "Tax Protest at Laiyang, Shandong, 1910: Commoner Organization Versus the County Political Elite," *Modern China* 6.1 (January 1980): 41–71; Roxann Prazniak, "Weavers and Sorceresses of Chuansha: The Social Origins of Political Activism Among Rural Chinese Women," *Modern China* 12.2 (April 1986): 202–229.

In a recent book Roxann Prazniak argues that the uprisings against the so-called "New Policies" entailed far more than protests over rising taxes. She holds that peasants and others in village China had imbibed a "rural culture of protest" that arose from the Taiping Rebellion, the Boxer Uprising, and other sources. This radical moral vision held in common among the farmers, laborers, and even some elites in a locality enabled those rural residents to construct networks of self-defense which they could bring to bear against threats posed by misuse of power. But they even sought to dismantle modernity itself, especially since they perceived the local self-government elites' version of the modernist project as a threat to their own precarious livelihoods. Prazniak looks at uprisings in several locations, and finds differing combinations of ingredients in each uprising, causing her to emphasize the "place-based" nature of the uprisings. See Roxann Prazniak, *Of Camel Kings and Other Things: Rural Rebels Against Modernity in Late Imperial China* (Lanham, Maryland: Roman and Littlefield Publishers, Inc., 1999), 257–66.

[4] For example, see "Zhongyang dangbu daibiao Ding Chaowu xunzi" (Admonitions from Central representative Ding Chaowu), in *Neizheng bu diyi minzheng huiyi jiyao*, ed., Neizhengbu diyi qi minzheng huiyi mishuqu (Shanghai, 1929), 284–85.

[5] Power is the ability to make others act in ways that they would not otherwise choose. Another common definition of power is "the ability to influence collective decision-making." In general, I prefer the first definition, though in many cases the latter one is useful. For discussion of the concepts of "elite" and "power," see Robert D. Putnam, *The Comparative Study of Political Elites* (Englewood Cliffs, N. J.: Prentice-Hall, 1976), especially 5–6, 15–19. I usually exclude from the category "local elites" certain major officeholders of the county government, for example the magistrates, since those persons were usually outsiders serving only briefly in the area they administered; they were both appointees and creatures of the provincial government. Nonetheless, in those situations in which magistrates and other high county appointees were local persons or stayed in office long enough to develop strong local roots, they would have to be considered local elites.

[6] For an example of the use of the concept of economic elites, see Putnam, *Comparative Study*, 25–26.

[7] Martin M. C. Yang, *Chinese Social Structure: A Historical Study* (Taipei: The National Book Company, 1971), 317; Sidney Gamble, *North China Villages: Social, Political, and Economic Activities Before 1933* (Berkeley: University of California Press, 1963), 50–51, cited in Philip C. C. Huang, *The Peasant Economy and Social Change in North China* (Stanford: Stanford University Press, 1985), 239.

[8] For accounts of the gentry and their roles in late Qing society, see T'ung-tsu Ch'ü, *Local Government in China Under the Ch'ing* (Cambridge, Mass.: Harvard University Press, 1962), 168–92; Chung-li Chang, *The Chinese Gentry: Studies on Their Role in Nineteenth-Century Chinese Society* (Seattle: University of Washington Press, 1955).

[9] The emphasis is mine. T'ung-tsu Ch'ü, *Local Government*, 168.

[10] James Hays, *The Hong Kong Region, 1850–1911* (Hamden, Conn.: Archon Books, The Shoe String Press, 1977), esp. 185–93. Also see Joseph W. Esherick and Mary Backus Rankin, "Introduction," in *Chinese Local Elites and Patterns of Dominance*, ed. by Joseph W. Esherick and Mary Backus Rankin (Berkeley: University of California Press, 1990), 9–13.

[11] The term "government-sponsored institutions" is from Keith Schoppa, and the discussion of such institutions in Jiangsu laid out in this book is informed by Schoppa's work on Zhejiang; see his *Chinese Elites and Political Change*, 31–39.

[12] Roger R. Thompson, *China's Local Councils in the Age of Constitutional Reform, 1898–1911* (Cambridge, Mass.: Council on East Asian Studies, Harvard University, 1995), 23–35, 70–87.

[13] Thompson, *China's Local Councils*, 184.

[14] Thompson, *China's Local Councils*, 72–73.

[15] R. Keith Schoppa, "Local Self-Government in Zhejiang, 1909–1927," *Modern China* 2.4 (October 1976): 504; Thompson, *China's Local Councils*, 109. Certainly the tenor of the Qing regulations, with their emphasis on oversight of the councils by county magistrates, governors, and governors general bears out this interpretation; see H. S. Brunnert and V. V. Hagelstrom, *Present Day Political Organization of China*, trans. from the Russian by A. Beltchenko and E. E. Moran (1911; reprint, Taipei: Ch'eng-wen 1971), 83. The Qing rulers also sought to deflect local elites from participation in politics by encouraging these new elite-managed assemblies to exert their whole effort on what the regime hoped would be essentially nonpolitical activities like education, social service, and public works (Schoppa, "Local Self-Government," 505).

[16] Schoppa, "Local Self-Government," 509–513; Philip A. Kuhn, "Local Self-Government Under the Republic," 277–80. Both Kuhn and Schoppa call attention to the key role played in the local self-government apparatus by the lower gentry.

[17] See this chapter for discussion of professional associations (pp. 22–23). For information on the periods of operation of provincial and local assemblies, see *Chuansha xianzhi* (1936) 19:1–39.

[18] During the period when local assemblies were banned in Chuansha, the director of that county's public finance office (*gongkuan gongchan chu*) presided over thirty meetings of a "local conference" composed of local administrative personnel and local gentry. The gazetteer indicates that Chuansha enjoyed the reality of local self-government without the name; see *Chuansha xianzhi*, (1936) 19:23a.

[19] On the method of appointment, see Sa Shijiong, et al., *Minguo zheng zhi shi* (Changsha: Shangwu yinshuguan, 1940), 628–29; Chen Boxin, *Zhongguo de difang zhidu ji qi gaige* (Changsha: Guangxi jianshe yanjiuhui, 1939), 60. Schoppa indicates that the power of county executive councils' in Zhejiang in the 1920s overshadowed that of the assemblies. However, it appears that some of Jiangsu's assemblies retained a considerable measure of authority—even in financial matters, where Schoppa argues the Zhejiang assemblies felt the loss of power most severely (*Chinese Elites and Political Change*, 34). In Jiangsu counties, executive councils sometimes deferred to the judgment of county assemblies. For example, in 1926, the Huaiyin County Executive Council, skeptical of the county government's request for defense funds, suggested that the county assembly ought to decide the matter. The assembly ultimately granted some of the money the government wanted (*Shi bao*, April 4, 1926, sec. 1, page number not clear, local report entitled "Qingjiang").

[20] Sa Shijiong, et al., *Minguo zheng zhi*, 628.

[21] For a rundown on the activities of the Chuansha County Assembly, see for example *Chuansha xianzhi*, 19:4b–9b.

[22] For one of *Shi bao*'s countless accounts of elections of managers by township-level assemblies, see the following report on Zhenjiang County: *Shi bao*, July 9, 1926, sec. 1, p. 1.

[23] For example, see Zhang Zhongwu, ed., *Shuyang xiangtu zhi lüe* (Taibei: Chen Tianmin, 1974), 36.

[24] Zhang, *Shuyang xiangtu*, 35–36. At least some parts of Jiangsu had *xiangdong* decades prior to the adoption of the local self-government system, though they were not appointed by assemblies. For information on local elites in Jiangsu in the 1860s, see Jonathan K. Ocko, *Bureaucratic Reform in Provincial China: Ting Jih-ch'ang in Restoration Jiangsu, 1857–1870* (Cambridge, Mass.: Council on East Asian Studies, Harvard University, 1983), especially 135–44.

[25] One example of such a person was Danyang County's Hu Yinjie; see *Danyang wenshi ziliao* 1 (Dec. 1982): 29. Another provincial assemblyman who was

tremendously influential on the county level was Feng County's Sun Jishi; see Sun Guangwu, "Sun Jishi bei sha de qianqian houhou" (Before and after Sun Jishi was killed), *Feng xian wenshi ziliao* 1 (December 1983): 143–44. For information on the franchise laws as well as the provincial and national focii of provincial assemblymen, see Thompson, *China's Local Councils*, 138–44.

[26] These figures are based on my own compilation of data included in the biography, election (exam degree), and local self-government sections of the *Chuansha xianzhi*. Because information in the gazetteers on degree holders is incomplete, our figures on gentry participation in local assemblies probably understate gentry dominance of those bodies, especially in the later years. Biographies are usually provided only for persons who were already dead at the time the gazetteer was written. Further, our figures do not count as gentry, for example, persons like the Shuyang County Assembly's Li Liangeng, who was the younger brother of prominent musician and former official Li Yinggeng, who had earned the *jinshi* degree. We should not exclude the possibility that Liangeng's talents, as the county gazetteer claims, "exceeded those of his elder brother," nor that he was every bit the "new culture maverick" (*xinchao pai*) of his stodgy lineage that the gazetteer describes (Zhang Zhongwu, ed., *Shuyang xiangtu*, 133). Yet it is reasonable to suspect that he benefited from his brother's achievements, prominence, and connections. Still my figures count him as a nongentry, even though he is from a gentry family. Although our sources only rarely tell us of family and lineage connections, the lists of assembly members reveal many persons who shared a surname and a syllable of their given names with a local degree-holder, a hint—albeit, not proof—that they might have been brothers. My figures also understate gentry influence on the Chuansha County Assembly, because I do not include as gentry the two persons (12 percent of all Chuansha assemblymen) who held the *yin* (hereditary) degree.

Roger Thompson has argued that rural elites and merchants were underrepresented in local assemblies (he calls them councils) that were formed on the basis of the 1909 regulations. He sees those early bodies as having been dominated almost exclusively by degree holders and those who had held positions as managerial elites in the late Qing era (Thompson, *China's Local Councils*, 141–61).

[27] I must rely on biographies in the gazetteers, which contain only biographies of persons who were already deceased at the time of writing. Therefore, my available sample of assembly members is probably unrepresentatively old.

[28] We have little systematic information on assemblymen in any area outside the Lower Yangzi core, but very fragmentary data on *xian* assemblymen for Shuyang County (in the North China zone) indicate that a higher percentage of assemblymen may have been degree-holders there than in Chuansha, and that the decline in gentry membership, if there was a decline, was less noticeable in

Shuyang (Zhang Zhongwu, ed., *Shuyang xiangtu,* 129–47). For information on the social background of GMD members, see this chapter (pp. 36-41).

[29] *Yuepu lizhi* (1933), 10:10–11.

[30] *Chuansha xianzhi, ce* 10, *juan* 18 *shang,* entire; *juan* 18 *xia,* 5a–6b; *juan* 16, 5a–37a.

[31] *Chuansha xianzhi, ce* 10, *juan* 18 *shang,* entire; *juan* 18 *xia* , 8; *juan* 16, 5a–37a.

[32] *Chuansha xianzhi, ce* 10, *juan* 16, 5a–37a.

[33] I base this observation on the biography sections of the Shuyang, Yuepu, and Chuansha gazetteers.

[34] *North China Herald,* September 8, 1928, p. 402.

[35] The term "professional associations" is, arguably, a mistranslation of *fatuan.* "Legally-constituted associations" or "legally-recognized associations" would be closer to the Chinese meaning. "Professional association" conjures up images of western-style associations of doctors, lawyers, historians, or other professional specialists who have banded together to establish and enforce the standards for their specialty and to exchange the latest findings in their field. Most *fatuan* really did not fit into this category, though a few, like lawyers' associations, might have. I have, however, decided to follow convention in translating the term. Landholders' associations seem to have been present only in a few *xian,* all of which were in the Lower Yangzi core. For a reference to one of them, see *Shi bao,* June 26, 1926, p. 2, sec., 1, col. 1.

[36] On the establishment of the chambers of commerce and the agricultural associations, see Wang Shuhuai, *Zhongguo xiandaihua,* 408–10, 421–32.

[37] Schoppa, *Chinese Elites and Political Change,* 34–35.

[38] *Shi bao,* April 7, 1926, sec. 1, p. 2, report on Zhenjiang.

[39] G. William Skinner, "Marketing and Social Structure in Rural China," *Journal of Asian Studies* 24 (November 1964) and 24 (February 1965). For one example of a nested system of chambers, see *Xu xiu Yancheng xianzhi* (1936), 6:6a–6b.

[40] In the years from 1914 on, some scholars see the *xian* elites on the defensive and their influence on the wane. See, for example, Marie-Claire Bergère, "The Chinese Bourgeoisie, 1911–37," in *The Cambridge History of China,* Vol. 12, *Republican China 1912–1949,* pt. 1, ed. John K. Fairbank (London: Cambridge University Press, 1983), 740–44. Although I strongly suspect that merchant influence on the provincial and national levels was waning, based on my reading of reports in *Shi bao,* it seems to me that their influence on county and subcounty affairs was still strong.

[41] For a case of acceptance of a suggested tax burden, see the *Shi bao* report of the Nantong Chamber's assumption of a levy for maintenance of a militia (April 21,

1926, sec. 1, p. 2). Earlier, the Nantong Chamber had rejected a special levy to support the local police (*Shi bao*, August 17, 1925, sec. 1, p. 2).

[42] For example, the Suzhou Chamber was consulted by the county government regarding bridge repairs (*Shi bao*, June 24, 1926, sec. 1, p. 2). The Yangzhou Chamber managed the repairs of the city wall (*Shi bao*, June 20, 1926, sec. 1, p. 1). On local defense, see the above note. The Yangzhou Chamber also was the body that decided to install running water in the city (*Shi bao*, March 29, 1926, sec. 1, p. 2).

[43] These militia played a key role in the revolution of 1911 on the local scene; see Wang Shuhuai, *Zhongguo xiandaihua*, 429; Young-tsu Wong, "Popular Unrest," 332.

[44] For one of the many reports on chambers providing funds for the war effort against the GMD, see the report on Yangzhou in *Shi bao*, March 10, 1927, sec. 1, p. 4.

[45] Barkan, "Nationalists, Communists," 403.

[46] *Suqian wenxian* 2 (January 1967): 156.

[47] On the distinction between lineages and clans, see Hugh D. R. Baker, *Chinese Family and Kinship* (New York: Macmillan, 1979), 49–70, 136–63.

[48] Li Changfu, *Fen sheng dizhi*, 131.

[49] See the biography of Shuyang County's Wang Chengji. (Zhang Zhongwu, *Shuyang xiangtu*, 139.)

[50] For example, see *Chuansha xianzhi* 21:8b–11b; *Yuepu li zhi* 9:1a–2b. Local gentry-merchants took the initiative to establish a Yuepu township militia in 1911 to deal with the chaos of the revolution; however, once an effective local government was set up, the militia became the township police force, funded and controlled by the county government.

[51] Another example of such merging of public and private roles is the common practice in parts of the Lower Yangzi core of using government tax agents not only for the public function of revenue collection but also for gathering land rents on privately owned land.

[52] See the description of government-established armed forces as well as village-level private militia in Zhang Zhongwu, *Shuyang xiangtu*, 69–70.

[53] On the militia elites of the North China area of the province, see Perry, *Rebels and Revolutionaries*, 84–94; Feng Hefa, *Zhongguo nongcun jingji ziliao*, 330–61; Zhang Zhongwu, *Shuyang xiangtu*, 69–70.

[54] This assertion on my part runs counter to the statement by John Lossing Buck's investigator that I cited at the beginning of a section in the previous chapter. For evidence supporting the view I state here, see the following estimates of the

numbers of religious professionals and attitudes toward religion or "superstition" in Zhao Ruheng, *Jiangsu shengjian*, vol. 2, *zhang* 8, 198–202, 204–209, 210–14.

[55] According to one source, which offered estimates which probably tend to be overly conservative, the most sizable temple landholdings were in Tai (over 40,000 *mu*), Xinghua (over 20,000 *mu*), Yancheng (over 30,000 *mu*), Tongshan (over 100,000 *mu*), Suqian (over 20,000 *mu*), Wu (2,700 *mu*), Wuxi (3,000 *mu*), Kunshan (1,000 *mu*) and Changshu (2,180 *mu*). See *Jiangsu sheng nongcun diaocha*, ed. Xingzheng yuan nongcun fuxing weiyuan hui (Shanghai: Shangwu yinshuguan, 1934), 3–6.

[56] *Agrarian China: Selected Source Materials From Chinese Authors*, trans. and compiled by the Research Staff of the Secretariat of the Institute of Pacific Relations (Chicago: University of Chicago Press, 1939), 12–13. This seems an exaggeration of the temple's holdings.

[57] On the comparative wealth of county- and township-level elites, see "Donghai Guanyun fen xian," 35.

[58] Martin M. C. Yang, *Chinese Social Structure*, 316–25.

[59] Twelve had traditional education, two had no education, and twelve of the biographies do not indicate what sort of education the merchant received. Five of the biographies are ambiguous about whether their subject's education was traditional or modern (*Chuansha xianzhi*, *ce* 10, *juan* 16, 18–35). Chuansha's gazetteer has much better coverage of merchants than that of any other Jiangsu *xian*. However, because it (like all gazetteers) includes only biographies of those who have already deceased, it is skewed in its coverage and probably understates the portion of the merchant class that had modern educations. The Shuyang County (North China zone) gazetteer, despite its broad coverage of local elites, lists only three merchants, none of whom is credited with a modern education. This is indicative of how much less important merchants were on the local scene in this zone than in the Lower Yangzi area (Zhang Zhongwu, *Shuyang xiangtu*, 135, 187).

[60] Richard Clarence Bush, "Industry and Politics in Kuomintang China: The Nationalist Regime and Lower Yangtze Cotton Mill Owners 1927–1937" (Ph.D. diss., Columbia University, 1978), 9, 10, 12, 32–34.

[61] Ash, *Land Tenure*, 9.

[62] Feng Hefa, *Zhongguo nongcun jingji lun*, 228; *Agrarian China*, 192–93.

[63] Chen Siling, "Tongshan qu nongmin ziwei gaikuang" (The circumstances of peasant self-defense in the Tongshan area) *Jiangsu yuebao* 4.4,6 (December 1, 1935):82 (nonconsecutive pagination); cf. Philip C. C. Huang, *The Peasant Economy and Social Change*, 71.

[64] Huang, *The Peasant Economy and Social Change*, 177–79.

[65] This pattern is most clearly visible in Yancheng and Pi Counties. On this question of rich peasant village elites, the division of Jiangsu into North China and Lower Yangzi portions is of limited usefulness. For example, one area in which the landholding parallels to some degree the pattern Huang sees is Qidong, which I include in the Lower Yangzi core, an area which shows little evidence of having rich peasant elites. I have included Qidong in the core, not because of *its* population density, but because it was surrounded by other high density *xian*. Therefore, the fact that it exhibits tenancy features of the North China zone and Lower Yangzi periphery may suggest that it really belongs more to the periphery than the core. See *Jiangsu sheng nongcun diaocha*, 8–9, 45, 92–99, 106–14, 118–34, 152–61, 170–85. However, whereas Huang distinguishes carefully between two types of rich peasants—those whose operations for the most part employed only family members and those whose operations used a great deal of long-term hired labor—the study cited here usually lumps all rich peasants together.

[66] Wu Shoupeng, "Xuhai ge shu," 342; Perry misreads the holdings as 4,000 and 2,000 *mu*. Perry, *Rebels and Revolutionaries*, 27.

[67] Wu Shoupeng, "Xuhai ge shu," 333, 342; Chen Siling, "Tongshan qu," 92–93; Liu Chengzhang, "Tongshan xian xiangcun xinyong ji qi yu diquan yidong zhi guanxi" in *Minguo ershi nian dai Zhongguo dalu tudi wenti ziliao*, vol. 90, ed. Xiao Zheng (Taibei: Chengwen chubanshe youxian gongsi, 1977), 47539–42.

[68] Zhang Zhongwu, *Shuyang xiangtu*, 12, 204.

[69] Alitto, "Rural Elites," 48; see also Wu Shoupeng, "Xuhai ge shu," passim.

[70] Wang Muhan, "Jiangsu yanken qu tudi zhengli quyi" (Humble opinions on the rectification of Jiangsu's salt-land reclamation area), *Dongfang zazhi* 31.24 (December 16, 1934): 37.

[71] Li Jixin, "Huainan yanken qu zhi ken zhi wenti" (Reclamation and settlement questions in the salt-land reclamation areas south of the Huai), *Dizheng yuekan* 3.5 (May 1935): 705–719.

[72] Wang Muhan, "Jiangsu yanken," 38.

[73] Samuel C. Chu, *Reformer in Modern China: Chang Chien, 1853–1926* (New York: Columbia University Press, 1965), 124.

[74] Ash, *Land Tenure*, 15.

[75] Ch'en Hung-ch'in, "Land Division Through the Land Development Companies in Northern Kiangsu," in *Agrarian China*, 39; also cited in Ash, *Land Tenure*, 15.

[76] Ch'en Hung-ch'in, "Land Division," 40.

[77] Nagano Akira, *Zhongguo tudi zhidu yanjiu*, trans. from the Japanese by Lu Pu (Shanghai: Chen Baohua, 1933), 174–75.

[78] Ash, *Land Tenure*, 11. Certainly, however, many of the urban-based landlords had only small, scattered holdings; see Bell, "Merchants, Peasants, and the State": The Organization and Politics of Chinese Silk Production, Wuxi County, 1870–1937" (Ph.D. diss., University of California, Los Angeles, 1985), 133.

[79] See for example, the information on Changshu County in *Jiangsu sheng nongcun diaocha*, esp., 202–245. One exception was the village of Shangtang, which had a resident landlord family holding between fifty and one hundred *mu*, an amount that would have qualified the household as wealthy. Land was more productive and worth more in the Lower Yangzi core than in the North China area; cf. Ash, *Land Tenure*, 10–11, 18–19. A more important exception is to be found in some of the Lower Yangzi core *xian* that lay north of the Yangzi, most notably Nantong. (Nagano Akira, *Zhongguo tudi*, 174–75.) There were, of course, exceptions to nearly all of the generalizations I draw here. For a more textured overview of the land tenure situation in Jiangsu, see Ash, *Land Tenure*, entire.

[80] Different names were used for this institution in different localities. For the classic account of these institutions, see Muramatsu Yuji, "A Documentary Study of Chinese Landlordism in the Late Ch'ing and the Early Republican Kiangnan," in Muramatsu Yuji, *Kindai Konan no sosan: Chugoku jinushi seido no kenkyu* (Tokyo: Tokyo Daigaku shuppankai, 1970), English section, 1–43. For an audacious, recent treatment of the history of these institutions, see Kathryn Bernhardt, *Rents, Taxes, and Peasant Resistance: The Lower Yangzi Region, 1840–1950* (Stanford: Stanford University Press, 1992).

[81] For the Yongzheng Emperor's edict in 1735 prescribing punishment for tenants who refused to pay land rent, see Kung-ch'üan Hsiao, *Rural China*, 393.

[82] Amy Fei-man Ma, "Local Self-Government," 47–84.

[83] Lynda Schaefer, "Merchants, Peasants, and the State," 186–200.

[84] Perry, *Rebels and Revolutionaries*, 45.

[85] "Donghai Guanyun fen xian ji shi benmo" (The whole story of the division of Donghai and Guanyun Counties), *Haizhou wenxian* "Special Issue" (January 1979). Wujin County's education circles were also split into "city" and "township" factions. See Xu Weiyong, "Minguo liunian de yici xuewu gaige" (The 1917 reform of educational affairs), *Wujin wenshi ziliao* 7 (December 1986): 77–84.

[86] See Zhang Ruoruan, "Donghai qu zhengzhi shikuang" (The political situation in the Donghai administrative inspectorate district), *Zheng heng yuekan* 1.11 (August 1934): 73.

[87] On the definition of factions, see Frank Belloni and Dennis C. Beller, "The Study of Factions," in Frank P. Belloni and Dennis C. Beller, eds., *Faction Politics: Political Parties and Factionalism in Comparative Perspective* (Santa Barbara, California: ABC Clio, Inc., 1978), 11; Joseph Bosco, "Taiwan Factions: *Guanxi*, Patronage, and the State in Local Politics," in Murray Rubenstein, ed., *The Other Taiwan: 1945 to the Present* (Armonk, New York: An East Gate Book, M. E. Sharpe, 1994), 114–15.

[88] For such analysis, see Carl H. Landé, "The Dyadic Basis of Clientelism," in Steffen W. Schmidt, et al., eds., *Friends, Followers, and Factions: A Reader in Political Clientelism* (Berkeley: University of California Press, 1977), xiii–xxxvi.

[89] For the quoted material and regarding factions among Chinese in Taiwan as groups rather than dyads, see Bosco, "Taiwan's Factions," 115, 124; J. Bruce Jacobs, *Local Politics in a Rural Chinese Cultural Setting: A Field Study of Mazu Township, Taiwan* (Canberra: Contemporary China Centre, Research School of Pacific Studies, Australian National University, 1980), 51. Lowell Dittmer has suggested that CCP factions have been passed on from one patron to another, more or less intact. He also depicts CCP factions as a mixture of *guanxi* networks based on face-to-face relations and groups coalesced through some degree of impersonal mass recruitment. See his "Chinese Informal Politics," *The China Journal* 34 (July 1995): 1–34. However, elsewhere, Dittmer downplays group orientation in Chinese culture ("Chinese Informal Politics," 10).

In chapter 4, treating GMD factionalism from 1927 through 1931, I discuss the survival of Jiangsu's CC Clique even though its founding leader, Li Shouyong, broke ties with it and joined the Blue Shirt (*Lanyishe/Fuxingshe/Lixingshe*) factional complex. This seems to me an example of a Jiangsu faction behaving—at least temporarily—as a group rather than a chain of dyads.

[90] Andrew J. Nathan, *Peking Politics, 1918–1923: Factionalism and the Failure of Constitutionalism* (Berkeley: University of California Press, 1976), 48.

[91] Nathan, *Peking Politics*, 50–54. In a number of other books and articles, however, Nathan has downplayed the uniqueness of Chinese culture. Citing a handful of cross-cultural statistical studies, Nathan states his doubt that "there is an empirical basis for any strong claim of Chinese distinctiveness" in the importance it places on *guanxi* and factions. See Andrew J. Nathan, *China's Transition* (New York: Columbia University Press, 1997), 136–51, esp. 142–46.

[92] Jacobs, *Local Politics*, 43.

[93] Jacobs, *Local Politics*, 41–51.

[94] Mayfair Mei-hua Yang, *Gifts, Favors, and Banquets*, 146–72. Andrew Kipnis also emphasizes change over time in the nature of *guanxi* production in Fengjia village in Shandong. He notes that in the 1960s through early 1980s, collectivized agriculture fostered the growth of clientelist ties to the village CCP

party secretary. Decollectivization and the rise of family farming subsequently led to farmers' cultivation of broader, extravillage networks of *guanxi* to garner loans and other business advantages; see Andrew Kipnis, *Producing Guanxi: Sentiment, Self and Subculture in a North China Village* (Durham, NC: Duke University Press, 1997), 127, 134–35.

[95] I base this on the many local memoir articles that I cite in the chapters on factionalism.

[96] Guy Alitto describes the flexible application of the label "local bullies and evil gentry" in the politics of southwest Henan. A local militia leader, Peng Yuting, who carried out a successful coup against the county government in 1930, saw the label applied to him by his factional enemies, and he returned the compliment when he spoke of the county-level faction he had overthrown; see Alitto's "Rural Elites in Transition: China's Cultural Crisis and the Problem of Legitimacy," *Select Papers From the Center For Far Eastern Studies* 3 (1978–79): 218–63, esp. 221, 236–37, 244–47, 249–50. However, it is also possible for factionalized communities to share an estimate of the moral quality of a local elite. Jacobs found that former tenants and former landlords from a variety of localities in Mazu Township, Taiwan were remarkably unanimous in their view about the relative "goodness" of particular local elites prior to land reform (Jacobs, *Local Politics*, 111).

[97] Although such accounts are legion, one of the most interesting is Arthur Henderson Smith, *Village Life in China: A Study in Sociology* (New York: Fleming H. Revell Company, 1899), 211–25.

[98] Kuhn, "Local Self-Government Under the Republic," 293; see also Stephen C. Averill, "The New Life in Action: The Nationalist Government in South Jiangxi, 1934–37," *China Quarterly* 88 (December 1981): 621, 625. My argument is similar to that made in Schoppa, *Chinese Elites and Political Change*, 55. In this passage Schoppa holds that *tuhao lieshen* "was used indiscriminately to describe an enemy of any social background . . . ranging from landlord types to urban politicians to academics and returning modern school graduates." In general, we cannot assume that we know a great deal about the social characteristics of someone identified in a source only as a *tuhao lieshen*.

[99] This observation is based on all cases I have encountered of persons labeled as *tuhao lieshen* and whose social or political position I know.

[100] I base this observation on my reading of local *wenshi ziliao* (memoir literature) accounts of the early history of local elite factions in Jiangsu counties. I have found one account that traces a faction back to the 1890s; all of the other memoirs I have seen track the factions back no further than the mid-to-late first decade of the twentieth century. For an example of a source that sees the rise of a

local faction as tied to an early assembly election under the self-government system, see Xu Weiyong, "Minguo liunian."

Commenting on Chinese society in the late nineteenth century, Arthur H. Smith says:

> There is not . . . that constant struggle between the "ins" and the "outs," which is seen in lands where the democracy is of a more flagrant type than in China. Yet even in China such contests do sometimes occur. We know of one village in which the public business had for some time been monopolized by a band of men who had subjected themselves to the criticisms of those who, although younger, felt sure that they were not on that account less capable. The result of the criticisms was that the incumbents withdrew from their places, leaving them to those who offered the criticisms, a method of adjustment which is known to be practiced in the government of the empire.
>
> But it is probable that the cases of such easy victory are relatively rare, for the reason that the "ins" have every opportunity to keep themselves in their position, and they are for the most part not at all sensitive to criticism, being quite content to reap the substantial benefits of their position, and to leave the talking to spectators. (Smith, *Village Life*, 229–30)

To be sure, the Qing bureaucracy was certainly subject to factional conflict, and conflict among local elites even before the dawn of the twentieth century was far from unknown. On factionalism in the Qing bureaucracy, see James M. Polachek, *The Inner Opium War* (Cambridge, Mass.: Council on East Asian Studies, Harvard University, 1992). On conflicts among Qing local elites, some clientelist in nature, some not, see Ocko, *Bureaucratic Reform*, 139–40; Kung-ch'üan Hsiao, *Rural China: Imperial Control in the Nineteenth Century* (Seattle: University of Washington Press, 1972), 319–20, 361–70, 419–20, 425.

[101] Nathan, *China's Transition*, 136–51.

[102] For Thompson's views, see *China's Local Councils*, 69, 136, 147, 155, 157, 160. In fact, Thompson is rather vague about exactly what system would have been appropriate for China. He only posits that the proper approach for China was something "[i]n between the state-enhancing authoritarian solution identified with officials like Zhao Erxun and the person-oriented exercise in local democracy championed by returned students" (*China's Local Councils*, 157).

In a later work, Thompson argues that factional conflict was stimulated by Western nations' insistence that Chinese Christians not be taxed to support traditional religious rituals and dramatic performances. The Qing state proceeded to strip away the religious side to the exercise of authority in local areas, and some elites also took up the cause of desacralizing local government, in many cases taking religious properties for secular purposes. Thompson sees this as an important cause of factional conflict, since some elites rose to defend the local religious properties and practices against attacks by other elites ("Cultural Imperialism," 14).

¹⁰³ Often counties were rent by factions based in groups of local schools. We would need to know a great deal more than we do now about the local self-government system before blaming its organizational approach for factional discord within education circles, particularly when much of that factionalism preceded the 1909 law; see Barry C. Keenan, *Imperial China's Last Classical Academies: Social Change in the Lower Yangzi, 1864–1911* (Berkeley: China Research Monograph, Institute of East Asian Studies, University of California, Center for Chinese Studies, 1994), 126. Wang Shuhuai has detailed what he sees as the reasons for the contentious local environment from 1906 through 1911. He argues that new taxes levied to foot the bill for China's modernization projects created much of the conflict. Some of the strife he describes took place *between* different professional circles (*jie*). It is not clear how a government approach that honored such circles would have headed off conflicts over resources (Wang Shuhuai, *Zhongguo xiandaihua*, 265, 167).

¹⁰⁴ This is suggested by Jia Ming in "Xinhai geming hou Suining zhengju de yanbian" (The evolution of Suining's political situation after the 1911 Revolution), *Suining wenshi ziliao* 4 (December 1988): 1.

¹⁰⁵ Xu Weiyong, "Minguo liunian," 83. This article also recounts a case of an educational reform project, pushed by provincial educational authorities (the Provincial Education Association), that severely polarized the Wujin political and educational scene ("Minguo liunian," 77 84).

¹⁰⁶ Stephen C. Averill, "Education and Local Elite Politics in Early Twentieth Century China," unpublished paper, 1996.

¹⁰⁷ John Fitzgerald, *Awakening China: Politics, Culture, and Class in the Nationalist Revolution* (Stanford: Stanford University Press, 1996).

¹⁰⁸ Zhang Xianwen, ed., *Zhonghua minguo shi gang* (Henan: Renmin chubanshe, 1986), 200–201.

¹⁰⁹ I have borrowed the term "counterelite" from Marvin Zonis, *The Political Elite of Iran* (Princeton: Princeton University Press, 1971), 39–79.

¹¹⁰ Gu Ziyang, *Jiangsu sheng dangwu yange* (n.p., 1936), GMDA no. 001/34, 2.

¹¹¹ Ibid. The ages given here are estimates based on the ages of party members in 1929 and on the fact that most were middle school students and teachers. See *Zhongguo Guomindang nianjian* (1929), ed. Zhongguo Guomindang dangshi shiliao bianzuan weiyuanhui, 747.

¹¹² Averill, "Education," 35.

¹¹³ "Jiangsu Xiao xian Jiangyin Jiangning Songjiang deng dangyuan rudang yuanshu," 1924, GMDA no. 435/69.

[114] "Jiangsu dangshi gaimo" (A model for Jiangsu party histories), *Jiangsu dangwu zhoukan* 25 (July 6, 1930): 84.

[115] Interview, Taibei, 1977.

[116] Chang Kuo-t'ao, *The Rise of the Chinese Communist Party, 1921–1927* (Lawrence: University of Kansas Press, 1971), 1: 602; Ho Ping-ti, *Studies on the Population of China, 1368–1953* (Cambridge, Mass.: Harvard University Press, 1959), 223.

[117] Yu Lin, "Jiangnan nongcun shuailuo de yige suoyin" (An index of decline in southern Jiangsu villages), *Xin chuangzao* 2.1,2 (July 22, 1932): 180.

[118] Robert North, with the collaboration of Ithiel de Sola Pool, *Kuomintang and Chinese Communist Elites* (Stanford: Stanford University Press, 1952), 48.

[119] Thomas Daniel Curran, "Education and Society in Republican China" (Ph.D. diss., Columbia University, 1986), 212–25.

[120] One source told me that most middle schools charged tuition, though a number of normal schools were tuition-free. Interview, Taibei, 1977.

[121] This is the general range of monthly costs per student as indicated in "Zhongyang qingnianbu dui Huaiyin zhongxue xuesheng zhi diaocha biao," 1927, GMDA no. 468/22.

[122] Curran, "Education and Society," 224.

[123] "Zhongyang qingnianbu dui Huaiyin zhongxue xuesheng," GMDA. See also Jin Weijian, ed., *Tongshan nongcun jingji diaocha* ([Zhenjiang]: Jiangsu sheng nongmin yinhang, 1931), 26.

[124] "Zhongyang qingnianbu dui Huaiyin zhongxue jiaozhiyuan zhi diaocha biao," 1927, GMDA no. 435/219.

[125] Since I am using percentile rankings devised for Tongshan County in the North China area of the province, and Songjiang is in the generally wealthier Lower Yangzi core, this surprisingly low average income may mean an average ranking *considerably* below 53 percentile. Jin Weijian, *Tongshan nongcun*, 26; "Jiangsu Xiao xian Jiangyin," GMDA.

[126] The average figure for members of the Songjiang first precinct was around 480 *yuan*. "Jiangsu Xiao xian Jiangyin," GMDA; Jin Weijian, *Tongshan nongcun*, 26.

[127] Interview, Taibei, July 1977 has provided the information on Feng party leaders. On economic percentiles, see Jin Weijian, *Tongshan nongcun*, 26.

[128] Interview, Taibei, July 1977.

[129] The financial insecurity is manifested in comments written on the Songjiang and Huaiyin forms. "Jiangsu Xiao xian Jiangyin," GMDA; Wu Tianhan et al., eds., *Zhongguo Guomindang Kunshan xian dang shi* (n.p., 1929), GMDA no. 435/177, 15.

[130] Chen Sibai, "Bimi qijian Zhenjiang dang shi cailiao shiling" (Miscellanea from materials on Zhenjiang party history in the secret period), *Jiangsu dangwu zhoukan* 25 (July 6, 1930): 98–102.

[131] On the division of the Jiangsu GMD into left and right wings, see the next chapter.

[132] *Jiangsu sheng dangbu dang shi*, 16; "Sun Wen zhuyi xuehui chengli jingguo ji qi yingxiang" (The events of the establishment of the Sunist Study Society and its influence), reprinted excerpt from *Zhonghua minguo shiliao yanjiu zhongxin diershijiu ci xueshu taolunhui jilu* (Taibei, n.d.), 327; "Zhongyang zuzhibu buzhang riji," 1925, GMDA no. 435/240, 2; John Israel, *Student Nationalism in China, 1927–1937* (Stanford: Stanford University Press, 1966), 5; *Zhongguo Guomindang Nanjing shi dangbu dang shi*, ed. Dang shi bianjishe (Nanjing, 1927), GMDA no. 001/83, 2.

Notes to Chapter 3

[1] George T. Yu, *Party Politics in Republican China: The Kuomintang, 1912–1924* (Berkeley; University of California Press, 1966), 172–75. Sun appointed veteran GMD members Mao Zuquan, Liu Yunzhao, and Di Kan as Jiangsu's delegates to the Congress, while Jiangsu's GMD Branch Congresses sent Gu Ziyang, Zhang Shushi, and Zhu Jixun. See Gu Ziyang, *Jiangsu sheng dangwu*, 3–4.

[2] Gu Ziyang, *Jiangsu sheng dangwu*, 4; *Jiangsu sheng dangbu dangshi*, 1–2. Prior to appointing this committee, on the recommendation of Jiangsu delegates, the GMD CEC had sent Liu Yunzhao, Zhu Jixun, and Mao Zuquan back to Jiangsu as the Jiangsu Provincial Party Affairs Preparatory Committee.

[3] Li Yunhan, *Cong rong gong dao qingdang* (1966; reprint, Taibei: Zhongguo xueshu zhuzuo jiangzhu weiyuanhui, 1973), 160. Zhu and Hou's sponsors were Shao Lizi and Ye Chucang.

[4] "Jiangsu Xiao xian Jiangyin," pledge documents for Zhu Jixun and Hou Shaoqiu.

[5] See Ge Jianshi, "Jiangsu dangwu de yidian zhanggu" (A few historical anecdotes about Jiangsu party affairs), in *Guofu yu Jiangsu*, ed. Li Hongru (1965; reprint, Taibei: Sanmin shuju, 1966), 127–30. Ge belittles Zhu, saying the Jingxian Middle School was really a small school with less than one hundred students, and therefore Zhu did not really deserve the respect that party leaders paid him. Of course, Ge's attitude toward Zhu was colored by the fact that they were from opposite factions in the party. Zhu was a leftist; that is, he favored the inclusion of Communists in the GMD. Ge was a member of the GMD right wing in the mid-1920s.

[6] Gu Ziyang, *Jiangsu sheng dangwu*, 3; *Jiangsu sheng dangbu dangshi*, 3.

[7] Donald W. Klein and Anne B. Clark, *Biographic Dictionary of Chinese Communism, 1921–1965* (Cambridge, Mass.: Harvard University Press, 1971) 1:569. The rightists without fail referred to Zhu as a Communist. One man I interviewed stated that Zhu was 80 percent Communist—whatever that means. Interview, Taibei, July 1977. At least one memoir cites Zhu as a Communist; see Cao Wenbin, "Jintan Guomindang zuopai zuzhi de shimo" (The beginning and the end of the organization of the left wing of the Nationalist Party in Jintan), *Jintan wenshi ziliao* 2 (May 1985): 8–18, especially 9.

[8] *Jiangsu sheng dangbu dangshi*, 4.

[9] Ge Jianshi, "Jiangsu dangwu," 127–30.

[10] Averill, "Education," 33.

[11] *Shen bao*, March 16, 1927, p. 7, col. 3. This article is Zhu's obituary.

[12] Evidence of Zhu's work in southern Jiangsu is in Jinshan County party pledge documents contained in "Jiangsu Xiao xian Jiangyin." Also see *Jiangsu sheng dangbu dangshi*, 10; Gu Ziyang, *Jiangsu sheng dangwu*, 5. For evidence of Hou's work in establishing the Wu County GMD, see "Jiangsu Wu xian dangbu gongzuo diaocha shixiang yilan," 1. For signs of Zhu's work in Kunshan County, see Wu Tianhan, et al. *Zhongguo Guomindang Kunshan*, 6, 9–10. *Shen bao*, March 16, 1927, p. 7, col. 3.

[13] Huang Jilu, et al., eds., *Geming renwu zhi* (Taibei: Zhongyang wenwu gongyingshe, 1973), 11: 371–75.

[14] Ibid.

[15] Ibid.; interview, Taibei, August 1977; Gu Ziyang, *Jiangsu sheng dangwu*, 2; "Jiangsu Xiao xian Jiangyin," Xiao County party pledge documents; "Suqian geming yundong" (Suqian County's revolutionary movement), *Suqian wenxian* 2 (January 1967): 21–22.

[16] Zhu Jixun, "Geming dang nali keyi youqing" (How can a revolutionary party lean to the right?), *Zhongguo Guomindang dierci quanguo daibiao dahui rikan* 1 (December 30, 1925): 1–2.

[17] *Zhongguo Guomindang Nanjing*, 1–3.

[18] "Jiangsu Xiao xian Jiangyin," Songjiang party entrance forms, nos. 4, 9, 11, 26, 32.

[19] Recall that it is far from clear that Zhu was actually a CCP member.

[20] *Jiangsu sheng dangbu dangshi*, 2–6; Richard Tze-yang Wang, "Wu Chih-hui: An Intellectual and Political Biography" (Ph.D. diss., University of Virginia, 1976), 209–20. The secretary of the provincial GMD headquarters Zhu hired was Huang Linshu.

[21] *Jiangsu sheng dangbu dangshi*, 7–10.

[22] Ibid.

[23] Ibid., 7–9, 12. Liu Yunzhao and Shen Jing no longer attended, Shen because he felt the need to devote his time to agricultural education, and Liu because he had been appointed a county magistrate in Henan. Liu was one of a tiny group of GMD members who had held positions of power prior to the Northern Expedition.

[24] *Zhongguo Guomindang Nanjing*, 5–10. The brouhaha began over the question of credentials required for participation in the election. Fan and the other rightists believed that only proof of membership application was required, but just before the election, speaking for the provincial committee, Zhu decreed that participation in the election required official party credentials. Reportedly Zhu had made such credentials available to CCP members, but Fan and his partisans never received the credentials they had requested for their members. Enraged at the prospect of losing an election they thought they should have won, Fan and the other rightists proceeded to beat up Zhu, Zhang Shushi, and the CCP members in attendance. Later Zhu, Zhang, and Liu Yazi asked the Guangzhou party center to expel Fan and the other Nanjing rightists for assaulting them and for disrupting the election. Shortly afterward, the party center revoked the memberships of the Nanjing rightist leaders.

[25] Ibid., 10–12; *Shen bao*, April 12, 1927, p. 14, cols. 1–2, read in conjunction with *Zhongguo Guomindang Nanjing*, 22, makes it clear that both leftists and rightists had their own Nanjing headquarters. It seems that Zhu moved quickly to establish a leftist Nanjing GMD after the rightists split away.

The rightist municipal GMD maintained close relations with the Shanghai Executive Committee, which Guangzhou had originally established as a branch of the Central Executive Committee to oversee party affairs in the Lower Yangzi region. Ye Chucang and other GMD members who opposed Communist membership in the party dominated the Shanghai Executive Committee.

[26] Fan Xiongyi and Shen Jing comprised the Standing Committee of the Restoration Committee. (*Jiangsu sheng dangbu dangshi*, 11–14). The new rightist GMD was disgusted at the refusal of Gu Ziyang and his northern Jiangsu GMD organizations to cooperate in its anti-Communist GMD. They claimed that Gu had sent Chen Qubing as his representative to the Restoration Conference, but later he denied that the proxy Chen had produced was genuine. Gu continued to be associated with the pro-Communist GMD until December 1926, a late switch of sides that some GMD members, probably correctly, felt was illustrative of Gu's left-leaning political philosophy. See *Jiangsu sheng dangbu dangshi*, 15; interview, Taibei, July 1977.

[27] *Jiangsu sheng dangbu dangshi*, 6, 10; Gu Ziyang, *Jiangsu sheng dangwu*, 6.

28 "Zuzhi bu huiyi jishi lu," 1924, GMDA no. 435/82.

29 Richard Tze-yang Wang, "Wu Chih-hui," 220–21.

30 *Jiangsu sheng dangbu dangshi*, 15.

31 As Sun's family and followers arrived in the Nanjing railroad station, Nanjing rightists destroyed the flags of the welcoming party sent by the leftists' Jiangsu party headquarters. The CCP, excluded from the memorial in the park, held its own service that, according to not-so-reliable rightist sources, was more of a celebration of Sun's death than a memorial. The Communists reportedly marked their "celebration" by hanging up red lanterns and parading around. See *Zhongguo Guomindang Nanjing*, 13–14.

On March 13, mourners met at the new gravesite of Sun Yat-sen on Xiaomao Mountain. Madame Sun, Sun Ke, Ma Chaojun, Deng Zeru, Ye Chucang, Yang Xingfo, and the Nanjing rightists participated in the service. Banished from the gathering by the rightists, the Communists and leftist Jiangsu GMD leaders were attacked and severely beaten by Fan's rightist group when they attempted to attend. Provincial GMD and CCP leader Hou Shaoqiu was the most seriously hurt, and a total of over sixty people were injured. The rightists deprecated the Communists' fear of fighting and particularly made fun of Hou Shaoqiu's cries for help as he was being beaten. They also bragged that their conduct displayed their "spirit of struggle" and claimed that Communists revealed an unrevolutionary nature by going to warlord police authorities to accuse the GMD rightists of assault (*Zhongguo Guomindang Nanjing*, 14–17).

32 The authoritative English language account of GMD central-level politics during this period is C. Martin Wilbur, "The Nationalist Revolution: From Canton to Nanking, 1923–28," in *The Cambridge History of China*, vol. 12, *Republican China, 1912–1949*, pt. 1, ed. John K. Fairbank (London: Cambridge University Press, 1983), 527–720.

33 *Zhongguo Guomindang bashi nian dashi nian biao*, 205; see also Wilbur, "The Nationalist Revolution," 620–23; Li Yunhan, *Cong rong gong*, 611.

34 *Zhongguo Guomindang Nanjing*, 223; see also Wilbur, "The Nationalist Revolution," 632–33; Gu Ziyang, *Jiangsu sheng dangwu*, 9–10. Certain secondary accounts argue that Chiang Kai-shek was in Nanjing by March 9, organizing the anti-Communist purge in that city. For example, see *Jiang Jieshi yanjiu zhuanji*, ed. Ningbo shifan xueyuan zhengshi xi Jiang Jieshi yanjiushi (N.p., 1988), vol. 1, 143–44; Wu Jinliang and Zhu Xiaoping, *Jiang shi jiazu quanzhuan* (Beijing: zhongguo wenshi chubanshe, 1998), 216.

35 *Zhongguo Guomindang bashi nian dashi nian biao*, 205.

36 Harold R. Isaacs, *The Tragedy of the Chinese Revolution* (1938; 2nd rev. ed., Stanford: Stanford University Press, 1961), 175–82; Anatol M. Kotenev, *New*

Lamps for Old: An Interpretation of Events in Modern China and Whither They Lead (Shanghai, 1931; reprint, New York: AMS Press reprint, N.Y., 1971), 268. The military forces Chiang deployed in Shanghai were commanded by Bai Chongxi.

[37] *Zhongguo Guomindang dierci quanguo daibiao dahui xuanyan ji jueyi an* (Guangzhou: Zhongyang zhixing weiyuanhui xuanchuanbu, 1926), 16, 53.

[38] Ibid., 60–61.

[39] Ibid., 31, 54. On the plethora of local-elite-controlled finance organs as well as GMD efforts to reign them in, see Philip A. Kuhn, "Local Taxation and Finance in Republican China," *Select Papers From the Center for Far Eastern Studies* 3 (1978–1979): 100–136. For an example of an explicit statement by a mass organization of the left GMD, though one heavily dominated by the CCP, against the existing local self-government system, see the diatribe by the Hunan Peasant Congress in Tanaka Tadao, *Guomin geming yu nongcun wenti*, trans. from the Japanese by Li Yuwen (Beiping: Jingcheng yinshu ju, 1932) 1: 26–27.

[40] *Zhongguo Guomindang dier ci quanguo daibiao dahui xuanyan*, 59–61.

[41] James Pinckney Harrison, *The Long March to Power: A History of the Chinese Communist Party, 1921–72* (New York: Praeger, 1972), 72; C. Martin Wilbur and Julie Lien-ying How, eds., *Documents on Communism, Nationalism, and Soviet Advisers in China, 1918–1927* (New York: Columbia University Press, 1956), 376.

[42] Zhongyang xuanchuanbu, ed., *Zhongguo Guomindang yu nongren* (Nanjing: Zhongyang xuanchuan bu, 1930), 54–56.

[43] Roy Hofheintz, Jr., *The Broken Wave: The Chinese Communist Peasant Movement, 1922–1928* (Cambridge, Mass.: Harvard University Press, 1977), 162. Later in this chapter I note a limited rent reduction campaign pressed by a peasant association of a Jiangsu county GMD branch.

[44] Isaacs, *The Tragedy*, 210–16.

[45] *Shen bao*, April 15, 1927, p. 9, cols. 4–5.

[46] See the section on contemporary society on the Songjiang County party entrance forms: "Jiangsu Xiao xian Jiangyin."

[47] The Peasant Department had issued instructions to the effect that the Guomindang mass movement was to develop connections with and infiltrate traditional secret societies, but it was not to mix its party-led peasant associations with the secret societies. He Yangling, ed., *Nongmin yundong* (Nanjing: Zhongguo Guomindang zhongyang dangwu xuexiao, 1928), *bian* 4, 39–40, 42–47, 59.

[48] Ibid., *bian* 4, 43.

[49] Wu Tianhan, et al., *Zhongguo Guomindang Kunshan*, 16–17.

⁵⁰ The sources consulted for this entire section on Zhou Shuiping include: *Jiangyin renmin geming shi* (Nanjing: Nanjing Daxue chubanshe, 1991), 10–11; Mao Huangshan, and Wang Shoupeng, "Jiefang qian de Jiangyin xinwen shiye" (The news business in Jiangyin before liberation), *Jiangyin wenshi ziliao* 8 (August 1987): 35; and Bernhardt, *Rents*, 197–99.

⁵¹ *Jiangyin renmin geming shi*, 10–11.

⁵² Bernhardt, *Rents*, 198.

⁵³ Jiang Xiyi, "Zhou Shuiping lieshi shilüe" (A short biographical account of martyr Zhou Shuiping), *Wenshi ziliao xuanji* (for Shazhou) 2 (no date): 81–88.

⁵⁴ Bernhardt, *Rents*, 197.

⁵⁵ "Xia Lin lieshi zhuan lu" (A brief biography of the martyr Xia Lin), *Danyang wenshi ziliao* 1 (December 1982): 18–19; Wang Goufu, "Dui Danyang geming shi de huiyi de diandi" (A brief reflection on Danyang's revolutionary history), *Danyang wenshi ziliao* 1 (December 1982): 28–29.

⁵⁶ "Xia Lin lieshi"; Wang Goufu, "Dui Danyang geming shi."

⁵⁷ He Yangling, *Nongmin, bian* 4, 48–50; "Jiang Zhe nongmin de tongku ji qi fankang yundong" (The privation of Jiangsu and Zhejiang peasants and their opposition movement), *Xiangdao zhoubao*, no. 179.

⁵⁸ Wang Zhitao, "Diyi ci Guo-Gong hezuo zai Qingpu" (The first cooperation between the Nationalists and Communists in Qingpu), *Qingpu wenshi* 6 (June 1991): 21.

⁵⁹ He Yangling, *Nongmin, bian* 5, 52–54; *Shen bao*, March 27, 1927, p. 8, col. 3; Zhang Shoufu, "Yijiuerqi nian Guo-Gong hezuo shiqi beifa jun gongke Songjiang muji ji" (An eyewitness account of the Northern Expeditionary Armies taking Songjiang during the period of the 1927 cooperation between the Nationalists and Communists), *Songjiang wenshi* 1 (October 1981): 33–36.

⁶⁰ He Yangling, *Nongmin, bian* 5, 52–54; *Shen bao*, March 27, 1927, p. 8, col. 3; Zhang Shoufu, "Yijiuerqi," 33–36; Chen Guisan, "Huiyi da geming shidai de Zhongguo Guomindang Songjiang xian dangbu" (Recalling the Songjiang County Chinese Nationalist Party in the era of the great revolution), *Songjiang wenshi* 1 (October 1981): 37–38.

⁶¹ Fang Kaijia, "Da geming qijian gongshen tuhao Chen Jinju" (The public trial of local bully Chen Jinju at the time of the great revolution), *Songjiang wenshi* 1 (October 1981): 40–42. Also see Yang Zaichuan, et al, "Chujue eba" (Executing an evil despot), *Jinshan wenshi ziliao* 7 (December 1988): 53–54.

⁶² *Shen bao*, April 9, 1927, p. 10, col. 2.

⁶³ He Yangling, *Nongmin, bian* 4, 46–48.

⁶⁴ He Yangling, *Nongmin, bian* 4, 50–59.

⁶⁵ Zhou Qixin, "Da geming shiqi Changshu Guomindang de dongtai" (Developments in the Changshu Guomindang at the time of the great revolution), *Wenshi ziliao jicun* 2 (December 1962; reprinted July 1984): 39–48.

⁶⁶ One former Jiangsu GMD leader intimated to me that the factionalism among existing local elites invaded the party. Interview, Taibei, 1977.

⁶⁷ "Jiangsu sheng dangbu duiyu zuzhi sheng zhengfu zhi jihua," 26–30. For the hostile attitude of the left GMD toward "local bullies and evil gentry," also see 7–8, 12, 17–19, 23, 33–34.

⁶⁸ *Shen bao*, March 18, 1927, p. 7, col. 5.

⁶⁹ *Shen bao*, March 21, 1927, p. 7, col. 1; *Shen bao*, March 20, 1927, p. 10, col. 1.

⁷⁰ *Shen bao*, March 22, 1927, p. 4, col. 4.

⁷¹ *Shen bao*, March 26, 1927, p. 5, col. 3.

⁷² *Shen bao*, April 2, 1927, p. 10, cols. 2–3.

⁷³ *Shen bao*, April 5, 1927, p. 10, col. 3.

⁷⁴ *Shen bao*, March 25, 1927, p. 4, col. 3.

⁷⁵ *Shen bao*, April 14, 1927, p. 10, col. 3.

⁷⁶ Ibid.; *Shen bao*, April 14, 1927, p. 1, col. 2.

⁷⁷ *Shen bao*, April 7, 1927, p. 8, col. 1.

⁷⁸ Rugao seems to have been such a place. See Lenore Barkan, "Patterns of Power: Forty Years of Elite Politics in a Chinese County," in Esherick and Rankin, *Chinese Local Elites*, 208–210.

⁷⁹ For a survey of the growth of anti-Communist thought in the GMD, see Li Yunhan, *Cong rong gong*, 398–412. My analysis of the Western Hills group differs in emphasis from that of Keith Schoppa ("Shen Dingyi and the Western Hills Group: 'What's a Man Like You Doing in a Group Like This?'" *Republican China* 16.1 [November 1990]: 35–50). Schoppa downplays ideological cohesion among the Western Hills adherents and argues that, therefore, the term "right wing" is a misleading appellation for them. On the question of ideological cohesion, I believe that although the group did debate the questions Schoppa notes, there were some commonalities among the positions of all, or almost all, of the speakers at the Shanghai Western Hills Congress in 1926. Central to my position is that none of the Western Hills leaders wanted mass organizations to carry out direct action against local elites. And although we have many instances of leftist GMD party branches promoting campaigns against local elites, I have yet to find one in which a Western Hills-associated party branch in Jiangsu did such a thing. To be sure, Shen Dingyi, whom Schoppa studies, had been a Communist and went on to press for rent reduction in Zhejiang, but Shen seems unrepresentative of the Western Hills group as a whole.

[80] Li Yunhan, *Cong rong gong,* 402, 410.

[81] Ju Zheng, ed., *Qingdang shilu* (Nanjing: Jiangnan wanbao, n.d.), 244.

[82] See Tao Qiqing, ed., *Quanmin geming yu guomin geming* (Shanghai: Guangmin shuju, 1929).

[83] Ju Zheng, *Qingdang shilu,* 29–30, 207, 244–45. For brief mention of local bullies and evil gentry, see Li Yunhan, "Jieshao Sun Wen zhuyi xuehui ji qi youguan wenjian" (Introducing the Sunist Study Society and documents related to it), reprint from *Zhongyang yanjiuyuan jindai shi yanjiuso jikan* 4 (Feb. 1974): 515; "Sun Wen zhuyi xuehui chengli," 346.

[84] Ju Zheng, *Qingdang shilu,* 249–50.

[85] Ibid., 181–84, 205, 244–45.

[86] Ibid., 181.

[87] Ibid., 205.

Notes to Chapter 4

[1] For example, see Guy Hunter, *Modernizing Peasant Societies: A Comparative Study in Asia and Africa* (New York: Oxford University Press, 1971), 40–41.

[2] Zhang Ruoyuan, "Donghai qu," 73.

[3] Andrew J. Nathan, "A Factionalism Model for CCP Politics," in Steffen W. Schmidt, et al., eds., *Friends, Followers, and Factions: A Reader in Political Clientelism* (Berkeley: University of California Press, 1977), 384. This arrangement, in which factional networks reached from the townships to the provincial and, eventually, all the way up to national levels, stands in contrast to the situation in Taiwan described by Joseph Bosco. He argues that in Taiwan all attempts in the 1950s to link county-level factions on an islandwide basis were suppressed by the GMD as a threat to party power (Bosco, "Taiwan's Factions," 122).

[4] Interview, Taibei, 1977.

[5] *Weiguangshe* members seem to have been somewhat more leftist than the succeeding county party leadership, and one of them, Teng Yangzhi, was an associate of provincial Anti-CC Clique leader Gu Ziyang, while another was Zhao Ruheng, a prolific writer who later compiled a widely used handbook on Jiangsu. The *Weiguang she* published a very useful history of the Kunshan party, though that book was later judged by conservative party officials to be "reactionary" (read "leftist"); see Wu Tianhan et al., *Zhongguo Guomindang Kunshan.* Also see "Jiangsu dangshi gaimo" (A model for Jiangsu party histories), *Jiangsu dangwu zhoukan* 25 (July 6, 1930): 95; *Zhongyang dangwu yuekan* 24 (July

1930): 75. The connection between Gu and Teng Yangzhi was supplied in an interview in Taibei in 1977.

[6] Whereas in central-level politics the term "CC Clique" referred to the totality of the Chen brothers' supporters, in this book I call that group the Organization Clique. In Jiangsu, "CC" designated one of several factions connected with the Chens. Very few observers of national politics have noticed that the term "CC Clique" meant something different in national politics than in Jiangsu. However, one analyst of national politics astutely argued that this name should be reserved for the Jiangsu network led by Li Shouyong and Wang Baoxuan. He argued that although Li and Wang were close to the Chen brothers, the Jiangsu CC Clique certainly did not "belong to the two Chens." This observer failed, however, to differentiate meaningfully between the various national networks that supported Chiang K'ai-shek; see He Fu, "San zhong quan hui qian Guomindang ge paixi zhi shi de fenxi" (An analysis of the history of the various factions of the Nationalist Party prior to the Third National Congress), *Shehui xinwen* 1.25 (December 15, 1932): 512.

[7] For such denials by the Chens see Wu Xiangxiang, ed., *Chen Guofu de yisheng* (Taibei: Zhuanji wenxue chubanshe, 1971), 12–15; Chen Lifu, "Wo suo zhidao de xianxiong Guofu" (The late brother Guofu whom I knew), *Zhuanji wenxue* 39.3 (September 1976): 12–14; Xu Yongping, *Chen Guofu zhuan* (Taibei: Zhengzhong shuju, 1978), 606–607, 781–83.

[8] Interviews, Taipei, 1977. One such Japanese report is *CC dan ni kansuru chosa* (Shanghai, 1939). For rather compelling evidence that there was at least some formal organization to the Organization Clique, see Liu Butong, "Guomindang de moying—'CC' tuan" (The devilish shadow of the Nationalist Party—the "CC" Clique), *Wenshi ziliao xuanji* 45 (first published, April 1964; reprinted, December 1980): 233.

[9] Howard L. Boorman, ed., *Biographical Dictionary of Republican China* (New York: Columbia University Press, 1967), 1: 202–204.

[10] Boorman, *Biographical Dictionary*, 1: 201–213. He is also said to have established there the Zhejiang Revolutionary Comrades Society to fight the CCP. Members of this organization were later to be key figures in the Organization Clique. See *CC dan ni kansuru chosa*, 6–7.

[11] Chen Shaoxiao, *Hei wang lu* (Hong Kong: Zhi cheng chubanshe, 1965), 289–90, 333–34; Yi Xun, *Jiang dang zhenxiang* (N.p.: Nanyang chubanshe, 1949), 56–58; Boorman, *Biographical Dictionary*, 1: 206–208.

[12] Chen Dunzheng, *Dong luan de huiyi* (Taibei: Yuan xia shushe, 1979), 29, 35; Liu Butong, "Guomindang de moying," 233. Chen Lifu states that this organization became active in 1935; see Ch'en Li-fu, *The Storm Clouds Clear Over China: The Memoir of Ch'en Li-fu 1900–1993*, ed. and comp. Sidney H. Chang

and Raymond H. Myers (Stanford, California: Hoover Institution Press, 1994), 142.

[13] Nathan, *Peking Politics*, 33.

[14] *CC dan ni kansuru chosa*, 23; *CC haomen ziben neimu*, ed. Jingji ziliao shi (Luoyang: Guanghua shudian, 1948), 3–4.

[15] Interview, Taibei, 1977.

[16] Ibid.

[17] For example, Shen Baixian, who served a term as Jiangsu's Commissioner of Reconstruction, was named as a close associate of the Chen brothers. Likewise, He Yushu, Jiangsu's Commissioner of Agriculture and Commissioner of Industry in the early part of the Nanjing Decade, was sometimes listed as an associate of the Organization Clique. See *CC dan ni kansuru chosa*, 11, 13, 23. However, this source must be used with care, since it lists Ge Jianshi as a member of the Organization group. This is most certainly inaccurate, as I establish later in this chapter. *CC dan ni kansuru chosa*, 64.

Unfortunately, clique politics in the government are even more difficult to follow than those within the party. A few episodes, however, are open to view. For example, some sources indicate that Chiang Kai-shek forced Chen Guofu, then provincial governor, to accept Gu Renfa, an affiliate of the Political Science Clique, as his Commissioner of Civil Affairs. It is said that Chen had Gu's strong-willed wife transported to the provincial capital at Zhenjiang so she could "discover" Gu's extramarital activities, precipitating embarrassing actions that drove Gu from office. Chen then installed his friend Yu Jingtang in the post. See Yi Xun, *Jiang dang zhenxiang*, 88–89; *CC dan ni kansuru chosa*, 15–16; Chen Guofu, *Su zheng huiyi* (Taibei: Zhengzhong shuju, 1951), 35, 123–24.

[18] A number of indications of Ye's working relation with the Chens exist. For one of these, see Boorman, *Biographical Dictionary*, 4: 29, which notes that Ye held a high position in the Jiangsu Provincial Farmer's Bank, an organization in the Chen brothers' network.

[19] Lloyd E. Eastman, "The Kuomintang in the 1930s," in *The Limits of Change*, ed. Charlotte Furth (Cambridge, Mass.: Harvard University Press, 1976), 196–200. Unfortunately, I have discovered few very revealing philosophical writings by the provincial partisans of the Organization Clique, so it is unknown how closely they hewed to this line which predominated among national spokesmen for the faction.

[20] For example, several factions tied to the Organization group maintained close ties with the Jiangsu Farmer's Bank and, on occasion, used it to aid members. (Interview, Taibei, 1977.)

[21] The anti-Western Hills organizations competing with the Practice Society were the New China Study Society (*Xin Zhong xueshe*), the New China Revolutionary Youth Society (*Xin Zhong geming qingnian she*), and the Grand Alliance (*Da tongmeng*); see Sima Xiandao, *Beifa hou zhi gepai sichao* (Beiping: Ying shan she chuban bu, 1930), 203–11; interview, Taibei, 1977. In many other sources, a *Xing Zhong hui* or *Xing Zhong she* is mentioned as a Hebei faction, and one of these may be the correct name of one of these societies (Chen Lifu, "Wo suo zhidao," 13).

Zhu Jianbai and Zhou Jieren, both Yancheng natives and Beijing University graduates, had probably affiliated with the CC group because of the Practice Society tie (interview, Taibei, 1977).

[22] My interviews in Taiwan establish Li Shouyong and Wang Baoxuan's leadership of the provincial CC Clique. This is also supported by Chong Gong, "Jiangsu sheng dangbu gepai de lishi ji qi huodong" (The movements and history of the various factions of the Jiangsu provincial party headquarters), *Shehui xinwen* 1.17 (November 21, 1932): 367. On the leadership roles of Qi Xiyong, Zhou Jieren, and Zhou Shaocheng, I also rely on my 1977 interviews in Taiwan as well as confidential correspondence from persons in Taiwan. But for confirmation, see "Su sheng dangbu gai xuan zhi qian hou" (Before and after the reelection of the Jiangsu provincial party branch), *Shehui xinwen* 1.28 (December 24, 1932): 554–55; Da Ke, "Su sheng dangbu xuanju zhi yimu" (The inside story of the election of the Jiangsu party branch), *Shehui xinwen* 2.5 (January 13, 1932): 50–52. On the leadership role of Li Shouyong and Qi Xiyong in the CC Clique, see Da Ke, "Jiangsu dangwu de lishi guan" (An historical view of Jiangsu party affairs), *Xiandai shiliao* (N.p., 1933), 1: 100.

People that I interviewed in Taiwan in the mid-1970s spoke of the group that Li joined both as the *Fuxingshe* and as the Blue Shirts. Recent analyses have argued that these groups were not identical. Frederic Wakeman has depicted a factional arrangement in which the innermost, secret, core group was the *Lixingshe*. According to his understanding, the *Lixingshe* treated the *Fuxingshe*, the Revolutionary Army Comrades Association, the Revolutionary Youth Comrades Association, and the Blue Shirts as its "front groups"; see Frederic Wakeman, Jr., "A Revisionist View of the Nanjing Decade: Confucian Fascism," *China Quarterly* 150 (June 1997): 409. Certain other scholars have argued that no group called itself the Blue Shirts; see Xu Youwei and Phillip Billingsley, "Behind the Scenes of the Xi'an Incident: The Case of the *Lixingshe*," *China Quarterly* 154 (June 1998): 284.

[23] Personal correspondence from Taiwan, 1984.

[24] Nathan, "A Factionalism Model," 385.

[25] These meetings took place some months before the CC and FF Cliques split. Thus, future CC leaders Li Shouyong and Qi Xiyong were included in the chats, as were Ye Xiufeng, Liu Jihong, and Jin Hesheng. Eventually, however, the ambition and commanding personalities of Li and Ye shattered whatever amity and collegiality had existed among the provincial cadres of the Chen brothers. Competition replaced friendship as Ye, commonly designated the head of the FF partisans, and Li jockeyed to place their friends in positions of power in the party (interviews, Taibei, 1977; personal correspondence from Taiwan, 1984).

One memoir identifies "the F. F. Group in Kiangsu Province" as one of several "political associations" established "[b]efore and during the Northern Expedition . . . to promote propaganda and to evade surveillance of the warlords"; see William L. Tung, *Revolutionary China: A Personal Account, 1926–1949* (New York: St. Martin's Press, 1973), 149. I believe, however, that the advent of this group had nothing to do with warlords, but was tightly related to the fight for position within the Guomindang.

[26] Ceng Yangfu cosponsored Ye's entry into the party. For seven months immediately after returning to China, Ye worked to support his family because of his father's death. In 1927 he entered the National Revolutionary Army and worked in its Secretariat. Ye's patron when he worked in the Investigation Section of the Organization Department was Zhang Daofan (interviews, Taibei, 1977; Chen Shaoxiao, *Hei wang lu*, 337, 356–61; see also 290–91 for more of Ye's activities.) Ye was said to have been a member of the secret "Blue and White Society," which included only the *crème de la crème* of the Organization Clique (Liu Butong, "Guomindang de moying," 233). For more on Ye and the Investigation Section, as well as the Central Statistical Bureau, see Zhang Wen, "Zhong Tong 20 nian" (Twenty years of the Central Statistical Bureau), *Jiangsu wenshi ziliao xuanji* 23 (August 1987; January 1988): 3–4, 95. However, this article includes inaccurate information on the time of the founding of the FF Clique.

[27] Interviews, Taibei, 1977; interview, New York City, 1982. For more information on the followers and strategies of Zhang Yuanyang, and a claim that he was temporarily aligned with the Reorganization Clique, see Da Ke, "Su sheng dangbu xuanju," 50–52; also "Su sheng dangbu gai xuan zhi qian hou," 552–55.

[28] Yang was Zhejiangese and Cao was an Anhui native, but Ma was from Wujin County in Jiangsu (confidential correspondence from Taiwan, 1984). See also "Su sheng dangbu zhi qian hou"; Chong Gong, "Jiangsu sheng dangbu ge pai," 367; Yang Gu, "Wo suo zhidao de Guomindang sheng, xian paixi qingkuang" (The Nationalist Party provincial and county factions as I know them), *Jiangdu wenshi ziliao xuan bian* 2 (December 1984): 16–20. For the ties of Ma and Yang to the Organization Clique, see Liu Butong, "Guomindang de moying," 237, 246.

[29] Interviews, Taibei, 1977. For more information on the Anti-CC Clique (though not all of it is correct), see Chong Gong, "Jiangsu sheng dangbu ge pai," 367–68; Da Ke, "Su sheng dangbu," 50–52. In the latter source Ge Jianshi is identified as leader of a so-called "Actual Power Faction," indicating that he had his own network of protégés, though most other sources consider Ge and his network as fitting under the Anti-CC umbrella. Also see Da Ke, "Jiangsu dangwu de lishi guan," 100–105, although this piece errs in naming Ge Jianshi as a part of the Reorganization Clique. This, I believe, stems from the fact that prior to early 1930, the Anti-CC and Reorganization Cliques cooperated very closely, leading observers to confuse the two. In fact, it may well be that the two cliques were not really completely separate and distinct factions until the events of late 1929 and 1930 drove them apart. See Da Ke, "Su sheng Guo daibiao fuxuan huaxu lu" (Interesting episodes in the reelection of Jiangsu's representatives to the National Assembly), *Shehui xinwen* 3.27 (June 21, 1933): 425.

[30] The source, when prompted, did agree with a suggestion that Gu might have wanted to move faster on land reform than did the party center. That Gu polled more votes among local peasant associations in the 1931 National Assembly (*Guomin huiyi*) elections than other candidates seems to bear out this idea (interviews, Taibei, 1977; some reports of votes for Gu by local peasant associations appear in *Shishi xinbao* [1931] March 24, sec. 1, p. 4, col. 8; March 28, sec. 1, p. 4, col. 6; March 21, sec. 1, p. 4, col. 5).

[31] On the Huangpu (Whampoa) Clique, see Hung-mao Tien, *Government and Politics in Kuomintang China, 1927–1937* (Stanford: Stanford University Press, 1972), 52–54.

[32] *Zhongyang zhoubao* 9.94 (March 24, 1930): 11. Another Anti-CC leader, Ni Bi, had been a commander of Huangpu forces in 1925; see *Zhonghua minguo shishi jiyao* for January through June 1925 (Taibei: Zhonghua minguo shiliao yanjiu zhongxin, 1975), 439. One of my interviewees suggested that Gu might have been close to Ding Weifen, though I have no confirmation of that.

[33] *Xinwen bao*, Feb. 7, 1930, sec. 3, p. 9, cols. 1–3.

[34] Ibid.; interview, Taibei, 1977. Although a later chapter will cite some of Ni Bi's rather radical rhetoric, it is perhaps also worth noting that he had played a key role in the bloody suppression of Communist-led unions in Ganzhou, Jiangxi, in March of 1927. See Zhang Xianwen and Fang Qingqiu, eds., *Jiang Jieshi quan zhuan* (Zhengzhou, Henan: Henan renmin chubanshe, 1996), 1: 182.

[35] Confidential correspondence from a former Jiangsu GMD leader resident in Taiwan, 1983.

[36] For a look at the views of Jiangsu's Reorganizationists, see *Zhongguo Guomindang zuo pai ABC*, ed. Jiangsu pinglun she (Beiping: Jiangsu pinglun she, 1930), passim, but especially 132–33 and 155–96.

[37] After the failure of the plot, Teng Gu left the country for a while. Lu Yinquan assumed the provincial clique's leadership. One source testifies that in Teng's absence the Jiangsu Reorganizationists split into three subfactions; see "Teng Gu de xin huodong" (The new actions of Teng Gu), *Shehui xinwen* 3.7 (April 21, 1933): 100. See also "Teng Gu jingxuan guo daibiao" (Teng Gu runs for the National Assembly), *Shehui xinwen* 3.17 (May 21, 1933): 261. For a brief biography of Teng, see "Minguo renwu xiao zhuan" (Short biographies of personalities of the Republic), *Zhuanji wenxue* 36.4 (April 1, 1980): 145.

[38] Zhang Hao, "Jiefang qian Guomindang zuzhi zai Siyang de shimo" (The beginning and end of Nationalist Party organization in Siyang prior to liberation), *Siyang wenshi ziliao* 4 (December 1986): 114–28.

[39] Lao Zhuo, "Jiefang qian Guomindang Pi xian neibu paibie douzheng" (Internal factional struggle in the Pi county Nationalist Party prior to liberation), *Pi xian wenshi ziliao* 2 (October 1984): 46–61.

[40] Ibid., 47.

[41] Ibid., 47–48.

[42] Ibid., 48–49.

[43] Ibid., 46–61. Although it has been argued that in most counties in post-WWII Taiwan only two factions competed, in Republican-era Jiangsu no such rule held true. Many counties had as many as three factions competing for posts. For the Taiwan case, see Bosco, "Taiwan's Factions," 134.

[44] Most accounts of GMD factions in Yancheng do not mention the older local elites' factions. For example, see Sun Shi'ao, "Guomindang Yancheng xian dangbu chou wen yi ze" (A bit of ugly information about the Yancheng County party headquarters), *Wenshi ziliao xuanji* 3 (March 1982): 99–103. For information on pre-Northern Expeditionary oligarchs' factions in Yancheng, see Zhang Shaoyi, "Xi'nan dang he Zhongyang dang" (The Southwest faction and the Central faction), *Wenshi ziliao xuanji* 3 (August 1982): 4–9; Zhou Mengzhuang, "Guanyu Yancheng Xi'nan dang yu Zhongyang dang zhi shimo" (Facts related to the beginning and end of Yancheng's Southwest and Central Cliques), *Yancheng xian wenshi ziliao* 1–2 (reprinted January 1984): 118–27. Zhou does speak of some degree of penetration of the GMD by the old cliques, but his account is rather vague on the issue. None of the many other accounts relating to Yancheng factionalism speak of any relation between the old factional structures and the new ones.

[45] Jia Ming, "Xinhai geming hou Suining zhengju de yanbian," 15.

[46] One of the recurring themes in Helen Chauncey's *Schoolhouse Politicians* is the tension between the GMD-connected, county-level educational apparatus and the township-level educational elites.

⁴⁷ See Chauncey, *Schoolhouse Politicians*, passim, on the power grab by county-based GMD counterelites; on Suqian factionalism, see "Guomindang Suqian xian lishi jianjie he paixi douzheng" (A brief introduction to the history of the Nationalist Party in Suqian and factional struggle), *Suqian wenshi ziliao* 2 (December 1983): 36–40.

⁴⁸ "Guomindang Suqian xian lishi," 36–40. The City Faction was connected with the province's Anti-CC Clique.

⁴⁹ Xu Shouhong, "Zaoqi de Guomindang Funing xian dangbu" (The Funing county party headquarters during the early period), *Funing wenshi ziliao* 4 (September 1989): 99–100.

⁵⁰ Sun Shi'ao, "Guomindang Yancheng xian dangbu chou wen yi ze," 99–103. Zhu Jianbai and Zhou Jieren were both provincial CC Clique leaders from Yancheng whom Li had helped to promote.

⁵¹ For example, Duan Muzhen was originally one of Gu's protégés, though he and Gu later had a falling out.

⁵² The information in this paragraph on Tongshan's cliques is found in the following sources: Zhang Shupei, "Guomindang shiqi Tongshan xian de bao'an, jingcha deng qingkuang" (The circumstances of peace preservation and police in Tongshan County during the period of the Nationalist Party), *Tongshan wenshi ziliao* 2 (May 1983): 65–74; Zhang Shupei, "Tongshan Guomindang gaikuang" (The situation of the Tongshan Nationalist Party), *Tongshan wenshi ziliao* 5 (August 1985): 72–98; "Guanyu Wang Gongyu xiansheng huiyi de shuoming he zhushi" (Explanations and annotations about Mr. Wang Gongyu's recollections), *Tongshan wenshi ziliao* 5 (August 1985) : 115–16; "Tongshan xian Goumindang lishi yange" (The evolution of the history of Tongshan's Nationalist Party), *Tongshan wenshi ziliao* 10 (April 1987): 33–43; Gu Jixun, "Gu Ziyang xiansheng shilüe" (A brief account of the life of Mr. Gu Ziyang), *Xuzhou wenshi ziliao* 9 (December 1988): 84.

⁵³ Yang Gu, "Wo suo zhidao de Guomindang sheng, xian paixi qingkuang" (The circumstances of the Nationalist Party provincial and county factions as I knew them), *Jiangdu wenshi ziliao xuan bian* 2 (December 1984): 16–20. For a rather different view, see Liu Rentao, "Guomindang Wang, Hong, Ye sanzhong weiyishi" (Anecdotes about the Nationalists' central committeemen Wang, Hong, and Ye), *Jiangdu wenshi ziliao xuan pian* 2 (December 1984): 21–24.

⁵⁴ Chu Shuxin, "Wo ren Guomindang san qu quzhang suo yi" (Trivial recollections of when I was the Nationalists' third ward headman), *Jingjiang wenshi ziliao* 6 (March 1986): 102–116.

⁵⁵ I base this observation on my survey of local memoir literature.

⁵⁶ Ling Xiao, "Jiefang qian Suqian de jijia baokan" (Several of Suqian's periodicals prior to liberation), *Suqian xian wenshi ziliao* 3 (August 1984): 89–100, especially 91–92. Some issues of this journal include the word *"xian"* in the title, some do not.

⁵⁷ Wu Yan, "Luanshi yingxiong Zhu Ji" (A hero of a troubled time, Zhu Ji), *Jingjiang wenshi ziliao* 9 (December 1989): 34–51, especially 36.

⁵⁸ Ibid., 34–37.

⁵⁹ Sun Shi'ao, "Guomindang Yancheng xian dangbu," 99–103.

⁶⁰ Chen Youzhai, "Jiefang qian Guomindang Huai'an xian dangbu paixi douzheng pianduan" (Some fragments of memories of factional struggles in the Huai'an County GMD prior to liberation), *Huai'an wenshi ziliao* 4 (October 1986): 106–15. This article includes references to other individuals shifting from Anti-CC to CC alliances. It is worth noting, however, that the article appears to include several factual errors. Specifically, some of the dates it gives are off by several years, and it is the only source I have seen that refers to Li Shouyong and Zhu Jianbai as part of a provincial DD Faction. Moreover, the author conflates the party purge of 1927 and the rectification of 1930.

⁶¹ Jiang Songping, "Zhongtong zai Haimen huodong qingkuang" (The activities and circumstances of the Central Statistical Bureau in Haimen), *Haimen xian wenshi ziliao* 5 (September 1986): 74–78.

⁶² Chen Youzhai, "Jiefang qian Guomindang Huai'an," 106–115.

⁶³ For details and documentation of factional battles in Jiangsu's GMD from 1927 to 1929, see appendix I and its notes.

⁶⁴ On the uprising in Yancheng, see "Yancheng xian dangbu gongzuo diaocha shixiang yilan" (A list of work investigation items for the Yancheng county party headquarters), April 1930, GMDA, 435/177, 100–108. For some of the issues energizing the Reorganization Clique, see Edmund S. K. Fung, "Anti-Imperialism and the Left Guomindang," *Modern China* 11.1 (January 1985): 39–76. Fung does not believe that the Reorganizationists ever constituted a viable alternative to existing GMD leadership.

⁶⁵ For Cai's leadership of Sword Societies, see *Shi bao*, December 27, 1929, p. 2; for his description, see *Shi bao*, November, 29, 1929, p. 2.

⁶⁶ For an account of the uprisings of the Liyang Big Sword Societies in 1928, see Zhang Zhenzhi, *Geming yu zongjiao* (Shanghai: Minzhi shuju, 1929), 165–85.

⁶⁷ Ibid., 168, 170; Jing Song, *Jiangsu zhengzhi zhuangkuang yu renwu de celüe* (N.p., 1929), 87; Ch'en Yung-fa, "The Wartime Communists and Their Local Rivals: Bandits and Secret Societies," *Select Papers From the Center for Far Eastern Studies* 3 (1978–1979): 15–18, 22–25, 30.

⁶⁸ In fact, lacking the evidence contained in *wenshi ziliao*, I jumped to just such a conclusion in "Probing KMT Rule: Reflections on Eastman's 'New Insights,'" *Republican China* 9.2 (December 1982): 28–39. For national- and provincial-level Reorganizationists' programs, see *Zhongguo Guomindang zuopai ABC*, 132–33 and 155–96.

⁶⁹ Huang Huaizhen, "'Liyang pinglun she' chengli qianhou yixie qingkuang" (A few circumstances of the founding and the entire history of the "Liyang Critic Society"), *Liyang wenshi ziliao* (for the municipality) 8 (December 1990): 90–92; Jiang Yushu, "Kangzhan qian Liyang Guomindang jishi" (A record of the actual events of the Liyang Nationalist Party prior to the War of Resistance), *Liyang wenshi ziliao* (for the county) 3 (January 1985): 164–72.

⁷⁰ For the Reorganizationists' use of this slogan, see Edmund S. K. Fung, "Anti-Imperialism," 66. On Cai's Shanghai source of money and his disbursement of it, see *Shi bao*, Nov. 24, 1929, p. 3. This estimate of wages of skilled workmen relates to Shanghai, where wages were higher than in the rest of Jiangsu; see Holmes Welch, *The Practice of Chinese Buddhism, 1900–1950* (Cambridge, Mass.: Harvard University Press, 1973), 225.

⁷¹ The newspaper accounts of this event are vague about the numbers of braves the Reorganization Clique and Swords had at their disposal. Most say "several thousand." For example, see *Shi bao*, November 29, 1929, p. 2.

⁷² Interview, Taibei, 1977.

⁷³ This account of the Liyang uprising relies on the following sources: interviews, Taibei, 1977; *Shi bao* (1929) Nov. 23, p. 2; Nov. 24, p. 3; Nov. 27, p. 3; Nov. 28, p. 2; Nov. 29, p. 2; Dec. 27, pp. 2–3; Qing Jiajie, "Guomindang Gaizu pai zai Liyang de huodong shi mo" (The movement of the Reorganization Clique of the Nationalist Party in Liyang from the beginning to the end), *Liyang xianzhi ziliao* 2 (June 1985): 144–45; Lu Jianzhong, "Guomindang Gaizu pai Liyang baodong shibai hou yi, er shi" (One or two things about the aftermath of the failed insurrection of the Nationalist Party's Reorganization Clique), *Liyang wenshi ziliao* 2 (January 1984): 30–34.

⁷⁴ On the mutinies of Peng and Shi, see: *Shi bao* (1929) Dec. 4, p. 2; Dec. 6, p. 2; Dec. 8, p. 2; Dec. 9, pp. 1–2; Dec. 10, pp. 1–3; Dec. 11, p. 2; Dec. 12, pp. 2–3; Dec. 13, pp. 2–3; Dec. 14, p. 2; *A Chronology of Twentieth Century China, 1904–1949* (Washington, D.C.: Center for Chinese Research Materials, Association of Research Libraries, 1973), 4: 544–50.

⁷⁵ On his nickname, see James E. Sheridan, *Chinese Warlord: The Career of Feng Yü-hsiang* (Stanford: Stanford University Press, 1966), 261.

⁷⁶ Interviews, Taibei, 1977; Gu Ziyang, *Jiangsu sheng dangwu*, 19; *Xinwen bao*, February 7, 1930, sec. 3, p. 9, cols. 1–3.

[77] Miao had earlier been a radio instructor at the Huangpu Academy, where he had been one of the leading lights in the Sunist Study Society. Surprisingly, considering the right-wing ideology of that group, he was temporarily labeled a Communist during the purge, but he was saved by the intervention of He Yingqin and Miao's fellow Wuxi resident, Wu Zhihui. Some outside Miao's small circle nicknamed Miao "the little Daoist priest" (xiao daoshi) in contemptuous reference to his father's religious profession. (Interview, Taibei, 1977; Boorman, *Biographical Dictionary*, 3: 36–37; Yi Xun, *Jiang dang zhenxiang*, 26–28, 65.)

[78] *Xinwen bao*, February 7, 1930, sec. 3, p. 9, cols. 1–3; Gu Ziyang, *Jiangsu sheng dangwu*, 19; interviews Taibei, 1977; *Jiangsu gaodeng fating gongbao*, nos. 3,4 (March, April 1930), *zhuanjian* section, 6–11.

[79] *Xinwen bao*, February 7, 1930, sec. 3, p. 9, cols. 1–3; Gu Ziyang, *Jiangsu sheng dangwu*, 19; interviews, Taibei, 1977.

[80] This Lin Biao was *not* the famous Communist general. Interview, Taibei, 1977.

[81] Gu Ziyang, *Jiangsu sheng dangwu*, 20–21.

[82] Interviews, Taibei, 1977; *Shen bao*, January 15, 1928, p. 8, col. 3; *Zhongyang zhengzhi xuexiao biye tongxue lu*, ed. Biye sheng zhidaobu (n.p., 1947), 7.

[83] Because Yang Xingqin and Cao Minghuan were two of the three members of the Standing Committee of the Rectification Committee, they controlled it; see Gu Ziyang, *Jiangsu sheng dangwu*, 21.

[84] For a reference to a Nanhui County Executive Committee member who fled because he had ties with Ge Jianshi, a provincial Anti-CC leader, see Shi Shunyuan, "Youguan Nanhui xian Guomindang de yi lin ban zhao" (A bit of a fragment relating to Nanhui County's Nationalist Party), *Nanhui xian wenshi ziliao* 4 (February 1988): 48–50.

[85] Interview, Taibei, 1977.

[86] The list of those elected appears in *Zhongyang ribao*, May 4, 1931, sec. 1, p. 2, col. 2. It is possible that some obscure Anti-CC elements whose names and connections are not known were elected.

[87] At least after the beginning of the rectification period, few disputes were recorded in public media on which we must rely.

[88] For example, see the references to disputes in Nanhui County and at the provincial level during the rectification period in Shi Shunyuan, "Youguan Nanhui xian," 50.

[89] Interview, Taibei, 1977.

[90] Gu Ziyang, *Jiangsu sheng dangwu*, 23.

[91] Ibid.; interviews, Taibei, 1977.

⁹² "Zhongyang zuzhi weiyuan hui xiaji dangbu zuzhi gongzuo baogao shencha huiyao," 1934, GMDA, 435/17, nos. 9 and 10, p. 3; no. 6.

⁹³ Gu Ziyang, *Jiangsu sheng dangwu*, 28–36.

⁹⁴ Ibid., 28; interview, Taibei, 1977.

⁹⁵ Gu Ziyang, *Jiangsu sheng dangwu*, 31.

⁹⁶ Ibid, 31–33.

⁹⁷ Ibid, 32.

⁹⁸ Ibid, 33–35.

⁹⁹ Ibid, 35–36.

¹⁰⁰ Nathan, "A Factionalism Model," 386.

¹⁰¹ Along similar lines, Tang Tsou has argued that all-or-nothing struggles were the general rule in CCP intraparty conflict. See Tang Tsou, "Chinese Politics at the Top: Factionalism or Informal Politics? Balance-of-Power Politics or a Game to Win All?" *The China Journal* 34 (July 1995): 95–156, esp. 120–25.

¹⁰² *Zhongguo Guomindang nianjian* (1929), ed. Zhongguo Guomindang dangshi shiliao bianzuan weiyuanhui, 598–603; (1934), *bian* 3, 142–46.

¹⁰³ "Funing xian dangbu gongzuo diaocha shixiang yilan," GMDA no. 435/172.

Notes to Chapter 5

¹ On disruption of communication between provincial and *xian* levels, see Wu Tianhan, et al., *Zhongguo Guomindang Kunshan*, 36.

² For example, Chiang's troops dispersed the Suzhou General Labor Union on April 13. See *Shen bao*, April 14, 1927, p. 6, col. 5; April 16, 1927, p. 9, col. 4. For evidence of suppression of the peasant associations in Guangzhou, see Liu Shaotang, ed., *Minguo da shi rizhi* (Taibei: Zhuanji wenxue chubanshe, 1973), vol. 1, 360. Suppression of peasant organizations also took place in some parts of Jiangsu, though I have not run across very detailed accounts of that suppression during the purge. Such suppression in Songjiang County is implied by the following articles: Chen Guisan, "Huiyi da geming shidai de Zhongguo Guomindang Songjiang xian dangbu," 36–39; Fang Kaijia, "Da geming qijian gongshen tuhao Chen Jinju," 40–42.

³ *Shen bao*, May 10, 1927, p. 6, cols. 4–5.

⁴ I describe such cases later in this chapter. The Baoshan County gazetteer describes another similar case. Before the purge, Baoshan party leaders had formally warned county and township political elites (addressing them as "evil gentry and corrupt managers") not to provide financial aid for warlord armies.

Soon thereafter Li Xinglian, a resident of the town of Luodian whom the gazetteer describes only as an "evil gentry," burst into the fourth ward party headquarters and hurled insults at Sun Yat-sen's picture. In reaction, the party clamored for punishment. However, Li went to Shanghai and persuaded (the gazetteer says "bribed") the political department of GMD General Bai Chongxi's commanderate to aid him. This was probably not an isolated occurrence, judging from the performance of the army and its political department in other counties.

With the formal announcement of the purge by the central party and government in Nanjing in April, the gazetteer reports that "local bullies and evil gentry" charged several loyal, non-Communist GMD members with being Communists. Li and his confederates, with the aid of some GMD members in Shanghai, lodged charges against eight Baoshan County GMD members. Although the General Political Department soon cleared them, the GMD's Twenty-sixth Army in Shanghai arrested three of them and closed the county party headquarters. The local party leaders were again cleared and released several weeks later, but only through the intervention of provincial party leader Ge Jianshi (a Baoshan native), Hu Hanmin, and Chiang Kai-shek. See *Baoshan xian zai xu zhi* (1931), 1:2–4b. See also "Baoshan dangwu gaikuang" (The general situation of Baoshan party affairs), *Jiangsu dangshang* 15 (November 4, 1928): 11–14.

[5] *Shen bao* (1927) April 26, p. 10, col. 1; April 29, p. 10, col. 3; May 4, p. 10, cols. 1–2; May 7, p. 9, col. 4.

[6] *Shen bao*, May 4, 1927, p. 5, col. 2.

[7] *Shen bao*, April 29, 1927, p. 10, col. 3.

[8] *Shen bao*, April 23, 1927, p. 9.

[9] *Shen bao*, April 2, 1927, p. 10, cols. 2–3; April 3, 1927, p. 16, col. 2. The Political Department of the army referred to the old county elites as "opportunist elements."

[10] *Shen bao*, April 2, 1927, p. 10, cols. 2–3; April 3, 1927, p. 16, col. 2.

[11] *Shen bao*, April 2, 1927, p. 10, cols. 2–3; April 3, 1927, p. 16, col. 2; "Beifa shiqi Jinshan yamen duo yin ji" (A record of the seizing by force of the Jinshan county government seal at the time of the Northern Expedition), *Jinshan wenshi ziliao* 5: 1–2. My copy of this article lacks a date.

[12] Yu Lin, "Jiangnan nongcun shuailuo," 169–81, passim. Yu reveals that 80 to 90 percent of the party members were youthful intelligentsia from landlord families.

[13] Ibid., 171, 172, 174.

[14] *Shen bao*, May 16, 1927, p. 5, col. 5.

[15] Ibid.

16 *Shen bao*, May 30, 1927, p. 4, col. 4.

17 *Shen bao*, May 16, 1927, p. 5, cols. 5–6.

18 For one such case, see Zhang Zhongwu, ed., *Shuyang xiangtu*, 182–85. I deal with this case below.

19 *Shen bao*, July 7, 1927, p. 7, col. 3.

20 *Shen bao*, July 14, 1927, p. 7, col. 1.

21 *Shen bao*, July 4, 1927, p. 9, cols. 2–3.

22 *Shen bao*, July 11, 1927, p. 7, col. 4.

23 Chauncey, *Schoolhouse Politicians*, 152.

24 *Shen bao*, July 29, 1927, p. 9, col. 2.

25 Ni Bi, "Jiangsu sheng dangwu qingkuang" (The state of Jiangsu provincial party affairs), *Jiangsu xunkan* 22,23 (January 1, 1929): 1–16.

26 Zhongguo Guomindang dangshi shiliao bianzuan weiyuan hui, ed., *Zhongguo Guomindang nianjian* (1929), 747, 751.

27 The term "May Fourth Movement" in its narrowest sense refers to the demonstrations and strikes that erupted on May 4, 1919, after the Chinese public learned that the Paris Peace Conference was handing to Japan the leasehold and concessions in China held by Germany prior to World War I. The Chinese had expected the great powers to return these areas to China. However, I use the term in its broadest sense, to refer to the iconoclastic intellectual ferment from the mid-teens through the early 1920s. See Tsetsung Chow, *The May Fourth Movement: Intellectual Revolution in Modern China* (Cambridge, Mass.: Harvard University Press, 1960).

28 Rankin, "State and Society," 273.

29 Marianne Bastid, *Educational Reform in Early Twentieth-Century China*, trans. from the French by Paul J. Bailey (Ann Arbor: Center for Chinese Studies, University of Michigan, 1988), 86, 149–53. For evidence that student unrest in middle-level schools continued from 1912–1927, see Chi Hung Liu, "A Study of Modern Education in Jiangsu Province, China" (M.A. thesis, University of Washington, 1932), 103.

30 Comintern and the CCP Central Committee abandoned any hope of perpetuating the "united front" in September 1927. This did not, however, explicitly rule out the use of GMD organizations as fronts for CCP activities. See Benjamin I. Schwartz, *Chinese Communism and the Rise of Mao* (Cambridge, Mass.: Harvard University Press, 1951), 90.

31 "Jiangsu Jiangbei feigong raoluan shikuang zhi diaocha" (Investigation of the circumstances of Communist disorders in northern Jiangsu), *Chan gong banyuekan* 5–6 (January 10, 1931): 82, cited in Barkan, "Nationalists, Communists," 470,

521. See also Zhong Sheng, "Jiangsu ge xian gongchandang baodong jingguo" (Communist insurrections in various Jiangsu counties), *Jiangsu xunkan* 1 (September 1, 1928): 48–49.

[32] Wang Xiuhua, "Lianshui xian zhong dangbu zhibu de zaoqi huodong" (Actions of the party branch in Lianshui during the early period), *Lianshui wenshi ziliao* 1 (December 1982): 36–45.

[33] On the cases of Wujin, Yangzhou, Dongtai, Yixing, and Lianshui, see *Jiangsu geming douzheng jilüe* (Beijing: Dang'an chubanshe, 1987), 249, 271, 275, 281, 296. On Shuyang, see Ge Shaoliang, "Guanyu 'yiliu' can'an zhi wo de huiyi" (My recollections of the January 6th Massacre), *Shuyang wenshi ziliao* 6 (November 1990): 12–35. On Qidong, see Yao Zhiren, "Da geming shiqi de jinan gongzuo" (Work in the period of the great revolution to deal with the difficulties), *Qidong wenshi xuanji* 5 (November 1986): 21–35; Shen Yigong, Zhang Xiafeng, and Yao Zhiren, "Yi liangci Guo-Gong hezuo zhong de Guomindang Qidong xian dangbu" (Remembering the Qidong County Nationalist Party branch at the time of the two periods of Nationalist-Communist cooperation), *Qidong wenshi xuanji* 3 (September 1985): 24–33; "Jianghai zhi bin de hongse fengbao" (The red tempest in the coastal area), *Qidong wenshi* 8:1–12 (date is missing from my copy). On Ganyu, see Sun Yiwu, "Ganyu xian diyige Gongchandang yuan—Zhang Jingtong" (Ganyu County's first Communist party member: Zhang Jingtong), *Ganyu xian wenshi ziliao* 7 (October 1989): 24–28.

[34] Barkan, "Nationalists, Communists," 94–95, 104, 108, 416. For an example of a non-Communist who played a role in attacks on local elites in Rugao, see references to Cheng Changwu on pages 94, 104.

[35] *North China Herald*, February 23, 1929, p. 301.

[36] On the government's suppression of *Jiangsu pinglun* as a part of its general crackdown against Reorganizationists and other leftists in 1929, see *Shishi xinbao*, August 5, 1929, sec. 1, p. 3; August 27, 1929, sec. 2, p. 2.

[37] No definition of the term "great" was supplied. *Zhongguo Guomindang zuopai ABC*, 129–96.

[38] See Ni Bi, "Jiangsu sheng dangwu qingkuang," 1–15, especially 10–15.

[39] For example, Xiao Zheng was both an intimate of the Chen brothers *and* an advocate of fundamental reform of China's land tenure system. See Xiao Zheng, *Tudi gaige wushinian: Xiao Zheng huiyi lu* (Taipei: Zhongguo dizheng yanjiusuo zong jingxiao Zhuanji wenxue chubanshe, 1980). Also the single most significant movement for reform in post-rectification Jiangsu was a land reform program for Qidong County advocated by Zhou Ruqian, whom one source identified as an Organization Clique associate (Interviews, Taibei, 1977). Additionally, on pages

125–28 see the account of the execution of Sun Jishi (as a "local bully") by Wang Gongyu, another person who was close to the Chen brothers.

[40] Li Shouyong, "Zai Jiangsu ban dang" (Managing the party in Jiangsu), *Jiangsu dang sheng* 6 (September 2, 1928): 6–16, esp. 8–9.

[41] *Shen bao*, August 2, 1927, p. 6, col. 1; August 7, 1927, p. 8, col. 1. In 1929, when accusations against "local bullies and evil gentry" had diminished in volume, the special court's remaining cases and its jurisdiction were handed over to the regular court system.

[42] The provincial government also provided these procedural protections. For example, see *Shen bao*, June 5, 1927, p. 6, col. 5; July 13, 1927, p. 7, col. 3.

[43] *Shen bao* (1927), August 1, p. 10, col. 6; November 5, p. 4, cols. 4–5; November 6, p. 9, cols. 4–6; December 10, p. 13, col. 2; (1928) January 17, p. 9, col. 3; January 11, p. 9, col. 6; He Yangling, *Nongmin, bian* 8, 79–80; *Zhongyang ribao*, April 19, 1928, sec. 2, p. 2, cols. 1–3.

[44] For an example of a mass organization that continued, see the reference to the Yancheng General Labor Union in *Zhongyang ribao*, May 17, 1928, sec. 2, p. 3, cols. 4–5. Also see *Zhongyang ribao* (1928), February 15, sec. 2, p. 2; February 23, sec. 2, p. 2; March 7, sec. 2, p. 2, col. 4; April 19, sec. 2, p. 2; June 14, sec. 2, p. 3; September 29, sec. 2, p. 4, cols. 3–4. On the party center's denunciations of disobedient local branches, see Ye Chucang's report in *Shishi xinbao*, May 7, 1929, sec. 1, p. 4, col. 5.

[45] This particular proposal was put forward by the Jiangsu Peasant Association's rectification committee. *Zhongyang ribao*, September 9, 1928, sec. 2, p. 4, cols. 1–2.

[46] *Zhongyang ribao*, January 11, 1932, sec. 1, p. 4, cols. 1–4.

[47] *Shishi xinbao*, February 29, 1930.

[48] *North China Herald*, March 2, 1929, p. 349, cols. 1–2.

[49] *North China Herald*, April 21, 1928, p. 98; September 8, 1928, p. 402, cols. 1–4.

[50] *North China Herald*, April 21, 1928, p. 98.

[51] *North China Herald*, March 2, 1929, p. 349, cols. 1–2.

[52] Ibid.

[53] Ibid.

[54] *North China Herald*, October 27, 1928, p. 133, cols. 5–6.

[55] Zhou Jianzhang, "Zhuiyi Donghai xian er, sanshi nian dai de wangshi" (Recollecting the past: the era of the twenties and thirties in Donghai County), *Lianyungang shi wenshi ziliao* 4 (August 1986): 13–30.

[56] Zhou Jianzhang, "Zhuiyi Donghai," 13–18.

[57] *Jiangsu jianshe ting gongbao* 15 (October 1, 1928): 127.

[58] Ibid., 127–28.

[59] Ibid., 127–28.

[60] Ibid., 128–29.

[61] *Zhongguo Guomindang dierjie zhongyang jiancha weiyuan hui baogao shu* (Report of the second supervisory committee of the Nationalist Party) (N.p., n.d.), 88. Internal evidence suggests that this was published in late 1928 or early 1929.

[62] Sun Yiwu, "Ganyu xian diyige Gongchandang yuan," 25–26.

[63] Ibid., 25–26; Sun Ziying and Song Yiqian, "Women suo zhidao de Zhu Shoushi xiansheng" (The Mr. Zhu Shoushi that we knew), *Ganyu xian wenshi ziliao* 7 (October 1989): 47–51.

[64] *Zhongyang ribao*, April 19, 1928, sec. 2, p. 2, cols. 1–3. A memoir produced in the People's Republic of China gives a different slant on this affair. It does not include any references to Zhang's statement about the GMD being harmed by the CCP. In fact, it suggests that Zhang took his life because he was distraught about the execution of two Communists. That is, of course, possible, but his troubled mental state was very likely more a result of the death of his younger brother, Zhang Jiren, who had been the leader of the county's peasant association. Jiren had apparently been killed in the county government's attempt to suppress the peasant association. See Xu Zhiyi, "Xu Zhiren zhuan lüe" (A brief biography of Xu Zhiren), *Jiading wenshi ziliao xuanji* 1: 167–70. (My copy of this article includes no date.)

[65] *Zhongyang ribao*, April 19, 1928, sec. 2, p. 2, cols. 1–3.

[66] Sun Guangwu, "Sun Jishi bei sha," 143–44.

[67] Chen Yifu, "Qingmo minchu de Feng xian jiaoyu gaikuang" (The situation of Feng County education in the late Qing and early Republic), *Feng xian wenshi ziliao* 9 (April 1991): 2–3.

[68] Sun Guangwu, "Sun Jishi bei sha," 144–46.

[69] Ibid., 146.

[70] Dong Yao, ed., "Beifa hou, Feng xian shouren xianzhang Wang Gongyu" (The first Feng County magistrate Wang Gongyu), *Feng xian wenshi ziliao* 4 (March 1986): 7–12.

[71] Ibid., 11.

[72] Ibid.

[73] Ibid.; Sun Guangwu, "Sun Jishi bei sha," 147. On the execution of Sun see also *Shi bao*, February 16, 1928, p. 3; February 20, 1928, p. 7.

[74] Sun Guangwu, "Sun Jishi bei sha," 147; Dong Yao, ed., "Beifa hou," 11–12; interview, Taibei, 1977.

[75] Chen Yifu, "Qingmo minchu," 4; interview, Taibei, 1977.

[76] Interview, Taibei, 1977; Dong Yao, ed., "Beifa hou," *Feng xian wenshi ziliao* 4 (March 1986): 7–14.

[77] Yang Binnong, "Qingmo minguo Feng xian jianwen zatan" (Miscellaneous observations on Feng County in the late Qing and Republican periods), *Feng xian wenshi ziliao* 4 (March 1986): 180.

[78] *Shen bao*, September 2, 1928, p. 14, col. 3.

[79] *Shen bao*, July 28, 1927, p. 9, col. 3. Part of this process can be seen in the Donghai County case in *Zhongyang ribao*, February 17, 1928, sec. 2, p. 2, cols. 1–2. See also *Shen bao*, July 11, 1927, p. 7, col. 4; *Shishi xinbao*, July 1, 1929, sec. 2, p. 2, col. 4.

[80] *Shen bao*, August 7, 1927, p. 8, col. 1.

[81] *Shen bao*, July 4, 1927, p. 10, col. 4.

[82] For example see Wu Tianhan, et al., *Zhongguo Guomindang Kunshan*, 34.

[83] Barkan, "Nationalists, Communists," 417–20.

[84] *Shen bao*, September 6, 1927, p. 6, col. 6.

[85] I have found over a hundred such cases mentioned, primarily in *Shen bao*, *Zhongyang ribao*, and *Shi bao*, though many other sources contain such reports.

[86] I suppose that it would be possible to argue that the provincial assembly members, whose cases I deal with in this chapter, were provincial rather than local elites. However, anecdotal evidence suggests that these men, in addition to playing political roles at the provincial level, exercised power at the county level.

[87] Yang Dongye, "Aiguo minzhu zhanshi Feng Yinong" (Patriotic, democratic soldier Feng Yinong), *Lianyungang shi wenshi ziliao* 5 (December 1987): 154–56.

[88] *Zhongyang ribao*, May 5, 1928, sec. 2, p. 4; *Funing xian xin zhi* (1934) 4:23b–24a.

[89] The Funing County gazetteer (cited above) lists twelve other provincial assembly members. None of them matches any of the over two hundred names I have collected of persons assaulted as "bullies." Of course, this is not conclusive proof that other Funing assembly members were not prosecuted, since my catalog of cases is quite incomplete.

[90] *Nanjing minguo ribao*, October 24, 1927, p. 5.

[91] Barkan, "Nationalists, Communists," 418.

[92] *Shi bao*, August 26, 1928, sec. 1, p. 4.

[93] Allegedly he had pocketed the money a merchant had paid for a brokerage license, but never produced the license. *Shi bao*, Nov. 25, 1927, sec. 2, p. 6; (1928) Jan. 15, p. 6; Feb. 3, sec. 2, p. 6; Feb. 4, sec. 2, p. 6; Mar. 1, p. 6; Mar. 2,

sec. 2, p. 7; April 12, sec. 2, p. 6; April 15, p. 6; *Zhongyang ribao*, April 12, 1928, sec. 2, p. 2.

[94] For the significance of county provisional committees and county special committees, see Appendix I. For the references on the two committees' support for action against Yao, see Xu Mengmei, Zheng Fengshi, and Di Dounan, "Huiyi Guomindang zai Taicang de dangwu huodong" (Reminiscing about the party affairs actions of the Nationalist Party in Taicang), *Taicang wenshi ziliao jicun* 2 (December 1984): 36–37.

[95] For the case of Qian Jingzhi, a township head (*xiang xingzheng juzhang*) in Kunshan County, see Wu Tianhan, et al., *Zhongguo Guomindang Kunshan*, 73.

[96] See the section of this chapter on party-government conflict.

[97] *Shi bao*, November 19, 1927, p. 3; January 9, 1928, sec. 2, p. 7.

[98] *Shishi xinbao*, July 20, 1929, sec. 2, p. 2, col. 9.

[99] Wu Tianhan, et al., *Zhongguo Guomindang Kunshan*, 74, 77, 90.

[100] In addition to the sources cited below, see Wu Qiang, "Yiliu can'an huiyi" (Reminiscences about the January 6th Massacre), *Shuyang wenshi ziliao* 2 (May 1985): 1–18. However, I believe that much of the information on GMD clique connections in this article is not accurate. Other articles on this event include Li Wangsu, "Ao qing bianxiang leng zhong kai" (Revealing pridefulness as it abates), *Shuyang wenshi ziliao* 1 (October 1984): 10–25. Some brief accounts contemporary with the event appear in *Zhongyang ribao* (1928) February 5, sec. 2, p. 3; June 28, sec. 2, p. 3; June 10, sec. 2, p. 3. Also see the accounts cited below.

[101] For the "Eight Local Bullies" designation for this clique, see "'Yi liu' can'an de shishi jingguo" (The actual events of the January 6th Massacre), *Shuyang wenshi ziliao* 6 (November 1990): 36–70. For the designation "East Faction" and information on the Cheng family's holdings and background, see "Sun Depei nianji gao (jielu)" (A draft of the years of Sun Depei [excerpt]), *Shuyang wenshi ziliao* 4 (March 1988): 47–48, 58; and Yang Hegao, "Da dizhu 'Cheng Zhentai' jia ye xingshuai shimo" (The rise and fall of the family property of great landlord Cheng Zhentai), *Shuyang wenshi ziliao* 2 (May 1985): 118–28. For the designation "Cheng Faction," see Zhang Zhongwu, *Shuyang xiangtu*, 182–83.

[102] "Sun Depei," 48.

[103] Ge Shaoliang, "Guanyu 'yiliu,'" 13–15.

[104] Ge Shaoliang, "Guanyu 'yiliu,'" 12–33; "Sun Depei," 47–49.

[105] Ge Shaoliang, "Guanyu 'yiliu,'" 28–30; Zhang Zhongwu, ed., *Shuyang xiangtu*, 142, 181–85.

[106] Ge Shaoliang, "Guanyu 'yiliu,'" 25.

[107] "'Yiliu' can'an de shishi jingguo" (The actual events of the January 6th Massacre), *Shuyang wenshi ziliao* 6 (November 1990): 65–67; Ge Shaoliang, "Guanyu 'yiliu,'" 30–35.

[108] "Sun Depei," 58.

[109] Zhang Zhongwu, ed., *Shuyang*, 182.

[110] Ge Shaoliang, "Guanyu 'yiliu,'" 33–35; "'Yiliu' can'an de shishi jingguo," 36–48.

[111] "'Yiliu' can'an shishi jingguo," 36–48.

[112] Ibid., 48–70.

[113] Ibid., 49–58.

[114] Ibid., 58–70; Zhang Zhongwu, ed., *Shuyang xiangtu*, 183–84.

[115] Zhang Zhongwu, ed., *Shuyang xiangtu*, 181–85; *Jiangsu sheng zhengfu gongbao* 62 (December 3, 1928): 32–35. See also "'Yiliu' can'an yihou" (After the January 6th Massacre), *Shuyang wenshi ziliao* 6 (November 1990): 71–84.

[116] Zhang Zhongwu, ed., *Shuyang xiangtu*, 184–85.

[117] We have already looked at the case of Sun Jishi, head of the Feng County Chamber of Commerce (pp. 125–28).

[118] Hua Gang, *Yijiuerwu nian zhi yijiuerqi nian de Zhongguo da geming shi* (Shanghai: Chungeng shudian, 1931), 316.

[119] *Shen bao*, August 8, 1927, p. 10, col. 4.

[120] These are 1933 figures from Zhao Ruheng, *Jiangsu shengjian*, vol. 1, *zhang* 2, 61–66.

[121] *Zhongguo Guomindang shangren yundong jingguo*, edited by Zhongguo Guomindang zhongyang shangrenbu (n. p.: Zhongguo Guomindang zhongyang shangren bu, 1927), 1–2.

[122] Ibid., 3–4.

[123] Ibid., 4–5.

[124] Ibid., 6. At least the Western Hills Nanjing municipal headquarters had such a department, so it is likely that the provincial headquarters also had one. Ju Zheng, *Qingdang shilu*, 85.

[125] *Zhongguo Guomindang shangren*, 11–12.

[126] Bu Zhongji, "Huang Lisan qi ren" (The man Huang Lisan), *Yancheng wenshi ziliao xuanji* 6:33–36. My copy lacks dates.

[127] *Shen bao*, August 15, 1927, p. 9, cols. 4–5.

[128] *Shen bao*, August 8, 1927, p. 10, col. 5.

[129] *Shen bao*, May 30, 1927, p. 8, col. 5.

[130] *Shen bao*, August 16, 1927, p. 10, col. 3.

[131] For example, the Nanhui County party passed on merchant requests that taxes not be increased. *Shishi xinbao*, June 22, 1929, sec. 2, p. 2, col. 3.

[132] For a report on one meeting between Chiang and his merchant allies, see *Shen bao*, July 6, 1927, p. 13, col. 1. On the terror tactics employed to force merchant contributions, see Isaacs, *Tragedy*, 181–82; also see Parks M. Coble, *The Shanghai Capitalists and the Nationalist Government, 1927–1937*. (Cambridge, Mass., Council on East Asian Studies, Harvard University, 1980), 32–40. On Chiang's ties in Shanghai and the GMD's links with certain factions of Shanghai merchants, see Joseph Fewsmith, *Party, State, and Local Elites in Republican China: Merchant Organizations and Politics in Shanghai, 1890–1930* (Honolulu: University of Hawaii Press, 1985), 115–66.

[133] Akira Iriye, *After Imperialism: The Search for a New Order in the Far East, 1921–1931* (Cambridge, Mass.: Harvard University Press, 1969), 193–205. On the boycotts, see also C. F. Remer, *A Study of Chinese Boycotts* (1933; reprint, Taipei: Ch'eng-wen, 1966), 137–40.

[134] *Zhongyang ribao*, October 19, 1928, sec. 2, p. 2, cols. 1–4.

[135] *Shishi xinbao*, November 24, 1931, sec. 2, p. 1, col. 8.

[136] *Zhongyang ribao*, October 19, 1928, sec. 2, p. 2, cols. 1–4.

[137] *Shishi xinbao*, April 28, 1929, sec. 2, p. 2, col. 6.

[138] *North China Herald*, July 13, 1929, p. 50.

[139] *Shishi xinbao*, November 1, 1931, sec. 1, p. 4, cols. 1–2.

[140] For example, see the report on the actions of students in Taicang County given in *Shishi xinbao*, January 14, 1932, sec. 2, p. 4. See also Israel, *Student Nationalism*, 57.

[141] Jiang Yigu, "30 niandai qianhou, Jiangyin xuesheng chajin Rihuo qingkuang de huiyi" (From the beginning to the end of the 1930s, recollections of the circumstances of Jiangyin students' prohibition of Japanese goods), *Jiangyin wenshi ziliao* 10 (September 1989): 88–89.

[142] *Shishi xinbao*, October 10, 1929, sec. 3, p. 2, col. 3.

[143] *Shishi xinbao* (1929) April 29, sec. 2, p. 3, col. 2; May 27, sec. 2, p. 2, col. 3; June 29, sec. 2, p. 1, col. 5; June 30, page number illegible; July 3, sec. 2, p. 2, col. 3.

[144] Cao Kemin, "Mijia de feizhang ji qi shehui de yingxiang" (The spiraling of rice prices and its social consequences), *Cunzhi* 1.6 (September 1, 1930): 8–10.

[145] *Shishi xinbao*, May 27, 1929, sec 2, p. 2, col. 3.

[146] On the concept of "scientism," see Daniel W. Y. Kwok, *Scientism in Chinese Thought, 1900–1950* (New Haven: Yale University Press, 1965).

[147] "Jiangsu Xiao xian Jiangyin," Songjiang documents, 76–94.

[148] I base this judgment on my survey of biographies in county-level *wenshi ziliao* from Jiangsu.

[149] Roger R. Thompson, "Cultural Imperialism," 6, passim; Duara, *Culture, Power, and the State*, 31–35, 118–48; David Johnson, "'Confucian' Elements in the Great Temple Festivals of Southeastern Shansi in Late Imperial Times," *T'oung Pao* 83 (1997): 126–61.

[150] C. K. Yang, *Religion in Chinese Society* (Berkeley: University of California Press, 1961), 366.

[151] Prasenjit Duara, "Knowledge and Power in the Discourse of Modernity: The Campaigns Against Popular Religion in Early Twentieth-Century China," *Journal of Asian Studies* 50.1 (February 1991): 67–83. Duara also covers this ground in *Rescuing History From the Nation*, 99, and elsewhere in chapter 3. In *Culture, Power, and the State*, Duara makes a number of points relevant to the question of state treatment of religious issues. He argues that local elites in North China often exerted social influence by serving as patrons of temples and managers of religious ceremonies. He notes that from the late nineteenth century through the 1930s the Chinese state attacked local religious institutions and extracted their wealth. Resistance was sharp, but short-lived. Local elites, who had early on played religious leadership roles in their communities, quickly shifted to a strategy of using the expanding state as a symbolic basis of their power. See Duara, *Culture, Power and the State*, 156, 157, 136–37.

[152] Ash, *Land Tenure*, 16–17; Zhao Ruheng, *Jiangsu shengjian*, vol. 2, *zhang* 8, 204–210; "Yancheng xian dangbu gongzuo diaocha shixiang yilan," 40–47.

[153] This account of the Yancheng Massacre and related circumstances relies on the following sources: "Yancheng xian dangbu gongzuo," 8–9; 34–35; *Shen bao*, October 10, 1928, p. 8; October 13, 1928, p. 11, col. 1; "Ling chaban Yancheng xianzhang Li Yicheng" (Order for investigation and handling of Yancheng magistrate Li Yicheng), *Jiangsu sheng zhengfu gongbao* 56:14; 58:52; *Zhongyang ribao* (1928) October 13, sec. 3, p. 1; October 16, sec. 2, p. 3, cols. 1–4; October 17, sec. 2, p. 3, cols. 1–3; October 17, sec. 2, p. 3, col. 8; October 18, sec. 2, p. 3, cols. 3–5, 6–7; Cai Bochuan, "Huoshao chenghuang miao" (The burning of the Temple of the City God), *Yancheng xian wenshi ziliao* 1,2 (reprinted January 1984): 47–53.

[154] Zhang Shaoyi, "Xi'nan dang," 4–9; Zhou Mengzhuang, "Guanyu Yancheng," 118–27.

[155] Zhang Shaoyi, "Xi'nan dang," 4–8; Gao Yuzai, "Hu Qidong xiansheng ersan shi" (Two or three things about Mr. Hu Qidong), *Yancheng wenshi ziliao xuanji* 4 (June 1986): 107–108; Zhou Mengzhuang, "Guanyu Yancheng," 118–26.

[156] Ai Wu and Wen Han, "Gaizu pai fenzi zai Yancheng suo yinqi de shibian" (The incident that was instigated by the Reorganization Clique elements in Yancheng), *Yancheng xian wenshi ziliao* 1,2 (January 1984): 54–57; Zhang Youwu, "Xia Song shengping shilüe" (A brief sketch of the life of Xia Song), *Jianhu wenshi xuanji* 3 (November 1989): 15–19.

[157] Interview, Taibei, 1977.

[158] *Shishi xinbao*, April 27, 1927, sec. 2, p. 3, col. 6; (1929) March 1, sec. 2, p. 2, col. 3; April 24, sec. 2, p. 2, col. 5; April 30, sec. 2, p. 2, cols. 5–6; Feng Hefa, ed., *Zhongguo nongcun jingji ziliao*, 357.

[159] *North China Herald*, March 23, 1929, p. 481.

[160] *Shi bao*, February 20, 1929, sec. 1, p. 4, cols. 1–2.

[161] *Shi bao*, February 20, 1929, sec. 1, p. 4.

[162] On the unpopularity of the calendar reform among Sword Society membership, see Zhang Zhenzhi, *Geming yu zongjiao*, 192–93. I suspect that the general feeling of the Sword Society membership was not far removed from that of the populace more generally.

[163] *Shi bao*, February 23, 1929, sec. 1, p. 3.

[164] *Shen bao*, February 21, 1929, p. 11, cols. 3–4. One source indicates that the "local bullies" had been investigated by the party and that the provincial government had ordered their arrest. However, it also argues that the government had never caught the accused individuals. This source also lists as leaders of the Suqian uprising people of neighboring counties who had been charged as "local bullies and evil gentry." See Ling Yanyu, "Xu lun Suqian shijian" (Continued discussion of the Suqian Incident), *Mingri zhi Jiangsu* 6 (June 1929): 17–33, esp. 18–19 (non-consecutive pagination). See also the article on the Suqian uprising in the April 1929 issue of this journal.

[165] *Shi bao*, February 23, 1929, sec. 1, p. 3.

[166] *Shen bao*, February 24, 1929, p. 11, col. 3.

[167] *Shishi xinbao*, April 20, 1929, sec. 3, p. 4, cols. 3–4.

[168] *Shen bao*, February 21, 1929, p. 11, cols. 3–4. One alternative interpretation of available news reports would be that some local chambers of commerce (i.e., from the county seat and various townships) were supporting the Swords while others were funding the military forces suppressing them. Most reports are ambiguous; they do not reveal whether the chambers of which they speak were based in the county seat or in some market town.

[169] For the list of those accused as "bullies" in Suqian, see *Shen bao*, February 21, 1929, p. 11, cols. 3–4. For background on Zhang and Liu, see *Suqian wenxian* 2 (January 1967): 19, 47, 52.

[170] *Shen bao*, February 21, 1929, p. 11, cols. 3–4; *Suqian wenxian* 2 (January 1967): 19, 47, 52.

[171] For such speculation, see *Shi bao*, February 25, 1929, sec. 1, p. 3.

[172] *Shen bao*, February 21, 1929, p. 11, cols. 3–4.

[173] Although one source (*Shi bao*, March 2, 1929, sec. 1–2, pp. 1–2) indicates that one person was not recovered, another (*Shishi xinbao*, April 4, 1929, sec. 3, p. 4) says all were restored to freedom. The magistrate fled Suqian in early March.

[174] Zheng Keming, "Suqian Xiaodao hui shimo" (The beginning and the end of the Suqian Small Sword Society), *Huaiyin wenshi ziliao* 2 (December 1984): 42–50; *Jiangsu geming douzheng jilüe*, 385, 388–89. Duara has described the Suqian conflict as a case of "bifurcated history," in which both sides in the struggle were animated by their own versions of utopia ("great unity," *datong*). The party's vision of the "shining new age" was countered by the rebels' yearnings for community that would be bound together by popular religion. Duara calls attention to the rebels' use of the name "Army of Great Unity" for their armed forces. See Duara, *Rescuing History*, 106.

[175] *Shishi xinbao* (1931) March 5, sec. 1, p. 4, cols. 9–10; March 7, sec. 1, p. 4, col. 7; March 9, sec. 2, p. 2, col. 9; March 22, sec. 1, p. 4, col. 12; Chen Guofu, *Su zheng huiyi*, 82.

[176] On the government's "temporary" opposition to confiscation of temple property, see "Guanli simiao xin li wei ban yiqian zhan reng qi jiu" (Until the articles on management of shrines and temples have been promulgated, temporarily maintain the status quo), *Jiangsu sheng zhengfu gongbao* 59 (November 12, 1928): 18–23; "Ling zhi simiao guanli diaoli zhan huan shixing" (Directing all to be aware that they should postpone putting into effect the "Articles on Temples and Shrines"), *Jiangsu sheng zhengfu gongbao* 168 (June 25, 1929): 6.

[177] Central University was independent of the provincial government, but it administered Jiangsu education as if it were a provincial department of education.

[178] "Xu xiansheng yuan cheng yi" (The original petitions of county magistrate Xu, 1), *Jiangsu sheng zhengfu gongbao* 59 (November 12, 1928): 19.

[179] Interview, Taibei, 1977.

[180] "Dahui shenxiang yu pochu mixin wenti" (Destruction of idols and the problem of eradication of superstition), *Jiangsu sheng zhengfu gongbao* 64 (December 17, 1928): 47–48; "Ling jin Rugao xian wei ling hui chenghuang miao" (Directing prohibition of Rugao County from destroying the Temple of

the City God in contravention of orders), *Jiangsu sheng zhengfu gongbao* 60 (November 19, 1928): 24–25.

[181] "Dahui shenxiang." This article also suggests that the provincial government differentiated between idols, which it considered fair game for idol smashing by local party branches, and substantial properties of religious institutions, which were to be protected.

[182] Chen Guofu, *Su zheng huiyi*, 82–83.

[183] Ibid.

[184] *Xinwen bao*, March 9, 1933, p. 8, col. 4.

[185] Chen Guofu, *Su zheng huiyi*, 82–87. This passage refers to government policy during Chen Guofu's term as provincial governor (October 1933–1937).

[186] Zhou Fohai, "Zenyang tuijin Su sheng yiwu jiaoyu" (How to push forward compulsory education in Jiangsu), *Jiangsu jiaoyu* 4.9 (September 15, 1935): 3.

[187] Chen Guofu, *Su zheng huiyi*, 102–103.

[188] Y. C. Wang, *Chinese Intellectuals and the West, 1872–1949* (Chapel Hill: University of North Carolina Press, 1966). This idea is a subtext at many points in the book, but see especially 182–85, 369, and 500.

[189] Hunter, *Modernizing Peasant Societies*, 46.

[190] Curran, "Education and Society," 180.

[191] Ibid., 196–97, 180–81.

[192] Ibid., 175–76, 178, 180, 200, 205, 237.

[193] Ibid., 178.

[194] Ibid., 179, 181, 182–88.

[195] *Shishi xinbao*, August 13, 1929, sec. 2, p. 2, col. 9.

[196] Noel R. Miner, "Chekiang: The Nationalist's Effort in Agrarian Reform and Construction, 1927–1937" (Ph.D. diss., Stanford University, 1973), 68–69, 72–76, 260; Noel R. Miner, "Agrarian Reform in Nationalist China: The Case of Rent Reduction in Chekiang, 1927–1937," in *China at the Crossroads: Nationalists and Communists, 1927–1949*, ed. F. Gilbert Chan (Boulder: Westview Press, 1980), 81.

[197] Wu Tianhan, et al., *Zhongguo Guomindang Kunshan*, passim, especially in the latter half of the book.

[198] Feng Yingzi, "Wushi nian qian de Kunshan diandi" (A little bit about the Kunshan of fifty years ago), *Kunshan wenshi* 1 (March 1983): 59–67.

[199] David Tsai, "Party-Government Relations in Kiangsu Province, 1927–1932," *Select Papers From the Center for Far Eastern Studies* 1 (1975–1976): 86–88.

200 Ibid., 90.

201 Ibid., 90–92.

202 Ibid., 93. After the CCP came to power in 1949 it also had trouble finding a satisfactory distribution of powers and responsibilities between party and government. However, according to Shiping Zheng, in the case of the CCP, the party's power greatly overshadowed that of the government. See Shiping Zheng, *Party vs. State in Post-1949 China: The Institutional Dilemma* (Cambridge: Cambridge University Press, 1997).

203 *Shen bao*, June 6, 1927, p. 8, cols. 3–4.

204 For use of the slogan, see Ye Chucang's article in *Zhongyang ribao*, June 8, 1928, sec. 2, p. 3.

205 Ye Chucang, "Jiangsu sheng xingzheng jinkuang" (The recent situation in Jiangsu provincial administration), *Zhongyang dangwu yuekan* 27 (October 1930): 147–51.

206 See Lu Ziquan, "Chenwei shiwei xuanchuan he Guomindang de fanpu" (The Chen dike demonstration and propaganda, and the Nationalist Party's counteroffensive), *Xinyi wenshi ziliao* 2 (June 1986): 57–75, especially 59–60. Another factor in party-government tension in one corner of Pi County was the domination of one ward branch GMD organization by Communists. An underground Communist cell, posing as the GMD ward branch, put together a sizable demonstration, replete with agitators chanting slogans tinged with the concept of class struggle, and denigrating Chiang Kai-shek and the Nationalist Party.

207 Ni Bi, "Duiyu Jiangsu ge xian zhengzhi de ganxiang he xiwang" (Opinions and hopes with regard to the politics of various Jiangsu counties), *Jiangsu xunkan* 2 (September 11, 1928): 12.

208 Ibid., 11–13.

209 Ibid.

210 Lloyd E. Eastman, *The Abortive Revolution*, 299–303. Eastman does not concentrate on the question of youth and government, but rather on corruption more generally.

211 *Shen bao*, December 14, 1927, p. 7, col. 5; *Shi bao*, December 13, 1927, sec. 1, pp. 2–3. Another article suggesting that the party approach to local elites varied by region appears in *Shen bao*, February 15, 1929, p. 11, cols. 4–6.

212 This paragraph, as well as succeeding ones on the Taixing fracas, are based on the following articles: *Shen bao* (1927) July 6, p. 10, col. 4; July 8, p. 9, cols. 1, 2 and 6, and p. 10, cols. 3 and 10; July 11, p. 7, col. 4; July 22, p. 9, col. 4; July 23, p. 9, cols. 2–3; July 28, p. 9, col. 3; August 1, p. 9, cols. 3–6; August 2, p. 6, col.

2; August 7, p. 8, col. 5; August 8, p. 9, col. 3; August 17, p. 10, col. 1. We have in this collection of articles sources from many perspectives, including those of a party member who was beaten, defenders of those who mounted the attack on the party, provincial GMD investigators who were sent to the scene, the county magistrate, He Yingqin, who was also the provincial commissioner of military affairs, and individual newspaper correspondents who seem to have been uncommitted to any side in the fray.

[213] Barkan, "Nationalists, Communists," 470. Li Yafei's self defense and his version of the events are given in *Shi bao*, July 19, 1927, sec. 3, (page number unclear).

[214] Yin Zhixiu, "Shen Yi tongzhi he Ru-Tai nongmin baodong" (Comrade Shen Yi and the peasant uprisings in Rugao and Taixing), *Jiangsu wenshi ziliao* 5: 71–98.

[215] *Shi bao*, July 19, 1927, sec. 3 (page number missing).

[216] *Shen bao*, July 11, 1927, p. 7, col. 6.

[217] On Shen Yi, see Zhong Sheng, "Jiangsu ge xian Gongchandang baodong," 48–49; Barkan, "Nationalists, Communists," 470–73; Yin Zhixiu, "Shen Yi tongzhi," 98.

[218] Yin Zhixiu, "Shen Yi tongzhi," 83–88; see also the articles in *Shi bao* and *Shen bao* cited above in notes 215 and 216.

[219] *Shen bao*, July 6, 1927, p. 10, col. 4; *Shen bao*, August 2, 1927, p. 6, col. 2.

[220] *Shen bao*, July 8, 1927, p. 10, col. 3.

[221] Shen did, however, enjoy the support of friends among local elites. After he was imprisoned, one Taixing gentry sent him 100 *yuan*, which Shen used to print a propaganda pamphlet for the peasant movement in the county. On this and other signs of Shen's relations to local elites, see Yin Zhixiu, "Shen Yi tongzhi," 83, 88.

[222] *Shen bao*, July 8, 1927, p. 9, col. 6 and p. 10, col. 1.

[223] *Shen bao*, August 1, 1927, p. 9, cols. 3–6.

[224] See *Shen bao*, July 22, 1927, p. 9, col. 4, for such a case in Funing County.

[225] *Shen bao*, February 15, 1929, p. 11, cols. 4–6.

[226] The main sources on the fight between Qiu Fu and the Kunshan County GMD are Wu Tianhan, et al., *Zhongguo Guomindang Kunshan*, 28–44; Yang Qimin, "Kunshan 'qingdang' qianhou dangzheng da shi ji" (A chronology of party and administrative events before and after the purge in Kunshan), *Kunshan wenshi* 4 (September 1985): 99–102; "Guomindang Kunshan xian dangbu dangwu gaikuang" (The circumstances of party affairs in the Kunshan County Nationalist Party branch), *Kunshan wenshi* 4 (September 1985): 96–98; Zhang Zhichen, "1927 nian da geming shiqi de Kunshan" (Kunshan at the time of the

great revolution of 1927), *Kunshan wenshi* 1 (March 1983): 45–49; Zhou Meichu, "Huai jiu" (Thinking of the past), *Kunshan wenshi* 1 (March 1983): 57–59. Although Zhang Zhichen states that Lu Donghao had not been involved in attacks on the local GMD, Wu Tianhan argues in some detail that a Lu Qi had been a leader in such assaults on the party. I suspect that these are two names for one individual. See Wu Tianhan, et al, *Zhongguo Guomindang Kunshan*, 38–40.

[227] Zhang Zhichen, "1927 nian da geming," 46–49; Wu Tianhan et al, *Zhongguo Guomindang Kunshan*, 28–44.

[228] Wu Tianhan et al., *Zhongguo Guomindang Kunshan*, 45–111, passim.

[229] Wu Tianhan et al, *Zhongguo Guomindang Kunshan*, passim.

[230] Jia Ming, "Xinhai geming hou Suining," 1–9.

[231] Ibid., 4.

[232] Ibid., 3–6. On the split between the Xia and Wang groups, see "Zhongguo Guomindang Jiangsu sheng Suining xian dangbu gongzuo diaocha shixiang yilan," February 20, 1930, 6–7. On the question of GMD ties with militia elites, see page 62.

[233] "Zhongguo Guomindang Jiangsu sheng Suining xian," 10; Jia Ming, "Xinhai geming hou Suining," 9–10.

[234] Jia Ming, "Xinhai geming hou Suining," 10.

[235] Ibid., 10–11.

[236] Ibid. The last two phrases each carry a double entendre. The first, which ends with the expression *xiaobian* (little pigtails) when spoken could also be taken as "he is simply piss." The second also suggests an alternate meaning: "he amplifies disorder."

[237] Ibid., 13–14.

[238] Ibid., 11; "Zhongguo Guomindang Jiangsu sheng Suining xian," 10–19, passim.

[239] Jia Ming, "Xinhai geming hou Suining," 14–18; "Zhongguo Guomindang Jiangsu sheng Suining xian," 6, 9, 22. For further references on Suining local elite factionalism and Li Zifeng, see: *Zhongyang ribao*, May 3, 1930, sec. 3, p. 2, col. 4; *Qianfeng* 11 (October 10, 1929): 28, 46; *Jiangsu sheng zhengfu gongbao* 83 (March 14, 1929): 14–16 and 86 (March 18, 1929): 15–16.

Notes to Chapter 6

[1] Miner, "Chekiang: The Nationalist's Effort," 74–77, 92–93. Although Miner does not explicitly blame the party center for the shift, the juxtaposition of Dai

Jitao's "negotiations" and the subsequent changes strongly imply that the party center was responsible.

² For just one of the many cases of this kind, see *Jiangsu dangwu zhoukan* 13 (April 12, 1930): 59–63.

³ See, for example, the minutes of a meeting of the provincial Organization Department in *Jiangsu dangwu zhoukan* 13 (April 12, 1930): 87–101.

⁴ Compare *Jiangsu dangwu zhoukan* with *Jiangsu dangsheng*, the organ of the Provincial Directorate, which controlled the Jiangsu party through most of 1928. Although the Directorate was a centrally-appointed committee, it showed more independence from the center than did the rectification committee of 1930 through 1931.

⁵ Pan Juemin, "Duiyu zhengli xian yixia geji dangbu de yijian" (An opinion with regard to rectifying the party branches below the county level), *Jiangsu dangwu zhoukan* 6 (February 16, 1930): 40–42.

⁶ *Jiangsu dangwu zhoukan* 13 (April 12, 1930): 60–61.

⁷ For example, the term appears only rarely in the official organ of the provincial rectification committee, *Jiangsu dangwu zhoukan*.

⁸ For an account of a typical meeting see *Zhongyang ribao*, January 16, 1930, sec. 2, p. 4. On an exceptional meeting in which measures against one particular local elite were passed, see *Zhongyang ribao*, May 3, 1930, sec. 3, p. 2, col. 4, In the latter case the provincial committee acted against Li Zifeng, the darling of a Suining County nonparty elite faction. This matter is treated at length in the previous chapter, pages 177–82. The Anhui Rectification Committee may not have been as cautious in its treatment of local elites; see *Zhongyang ribao*, February 26, 1931, sec. 2, p. 1, cols. 1–2. For other exceptional cases, see *Sumin zhoubao* 46 (May 19, 1930): 18 and *Sumin zhoubao* 45 (May 11, 1930): 12–13.

⁹ Gong Xinzhai and Luo Zhiyuan, "Jiangsu gexian xianzheng canguan jiyao" (A record of an inspection of county governments in various Jiangsu districts), *Jiangsu yuebao* 4.5,6 (December 1, 1935): 46, 50.

¹⁰ For the earlier attitude, see Wu Tianhan, et al., *Zhongguo Guomindang Kunshan*, 47.

¹¹ *Zhongyang ribao*, February 3, 1930.

¹² *Zhongyang ribao*, May 9, 1930, sec. 2, p. 4.

¹³ *Jiangsu dangwu zhoukan* 13 (April 12, 1930): 83.

¹⁴ *Jiangsu dangwu zhoukan* 25 (July 6, 1930): 111–12.

¹⁵ *Zhongyang ribao*, May 9, 1930, sec. 2, p. 4, col. 1.

¹⁶ *Zhongyang ribao*, July 19, 1930, sec. 2, p. 4.

¹⁷ This conclusion is the result of my survey of a variety of media sources from the early to mid-1930s, including *Shen bao, Jiangsu dangwu zhoukan, Shishi xinbao,* and *Xinwen bao,* as well as documents in the GMD archives in Taiwan.

¹⁸ In Suining, the provincial rectification committee supported the county party in a dispute with a *xian* magistrate that had begun before rectification. See *Shishi xinbao,* September 6, 1929, sec. 2, p. 1, col. 8; *Zhongyang ribao,* sec. 2, p. 4. Also see the complex and contorted history of the county GMD's fight with nonparty elites in "Zhongguo Guomindang Jiangsu sheng Suining xian dangbu." Also, on a case of party-government strife that stemmed, in part, from residual radicalism in a *xian* GMD branch, see Zhao Baojue, "Guomindang Qidong xian dangbu ji qi dang zheng jiufen" (The Qidong County party branch and its party-government dispute), *Qidong wenshi xuanji* 2 (April 1985): 48–51.

¹⁹ The source states that Chen became governor in 1934, but in reality the year was 1933. See Zhang Shupei, "Tongshan xian Guomindang gaikuang" (The situation of the Tongshan County Nationalist Party), *Tongshan wenshi ziliao* 5 (August 1985): 74–75.

²⁰ Pan Juemin, "Duiyu zhengli xian yixia geji dangbu de yijian," 40–42.

²¹ *Zhongyang ribao,* May 9, 1930, sec. 2, p. 4, col. 1.

²² *Jiangsu dangwu zhoukan* 30 (April 12, 1930): 62–64.

²³ *Jiangsu dangwu zhoukan* 25 (July 6, 1930): 111–12.

²⁴ See the section above, entitled "Party-Government Relations," pp. 164–83.

²⁵ A number of statements in Chen Lifu's memoirs lead one to believe that Chen equated loyalty to the GMD to personal loyalty to Chiang. See Ch'en Li-fu, *Storm Clouds,* passim, but esp. 1, 67, 136, 234–35.

²⁶ I see evidence for this in many sections of Chen Guofu's *Su zheng huiyi,* but see especially pages 137–40.

²⁷ See *Guoli zhengzhi daxue shi shiliao huibian* (Taibei, 1977), passim, but esp. see 2: 15. On the degree of the Chens' influence at the Central Party Affairs Academy, see Ch'en Li-fu, *Storm Clouds,* 195–98.

²⁸ Israel, *Student Nationalism,* 18, 23.

²⁹ A cynic might note that this approach left the appointment of local and provincial party leaders largely in the hands of the Central Organization Department, which was controlled by Zhou's friends. In fact, for several years the party followed this top-down method of filling leadership positions.

³⁰ "Geming gaochao zaiqi de qianye zhi zhunbei—Zhou Houjun shi zai sheng dangbu zongli jinian zhou zhi yanci—xian gei Jiangsu quan sheng de geming tongzhi" (Preparing for the reprise of the high tide of revolution—Mr. Zhou Houjun's talk at the provincial party headquarters' Sun Yat-sen remembrance

celebration—a lecture that he [Zhou] contributed to the revolutionary comrades of the entirety of Jiangsu province), *Susheng yuekan* 1.3,4 (October 1933): 1–8.

[31] Fewsmith, *Party, State and Local Elites*, 160.

[32] *Zhongguo jingji nianjian* (1934), *zhang* 13, 22–41; (1935), *xubian*, vol. 7 (but this edition is a reprint with vol. 18 on its spine), *zhang* 14, 61–69.

[33] See "Jiangsu sheng shangmin xiehui ji Tongshan xian shangmin xiehui gaizu jiufen," NTHA 1(1)-3099; "Jiangsu sheng Tongshan xian shangmin xiehui gaizu jiufen," NTHA 1(1)-3100.

[34] Chen Zhongyan, "Xuzhou shanghui zuzhi jianshi" (An outline history of the Xuzhou Chamber of Commerce organization), *Xuzhou wenshi ziliao* 7 (November 1986): 174–86, especially 176–77.

[35] "Qian Sunqing yu Wuxi xian shanghui" (Qian Sunqing and the Wuxi County Chamber of Commerce), *Wuxi wenshi ziliao* 1 (September 1980): 69–78. See also Li Tiping, "Xiri de Qingfeng chaye—jiu shehui Wuxi shishen de 'julebu'" (The Qingfeng teahouse of former days—the club of the Wuxi gentry of the old society), *Wuxi wenshi ziliao* 13 (March 10, 1986): 116–28.

[36] "Qian Sunqing," 72–74.

[37] Ibid., 73–75.

[38] This explanation of the party's role is based on countless newspaper and journal articles. But for one such article on each subject, see: *Shishi xinbao*, February 7, 1931, sec. 2, p. 2, col. 3 (on training militia); *Jiangsu dangwu zhoukan* 23 (June 22, 1930): 86–88 (on censorship); *Xinwen bao*, March 24, 1933, sec. 1, p. 4, col. 8 (on the party and cooperatives); *Zhongyang ribao*, May 9, 1930, sec. 2, p. 4, col. 1 (on the propaganda role); Li Zonghuang, "Difang zizhi zhi guoqu yu jianglai" (The past and future of local self-government), *Difang zizhi* 3 (September 30, 1935): 443–46 (on local self-government); Zhao Ruheng, *Jiangsu shengjian*, vol.1, *zhang* 2, 20 (on mass education).

[39] For more information on *xiangzhang* elections, see Geisert, "Power and Society, 183.

[40] Chu Shuxin, "Wo ren Guomindang," 102–16.

[41] Zhang Shupei, "Guomindang shiqi Tongshan xian," 68–70.

[42] Wang Ke-wen, "The Kuomintang in Transition: Ideology and Factionalism in the 'National Revolution,' 1924–1932" (Ph.D. diss., Stanford University, 1985), 235; So Wai-chor, *The Kuomintang Left*, 62.

[43] So Wai-chor, *The Kuomintang Left*, 75.

[44] Ibid., 81.

[45] Ibid., 118.

⁴⁶ Ibid., passim.

⁴⁷ The number of pages the chronology (*Jiangsu geming douzheng jilüe*) devotes to recounting CCP activity in Jiangsu per year is as follows: 1924: 14 pages; 1925: 63 pages; 1926: 39 pages; 1927: 98 pages; 1928: 78 pages; 1929: 77 pages; 1930: 83 pages; 1931: 60 pages; 1932: 56 pages; 1933: 33 pages; 1934: 15 pages; 1935: 24 pages; 1936: 16 pages.

This method for arriving at the levels of CCP activity in the various years is, to be sure, far from perfect. The increasing severity of media censorship in Jiangsu that started around 1930 might be partially responsible for the appearance that Communist-led disorders decreased after that time. Certainly by the 1930s the media were sanitized to downplay unrest in the province. The chronology compilers probably relied, at least to some degree, on those censored newspapers and magazines to construct the chronology. However, the compilers had other sources, including memoirs and CCP documents. In general, the information in local *wenshi ziliao* seems to support the idea that the provincial CCP was in a much tougher spot from 1931 to 1937 than it had been in the late 1920s. Memoirs suggest a reduced size and activity level for the Jiangsu CCP in this latter period.

⁴⁸ For just one among the multitudes of such cases, see the account of Communist Party activities in Chuansha County in Qiao Dingren, "Xin minzhu zhuyi geming shiqi Zhong Gong Chuansha zuzhi shi ziliao jian ji" (A simple compendium of materials on the history of the Chinese Communist Party's Chuansha organization during the period of the new democratic revolution), *Chuansha wenshi ziliao* 1 (June 1989): 5–10.

Patricia Stranahan's recent book reveals that the Shanghai CCP also hit upon hard times in the early 1930s for many of the same reasons that I suggest for the Jiangsu CCP. Nonetheless, Stranahan argues that by 1936 and 1937 the Shanghai CCP was to some extent recovering by virtue of the new policy of allowing members and local units of the party to involve themselves in anti-Japanese national salvation organizations. These organizations provided cover and a venue for increasing social connections of the CCP. It is possible that some of this kind of networking was going on outside of Shanghai in the Jiangsu hinterland by the mid-1930s, though I am presently unable to shine much light on this issue. See Patricia Stranahan, *Underground: The Shanghai Communist Party and the Politics of Survival* (Lanham, Maryland: Rowman and Littlefield Publishers, Inc., 1998), 121, and passim.

⁴⁹ On the laws on Communists who turned themselves in, see references in Jiang Songping, "Kangzhan qian 'Zhong Tong' zai Nantong de huodong" (Activities of the Central Statistical Bureau in Nantong before the War of Resistance), *Nantong wenshi ziliao xuanji* 4 (November 1984): 41. On the defections of Communists, see the 1930–1936 sections of *Jiangsu geming douzheng jilüe*.

⁵⁰ Ch'en Lifu, *Storm Clouds*, 65.

⁵¹ Zhang Shupei, "Guomindang 'Zhong Tong ju' zai Xuzhou" (The Nationalists' Central Statistical Bureau in Xuzhou), *Xuzhou wenshi ziliao* 1 (April 1981): 144–50.

⁵² Far and away the most famous of these turncoat intelligence agents was Gu Shunzhang, about whom much has been written. *Zhong Tong tegong milu* (Secret accounts of the special affairs work of the Central Statistical Bureau) is the title of volume 45 of *Jiangsu wenshi ziliao xuanji*. This compilation contains six articles on Gu.

⁵³ Barkan, "Nationalists, Communists," 473–519; *Jiangsu geming douzheng jilüe* has several entries for 1930 tracing at least some of this.

⁵⁴ The regime had always, to some degree, encouraged defections, and it had at least some success on that score in the late 1920s. For example, *Jiangsu geming douzheng jilüe* includes several examples of defections; this compilation notes the damage that these earlier instances of disloyalty brought to the CCP, but the post-1930 cases seem to have been more destructive to the party.

Further, even the Reeducation Institute, which was essentially a prison, had an earlier counterpart, known as the *Ganhua yuan*. See *Jiangsu geming douzheng jilüe*, 330.

⁵⁵ On the Reeducation Institute, see Zhang Wen, *Tegong*, 29–33; Zhang Guodong, "Fanxing yuan" (The Reeducation Institute), *Jiangsu wenshi ziliao* 45 (September 1991): 129–32, issue entitled "Zhong Tong tegong milu" (Secret writings on the Central Statistical Bureau's special affairs work); Guan Wenwei, "Suzhou Fanxing yuan zhenxiang" (The truth about the Suzhou Reeducation Institute), *Jiangsu wenshi ziliao* 45 (September 1991): 282–94, issue entitled "Zhong Tong tegong milu."

⁵⁶ Zhang Wen, *Tegong*, 26–29; Zhang Guolian, "Fanxing yuan," 129–31.

⁵⁷ Zhang Guodong, "Fanxing yuan," 131–32; *Jiangsu geming douzheng jilüe*, 593.

⁵⁸ Guan Wenwei, "Suzhou Fanxing yuan," 284.

⁵⁹ See Zhang Shupei, "Guomindang 'Zhong Tong ju,'" 144–63. It is worth noting that though the GMD regime's laws suggested that those Communists who turned themselves in and repented of their ideological errors would be well treated, some of the turncoats were executed by the regime, as shown in this article. On the situation in Nantong, see Jiang Songping, "Kangzhan qian 'Zhongtong,'" 41–51.

⁶⁰ For similar situations in other Jiangsu counties, see *Jiangsu geming douzheng jilüe*. On particular localities, see the following pages: Yixing (677), Pi (677), Yangzhou (677); Wujin (675), Feng (685), Rugao (683); Qidong, (683); Taixing (683); Yancheng (690); Pei (689), Suqian (671), and Wujiang (701). It is also

worth noting that the provincial committee of Jiangsu's CCP was also wracked by defections and effective secret police work (696).

Notes to Chapter 7

[1] Helen R. Chauncey, *Schoolhouse Politicians*, 146–72.

[2] Philip A. Kuhn, "Local Taxation and Finance in Republican China," 122–31.

[3] See, for example, Lenore Barkan, "Patterns of Power," 209–213, as well as Lynda Shaefer Bell, "From Comprador to County Magnate: Bourgeois Practice in the Wuxi County Silk Industry," in Joseph W. Esherick and Mary Backus Rankin, *Chinese Local Elites*, 113–39. I have covered some of this ground in Geisert, "Power and Society," 167–258.

[4] Hsi-sheng Ch'i, *Nationalist China at War: Military Defeats and Political Collapse, 1937–45* (Ann Arbor: University of Michigan Press, 1982), 234.

[5] Jiangsu sheng zhengfu mishu chu, ed., *San nian lai Jiangsu sheng zheng shuyao* (Zhenjiang: Jiangsu sheng zhengfu mishu chu disan ke, 1936), *bao'an* section, introduction, p. 1.

[6] Yung-fa Ch'en, *Making Revolution: The Communist Movement in Eastern and Central China, 1937–1945* (Berkeley: University of California Press, 1986), 447–97, passim; David M. Paulson, "Nationalist Guerrillas in the Sino-Japanese War: The 'Diehards' of Shandong Province," in *Single Sparks: China's Rural Revolutions*, ed. Kathleen Hartford and Steven M. Goldstein (Armonk, New York: M. E. Sharpe, 1989), 128–50. Although Paulson writes mainly about Shandong Province, the conditions he describes are very much like those in the North China zone of Jiangsu. However, F. Garvin Davenport believes that Zhejiang stands as an example of rather effective wartime governance and resistance to the Japanese. He argues that the GMD state largely retained control in southern Zhejiang and used its base there to launch partially effective initiatives aimed at reestablishing a foothold in northern Zhejiang, which had been subject to incursion and fitful dominion by the Japanese. See F. Garvin Davenport, "Resistance is State-Building: The GMD's Attempts at Political Consolidation of Zhejiang, 1937–1945," unpublished paper presented at the annual meeting of the Association for Asian Studies, Washington, D.C., March 1998.

Recently, Gregor Benton has written about Jiangsu during the war against Japan. He points out that the GMD's provincial government continued to operate after the Japanese had taken over major cities and lines of communication and transportation. He argues that the GMD's surviving (or reconstituted) government bureaucracy in the section of Jiangsu south of the Yangzi was strong enough to pose significant problems for the parts of the Communist Party's New

Fourth Army in the area. The GMD's wartime bureaucracy and military in the portion of Jiangsu north of the Yangzi were factionalized on the basis of localistic chauvinism and military clique ties, giving the Communists a chance to ally with disgruntled elements of the GMD forces. Consequently, in the early 1940s the Communists' New Fourth Army defeated the GMD regime's northern Jiangsu components. See Gregor Benton, *The New Fourth Army: Communist Resistance Along the Yangtze and the Huai, 1938–1941* (Berkeley: University of California Press, 1999), 100, 110, 132, 139, 316, 351, 419, 423, 481, 495–96, 716, 720. On page 32 Benton emphasizes the strength and density of the GMD's governmental and military apparatus in northern Jiangsu, a picture somewhat at odds with information given elsewhere in his book.

On the lack of unity of GMD forces in northern Jiangsu during the war, see Benton, *New Fourth Army*, 481. Benton defends GMD forces against the charge that they were uniformly collaborationist, though he cites cases of collaboration (139, 314–15). There is little in Benton or any other secondary source I have seen on Jiangsu during the war to suggest that organization of the masses by the Nationalist Party was of much help in the war effort, though the GMD's intelligence organs played a role in China's fight with Japan. (For one brief mention of a GMD organizational effort that looks more like an intelligence operation than mass mobilization, see Ch'en, *Making Revolution*, 464.) Benton does write about an effective mobilization effort in Anhui, led by Li Zongren and the Guangxi Military Clique, with CCP help (106, 716). Benton also finds that during the Nanjing Decade the GMD regime had alienated certain gentry leaders, thereby predisposing them to cooperate with the Communist Party during the war (199–202).

It is certainly not the case that GMD forces did not offer resistance to invading Japanese armies in Jiangsu, particularly at first. In the opening stage of the war, GMD armies fought well-known engagements in Jiangsu, such as the battles of Shanghai and Xuzhou. However, as the war dragged on, the party did not offer as much aid in the effort as it could have if it had been more experienced at and adapted to the task of mass organization.

[7] Paulson, "Resistance," 136; Benton, *New Fourth Army*, 139. See also Ch'en, *Making Revolution*, 459, 474, 483, 484.

[8] Yung-fa Ch'en, "The Making of a Revolution: The Communist Movement in Eastern and Central China, 1937–1945" (Ph.D. diss., Stanford University, 1980), 1: 244–64.

[9] I base this observation on my reading of county-level *wenshi ziliao*.

[10] Lloyd E. Eastman, *Seeds of Destruction: Nationalist China in War and Revolution, 1937–1949* (Stanford: Stanford University Press, 1984), 129.

Notes to Appendices

Appendix 1

[1] The Jiangsu Provincial Purge Committee consisted of Yu Xinyi, Ge Jianshi (Western Hills and Anti-CC), Wang Boling, Ye Chucang, Li Shouyong (CC), Zhou Shushan (Organization), Jin Hesheng (FF), Liu Jihong (FF), Ye Xiufeng (FF), and Li Yiping (see Gu Ziyang, *Jiangsu sheng dangwu*, 12; interviews, Taibei, 1977). The members of the original JSC were Li Zhiyun, Gu Ziyang (Anti-CC), Ge Jianshi (Western Hills and Anti-CC), Zhou Jieren (CC), Feng Shiqi (Western Hills), Liao Shishao, and Zou Guangheng (Gu, *Jiangsu sheng dangwu*, 10–12). On Zhou Shushan's ties to the Organization Department, see *Who's Who in China, 1918–1950*, compiled by Jerome Cavanaugh (Hong Kong: Chinese Materials Center, 1982), 58. On the factional connections of the rest of the persons mentioned, see Appendix II.

[2] *Shen bao*, April 30, 1927, p. 5, col. 6; *Zhongguo Guomindang Nanjing*, 24–28.

[3] *Shen pao*, May 30, 1927, p. 4, col. 4.

[4] Gu Ziyang, *Jiangsu sheng dangwu*, 11.

[5] Ibid., 10–11.

[6] *Shen bao*, July 24, 1927, p. 10, col. 5.

[7] For example, CC leader Li Shouyong introduced Cao Minghuan, who would later emerge as an important provincial associate of the Organization Clique, into the Jiangning County Party Purge Committee (*Shen bao*, July 30, 1927, p. 9, col. 5). Cao would later break with the CC network to form the Yang-Ma-Cao Clique, which like the CC Clique was a provincial appendage of the national Organization Clique.

[8] For example, CC leader Li Shouyong sometimes jointly introduced committee members with FF group partisan Jin Hesheng (*Shen bao*, July 27, 1927, p. 9, col. 4). One source in Taiwan informed me that the CC and FF Cliques were originally part of the same network of relations. Over time, however, the egos and personalities of Ye Xiufeng and Li Shouyong were such that each had to create his own grouping to compete with the other.

[9] *Shen bao*, June 24, 1927, p. 4, col. 1.

[10] Li Yunhan, *Cong rong gong*, 758.

[11] Donald A. Jordan, *The Northern Expedition: China's National Revolution of 1926–1928* (Honolulu: University of Hawaii Press, 1976), 136–37.

[12] *Shen bao*, August 21, 1927, p. 10, col. 2.

[13] Li Yunhan, *Cong rong gong*, 762–78; T'ang Leang-li, *The Inner History of the Chinese Revolution* (New York: E. P. Dutton and Co., 1930), 295–315; *Shen bao* (1927) November 3, p. 4, col. 3; November 6, p. 4, col. 3.

[14] Gu Ziyang, *Jiangsu sheng dangwu*, 12; *Shen bao*, October 14, 1927, p. 6, col. 1; October 24, 1927, p. 5, col. 1.

[15] The committee consisted of Gao Fang (Western Hills), Yang Sili (Western Hills), Guo Fuzeng, Li Shouyong (CC), Ge Jianshi (former member of the Sunist Study Society), Liu Bingchen (Western Hills), Shen Jing (Western Hills), Jiang Ziying (Western Hills), Miao Bin (former member of the Sunist Study Society), He Minhun (Guangxi Clique), and Niu Minhua. See Gu Ziyang, *Jiangsu sheng dangwu*, 12; "Wei 'yiyi erer can'an' gao quan guo tongzhi tongbao" (Telling the comrades of the entire nation about the November 22 Massacre) in "Yiyi erer can'an," (clippings), 1927, GMDA, 468/20; *Jiangsu dangsheng*, 12, 16; "Sun Wen zhuyi xuehui chengli," 328; interviews, Taibei, 1977.

[16] *Shen bao*, October 17, 1927, p. 3, col. 2; November 7, 1927, p. 6, cols. 5–6.

[17] For example, the Jiangyin County Special Committee apparently did so. *Shen bao*, November 13, 1927, p. 10, col. 3.

[18] *Shen bao*, December 10, 1927, p. 10, col. 3.

[19] However, the CSC claimed that Jiangsu and Nanjing party headquarters denied disseminating any such pronouncement. *Shen bao*, September 28, 1927, p. 4, col. 1; September 29, 1927, p. 6, col. 6.

[20] *Shen bao*, September 17, 1927, p. 6, col. 6. The epithets "opportunist," "rotten," and "bureaucratic" were labels often applied to the Western Hills group.

[21] "Su dangbu cheng zhongyang yao jian" (The Jiangsu party headquarters petitions the central headquarters about important items), in "Jian bao," 1927.

[22] Gu Ziyang, *Jiangsu sheng dangwu*, 13; *Shen bao*, November 19, 1927, p. 7, col. 6; November 21, 1927, p. 3.

[23] Chen Shaoxiao, *Hei wang lu*, 287–89. Chen Lifu denied the existence of the Central Club. See Chen Lifu, "Wo so zhidao."

[24] Interview, Taibei, 1977.

[25] *Zhongyang ribao*, February 28, 1928, sec. 2, p. 2, cols. 1–3; Li Shouyong, "Duan Shuyi xiansheng yu wo" (Mr. Duan Xipeng and me), *Zhuanji wenxue* 30.3 (March 1977): 21.

[26] See Li Shouyong, "Duan Shuyi"; Fang Qingru, "Zhongyang dangwu xuexiao" (Central Party Affairs Academy), in *Guoli zhengzhi daxue shi shiliao huibian*, ed. by Guoli zhengshi daxue xiaoshi bianyin weiyuan hui (Taibei, Guoli zhengzhi xiaozhang shi, 1977) 1: 221–22; Yi Xun, *Jiang dang zhenxiang*, 30–31.

[27] For example, the Wu County party did so. *Shen bao*, December 11, 1927, p. 9, col. 4.

[28] *Shen bao*, December 10, 1927, p. 10, col. 3.

[29] *Shen bao*, December 11, 1927, p. 9, col. 4; January 4, 1928, p. 10, col. 3; January 13, 1928, p. 10, col. 3.

[30] Interview, Taibei, 1977; *Shen bao*, December 14, 1927, p. 10; December 22, 1927, p. 10, col. 6; January 4, 1928, p. 10, cols. 4–5.

[31] *Shen bao*, December 29, 1927, p. 6, col. 6. One recent book argues that the popular outrage and blame for the tragedy focused specifically upon Ge Jianshi (as Western Hills faction member in late 1927). See Song Ping, *Jiang Jieshi: zong siling, weiyuan zhang, zongcai, zhuxi, zongtong* (Hong Kong: Liwen chubanshe, 1992), 180. In fact, contemporary sources spread the blame for the massacre among several Western Hills figures.

[32] Gu Ziyang, *Jiangsu sheng dangwu*, 13; interviews, Taibei, 1977.

[33] *Shen bao*, January 30, 1928, p. 10, col. 5.

[34] Gu Ziyang, *Jiangsu sheng dangwu*, 14; *Zhongyang dangwu yuekan* 1 (June 1928): appendix. On Feng Ti's Huangpu connections, see *Shishi xinbao*, October 20, 1929, sec. 1, p. 2, col. 6. Leng Xin was part of the first graduating class of Huangpu Military Academy. See Xu Youchun, ed., *Minguo renwu da cidian* (Shijiazhuang: Hebei renmin chubanshe, 1991), 410.

[35] Chen Sibai, "Lüe tan Guomindang Jiangsu sheng dangbu dangwu douzheng" (Briefly speaking of the party affairs struggle in the Jiangsu branch of the Nationalist Party), *Wenshi ziliao xuanji* (Yancheng version) 3 (August 1982): 92–98.

[36] I assume Gu had to be aiding Chen, since Chen was in charge of recruiting in Shanghai, while Gu supplied students from northern Jiangsu. Those recruits must have passed through Chen's office. (See Boorman, *Biographical Dictionary*, 1: 203; Huang Jilu, et al., *Geming renwu zhi*, 11: 372.)

[37] On Teng's association with Wang's Reorganization Clique and with Wang himself, I depend on my 1977 interviews in Taibei, as well as correspondence with former provincial GMD leaders. But also see *Zhuanji wenxue* 36.4 (Jan. 4, 1980): 145; Da Ke, "Susheng dangbu xuanju zhi yi mu," 50–52; "Teng Gu jing xuan guo daibiao" (Teng Gu runs for the National Assembly), *Shehui xinwen* 3.17 (May 21, 1932): 261; "Teng Gu de xin huodong" (The new actions of Teng Gu), *Shehui xinwen* 3.7 (April 21, 1933): 100. On the attitude of the CEC, see Patrick Cavendish, "The 'New China,'" 53.

[38] Feng Ti started out as head of the provincial Organization Department, but he soon resigned, and Anti-CC stalwart Ni Bi took over his duties (Gu Ziyang, *Jiangsu sheng dangwu*, 14; interviews, Taibei, 1977). For evidence of Ye's absence,

see *Zhongyang ribao*, May 17, 1928, sec. 2, p. 3, cols. 4–5; May 22, 1928, sec. 2, p. 3; and many other accounts of standing committee meetings. Gu is correct that Qian Dajun was also a member of the Directorate; see *Zhongyang ribao*, April 26, 1928, sec. 2, p. 3, col. 2.

[39] Chen Sibai, "Lüe tan," 95.

[40] *Zhongyang ribao*, June 20, 1928, sec. 2, p. 3.

[41] *Zhongguo Guomindang dier jie zhongyang zhixing weiyuanhui diwu ci quanti huiyi jilu* (Nanjing: Zhongyang mishu chu, 1928), appendix of proposals to the Third National Congress.

[42] *Shen bao* (1928) November 1, p. 4, col. 1; November 3, p. 4, col. 5; November 4, p. 4, cols. 4–5 and p. 7, col. 6; November 5, p. 4, cols. 2–3; p. 9, col. 4: November 7, p. 7, cols. 4–5; p. 8, col. 4.

[43] *Zhongyang zhoubao* 39 (March 4, 1929): 2; *North China Herald*, February 23, 1929, p. 301.

[44] On Miao's protection by He, see Boorman, *Biographical Dictionary*, 3: 36; the information on Miao's ties to Chiang come from my 1977 interviews in Taiwan. Zhang's ties to Soong are implied by the fact that Zhang held a high position in Soong's Finance Ministry (see Xu Youchun, *Minguo renwu*, 963). On Zhang Naiyan's relation to Zhang Jingjiang, I rely on my interviews.

[45] My view is contrary to that of Yang Gu in "Wo suo zhidao de Guomindang," 16–20. Yang sees Miao as tied to the Organization Clique. Based on my interviews in Taiwan, I doubt that this was so.

[46] The members of this provincial executive committee were Wang Baoxuan (CC), Teng Gu (Reorganization Clique, with ties to Anti-CC), Ni Bi (Anti-CC), Gu Ziyang (Anti-CC), Zhou Jieren (CC), Zhu Jianbai (CC), Ge Jianshi (Anti-CC), Ye Chucang (Organization, though as a senior figure he may sometimes have transcended cliques), and Qi Xiyong (CC) (interviews, Taipei, 1977; Gu Ziyang, *Jiangsu sheng dangwu*, 16–17; also see Appendix 2).

[47] *Zhongyang zhoubao* 39 (March 4, 1929): 2; *North China Herald*, February 23, 1929, p. 301; Gu Ziyang, *Jiangsu sheng dangwu*, 17–18.

[48] *Zhongyang zhoubao* 39 (March 4, 1929): 2.

[49] Gu Ziyang, *Jiangsu sheng dangwu*, 17.

[50] Ibid., 18.

[51] *Shen bao*, June 10, 1929, p. 8, col. 5.

[52] Gu Ziyang, *Jiangsu sheng dangwu*, 18; *Shishi xinbao*, August 26, 1929, sec. 1, p. 3, col. 4; August 27, 1929, sec. 1, p. 3, col. 1.

Appendix 2

[1] In order to simplify the text and notes of this section, I only provide one source for each individual's factional membership. Obviously, more sources exist which speak to the issue of the factional backgrounds of many or most of these people, but to list all of those materials for each and every one of the individuals would be very complex and take a great deal of space. Quite a few of these factional identifications were confirmed by my interviews in Taibei in 1977.

[2] Chen Sibai, "Lüetan," 92–98.

[3] Da Ke, "Jiangsu dangwu de lishi guan," 98–105.

[4] Chong Gong, "Jiangsu sheng dangbu gepai," 367–68.

[5] Da Ke, "Su sheng dangbu xuanju zhi yimu," 51–53.

[6] "Su sheng dangbu gaixuan zhi qianhou" (At about the time of the reelection of the Jiangsu provincial party headquarters), *Shehui xinwen* 1.28 (December 24, 1932): 554–56.

[7] Da Ke, "Su sheng Guo daibiao fuxuan huaxu lu" (Colorful incidents in the reelection of Jiangsu's National Assemblymen), *Shehui xinwen* 3.27 (June 21, 1932): 425–26.

[8] "Su quan hui huaxu lu" (Colorful incidents of the Jiangsu Congress), *Shehui xinwen* (January 10, 1933): 435–36.

[9] *Jiangsu dangsheng*, passim.

[10] Gu Ziyang, *Jiangsu sheng dangwu*, passim.

Appendix 3

[1] Information on Zhou Ruqian's connection with Zhou Shaocheng comes from a letter (September 1983) to me from a former provincial party leader who was living in Taiwan. For Zhou's protection of Communists, see Shen Yigong, et al., "Yici liangci Guo-Gong hezuo," 24–33, as well as Zhou Ruliang and Zhou Xiehe, "Yi Zhou Ruqian xiansheng" (Remembering Mr. Zhou Ruqian), *Qidong wenshi xuanji* 5 (November 1986): 80–85.

[2] For description and history of this dual ownership system, see Bernhardt, *Rents*, passim, but esp. 24–27.

[3] For brief references to this original plan, see Zhou Ruliang and Zhou Xiehe, "Yi Zhou Ruqian," 83; and Zhang Shiming, "Qidong Guomindang shi jilüe" (A sketch of the history of the Qidong Nationalist Party), *Qidong wenshi xuanji* 2 (April 1985): 52–53.

[4] For Zhou's justifications, see the first sentence of Lu Yanghao, "Yizhuan Chong ren zai Qi diquan wenti zhi yanjiu" (Research on the question of transferring the

Qidong land rights of Chongming residents), *Jiangsu yanjiu* 3.1 (April 31, 1937): nonconsecutive pagination.

[5] Actually, only something over 60 percent of the land in Qidong was owned by persons who still resided in Chongming. Another 19.5 percent was held by Chongming natives who had moved to Qidong. See Liu Xiuqing, "Qidong zu dian wenti yu fuzhi zigeng nong yundong" (The Qidong tenancy question and supporting the movement for "self-tilling peasants"), *Dizheng yuekan* 5.2, 3 (March 1937): 322–23. Zhou's plan was ambiguous on the question of how it would handle those recent Qidong residents.

[6] *Agrarian China*, 26–30.

[7] For information on the Qidong land reform problem that supports this and preceding paragraphs, see *Agrarian China*, 341–42; Liu Xiuqing, "Qidong zu dian"; Lu Yanghao, "Yizhuan Chong ren," passim.

[8] Interviews, Taibei, 1977.

[9] *Agrarian China*, 30; Wang Fengxin, "Ping *Xin Qidong bao* 'Yizhuan Chongren zai Qi diquan zhi jiantao'" (Criticizing the *New Qidong Gazette*'s "Discussion of transferring the Qidong land rights of Chongming residents"), *Jiangsu yanjiu* 3.1 (January 31, 1937): nonconsecutive pagination; Lu Yanghao, "Yizhuan Chong jen."

[10] Zhang Zhiming, "Qidong Guomindang," 53; Zhou Ruliang and Zhou Xiehe, "Yi Zhou Ruqian," 83; Zhou Ruiying, Zhou Cuntao, Zhou Xuemei, and Zhou Cunhe, "Huiyi fuqin Zhou Ruqian" (Remembering our father, Zhou Ruqian) *Qidong wenshi xuanji* 5 (November 1986): 89–92.

Glossary

Names of people listed as authors in the bibliography are not included here.

Ba tulie 八土劣
Bai Baoshan 白寶山
Bai Chongxi 白崇禧
Batan 八灘
Bao (clique) 鮑
bao'an dui 保安隊
Baoweituan bangongting 保衛團辦公廳
Bei dang 北黨
Bei pai 北派
Beixiang pai 北鄉派
boshi tuan 薄屎團
buheli 不合理

Cai Hanyu 蔡漢餘
Caiqiao 蔡橋
canshihui 參事會
Cao Binggan 曹炳乾
Cao Minghuan 曹明煥
Caoyan 草堰
Ceng Yangfu 曾養甫
Changren (township) 長人
Chen Boming 陳伯明
Chen Cheng 陳誠
Chen Gongbo 陳公博
Chen Jianbo 陳鑒波
Chen Jinju 陳金聚
Chen Kanghe 陳康和
Chen Qimei 陳其美

Chen Qubing 陳去病
Chen Ruyi 陳如翼
Chen Weishan 陳惟善
Chen Xiekun 陳燮坤
Chen Yaxuan 陳亞軒
Chen Zhongming 陳重明
Cheng Changwu 成昌吾
Cheng Ruyuan 程如垣
Cheng Zhaoshi 程肇湜
Cheng pai 城派
Chenyang 陳洋
Chiang Kai-shek (Jiang Jieshi) 蔣介石
cun nonghui 村農會

Da tongmeng 大同盟
Dai jia dang 戴家黨
Dai Jitao 戴季陶
Dai Jizhi 戴楫之
Dai pai 戴派
danghu lianhehui 當戶聯合會
danghua jiaoyu 黨化教育
Dangxiao pai 黨校派
dadao 打倒
dang yi 黨義
Dao Dai pai 倒戴派
daopo 道婆
Deng Zeru 鄧澤如

Di Kan 狄侃
Di Ying 狄膺
Dianhu hezuo zijiuhui 佃戶合作自救會
dibao 地保
difang shili 地方勢力
Ding Weifen 丁惟汾
dipi 地痞
dipi liumang 地痞流氓
Dong Hancha 董漢槎
Dongbei pai 東北派
Dong dang 東黨
Donggou 東溝
Dongkan 東坎
Dongnanxiang xueshe 東南鄉學社
Dong pai 東派
dongshi 董事
dongshihui 董事會
Dongyue (Temple) 東嶽
Duan Muzhen 段木真
ducha zhuanyuan 督察專員
dujun
dushu hui 讀書會

Er pai 二派

Fan CC pai 反CC派
Fan Xiongyi 范雄毅
fanri hui 反日會
Fanxing yuan 反省院
fatuan 法團
fei Jiangsu ren pai 非江蘇人派
fenfei tou 糞肥頭
Feng Jufen 馮菊芬
Feng Shaozhan 馮少瞻
Feng Shiqi 馮士奇
Feng Ti 酆悌
Feng Yuxiang 馮玉祥

fuhua 腐化
fuhua ehua 腐化惡化
Fuxingshe 復興社

Gaizu pai 改組派
Ganhua yuan 感化院
ganshi 幹事
Gao Fang 高方
Gao Juemin 高覺民
Gao Yuesheng 高嶽生
Ge Jincheng 葛錦城
Geng Xuannian 耿萱年
gong'an juzhang 公安局長
Gonghedang 共和黨
gongkuan gongchan chu 公款公產處
gongsheng 貢生
Gongyi (Middle School) 公益
Goudun 溝墩
Gu Nancun 顧南村
Gu Renfa 辜仁發
Gu Shunzhang 顧順章
Gu Xiping 顧希平
Gu Zifang 顧子芳
guanxi 關系
Gushan 顧山
Guanhu 官湖
Guo Fuzeng 郭福增
Guo Yin'gao 郭寅皋
Guojia zhuyi [pai] 國家主義[派]
Guomin huiyi 國民會議
Guomindang 國民黨

Haizhou 海州
haoshen 豪紳
He Haiqiao 何海樵
He Minhun 何民魂
He Xuyou 何續友
He Yingqin 何應欽

He Yushu 何玉書
Hengsha 橫沙
Hou Shaoqiu 侯紹裘
Hu Hanmin 胡漢民
Hu Yinjie 胡尹皆
huan 緩
Huanlong 環龍
Huang Jinrong 黃金榮
Huang Linshu 黃麟書
Huang Lisan 黃立三
Huang Renyan 黃仁言
Huang Songtao 黃松濤
Huang Zhian 黃志安
Huangpu 黃埔
Hudang jiuguo jun 護黨救國軍
huifu tebie weiyuanhui 恢復特別委員會
Huimen 慧門

jiabei quanding 加倍圈定
jiandu 監督
Jiang Ziying 蔣子英
Jiangbei 江北
Jiangnan 江南
Jiangsu dangwu zhoukan 江蘇黨務周刊
Jiangsu pinglun 江蘇評論
Jiangsu sheng dangwu zhengli weiyuanhui 江蘇省黨務整理委員會
Jiangsu sheng linshi zhixing weiyuanhui 江蘇省臨時執行委員會
Jiangsu sheng nongmin xiehui choubei hui 江蘇省農民協會籌備會
jiansheng 監生
Jianye 建業
Jiaoyu hui 教育會
jiaoyu xiehui 教育協會
jie 界

jigang 紀綱
Jile (Temple) 極樂
Jin Hesheng 靳鶴聲
Jin Pinsan 金品三
Jingxian 景賢
jinshi 進士
jiu shili 舊勢力
jiuji yuan 救濟院
Juntuncun 軍屯村
juren 舉人
juren jiating 舉人家庭

keshui zajuan 苛稅雜捐

Lan Bohua 蘭伯華
Lanyishe 藍衣社
Leng Xin 冷欣
Li Bingxin 李炳新
Li Dazhao 李大釗
Li Houji 李厚基
Li Jingzhai 李敬齋
Li Liangeng 李聯庚
Li Mingyang 李明揚
Li Tongfu 李通甫
Li Xinglian 李星聯
Li Yafei 李亞飛
Li Yicheng 李一誠
Li Yi'e 李一諤
Li Yinggeng 李映庚
Li Yiping 李一平
Li Zhiyun 李志雲
Li Zifeng 李子峰
Li Ziyi 李子一
Liang Cunren 梁存仁
Liao Shishao 廖世劭
Limen 理門
Ling Shaozu 凌紹祖
Lishe 禮社

Liu Bingchen　劉炳晨
Liu Chengrui　劉成瑞
Liu Chuanjing　劉傳經
Liu Jihong　劉季洪
Liu Menghou　劉孟侯
Liu Shengping　劉昇平
Liu Shirong　劉士榮
Liu Tianzhan　劉天展
Liu Xifan　劉錫藩
Liu Yanxiang　劉硯香
Liu Yazi　柳亞子
Liu Yunzhao　劉雲昭
Liu Zhendian　劉振殿
Liu Zihou　劉子厚
Liu Zisheng　劉子聲
Lixingshe　力行社
Liyang pinglun　溧陽評論
Lu Dun　魯鈍
Lu Donghao　陸東皓
Lu Qi　陸起
Lu Wenfeng　陸文鳳
Lu Yinquan　盧印泉
Luhe　鹿河
Luo Jigang　駱繼綱
Luodian　羅店
Lücheng　呂城

Ma Chaojun　馬超俊
Ma Yinbing　馬飲冰
Ma Yuanfang　馬元放
Mao Dun　矛盾
Mao Zuquan　茅祖權
Meng Guangtai　孟廣泰
Miao Bin　繆斌
Minguo ribao　民國日報
Minsheng ribao　民生日報
minzhi　民治
Minzhi xuehui　民治學會

Mo Baichou　莫伯籌
mu　畝

Ni Bingruo　倪冰若
Niu Changyao　鈕長耀
Niu Jianchu　牛踐初
Niu Minhua　鈕民華
Niu Yongjian　鈕永建
nongmin cujinhui　農民促進會
nongmin zijiuhui　農民自救會

Pan　潘
Pan Guojun　潘國俊
Peng Jianzhang　彭建章
pingmin　平民
pingmin jiaoyu cujinhui
　　平民教育促進會
Pu Rongqian　浦容潛
Pukou　浦口
Punan　浦南

Qi Shuzu　祁述祖
Qi Xiyong　祁錫勇
Qian Dajun　錢大鈞
Qian Jingzhi　錢敬植
Qian Sunqing　錢孫卿
Qin Xiaolu　秦效魯
Qing bang　青幫
Qingbaishe　青白社
Qingjiang　清江
Qingli Dongnanxiang xueshe caichan weiyuanhui　清理東南鄉學社財產委員會
Qiu Fu　秋復
Qiu Jin　秋瑾
Qiu Youzhen　邱有珍
Qiu Yugu　邱愚谷
qu　區

qu fenbu 區分部
quzhang 區長
quanmin geming 全民革命

ren'ai 仁愛
Rong Desheng 榮德生
Rong Zongjing 榮宗敬

San pai 三派
Sanwu she 三五社
sasao hui 灑掃會
Sha Bingyuan 沙炳元
Shan Xintian 單心田
shangmin xiehui 商民協會
Shangmin yundong jiangxisuo 商民運動講習所
shang you tiantang, xia you Su-Hang 上有天堂，下有蘇杭
Shao Lizi 邵力子
Shen Baixian 沈百先
Shen Dingyi 沈定一
Shen Jing 沈兢
Shen Susheng 沈素生
Shen Yi 沈毅
Sheng Xiru 盛翕如
shengyuan 生員
shenshang 紳商
Shenxin 申新
shi 市
Shi Shanglin 侍上林
shi xingzhengju 市行政局
Shi Yiqian 施軼千
Shi Yousan 石友三
shidafu 士大夫
shidong 市董
shifu 師傅
shoujiu wushizhe 守舊無識者
Shu sheng 沭聲

Sijing 泗涇
sishu 私塾
Song Zhenlun 宋鎮崙
Subei 蘇北
sufan 肅反
sufan zhuanyuan 肅反專員
Sun Chuanfang 孫傳芳
Sun Dachen 孫達忱
Sun Gong 孫恭
Sun Jingya 孫鏡亞
Sun Jishi 孫基士
Sun Ke 孫科
Sun Yat-sen 孫逸仙
Su'nan 蘇南
Suqian minbao 宿遷民報
Suqian ribao 宿遷日報

Taiyuangong (store) 泰源公
Tan Pingshan 譚平山
Tang Guohua 唐國華
Tang Qiyu 唐啓宇
Teng Gu 滕固
Teng Yangzhi 滕仰支
tewu 特務
Tewu shi 特務室
tezhong xingshi fating 特種刑事法庭
tianye gonghui 田業公會
Tongmenghui 同盟會
tongxianghui 同鄉會
tongye gonghui 同業公會
tu 圖
tudong 圖董
tu huangdi 土皇帝
tuhao lieshen 土豪劣紳

Wang Baoxuan 汪寶暄
Wang Boling 王柏齡
Wang Bingheng 王秉衡

Wang Changhao 王長浩
Wang Changjiang 王長江
Wang Chengji 王承基
Wang Gongyu 王公璵
Wang Jingwei 汪精衛
Wang Lantian 王藍田
Wang Shan 王禪
Wang Xianghe 王相和
Wang Xizhai 王錫齋
Wang Yushu 王玉樹
Wang Yuzi 王雨滋
Wang Ziyun 王子雲
Wang Zuoliang 王佐良
Weiguangshe 微光社
Weisheng lun 唯生論
Weng Hanzhong 翁翰中
wenshi ziliao 文史資料
Wu Baofeng 吳葆豐
Wu Baojin 武葆岑
Wu Shaoxi 吳少溪
Wu Yicang 吳倚滄
Wu Zhihui 吳稚輝
Wuhuading (Temple) 五華頂

Xi dang 西黨
Xi Yutang 奚玉堂
Xia Lin 夏霖
Xia Zicheng 夏子城
xiang 鄉
xiang xingzheng juzhang 鄉行政局長
xiang zhengwu weiyuan 鄉政務委員
xiangdong 鄉董
Xianglin 享林
Xiang pai 鄉派
xiangzhang 鄉長
xiangzuo 鄉佐
Xiaodao hui 小刀會
xiao daoshi 小道士

Xiao Jishan 蕭吉珊
xiao zhuge 小諸葛
xiaobian 小辮
xiaokang 小康
Xie Dengyu 謝澄宇
Xie Lunxian 謝侖仙
Xin Su ribao 新宿日報
Xin Zhenjiang bao 新鎮江報
Xin Zhong geming qingnian she 新中革命青年社
Xin Zhong xueshe 新中學社
Xi'nan dang 西南黨
Xi'nan pai 西南派
xinchao pai 新潮派
Xing guang 星光
Xing she 星社
Xing Zhong hui 興中會
Xing Zhong she 興中社
Xinpu 新浦
Xi pai 西派
Xixiang pai 西鄉派
xiucai 秀才
Xu (clique in Suining) 徐
Xu Enceng 徐恩曾
Xu Wentian 徐聞天
Xu Ximing 徐西明
Xue (family in Wuxi) 薛

Yan Xishan 閻錫山
Yang Fang 楊放
Yang Sili 楊思禮
Yang Tongshou 楊彤綬
Yang Xingfo 楊杏佛
Yang Xingqin 楊興勤
Yang-Ma-Cao 楊馬曹
yangxue tang 洋學堂
Yao Erjue 姚爾覺
Yao Heling 姚鶴齡

Ye Xiufeng 葉秀峰
Yexie 葉楒
yi dang zhi guo 以黨治國
Yilin 益林
yin 胤
yingfu 應付
Yi pai 一派
yishihui 議事會
Yiwei xingqi yanshuohui 已未星期演說會
Yiyi erer can'an 一一二二慘案
Yu Huaizhong 于懷忠
Yu Jingtang 余井塘
Yu Xiaqing 虞洽卿
Yu Xinyi 余心一
Yu Yichen 虞翊臣
yuan 元
Yuan Shikai 袁世凱
Yuepu 月浦
yunie 餘孽
Yunong hushui gongsi 裕農戽水公司

Zhang Baopei 張葆培
Zhang Daofan 張道藩
Zhang Fakui 張發奎
Zhang Gongren 張公任
Zhang Hongye 張宏業
Zhang Jian 張謇
Zhang Jingjiang 張靜江
Zhang Jingtong 張競同
Zhang Jiren 張吉人
Zhang Laifang 張來方
Zhang Minquan 張民權
Zhang Naiyan 張乃燕
Zhang Qingping 張慶平
Zhang Renjie 張人傑
Zhang Shishi 張師石
Zhang Shouyong 張壽鏞

Zhang Shushi 張曙時
Zhang Wenming 張文明
Zhang Xiaoyou 張孝友
Zhang Yuanyang 張淵揚
Zhang Zhi 張芝
Zhang Ziqin 張梓琴
Zhang Zongchang 張宗昌
Zhangyan 張堰
Zhao Yuzheng 趙毓政
zhen gongsuo 鎮公所
zhenya 鎮壓
zhidaoyuan 指導員
zhidao weiyuanhui 指導委員會
Zhongshan si 中山寺
Zhongshan zhuyi shijian she 中山主義實踐社
Zhongshi tongzhi julebu 忠實同志俱樂部
Zhongyang dang 中央黨
Zhongyang julebu 中央俱樂部
Zhongyang tebie weiyuanhui 中央特別委員會
Zhou Fengjing 周鳳鏡
Zhou Houjun 周厚鈞
Zhou Huapeng 周化鵬
Zhou Jieren 周傑人
Zhou Ruqian 周儒謙
Zhou Shaocheng 周紹成
Zhou Shuiping 周水平
Zhou Shushan 周曙山
Zhou Xiaoshi 周效實, 周肖實
Zhou Xu 周需
Zhou Zhongchen 周仲辰
Zhu Ji 朱驥
Zhu Jianbai 朱堅白
Zhu Laohu 朱老虎
Zhu Limin 朱立民
Zhu Shaoliang 朱紹良

Zhu Shoushi　朱壽石
Zhujing　朱涇
zongdong　總董
zong tuanzhang　總團長
Zou Guangheng　鄒廣恆
zuzhan　租棧

Bibliography

Sources in Chinese and Japanese

Ai Wu 愛吾 and Wen Han 文漢. "Gaizu pai fenzi zai Yancheng suo yinqi de shibian" 改組派分子在鹽城所引起的事變 (The incident that was instigated by the Reorganization Clique elements in Yancheng). *Yancheng xian wenshi ziliao* 鹽城縣文史資料 1,2 (reprinted January 1984): 54–57.

"Baoshan dangwu gaikuang" 寶山黨務概況 (The general situation of Baoshan party affairs). *Jiangsu dangsheng* 江蘇黨聲 15 (November 4, 1928): 11–14.

Baoshan xian zai xu zhi 寶山縣再續志 (Another continuation of the Baoshan County gazetteer). 1931.

"Beifa shiqi Jinshan yamen duo yin ji" 北伐時期金山縣衙門奪印記 (A record of the seizing by force of the Jinshan County government seal at the time of the Northern Expedition). *Jinshan wenshi ziliao* 金山文史資料 5 (n.d.): 1–2.

Bu Zhongji 卜忠吉. "Huang Lisan qi ren" 黃立三其人 (The man Huang Lisan). *Yancheng wenshi ziliao xuanji* 鹽城文史資料 6:33–36.

Cai Baichuan 蔡佰川. "Huoshao chenghuang miao" 火燒城隍廟 (The burning of the temple of the city god). *Yancheng xian wenshi ziliao* 鹽城縣文史資料 1,2 (reprinted January 1984): 47–53.

Cao Kemin 曹克敏. "Mijia de feizhang ji qi shehui de yingxiang" 米價的飛漲及其社會的影響 (The spiraling of rice prices and its social consequences). *Cunzhi* 村治 1.6 (September 1, 1930): 8–10.

Cao Wenbin 曹文彬. "Jintan Guomindang zuopai zuzhi de shimo" 金壇國民黨左派組織的始末 (The beginning and the end of the organization of the left wing of the Nationalist Party in Jintan). *Jintan wenshi ziliao* 金壇文史資料 2 (May 1985): 8–18.

CC dan ni kansuru chosa CC團に關する調査 (An investigation of the CC Clique). Prepared by the Special Investigative Section of the Japanese ministry in China. Shanghai, 1939.

CC hao men ziben neimu CC豪門資本內幕 (The inside story of the influential CC family), edited by Jingji ziliao shi 經濟資料室 (Material Room on the Economy). Luoyang: Guanghua shudian, 1948.

Chen Boxin 陳柏心. *Zhongguo de difang zhidu ji qi gaige* 中國的地方製度及其改革 (China's local systems and their reform). Changsha: Guangxi jianshe yanjiuhui, 1939.

Chen Dunzheng 陳敦正. *Dong luan de huiyi* 動亂的回憶 (Recollections of turmoil). Taibei: Yuan xia shushe, 1979.

Chen Guisan 陳貴三. "Huiyi ta geming shidai de Zhongguo Guomindang Songjiang xian dangbu" 回憶大革命時代的中國國民黨松江縣黨部 (Recalling the Chinese Nationalist Party headquarters at the time of the great revolution). *Songjiang wenshi* 松江文史 1 (October 1981): 36–39.

Chen Guofu 陳果夫. *Su zheng huiyi* 蘇政回憶 (Reflections on Jiangsu administration). Taibei: Zhengzhong shuju, 1951.

Chen Lifu 陳立夫. "Wo suo zhidao de xianxiong Guofu" 我所知道的先兄果夫 (The late brother Guofu whom I knew). *Zhuanji wenxue* 傳記文學 29.3 (September 1976): 12–14.

Chen Shaoxiao 陳少校. *Hei wang lu* 黑網錄 (Record of the Black Net). Hong Kong: Zhi cheng chubanshe, 1965.

Chen Sibai 陳斯白. "Bimi qijian Zhenjiang dang shi cailiao shiling" 祕密其間鎮江黨史材料拾零 (Miscellanea from materials on Zhenjiang party history in the secret period). *Jiangsu dangwu zhoukan* 江蘇黨務周刊 25 (July 6, 1930): 98–102.

———. "Lüe tan Guomindang Jiangsu sheng dangbu dangwu douzheng" 略談國民黨江蘇省黨部黨務鬥爭 (Briefly speaking of the party affairs struggle in the Jiangsu branch of the Nationalist Party). *Wenshi ziliao xuanji* 文史資料選輯 (Yancheng version) 3 (August 1982): 92–98.

Chen Siling 陳斯齡. "Tongshan qu nongmin ziwei gaikuang" 銅山區農民自衛概況 (The circumstances of peasant self-defense in the Tongshan area). *Jiangsu yuebao* 江蘇月報 4.4,6 (December 1, 1935): 78–97.

Chen Yifu 陳益甫. "Qingmo minchu de Feng xian jiaoyu gaikuang" 清末民初的豐縣教育概況 (The situation of Feng County education in the late Qing and early Republic). *Feng xian wenshi ziliao* 豐縣文史資料 9 (April 1991): 1–6.

Chen Youzhai 陳幼齋. "Jiefang qian Guomindang Huai'an xian dangbu paixi douzheng pianduan" 解放前國民黨淮安縣黨部派系鬥爭片斷 (Fragments of memories of factional struggles in the Huai'an County Nationalist Party prior to liberation). *Huai'an wenshi ziliao* 淮安文史資料 4 (October 1986): 106–115.

Chen Zhongyan 陳仲言. "Xuzhou shanghui zuzhi jianshi" 徐州商會組織簡史 (An outline history of the Xuzhou chamber of commerce organization). *Xuzhou wenshi ziliao* 徐州文史資料 7 (November 1986): 174–86.

Chong Gong 充公. "Jiangsu sheng dangbu gepai de lishi ji qi huodong" 江蘇省黨部各派的歷史及其活動 (The movements and history of the various factions of the Jiangsu provincial party headquarters). *Shehui xinwen* 社會新聞 1.17 (November 21, 1932).

Chu Shuxin 褚樹信. "Wo ren Guomindang san qu quzhang suo yi" 我任國民黨三區區長瑣憶 (Trivial recollections of when I was the Nationalists' third ward headman). *Jingjiang wenshi ziliao* 靖江文史資料 6 (March 1986): 102–116.

Chuansha wenshi ziliao 川沙文史資料 (Materials on the Culture and History of Chuansha). 1989–1990.

Chuansha xianzhi 川沙縣志 (Gazetteer of Chuansha County). 1936.

Cunzhi 村治 (Village Government). Beiping, 1929–1933.

Da Ke 大可. "Jiangsu dangwu de lishi guan" 江蘇黨務的歷史觀 (An historical view of Jiangsu party affairs). *Xiandai shiliao* 現代史料 (N.p., 1933), vol. 1.

———. "Su sheng dangbu xuanju zhi yimu" 蘇省黨部選舉之一幕 (The inside story of the election of the Jiangsu party branch). *Shehui xinwen* 社會新聞 2.5 (January 13, 1932): 50–52.

———. "Su sheng Guo daibiao fuxuan huaxu lu" 蘇省國代表複選花絮錄 (Colorful incidents in the reelection of Jiangsu's National Assemblymen). *Shehui xinwen* 社會新聞 3.27 (June 21, 1932): 425–26.

"Dahui shenxiang yu pochu mixin wenti" 打毀神像與破除迷信問題 (Destruction of idols and the problem of eradication of superstition). *Jiangsu sheng zhengfu gongbao* 江蘇省政府公報 64 (December 17, 1928): 47–48.

Danyang wenshi ziliao 丹陽文史資料 (Materials on the Culture and History of Danyang). Edited by Zheng xie Danyang xian wenshi ziliao yanjiu weiyuanhui 政協丹陽縣文史資料研究委員會 (Committee for Research on Materials on the Culture and History of the Political Consultative Conference for Danyang County), 1982–1986.

Dizheng yuekan 地政月刊 (The Journal of Land Economics). Nanjing, 1933–1937.

Dong Yao 董堯, ed. "Beifa hou, Feng xian shouren xianzhang Wang Gongyu" 北伐後, 豐縣首任縣長王公璵 (The first Feng County magistrate Wang Gongyu). *Feng xian wenshi ziliao* 豐縣文史資料 4 (March 1986): 7–12.

Dongfang zazhi 東方雜志 (Eastern Miscellany). Shanghai, 1927–1937.

"Donghai Guanyun fen xian ji shi benmo" 東海灌雲分縣紀事本末 (The whole story of the separation of Donghai and Guanyun counties). *Haizhou wenxian* 海州文獻 "Special Issue" 1 (January 1979):35–37

Fang Kaijia 方開甲. "Da geming qijian gongshen tuhao Chen Jinju" 大革命期間公審土豪陳金聚 (The public trial of local bully Chen Jinju at the time of the great revolution). *Songjiang wenshi* 松江文史 1 (October 1981): 40–42.

Fang Qingru 方青儒. "Zhongyang dangwu xuexiao" 中央黨務學校 (Central Party Affairs Academy). In *Guoli zhengzhi daxue shi shiliao huibian* 國立政治大學史史料彙編, edited by Guoli zhengzhi daxue xiaoshi bianyin weiyuanhui 國立政治大學校史編印委員會. Taibei: Guoli zhengzhi xiaozhang shi 國立政治大學校長室, 1977, vol. 1.

Feng Hefa 馮和法, ed. *Zhongguo nongcun jingji lun* 中國農村經濟論 (On the Chinese rural economy). Shanghai: Liming shudian, 1936.

———, ed. *Zhongguo nongcun jingji ziliao* 中國農村經濟資料 (Materials on the Chinese rural economy). Shanghai: Liming shuju, 1935.

Feng xian wenshi ziliao 豐縣文史資料 (Materials on the Culture and History of Feng County). 1983–1991.

Feng Yingzi 馮英子. "Wushi nian qian de Kunshan diandi" 五十年前的昆山點滴 (A little bit about the Kunshan of fifty years ago). *Kunshan wenshi* 昆山文史 1 (March 1983): 59–67.

"Funing xian dangbu gongzuo diaocha shixiang yilan" 阜寧縣黨部工作調查事項一覽 (A list of work investigation items for the Funing County party branch). GMDA no. 435/172.

Funing xian xin zhi 阜寧縣新志 (New gazetteer for Funing County). 20 juan, 10 vols. 1934.

Funing wenshi ziliao 阜寧文史資料 (Materials on the Culture and History of Funing). 1984–1990.

Ganyu xian wenshi ziliao 贛榆縣文史資料 (Materials on the Culture and History of Ganyu County). 1984–1990.

Gao Yuzai 高鬱哉. "Hu Qidong xiansheng ersan shi" 胡啓東先生二三事 (Two or three things about Mr. Hu Qidong). *Yancheng wenshi ziliao xuanji* 鹽城文事資料選輯 4 (June 1986): 107–108.

Ge Jianshi 葛建時. "Jiangsu dangwu de yidian zhanggu" 江蘇黨務的一點掌故 (A few historical anecdotes about Jiangsu party affairs). In *Guofu yu Jiangsu* 國父與江蘇 (The father of the country and Jiangsu), edited by Li Hongru 李鴻儒. 1965; reprint, Taibei: Sanmin shuju, 1966.

Ge Shaoliang 葛紹亮. "Guanyu 'yiliu' can'an zhi wo de huiyi" 關于'一六'慘案之我的回憶 (My recollections of the January 6th Massacre). *Shuyang wenshi ziliao* 沭陽文史資料 6 (November 1990): 12–35.

"Geming gaochao zaiqi de qianye zhi zhunbei—Zhou Houjun shi zai sheng dangbu zongli jinian zhou zhi yanci—xian gei Jiangsu quan sheng de geming tongzhi" 革命高潮再起的前夜之準備—周厚鈞氏在省黨部總理紀念周之演辭—獻給江蘇全省的革命同志 (Preparing for the reprise of the high tide of revolution—Mr. Zhou Houjun's talk at the provincial party headquarters' Sun Yat-sen remembrance celebration—a lecture that he [Zhou] contributed to the revolutionary comrades of the entirety of Jiangsu Province). *Susheng yuekan* 蘇聲月刊 1.3,4 (October 1933): 1–8.

GMDA [Guomindang Archives]. Historical Materials Research Center of the Republic of China. Yangmingshan, Taibei, Taiwan.

Gong Xinzhai 龔心齋, and Luo Zhiyuan 羅志淵. "Jiangsu gexian xianzheng canguan jiyao" 江蘇各縣縣政參觀紀要 (A record of an inspection of county governments in various Jiangsu districts). *Jiangsu yuebao* 江蘇月報 4.5,6 (December 1, 1935): 41–50.

Gu Jixun 顧積珣. "Gu Ziyang xiansheng shilüe" 顧子揚先生事略 (A brief account of the life of Mr. Gu Ziyang). *Xuzhou wenshi ziliao* 徐州文史資料 9 (December 1988): 80–88.

Gu Ziyang 顧子揚. *Jiangsu sheng dangwu yange* 江蘇省黨務沿革 (The evolution of Jiangsu provincial party affairs). N.p., 1936. GMDA no. 001/34.

"Guanli simiao xin li wei ban yiqian zhan reng qi jiu" 管理寺廟新例未頒以前暫仍其舊 (While the articles on management of shrines and temples have not yet been promulgated, temporarily maintain the status quo). *Jiangsu sheng zhengfu gongbao* 江蘇省政府公報 59 (November 12, 1928): 18–23.

Guan Wenwei 管文蔚. "Suzhou Fanxing yuan zhenxiang" 蘇州反省院真相 (The truth about the Suzhou Reeducation Institute). *Jiangsu wenshi ziliao* 江蘇文史資料 45 (September 1991): 282–94, issue entitled "Zhong Tong tegong milu" 中統特工祕錄.

"Guanyu Wang Gongyu xiansheng huiyi de shuoming he zhushi" 關于王公璵先生回憶的說明和注釋 (Explanations and annotations about Mr. Wang Gongyu's recollections). *Tongshan wenshi ziliao* 銅山文史資料 5 (August 1985): 115–16.

Guo Xuyin 國緒印, ed. *Guomindang paixi douzheng shi* 國民黨派系鬥爭史 (The history of factional struggle in the Nationalist Party). Shanghai: Renmin chubanshe, 1992.

Guoli zhengzhi daxue shi shiliao huibian 國立政治大學史史料彙編 (Collection of materials on the history of National Political University). Edited by Guoli zhengzhi daxue xiaoshi bianyin weiyuanhui 國立政治大學校史編印委員會 (The committee for editing and printing the school history of National Political University). 2 vols. Taibei: Guoli zhengzhi daxue xiaozhang shi, 1977.

"Guomindang Kunshan xian dangbu dangwu gaikuang" 國民黨昆山縣黨部黨務概況 (The circumstances of party affairs in the Kunshan County Nationalist Party branch). *Kunshan wenshi* 昆山文史 4 (September 1985): 96–98.

"Guomindang Suqian xian lishi jianjie he paixi douzheng" 國民黨宿遷縣歷史簡介和派系鬥爭 (A brief introduction to the history of the Nationalist Party in Suqian and factional struggle). *Suqian wenshi ziliao* 宿遷文史資料 2 (December 1983): 36–40.

Haimen xian wenshi ziliao 海門縣文史資料 (Materials on the Culture and History of Haimen County). 1985–1991.

Haizhou wenxian 海州文獻 (Literature on Haizhou). "Special Issue" (January 1979).

He Fu 何甫. "San zhong quan hui qian Guomindang ge paixi zhi shi de fenxi" 三中全會前國民黨各派系之史的分析 (An analysis of the history of the various factions of the Nationalist Party prior to the Third National Congress). *Shehui xinwen* 社會新聞 1.25 (December 15, 1932): 511–12.

He Yangling 賀揚靈, ed. *Nongmin yundong* 農民運動 (The Peasant Movement). Nanjing: Zhongguo Guomindang Zhongyang dangwu xuexiao, 1928.

Hua Gang 華崗. *Yijiuerwu nian zhi yijiuerqi nian de Zhongguo da geming shi* 一九二五年至一九二七年的中國大革命史 (History of the Great Chinese Revolution, 1925–1927). Shanghai: Chungeng shudian, 1931.

Huai'an wenshi ziliao 淮安文史資料 (Materials on the Culture and History of Huai'an). 1985–1989.

Huaiyin wenshi ziliao 淮陰文史資料 (Materials on the Culture and History of Huaiyin). Edited by Zhongguo renmin zhengzhi xieshang huiyi Jiangsu sheng Huaiyin shi weiyuanhui wenshi ziliao yanjiu weiyuanhui 中國人民政治協商會議江蘇省淮陰市委員會文史資料研究委員會 (Committee for Research on Materials on Culture and History of the Huaiyin, Jiangsu, Municipality Committee of the Chinese People's Political Consultative Conference). 1983–1989.

Huang Huaizhen 黃懷楨. "'Liyang pinglun she' chengli qianhou yixie qingkuang" '溧陽評論社'成立前後一些情況 (A few circumstances of the founding and the entire history of the "Liyang Critic Society"). *Liyang wenshi ziliao* 溧陽文史資料 (for the municipality) 8 (December 1990): 90–92.

Huang Jilu 黃季陸, Xiao Jizong 蕭繼宗, and Du Yuanzai 杜元載, eds. *Geming renwu zhi* 革命人物誌 (Records of revolutionary personages). 14 vols. Taibei: Zhongyang wenwu gongyingshe, 1973.

"Ji ban ge di gaizu pai" 緝辦各地改組派 (On the arrest and handling of various localities' Reorganization Clique personnel). NTHA no. 1(2)–172.

Jia Ming 賈銘. "Xinhai geming hou Suining zhengju de yanbian" 辛亥革命後睢寧政局的演變 (The evolution of Suining's political situation after the 1911 Revolution). *Suining wenshi ziliao* 睢寧文史資料 4 (December 1988): 1–20.

Jiading wenshi ziliao xuanji 嘉定文史資料選輯 (Selected Materials on the Culture and History of Jiading). 1987–1991.

"Jian bao" 剪報 (Newspaper clippings). 1927. GMDA no. 432/15.

Jiang Jieshi yanjiu zhuanji 蔣介石研究專輯, vol. 1. Edited by Ningbo shifan xueyuan zhengshi xi Jiang Jieshi yanjiushi 寧波師範學院政史系蔣介石研究室. N. p., 1988.

Jiang Songping 姜頌平. "Kangzhan qian 'Zhong Tong' zai Nantong de huodong" 抗戰前"中統"在南通的活動 (Activities of the Central Statistical Bureau in Nantong before the War of Resistance). *Nantong wenshi ziliao xuanji* 南通文史資料選輯 4 (November 1984): 41–51.

———. "Zhong Tong zai Haimen huodong qingkuang" 中統在海門活動情況 (The activities and circumstances of the Central Statistical Bureau in Haimen). *Haimen xian wenshi ziliao* 海門縣文史資料 5 (September 1986): 74–78.

Jiang Xiyi 蔣希益. "Zhou Shuiping lieshi shilüe" 周水平烈士事略 (A short biographical account of martyr Zhou Shuiping). *Wenshi ziliao xuanji* 文史資料選輯 (for Shazhou 沙州) 2 (no date): 81–88.

Jiang Yigu 蔣貽谷. "30 niandai qianhou Jiangyin xuesheng chajin Rihuo qingkuang de huiyi" 30年代前後江陰學生查禁日貨情況的回憶 (From the beginning to the end of the 1930s, recollections of the circumstances of Jiangyin students' prohibition of Japanese goods). *Jiangyin wenshi ziliao* 江陰文飾資料 10 (September 1989): 88–89.

Jiang Yushu 姜玉書. "Kangzhan qian Liyang Guomindang jishi" 抗戰前溧陽國民黨紀實 (A record of the actual events of the Liyang Nationalist Party prior to the War of Resistance). *Liyang xian wenshi ziliao* 溧陽縣文史資料 3 (January 1985): 164–72.

"Jiang Zhe nongmin de tongku ji qi fankang yundong" 江浙農民的痛苦及其反抗運動 (The privation of Jiangsu and Zhejiang peasants and their opposition movement). *Xiangdao zhoubao* 嚮導周報, no. 179.

Jiangdu wenshi ziliao xuan bian 江都文史資料選編 (Selected Compilations of Material on the Culture and History of Jiangdu County). 1983–1988.

"Jianghai zhi bin de hongse fengbao" 江海之濱的紅色風暴 (The red tempest in the coastal area). *Qidong wenshi* 啓東文史 8:1–12.

Jiangsu baojia 江蘇保甲 (Jiangsu Mutual Security Groups). Zhenjiang, 1935–1936.

Jiangsu dangsheng 江蘇黨聲 (The Voice of the Jiangsu Party). Nanjing, October–November, 1928.

"Jiangsu dangshi gaimo" 江蘇黨史楷模 (A model for Jiangsu party histories). *Jiangsu dangwu zhoukan* 江蘇黨務周刊 25 (July 6, 1930): 83–102.

Jiangsu dangwu zhoukan 江蘇黨務周刊 (Jiangsu Party Affairs Weekly). Zhenjiang, 1930–1931.

Jiangsu gaodeng fating gongbao 江蘇高等法庭公報 (Gazette of the Supreme Court of Jiangsu), nos. 3, 4 (bound together). Zhenjiang, March, April 1930.

Jiangsu geming douzheng jilüe 江蘇革命鬥爭紀略 (A Sketch of Revolutionary Struggle in Jiangsu). Edited by Zhonggong Jiangsu sheng wei dang shi gongzuo weiyuanhui 中共江蘇省委黨史工作委員會 (Party History Work Committee of the Jiangsu Provincial Committee of the Chinese Communist Party) and the Jiangsu sheng dang'an guan 江蘇省檔案館 (Jiangsu Provincial Party Archives). Beijing: Dang'an chubanshe, 1987.

Jiangsu jianshe ting gongbao 江蘇建設廳公報 (Jiangsu Reconstruction Commission Gazette). Zhenjiang, 1928.

Jiangsu sheng dangbu dang shi 江蘇省黨部黨史 (History of the Jiangsu provincial party headquarters). N.p., 1927. GMDA no. 481/13.

"Jiangsu sheng dangbu duiyu zuzhi sheng zhengfu zhi jihua" 江蘇省黨部對于組織省政府之計劃 (The plans of the Jiangsu provincial party headquarters with regard to organizing a provincial government). Date given is 1926 but internal evidence suggests early 1927. GMDA no. 435/145.

Jiangsu sheng nongcun diaocha 江蘇省農村調查 (A rural investigation of Jiangsu Province). Edited by Xingzhengyuan nongcun fuxing weiyuanhui 行政院農村復興委員會. Shanghai: Shangwu yinshuguan, 1934.

"Jiangsu sheng shangmin xiehui ji Tongshan xian shangmin xiehui gaizu jiufen" 江蘇省商民協會及銅山縣商民協會改組糾分 (Reorganization disputes among Jiangsu province's merchant associations and Tongshan County's merchant association). NTHA no. 1(1)–3099.

"Jiangsu sheng Tongshan xian shangmin xiehui gaizu jiufen" 江蘇省銅山縣商民協會改組糾分 (Reorganization disputes of the Tongshan County Merchant Association). NTHA no. 1(1)–3100.

Jiangsu sheng zhengfu gongbao 江蘇省政府公報 (Jiangsu Provincial Government Gazette). Nanjing, Zhenjiang, 1927–1936.

Jiangsu sheng zhengfu mishu chu 江蘇省政府祕書處 (Secretariat of the Jiangsu provincial government), ed. *Sannian lai Jiangsu sheng zheng shuyao* 三年來江蘇省政述要 (A sketch of administration in Jiangsu for the past three years). 2 vols. Zhenjiang: Jiangsu sheng zhengfu mishu chu disan ke, 1936.

Jiangsu wenshi ziliao xuanji 江蘇文史資料選輯 (Materials on the Culture and History of Jiangsu). N.p., 1981–1991.

"Jiangsu Wu xian dangbu gongzuo diaocha shixiang yilan" 江蘇吳縣黨部工作調查事項一覽 (A list of work investigation items for the Wu County, Jiangsu party headquarters). 1936. GMDA no. 435/175.

"Jiangsu Xiao xian Jiangyin Jiangning Songjiang deng dangyuan rudang yuanshu" 江蘇蕭縣江陰江寧松江等黨員入黨願書 (Party member entrance pledge documents for Xiao, Jiangyin, Jiangning, and Songjiang counties). 1924. GMDA no. 435/69.

Jiangsu xunkan 江蘇旬刊 (Jiangsu Ten Day Journal). Nanjing, 1928–1929.

Jiangsu yanjiu 江蘇研究 (Research on Jiangsu). Shanghai, 1925–1937.

Jiangsu yuebao 江蘇月報 (Jiangsu Monthly). Zhenjiang, 1934–1935.

Jiangyin renmin geming shi 江陰人民革命史 (History of the Jiangyin people's revolution). Nanjing: Nanjing daxue chubanshe, 1991.

Jiangyin wenshi ziliao 江陰文史資料 (Materials on the Culture and History of Jiangyin). 1983–1989.

Jianhu wenshi xuanji 建湖文史選集 (Selections on the Culture and History of Jianhu). 1986–1988.

Jin Weijian 金維堅, ed. *Tongshan nongcun jingji diaocha* 銅山農村經濟調查 (An investigation of the Tongshan County rural economy). [Zhenjiang]: Jiangsu sheng nongmin yinhang, 1931.

Jing Song 鏡松. *Jiangsu zhengzhi zhuangkuang yu renwu de celüe* 江蘇政治狀況與任務的策略 (Jiangsu's political situation and the measures that meet the task). N.p., 1929.

Jingjiang wenshi ziliao 靖江文史資料 (Materials on the Culture and History of Jingjiang). 1982–1989.

Jinshan wenshi ziliao 金山文史資料 (Materials on the Culture and History of Jinshan County). 1984–1988.

Jintan wenshi ziliao 金壇文史資料 (Materials on the Culture and History of Jintan). 1984–1988.

Ju Zheng 居正, ed. *Qingdang shilu* 清黨實錄 (The true records of the party purge). Nanjing: Jingnan wanbao, n.d.

Kunshan wenshi 昆山文史 (Materials on the Culture and History of Kunshan). 1983–1990.

Lao Zhuo 老拙. "Jiefang qian Guomindang Pi xian neibu paibie douzheng" 解放前國民黨邳縣內部派別鬥爭 (Internal factional struggle in the Pi County Nationalist Party prior to liberation). *Pi xian wenshi ziliao* 邳縣文史資料 2 (October 1984): 46–61.

Li Changfu 李長傅. *Fen sheng dizhi: Jiangsu* 分省地誌：江蘇 (Province-by-province gazetteers: Jiangsu). Shanghai: Zhonghua shuju youxian gongsi, 1936.

Li Hongru 李鴻儒, ed. *Guofu yu Jiangsu* 國父與江蘇 (The father of the country [Sun Yat-sen] and Jiangsu). 1965. Reprint, Taibei: Sanmin shuju, 1966.

Li Jixin 李積新. "Huainan yanken qu zhi ken zhi wenti" 淮南鹽墾區之墾殖問題 (Reclamation and settlement questions in the salt-land reclamation areas south of the Huai). *Dizheng yuekan* 地政月刊 3.5 (May 1935): 705–719.

Li Shouyong 李壽雍. "Duan Shuyi xiansheng yu wo" 段書貽先生與我 (Mr. Duan Xipeng and me). *Zhuanji wenxue* 傳記文學 30.3 (March 1977): 20–24.

———. "Zai Jiangsu ban dang" 在江蘇辦黨 (Managing the party in Jiangsu). *Jiangsu dang sheng* 江蘇黨聲 6 (September 2, 1928): 6–16.

Li Tiping 李惕平. "Xiri de Qingfeng chashu—jiu shehui Wuxi shishen de 'julebu'" 昔日的清風茶墅—舊社會無錫士紳的"俱樂部" (The Qingfeng teahouse of former days—the club of the Wuxi gentry of the old society). *Wuxi wenshi ziliao* 無錫文史資料 13 (March 10, 1986): 116–28.

Li Wangsu 李望蘇. "Ao qing bianxiang leng zhong kai" 敖情偏向冷中開 (Revealing pridefulness as it abates). *Shuyang wenshi ziliao* 沭陽文史資料 1 (October 1984): 10–25.

Li Yunhan 李雲漢. *Cong rong gong dao qingdang* 從容共到清黨 (From the admission of the Communists to the party purge). 1966. Taibei: Zhongguo xueshu zhuzuo jiangzhu weiyuanhui, 1973.

———. "Jieshao Sun Wen zhuyi xue hui ji qi youguan wenjian" 介紹孫文主義學會及其有關文件 (Introducing the Sunist Study Society and documents related to it). Reprinted from *Zhongyang yanjiu yuan jindai shi yanjiu so jikan* 中央研究院近代史研究所集刊 (Quarterly of the Institute of Modern History of the Academia Sinica) 4 (February 1974): 497–522.

Li Zonghuang 李宗黃. "Difang zizhi zhi guoqu yu jianglai" 地方自治之過去與將來 (The past and future of local self-government). *Difang zizhi* 地方自治 3 (September 30, 1935): 443–46.

Lianshui wenshi ziliao 漣水文史資料 (Materials on the Culture and History of Lianshui). 1982–1990.

Lianyungang shi wenshi ziliao 連雲港市文史資料 (Materials on the Culture and History of Lianyungang Municipality). 1983–1989.

"Ling chaban Yancheng xianzhang Li Yicheng" 令查辦鹽城縣長李一誠 (Order for investigation and handling of Yancheng magistrate Li Yicheng). *Jiangsu sheng zhengfu gongbao* 江蘇省政府公報 56 (October 1928): 14.

"Ling jin Rugao xian wei ling hui chenghuang miao" 令禁如皋縣違令毀城隍廟 (Directing prohibition of Rugao County from destroying the Temple of the City God in contravention of orders). *Jiangsu sheng zhengfu gongbao* 江蘇省政府公報 60 (November 19, 1928): 24–25.

Ling Xiao 凌霄. "Jiefang qian Suqian de jijia baokan" 解放前宿遷的幾家報刊 (Several of Suqian's periodicals prior to liberation). *Suqian xian wenshi ziliao* 宿遷縣文史資料 3 (August 1984): 89–93.

Ling Yanyu 凌雁雨. "Xu lun Suqian shijian" 續論宿遷事件 (Continued discussion of the Suqian incident). *Mingri zhi Jiangsu* 明日之江蘇 6 (June 1929): 17–33.

"Ling zhi simiao guanli iaoli zhan huan shixing" 令知寺廟管理條例暫緩施行 (Directing all to be aware that they should postpone putting into effect the "Articles on Temples and Shrines"). *Jiangsu sheng zhengfu gongbao* 江蘇省政府公報 168 (June 25, 1929): 6.

Liu Butong 劉不同. "Guomindang de moying—'CC' tuan" 國民黨的魔影—"CC"團 (The devilish shadow of the Nationalist Party—the "CC" Clique). *Wenshi ziliao xuanji* 文史資料選輯 (Beijing edition) 45 (first published April 1964; reprinted December 1980): 231–54.

Liu Chengzhang 劉承章. "Tongshan xian xiangcun xinyong ji qi yu diquan yidong zhi guanxi" 銅山縣鄉村信用及其與地權移動之關系 (Tongshan County rural credit and its relation to shifts in land ownership). M.A. thesis, Graduate School of Land Economics of Central Political Academy, Nanjing. In *Minguo ershi niandai Zhongguo dalu tudi wenti ziliao* 民國二十年代中國大陸土地問題資料 (Materials on the land question in the Chinese mainland in the 1930s). Vol. 90. Edited by Xiao Zheng. Taibei: Chengwen chubanshe youxian gongsi, 1977.

Liu Rentao 劉仁濤. "Guomindang Wang, Hong, Ye san zhong wei yishi" 國民黨王, 洪, 葉三中委軼事 (Anecdotes about the Nationalists' central committeemen Wang, Hong, and Ye). *Jiangdu wenshi ziliao xuanpian* 江都文史資料選編 2 (December 1984): 21–24.

Liu Shaotang 劉紹唐, ed. *Minguo da shi rizhi* 民國大事日誌 (Daily chronology of the great events of the republic). Vol. 1. Taibei: Zhuanji wenxue chubanshe, 1973.

Liu Xiuqing 劉岫青. "Qidong zu dian wenti yu fuzhi zigeng nong yundong" 啓東租佃問題與扶植自耕農運動 (The tenancy question and supporting the movement for "self-tilling peasants"). *Dizheng yuekan* 地政月刊 5.2, 3 (March 1937): 322–23.

Liyang xianzhi ziliao 溧陽縣志資料 (Materials for the Gazetteer for Liyang County). Edited by Liyang xian difangzhi bangongshi 溧陽縣地方志班公室 (The Office of the Liyang County Local Gazetteer). 1984–1985.

Liyang wenshi ziliao 溧陽文史資料 (Materials on the Culture and History of Liyang). 1983–1990. (Some of these issues were edited by the People's Political Consultative Conference for Liyang municipality, and some were edited by the People's Political Consultative Conference for Liyang County.)

Lu Jianzhong 陸建中. "Guomindang Gaizu pai Liyang baodong shibai hou yi, er shi" 國民黨改組派溧陽暴動失敗後一,二事 (One or two things about the aftermath of the failed insurrection of the Nationalist Party's Reorganization Clique). *Liyang wenshi ziliao* 溧陽文史資料 2 (January 1984): 30–34.

Lu Yanghao 陸養浩. "Yizhuan Chong ren zai Qi diquan wenti zhi yanjiu" 移轉崇人在啓地權問題之研究 (Research on the question of transferring the

Qidong land rights of Chongming residents). *Jiangsu yanjiu* 江蘇研究 3.1 (April 31, 1937): nonconsecutive pagination.

Lu Ziquan 陸子權. "Chenwei shiwei xuanchuan he Guomindang de fanpu" 陳圩示威宣傳和國民黨的反撲 (The Chen dike demonstration and propaganda, and the Nationalist Party's counteroffensive). *Xinyi wenshi ziliao* 新沂文史資料 2 (June 1986): 57–75.

Mao Huangshan 矛黃山 and Wang Shoupeng 王壽彭. "Jiefang qian de Jiangyin xinwen shiye" 解放前的江陰新聞事業 (The news business in Jiangyin before liberation). *Jiangyin wenshi ziliao* 江陰文史資料 8 (August 1987): 33–40.

Mingri zhi Jiangsu 明日之江蘇 (The Jiangsu of Tomorrow). 1929–1930.

"Minguo renwu xiao zhuan" 民國人物小傳 (Short biographies of personalities of the Republic). *Zhuanji wenxue* 傳記文學 36.4 (April 1, 1980): 145.

Muramatsu Yuji 村松祐次. *Kindai Konan no sosan: Chugoku jinushi seido no kenkyu* 近代江南の租棧：中國地主製度の研究 (Bursaries in Jiangnan in the modern period: Studies of the Chinese landlord system). Tokyo: Tokyo Daigaku shuppankai, 1970.

Nagano Akira 長野朗. *Zhongguo tudi zhidu yanjiu* 中國土地製度研究 (Research on China's land system), translated from the Japanese by Lu Pu 陸璞. Shanghai: Chen Baohua, 1933.

Nanhui xian wenshi ziliao 南匯縣文史資料 (Materials on the Culture and History of Nanhui County. 1987–1991.

Nanjing minguo ribao 南京民國日報 (Nanjing Republican Daily News). 1927.

Nantong wenshi ziliao xuanji 南通文史資料選輯 (Compilation of Materials on the Culture and History of Nantong Municipality). 1981–1989.

NHTA [Number Two Historical Archives]. Nanjing, China.

Ni Bi 倪弼. "Duiyu Jiangsu ge xian zhengzhi de ganxiang he xiwang" 對於江蘇各縣政治的感想和希望 (Opinions and hopes with regard to the politics of various Jiangsu counties). *Jiangsu xunkan* 江蘇旬刊 2 (September 11, 1928): 11–13.

———. "Jiangsu sheng dangwu qingkuang" 江蘇省黨務情況 (The state of Jiangsu provincial party affairs). *Jiangsu xunkan* 江蘇旬刊 22,23 (January 1, 1929): 1–16.

Pan Juemin 潘覺民, "Duiyu zhengli xian yixia geji dangbu de yijian" 對於整理縣以下各級黨部的意見 (An opinion with regard to rectifying the party branches below the county level). *Jiangsu dangwu zhoukan* 江蘇黨務周刊 6 (February 16, 1930): 40–42.

Pi xian wenshi ziliao 邳縣文史資料 (Materials on the Culture and History of Pi County). 1983–1991.

"Qian Sunqing yu Wuxi xian shanghui" 錢孫卿與無錫縣商會 (Qian Sunqing and the Wuxi County Chamber of Commerce). *Wuxi wenshi ziliao* 無錫文史資料 1 (September 1980): 69–78.

Qianfeng 前鋒 (Vanguard). Nanjing. 1929.

Qiao Dingren 喬鼎人. "Xin minzhu zhuyi geming shiqi Zhong Gong Chuansha xian zuzhi shi ziliao jian ji" 新民主主意革命時期中共川沙縣組織史資料簡輯

(A simple compendium of materials on the history of the Chinese Communist Party's Chuansha County organization during the period of the new democratic revolution). *Chuansha wenshi ziliao* 1 (June 1989): 5–10.

Qidong wenshi 啓東文史 (The Culture and History of Qidong). 1989–1991.

Qidong wenshi xuanji 啓東文史選輯 (Selected Materials on the Culture and History of Qidong). 1984–1987.

Qing Jiajie 慶家節. "Guomindang gaizu pai zai Liyang de huodong shi mo" 國民黨改組派在溧陽的活動始末 (The movement of the Reorganization Clique of the Nationalist Party in Liyang from the beginning to the end). *Liyang xianzhi ziliao* 溧陽縣志資料 2 (June 1985): 144–45.

Qingpu wenshi 青浦文史 (The Culture and History of Qingpu). 1989–1991.

Sa Shijiong 薩師炯, Qian Duansheng 錢端昇, Guo Denghao 郭登皞, Lin Qiongguang 林瓊光, Yang Hongnian 楊鴻年, Lü Enlai 呂恩萊, Feng Zhen 馮震. *Minguo zheng zhi shi* 民國政製史. Changsha: Shangwu yinshuguan, 1940.

Shehui xinwen 社會新聞 (The Society Mercury). Shanghai, 1932–1937.

Shen bao 申報 (The Shun Pao). Shanghai, 1927–1937.

Shen Yigong 沈軼公, Zhang Xiafeng 張俠風, and Yao Zhiren 姚志仁, "Yi liangci Guo-Gong hezuo zhong de Guomindang Qidong xian dangbu" 憶兩次國共合作中的國民黨啓東縣黨部 (Remembering the Qidong County Nationalist Party branch at the time of the two periods of Nationalist-Communist cooperation). *Qidong wenshi xuanji* 啓東文史選輯 3 (September 1985): 24–33.

Shi bao 時報 (The Times). Shanghai, 1925–1930.

Shi Shunyuan 石順淵. "Youguan Nanhui xian Guomindang de yi lin ban zhao" 有關南匯縣國民黨的一鱗半爪 (A bit of a fragment relating to Nanhui County's Nationalist Party). *Nanhui xian wenshi ziliao* 南匯縣文史資料 4 (February 1988): 48–50.

Shishi xinbao 時事新報 (The China Times). Shanghai, 1928–1937.

Shuyang wenshi ziliao 沭陽文史資料 (Materials on the Culture and History of Shuyang County). 1984–1990.

Sima Xiandao 司馬仙島. *Beifa hou zhi gepai sichao* 北伐後之各派思潮 (The doctrines of the various cliques after the Northern Expedition). Beiping: Ying shan she chubanbu, 1930.

Siyang wenshi ziliao 泗陽文史資料 (Materials on the Culture and History of Siyang). 1983–1990.

Songjiang wenshi 松江文史 (The Culture and History of Songjiang). 1981–1991.

Song Ping 宋平. *Jiang Jieshi: zong siling, weiyuan zhang, zongcai, zhuxi, zongtong* 蔣介石：總司令，委員長，總裁，主席，總統 (Chiang Kai-shek: Commander in chief, generalissimo, director-general, chairman, president). Hong Kong: Liwen chubanshe, 1992.

"Su quan hui huaxu lu" 蘇全會花絮錄 (Colorful incidents of the Jiangsu Congress). *Shehui xinwen* 社會新聞 (January 10, 1933): 435–36.

"Su sheng dangbu gai xuan zhi qian hou" 蘇省黨部改選之前後 (Before and after the reelection of the Jiangsu provincial party branch). *Shehui xinwen* 社會新聞 1.28 (December 24, 1932): 554–55.

Suining wenshi ziliao 睢寧文史資料 (Materials on the Culture and History of Suining). 1984–1990.

Sumin zhoubao 蘇民周報 (Jiangsu Citizen's Weekly). Nanjing, 1929–1930.

"Suqian geming yundong" 宿遷革命運動 (Suqian County's revolutionary movement). *Suqian wenxian* 宿遷文獻 2 (January 1967): 18–24.

Suqian wenshi ziliao 宿遷文史資料 (Materials on the Culture and History of Suqian). 1983–1987.

Suqian wenxian 宿遷文獻 (Literature on Suqian County). No. 2 (January 1967).

"Su sheng dangbu gaixuan zhi qianhou" 蘇省黨部改選之前後(At about the time of the reelection of the Jiangsu provincial party headquarters), *Shehui xinwen* 社會新聞 3.27 (June 21, 1932): 425–26.

Susheng yuekan 蘇聲月刊 (The Voice of Jiangsu Monthly). Zhenjiang, 1933–1935.

"Sun Depei nianji gao (jielu)" 孫德培年紀稿(節錄) (A draft of the years of Sun Depei [excerpt]). *Shuyang wenshi ziliao* 沭陽文史資料 4 (March 1988): 46–61.

Sun Guangwu 孫光武. "Sun Jishi bei sha de qianqian houhou" 孫基士被殺的前前後後 (Before and after Sun Jishi was killed). *Feng xian wenshi ziliao* 豐縣文史資料 1 (December 1983): 143–47.

Sun Shi'ao 孫石鰲. "Guomindang Yancheng xian dangbu chou wen yi ze" 國民黨鹽城縣黨部醜聞一則 (A bit of ugly information about the Yancheng County party headquarters). *Wenshi ziliao xuanji* 文史資料選輯 3 (March 1982): 99–103.

"Sun Wen Zhuyi xue hui chengli jingguo ji qi yingxiang" 孫文主義學會成立經過及其影響 (The events of the establishment of the Sunist Study Society and its influence). Reprinted excerpt from *Zhonghua minguo shiliao yanjiu zhongxin diershijiu ci xueshu taolunhui jilu* 中華民國史料研究中心第二十九次學術討論會記錄 (Minutes of the twenty-ninth conference of the Seminar of the Historical Materials Research Center of the Republic of China). Taibei, n.d.

Sun Yiwu 孫宜武. "Ganyu xian diyige Gongchandang yuan—Zhang Jingtong" 贛榆縣第一個共產黨員張竟同 (Ganyu County's first Communist Party member—Zhang Jingtong). *Ganyu xian wenshi ziliao* 贛榆縣文史資料 7 (October 1989): 24–28.

Sun Ziying 孫子英, and Sun Yiqian 孫宜謙. "Women suo zhidao de Zhu Shoushi xiansheng" 我們所知道的朱壽石先生 (The Mr. Zhu Shoushi that we knew). *Ganyu xian wenshi ziliao* 贛榆縣文史資料 7 (October 1989): 47–51.

Taicang wenshi ziliao jicun 太倉文史資料輯存 (Compilation of Materials on the Culture and History of Taicang). 1984–1991.

Tanaka Tadao 田中忠夫. *Guomin geming yu nongcun wenti* 國民革命與農村問題 (The national revolution and the rural question). Translated from the Japanese by Li Yuwen 李育文. 2 vols. Beiping: Jingcheng yinshuju, 1932.

Tao Qiqing 陶其情, ed. *Quanmin geming yu guomin geming* 全民革命與國民革命 (Revolution of the whole people or national citizens' revolution?) Shanghai: Guangming shuju, 1929.

"Teng Gu de xin huodong" 騰固的新活動 (The new actions of Teng Gu). *Shehui xinwen* 社會新聞 3.7 (April 21, 1933): 100.

"Teng Gu jingxuan guo daibiao" 騰固競選國代表 (Teng Gu runs for the National Assembly). *Shehui xinwen* 社會新聞 3.17 (May 21, 1933): 261.

Tongshan wenshi ziliao 銅山文史資料 (Materials on the Culture and History of Tongshan). 1982–1990.

"Tongshan xian Guomindang lishi yange" 銅山縣國民黨歷史沿革 (The evolution of the history of Tongshan's Nationalist Party). *Tongshan wenshi ziliao* 銅山文史資料 7 (April 1987): 33–43.

Wang Fengxin 王逢辛. "Ping *Xin Qidong bao* 'Yizhuan Chongren zai Qi diquan zhi jiantao'" 評新啓東報移轉崇人在啓地勸之檢討 (Criticizing the *New Qidong Gazette*'s "Discussion of transferring the Qidong land rights of Chongming residents"). *Jiangsu yanjiu* 江蘇研究 3.1 (January 31, 1937): nonconsecutive pagination.

Wang Goufu 王緱甫. "Dui Danyang geming shi de huiyi de diandi" 對丹陽革命史的回憶的點滴 (A brief reflection on Danyang's revolutionary history). *Danyang wenshi ziliao* 丹陽文史資料 1 (December 1982): 28–29.

Wang Muhan 王慕韓. "Jiangsu yanken qu tudi zhengli quyi" 江蘇鹽墾區土地整理芻議 (Humble opinions on the rectification of Jiangsu's salt-land reclamation area). *Dongfang zazhi* 東方雜誌 31.24 (December 16, 1934): 37–46.

Wang Shuhuai 王樹槐. *Zhongguo xiandaihua de quyou yanjiu: Jiangsu sheng, 1860–1916* 中國現代化的區域研究: 江蘇省, 1860–1916 (Regional research on China's modernization: Jiangsu Province, 1860–1916). Taibei: Zhongyang yanjiu yuan jindai shi yanjiusuo, 1984.

Wang Xiuhua 王岫華. "Lianshui xian zhong dang zhibu de zaoqi huodong" 漣水縣中黨支部的早期活動 (Actions of the party branch in Lianshui during the early period). *Lianshui wenshi ziliao* 漣水文史資料 1 (December 1982): 36–45.

Wang Yijin 汪疑今. "Zhongguo jindai renkou yidong zhi jingji de yanjiu" 中國近代人口移動之經濟的研究 (Research on the economics of Chinese migration in the modern era). *Zhongguo jingji* 中國經濟 4.5 (May 1937): nonconsecutive pagination.

Wang Zhitao 王志濤. "Diyi ci Guo-Gong hezuo zai Qingpu" 第一次國共合作在青浦 (The first cooperation between the Nationalists and Communists in Qingpu). *Qingpu wenshi* 青浦文史 6 (June 1991): 15–30.

Wenshi ziliao jicun 文史資料輯存 (Compilations of Archived Materials on Culture and History). Compiled by Zhongguo renmin zhengzhi xieshang huiyi Jiangsu sheng Changshu shi weiyuanhui wenshi ziliao yanjiu weiyuanhui 中國人民政治協商會議江蘇省常熟市委員會文史資料研究委員會 (The Committee on Research on Materials on the Culture and History of the Changshu Municipality, Jiangsu Province, Chinese People's Political Consultative Conference). 1961–1991.

Wenshi ziliao xuanji 文史資料選輯 (Selected Materials on Culture and History). Compiled by Zhongguo renmin zhengzhi xieshang huiyi Jiangsu sheng Shazhou xian weiyuanhui wenshi ziliao yanjiu weiyuanhui 中國人民政治協商會議江蘇省沙州縣委員會文史資料研究委員會 (The Committee on Research on Materials on the Culture and History of Shazhou County, Jiangsu, Chinese People's Political Consultative Conference). 1983–1986 (and some prior volumes that lack dates).

Wenshi ziliao xuanji 文史資料選輯 (Selected Materials on Culture and History). Compiled by Zhongguo renmin zhengzhi xieshang huiyi Jiangsu sheng Yancheng xian weiyuanhui wenshi ziliao yanjiu weiyuanhui 中國人民政治協商會議江蘇省鹽城縣委員會文史資料研究委員會 (The Committee on Research on Materials on Culture and History of Yancheng County, Jiangsu, Chinese People's Political Consultative Conference). 1982.

Wu Jinliang 吳金良, and Zhu Xiaoping 朱小平. *Jiang shi jiazu quan zhuan* 蔣氏家族全傳, vol. 1. Beijing: Zhongguo wenshi chubanshe, 1998.

Wu Qiang 吳強. "Yiliu can'an huiyi" 一六慘案回憶 (Reminiscences about the January 6th Massacre). *Shuyang wenshi ziliao* 沭陽文史資料 2 (May 1985): 1–18.

Wu Shoupeng 吳壽彭. "Xu Hai ge shu" 徐海各屬 (The various parts of the Hsu-Hai district). In *Zhongguo nongcun jingji ziliao* 中國農村經濟資料, edited by Feng Hefa 馮和法. Shanghai: Liming shuju, 1935.

Wu Tianhan 吳天憾, Zhao Huaibi 趙懷璧, Wang Dasan 王達三, and Zhao Ruheng 趙如珩. *Zhongguo Guomindang Kunshan xian dang shi* 中國國民黨昆山縣黨史 (History of the Kunshan County Nationalist Party). N.p., 1929. GMDA no. 435/177.

Wu Xiangxiang 吳相湘, ed. *Chen Guofu de yisheng* 陳果夫的一生 (The life of Chen Guofu). Taibei: Zhuanji wenxue chubanshe, 1971.

Wu Yan 吳岩. "Luanshi Yingxiong Zhu Ji" 亂世英雄朱驥 (Hero of a troubled time, Zhu Ji). *Jingjiang wenshi ziliao* 靖江文史資料 9 (December 1989): 34–51.

Wujin wenshi ziliao 武進文史資料 (Materials on the Culture and History of Wujin). 1982–1991.

Wuxi wenshi ziliao 無錫文史資料 (Materials on the Culture and History of Wuxi Municipality). 1980–1990.

Wuxi xian zhengfu 無錫縣政府 (Wuxi County government), ed. *Wuxi gailan* 無錫概覽 (A General Look at Wuxi). Wuxi, 1935.

"Xia Lin lieshi zhuan lu" 夏霖烈士傳略 (A brief biography of the martyr Xia Lin). *Danyang wenshi ziliao* 丹陽文史資料 1 (December 1982): 16–22.

Xiandai shiliao 現代史料 (Historical materials relating to the contemporary period). 3 vols. N.p., 1933.

Xiangdao zhoubao 響導周報 (The Guide Weekly). Shanghai, Guangzhou, 1922–1927.

Xiao Zheng 蕭錚. *Tudi gaige wushinian: Xiao Zheng huiyi lu* 土地改革五十年：蕭錚會議錄 (Fifty years of land reform: The memoirs of Xiao Zheng). Taibei: Zhongguo dizheng yanjiu suo zong jingxiao Zhuanji wenxue chubanshe, 1980.

Xinwen bao 新聞報 (The News). Shanghai, 1930–1933.

Xinyi wenshi ziliao 新沂文史資料 (Materials on the Culture and History of Xinyi). 1985–1988.

Xu Mengmei 徐夢梅, Zheng Fengshi 鄭風石, and Di Dounan 狄鬥南. "Huiyi Guomindang zai Taicang de dangwu huodong" 回憶國民黨在太倉的黨務活動 (Reminiscing about the party affairs actions of the Nationalist Party in Taicang). *Taicang wenshi ziliao jicun* 太倉文史資料輯存 2 (December 1984): 34–45.

Xu Shouhong 徐壽洪. "Zaoqi de Guomindang Funing xian dangbu" 早期的國民黨阜寧縣黨部 (The Funing County party headquarters during the early period). *Funing wenshi ziliao* 阜寧文史資料 4 (September 1989): 95–102.

Xu Weiyong 徐維鏞. "Minguo liunian de yici xuewu gaige" 民國六年的一次學務改革 (An education reform from 1917). *Wujin wenshi ziliao* 武進文史資料 7 (December 1986): 77–84.

"Xu xianzhang yuan cheng yi" 徐縣長原呈一 (The original petitions of County Magistrate Xu, 1). *Jiangsu sheng zhengfu gongbao* 江蘇省政府公報 59 (November 12, 1928): 19.

Xu xiu Yancheng xian zhi 續修鹽城縣志 (A continuation and revision of the gazetteer for Yancheng County). 1936.

Xu Yongping 徐詠平. *Chen Guofu zhuan* 陳果夫傳 (Biography of Chen Guofu). Taibei: Zhengzhong shuju, 1978.

Xu Youchun 徐友春, ed. *Minguo renwu da cidian* 民國人物大辭典 (Dictionary of Republican-era personages). Shijiazhuang: Hebei renmin chubanshe, 1991.

Xu Zhiyi 徐植義. "Xu Zhiren zhuan lüe" 徐植仁傳略 (A brief biography of Xu Zhiren). *Jiading wenshi ziliao xuanji* 嘉定文史資料選輯 1 (n.d.): 167–70.

Xuzhou wenshi ziliao 徐州文史資料 (Materials on the Culture and History of Xuzhou). 1981–1990.

"Yancheng xian dangbu gongzuo diaocha shixiang yilan" 鹽城縣黨部工作調查事項一覽 (A list of work investigation items for the Yancheng County party headquarters). April 1930. GMDA no. 435/177.

Yancheng xian wenshi ziliao 鹽城縣文史資料 (Materials on the Culture and History of Yancheng County). Edited by Zhongguo renmin zhengzhi xieshang huiyi Yancheng shi jiaoqu weiyuanhui wenshi ziliao weiyuanhui 中國人民政治協商會議鹽城市郊區委員會文史資料委員會 (Committee for Research on Materials on Culture and History for Yancheng Municipality's Suburban Area of the Chinese People's Political Consultative Conference). 1984.

Yancheng wenshi ziliao xuanji 鹽城文史資料選輯 (Selected Materials on the Culture and History of Yancheng). Edited by Zhongguo renmin zhengzhi xieshang huiyi Jiangsu sheng Yancheng shi weiyuanhui wenshi ziliao yanjiu weiyuanhui 中國人民政治協商會議江蘇省鹽城市委員會文史資料研究委員會 (Committee for Research on Materials on Culture and History of the Yancheng, Jiangsu, Municipality Committee of the Chinese People's Political Consultative Conference). 1984–1990.

Yang Binnong 楊邠農. "Qingmo minguo Feng xian jianwen zatan" 卿末民國豐縣見聞雜談 (Miscellaneous observations on Feng County in the late Qing and Republican periods). *Feng xian wenshi ziliao* 豐縣文史資料 4 (March 1986): 179–91.

Yang Dongye 揚東野. "Aiguo minzhu zhanshi Feng Yinong" 愛國民主戰士馮逸農 (Patriotic, democratic soldier Feng Yinong). *Lianyungang shi wenshi ziliao* 連雲港市文史資料 5 (December 1987): 152–59.

Yang Gu 楊谷. "Wo suo zhidao de Guomindang sheng, xian paixi qingkuang" 我所知道的國民黨省，縣派系情況 (The Nationalist Party provincial and county factions as I know them). *Jiangdu wenshi ziliao xuan bian* 江都文史資料 選編 2 (December 1984): 16–20.

Yang Hegao 楊鶴高. "Da dizhu 'Cheng Zhentai' jia ye xingshuai shimo" 大地主"程震泰"家業興衰始末 (The rise and fall of the family property of great landlord Cheng Zhentai). *Shuyang wenshi ziliao* 沭陽文史資料 2 (May 1985): 118–28.

Yang Qimin 楊其民. "Kunshan 'qingdang' qianhou dangzheng da shi ji" 昆山"清黨"前後黨政大事記 (A chronology of party and administrative events before and after the purge in Kunshan). *Kunshan wenshi* 昆山文史 4 (September 1985): 99–102.

Yang Zaichuan 楊在川, et al. "Chujue eba" 處決惡霸 (Executing an evil despot). *Jinshan wenshi ziliao* 金山文史資料 7 (December 1988): 53–54.

Yao Zhiren 姚志仁. "Da geming shiqi de jinan gongzuo" 大革命時期的濟難工作 (Work in the period of the great revolution to deal with the difficulties). *Qidong wenshi xuanji* 啟東文史選輯 5 (November 1986): 21–35.

Ye Chucang 葉楚傖. "Jiangsu sheng xingzheng jinkuang" 江蘇省行政近況 (The recent situation in Jiangsu provincial administration). *Zhongyang dangwu yuekan* 中央黨務月刊 27 (October 1930): 147–51.

Yi Xun 翊勳. *Jiang dang zhenxiang* 蔣黨真相 (The truth about Chiang Kai-shek's factions). N.p.: Nanyang chubanshe, 1949.

"'Yiliu' can'an de shishi jingguo" "一六"慘案的事實經過 (The actual events of the January 6th Massacre). *Shuyang wenshi ziliao* 沭陽文史資料 6 (November 1990): 36–70.

"'Yiliu' can'an yihou" "一六"慘案以後 (After the January 6th Massacre). *Shuyang wenshi ziliao* 沭陽文史資料 6 (November 1990): 71–84.

"Yiyi erer can'an" 一一二二慘案 (The November 22 massacre). GMDA no. 468/20.

Yin Zhixiu 尹之秀. "Shen Yi tongzhi he Ru-Tai nongmin baodong" 沈毅同志和如泰農民暴動 (Comrade Shen Yi and the peasant uprisings in Rugao and Taixing). *Jiangsu wenshi ziliao* 江蘇文史資料 5 (n.d.): 71–98.

Yu Lin 余霖. "Jiangnan nongcun shuailuo de yige suoyin" 江南農村衰落的一個索引 (An index of decline in southern Jiangsu villages). *Xin chuangzao* 新創造 (New Creation) 2.1, 2 (July 22, 1932): 169–81.

Yuepu li zhi 月浦里志 (Gazetteer for the Yuepu locality). 1933.

Zhang Guodong 張國棟. "Fanxing yuan" 反省院 (The Reeducation Institute). *Jiangsu wenshi ziliao* 江蘇文史資料 45 (September 1991): 129–32.

Zhang Hao 張浩. "Jiefang qian Guomindang zuzhi zai Siyang de shimo" 解放前國民黨組織在泗陽的始末 (The beginning and end of Nationalist Party organization in Siyang prior to liberation). *Siyang wenshi ziliao* 泗陽文史資料 4 (December 1986): 114–28.

Zhang Ruoruan 張若阮. "Donghai qu zhengzhi shikuang" 東海區政治實況 (The political situation in the Donghai administrative inspectorate district). *Zheng heng yuekan* 政衡月刊 (Administrative Assessment Monthly) 1.11 (August 1934): 71–92.

Zhang Shaoyi 張少逸. "Xi'nan dang he Zhongyang dang" 西南黨和中央黨 (The Southwest Faction and the Central Faction). *Wenshi ziliao xuanji* 文史資料選輯 3 (August 1982): 4–9.

Zhang Shiming 張士明. "Qidong Guomindang shi jilüe" 啓東國民黨史記略 (A sketch of the history of the Qidong Nationalist Party). *Qidong wenshi xuanji* 啓東文史選輯 2 (April 1985): 52–53.

Zhang Shoufu 張壽甫. "Yijiuerqi nian Guo-Gong hezuo shiqi beifajun gongke Songjiang muji ji" 一九二七年國共合作時其北伐軍攻克松江目擊記 (An eyewitness account of the Northern Expeditionary Armies taking Songjiang during the period of the 1927 cooperation between the Nationalists and Communists). *Songjiang wenshi* 松江文史 (October 1981): 33–36.

Zhang Shupei 張樹培. "Guomindang shiqi Tongshan xian de bao'an jingcha deng qingkuang" 國民黨時期銅山縣的保安警察等情況 (The circumstances of peace preservation and police in Tongshan County during the period of the Nationalist Party). *Tongshan wenshi ziliao* 銅山文史資料 2 (May 1983): 65–74.

———. "Guomindang 'Zhong Tong ju' zai Xuzhou" 國民黨'中統局'在徐州 (The Nationalists' 'Central Statistical Bureau' in Xuzhou). *Xuzhou wenshi ziliao* 徐州文史資料 1 (April 1981): 144–83.

———. "Tongshan Guomindang gaikuang" 銅山國民黨概況 (The situation of the Tongshan Nationalist Party). *Tongshan wenshi ziliao* 5 (August 1985): 72–98.

Zhang Wen 張文. "Zhong Tong 20 nian" 中統20年 (Twenty years of the Central Statistical Bureau). *Jiangsu wenshi ziliao xuanji* 江蘇文史資料選輯 23 (August 1987; January 1988): 1–115.

Zhang Wen, et al. *Tegong zong bu—Zong Tong* 特工總部—中統 (A general collection on special affairs work—the Central Statistical Bureau). N.p., n.d.

Zhang Xianwen 張憲文. *Zhonghua minguo shi gang* 中華民國史綱 (An outline of the history of the Republic of China). Henan: Renmin chubanshe, 1986.

Zhang Xianwen, and Fang Qingqiu 方慶秋, eds. *Jiang Jieshi quan zhuan* 蔣介石全傳 (The complete biography of Chiang Kai-shek). 2 vols. Zhengzhou: Henan renmin chubanshe, 1996.

Zhang Yimin 張益民. "1927–1937: Nanjing Guomindang zhengquan yu Jiang Zhe dizhu haoshen" 1927–1937: 南京國民黨政權與江浙地主豪紳 (The Nanjing Nationalist Party regime and the powerful landlord gentry of Jiangsu and Zhejiang, 1927–1937). *Dang'an yu lishi* 檔案與歷史 (Archives and History) (February 1989): 56–62.

Zhang Youwu 張友武. "Xia Song shengping shilüe" 夏嵩生平事略 (A brief sketch of the life of Xia Song). *Jianhu wenshi xuanji* 建湖文史選輯 3 (November 1989): 15–19.

Zhang Zhenzhi 張振之. *Geming yu zongjiao* 革命與宗教 (Revolution and religion). Shanghai: Minzhi shuju, 1929.

Zhang Zhichen 張之琛. "1927 nian da geming shiqi de Kunshan" 1927年大革命時期的昆山 (Kunshan at the time of the great revolution of 1927). *Kunshan wenshi* 昆山文史 1 (March 1983): 45–49.

Zhang Zhongwu 張仲五, ed. *Shuyang xiangtu zhi lüe* 沭陽鄉土志略 (A gazetteer of the Shuyang locality). Taibei: Chen Tianmin, 1974.

Zhao Baojue 趙寶玨. "Guomindang Qidong xian dangbu ji qi dang zheng jiufen" 國民黨啓東縣黨部及其黨政糾紛 (The Qidong County party branch and its party-government dispute). *Qidong wenshi xuanji* 啓東文史選輯 2 (April 1985): 48–51.

Zhao Ruheng 趙如珩, ed. *Jiangsu shengjian* 江蘇省鑒 (Jiangsu Provincial Handbook). 2 vols. Shanghai: Xin Zhongguo jianguo xueshe, 1935.

Zheng Keming 鄭克明. "Suqian xiao dao hui shimo" 宿遷小刀會始末 (The beginning and the end of the Suqian Small Sword Society). *Huaiyin wenshi ziliao* 淮陰文史資料 2 (December 1984): 42–50.

Zhong Sheng. "Jiangsu ge xian Gongchandang baodong jingguo" 江蘇各縣共產黨暴動經過 (Communist insurrections in various Jiangsu counties). *Jiangsu xunkan* 江蘇旬刊 (September 1, 1928): 48–49.

Zhong Tong tegong milu 中統特工秘錄 (Secret accounts of the special affairs work of the Central Statistical Bureau). Volume 45 of *Jiangsu wenshi ziliao* 江蘇文史資料.

Zhongguo Guomindang bashi nian dashi nian biao 中國國民黨八十年大事年表 (A chronology of the great events of the past eighty years of the Chinese Nationalist Party). Edited by Zhongguo Guomindang zhongyang weiyuanhui dangshi weiyuanhui 國民黨中央委員會黨史委員會. Taibei: Zhongguo Guomindang zhongyang weiyuanhui dang shi weiyuanhui, 1974.

Zhongguo Guomindang dangshi shiliao bianzuan weiyuanhui 中國國民黨黨史史料編纂委員會, ed. *Zhongguo Guomindang nianjian* 中國國民黨年鑒 (Yearbook of the Chinese Nationalist Party). 1929, 1934.

Zhongguo Guomindang dierci quanguo daibiao dahui rikan 中國國民黨第二次全國代表大會日刊 (Chinese Nationalist Party Second National Congress daily). Guangzhou, 1926.

Zhongguo Guomindang dierci quanguo daibiao dahui xuanyan ji jueyi an 中國國民黨第二次全國代表大會宣言及決議案 (Propaganda and decisions of the Second National Congress of the Chinese Nationalist Party). Guangzhou: Zhongyang zhixing weiyuanhui xuanchuan bu, 1926.

Zhongguo Guomindang dierjie zhongyang jiancha weiyuanhui baogao shu 中國國民黨第二屆中央監察委員會報告書 (Report of the Second Central Supervisory Committee of the Nationalist Party). N.p., n.d.

Zhongguo Guomindang dier jie zhongyang zhixing weiyuanhui diwu ci quanti huiyi jilu 中國國民黨第二屆中央執行委員會第五次全體會議記錄 (Minutes of the Fifth Plenum of the Second Central Executive Committee of the Chinese Nationalist Party). Nanjing: Zhongyang mishu chu, 1928.

"Zhongguo Guomindang Jiangsu sheng Suining xian dangbu gongzuo diaocha shixiang yilan" 中國國民黨江蘇省睢寧縣黨部工作調查事項一覽 (A list of work investigation items for the Suining County, Jiangsu Province, Chinese Nationalist Party). February 20, 1930. GMDA no. 435/174.

Zhongguo Guomindang Nanjing shi dangbu dang shi 中國國民黨南京市黨部黨史 (History of the Nanjing headquarters of the Chinese Nationalist Party). Edited by Dang shi bianjishe 黨史編輯社 (Party History Editing Society). Nanjing, 1927. GMDA no. 001/83.

Zhongguo Guomindang shangren yundong jingguo 中國國民黨商人運動經過 (The development of the merchant movement of the Chinese Nationalist Party). Edited by Zhongguo Guomindang zhongyang shangren bu 中國國民黨中央商人部 (The merchant's department of the Chinese Nationalist Party). N.p.: Zhongguo Guomindang zhongyang shangren bu, 1927. GMDA no. 435/113.

Zhongguo Guomindang yu nongren 中國國民黨與農人 (The Chinese Nationalist Party and the peasants). Edited by Zhongyang xuanchuan bu 中央宣傳部 (The central propaganda department). Nanjing: Zhongyang xuachuan bu, 1930.

Zhongguo Guomindang zuo pai ABC 中國國民黨左派ABC (The ABC's of the left wing of the Chinese Nationalist Party). Edited by Jiangsu pinglunshe 江蘇評論社 (The Jiangsu Critic). Beiping: Jiangsu pinglunshe, 1930.

Zhongguo jingji nianjian 中國經濟年鑒 (Chinese economic handbooks). Shanghai: Shangwu yinshuguan, 1934–1935.

Zhonghua minguo shishi jiyao 中華民國史事紀要 (A record of important facts about historical events of the Republic of China). For January through June 1925. Taibei: Zhonghua minguo shiliao yanjiu zhongxin, 1975.

"Zhongyang dangbu daibiao Ding Chaowu xunci" 中央黨部代表丁超五訓詞 (Admonitions from central representative Ding Chaowu). In *Neizheng bu diyi minzheng huiyi jiyao* 內政部第一民政會議紀要 (A record of important facts from the First Civil Affairs Conference of the Ministry of the Interior), edited by Neizhengbu diyi qi minzheng huiyi mishu chu 內政部第一期民政會議祕書處 (Secretariat of the First Conference of the Ministry of the Interior). Shanghai, 1929.

Zhongyang dangwu yuekan 中央黨務月刊 (Central Party Affairs Monthly). Nanjing, 1928–1931.

"Zhongyang qingnianbu dui Huaiyin zhongxue jiaozhiyuan zhi diaocha biao" 中央青年部對淮陰中學教職員之調查表 (Investigation forms of the Central Youth Department with regard to Huaiyin Middle School staff and teachers). 1927. GMDA no. 435/219.

"Zhongyang qingnianbu dui Huaiyin zhongxue xuesheng zhi diaocha biao" 中央青年部對淮陰中學學生之調查表 (Investigation forms of the Central Youth

Department with regard to Huaiyin Middle School students). 1927. GMDA no. 468/22.

Zhongyang ribao 中央日報 (Central Daily News). Shanghai, Nanjing, 1928–1935.

Zhongyang zhengzhi xuexiao biye tongxue lu 中央政治學校畢業同學錄 (A record of the alumni of the Central Political Academy). Edited by Biye sheng zhidao bu 畢業生指導部 (The Alumni Office). N.p., 1947.

Zhongyang zhoubao 中央周報 (Central Weekly Report). Nanjing, 1928–1932.

"Zhongyang zuzhi weiyuanhui xiaji dangbu zuzhi gongzuo baogao shencha huiyao" 中央組織委員會下級黨部組織工作報告審查彙要 (The Central Organization Committee's compiled reviews of the organization work reports of lower-level party branches). 1934. GMDA no. 435/17.

"Zhongyang zuzhibu buzhang riji" 中央組織部部長日記 (A daily record of the chairman of the Central Organization Department). 1925. GMDA no. 435/240.

Zhou Fohai 周佛海. "Zenyang tuijin Su sheng yiwu jiaoyu" 怎樣推進蘇省義務教育 (How to push forward compulsory education in Jiangsu). *Jiangsu jiaoyu* 江蘇教育 (Jiangsu Education) 4.9 (September 15, 1935): 1–3.

Zhou Jianzhang 周建章. "Zhuiyi Donghai xian er, sanshi nian dai de wangshi" 追憶東海縣二三十年代的往事 (Recollecting the past: The era of the twenties and thirties in Donghai County). *Lianyungang shi wenshi ziliao* 連雲港市文史資料 4 (August 1986): 13–30.

Zhou Meichu 周梅初. "Huai jiu" 懷舊 (Thinking of the past). *Kunshan wenshi* 昆山文史 1 (March 1983): 57–59.

Zhou Mengzhuang 周夢莊. "Guanyu Yancheng Xi'nan dang yu Zhongyang dang zhi shimo" 關于鹽城西南黨與中央黨之始末 (Facts related to the beginning and end of Yancheng's Southwest and Central Cliques). *Yancheng xian wenshi ziliao* 鹽城縣文史資料 1,2 (reprinted January 1984): 118–27.

Zhou Qixin 周啓新. "Da geming shiqi Changshu Guomindang de dongtai" 大革命時期常熟國民黨的動態 (Developments in the Changshu Guomindang at the time of the great revolution). *Wenshi ziliao jicun* 文史資料輯存 2 (December 1962; reprinted July 1984): 39–48.

Zhou Ruiying 周瑞英, Zhou Cuntao 周村陶, Zhou Xuemei 周雪梅, and Zhou Cunhe 周村和. "Huiyi fuqin Zhou Ruqian" 回憶父親周儒謙 (Remembering our father, Zhou Ruqian). *Qidong wenshi xuanji* 啓東文史選輯 5 (November 1986): 89–92.

Zhou Ruliang 周儒良, and Zhou Xiehe 周協和. "Yi Zhou Ruqian xiansheng" 憶周儒謙先生 (Remembering Mr. Zhou Ruqian). *Qidong wenshi xuanji* 啓東文史選輯 5 (November 1986): 80–85.

Zhu Jixun 朱季恂. "Geming dang nali keyi youqing" 革命黨那里可以右傾 (How can a revolutionary party lean to the right?). *Zhongguo Guomindang dierci quanguo daibiao dahui rikan* 中國國民黨第二次全國代表大會日刊 1 (December 30, 1925): 1–2.

Zhuanji wenxue 傳記文學 (Biographical Literature). Taibei, 1965–1980.

"Zuzhi bu huiyi jishi lu 組織部會議記事錄 (A record of the meetings of the Organization Department). 1924. GMDA no. 435/82.

Sources in English

Agrarian China: Selected Source Materials From Chinese Authors. Translated and compiled by the Research Staff of the Secretariat, Institute of Pacific Relations. Chicago: University of Chicago Press, 1939.

Alitto, Guy S. "Rural Elites in Transition: China's Cultural Crisis and the Problem of Legitimacy." *Select Papers from the Center for Far Eastern Studies* 3: 218–63 (1978–79).

Ash, Robert. *Land Tenure in Pre-Revolutionary China: Kiangsu Province in the 1920s and 1930s.* London: Contemporary China Institute, School of Oriental and African Studies, University of London, 1976.

Averill, Stephen C. "Education and Local Elite Politics in Early Twentieth Century China." Unpublished paper, 1996.

———. "The New Life in Action: The Nationalist Government in South Jiangxi, 1934–37." *China Quarterly* 88 (December 1981): 594–628.

———. "The Origins of the Futian Incident." In *New Perspectives on the Chinese Communist Revolution*, edited by Tony Saich and Hans van de Ven. Armonk, N.Y.: M. E. Sharpe, 1995.

Bailey, F. G. "The Definition of Factionalism." In *A House Divided?: Anthropological Studies of Factionalism*, edited by M. Silverman and R. F. Salisbury. Newfoundland, Canada: Institute of Social and Economic Research, Memorial University of Newfoundland, University of Toronto Press, 1977.

Baker, Hugh D. R. *Chinese Family and Kinship.* New York: Macmillan, 1979.

Barkan, Lenore. "Nationalists, Communists, and Rural Leaders: Political Dynamics in a Chinese County, 1927–1937." Ph.D. diss., University of Washington, 1983.

———. "Patterns of Power: Forty Years of Elite Politics in a Chinese County." In *Chinese Local Elites and Patterns of Dominance*, edited by Joseph W. Esherick and Mary Backus Rankin. Berkeley: University of California Press, 1990.

Bastid, Marianne. *Educational Reform in Early Twentieth-Century China.* Translated from the French by Paul J. Bailey. Ann Arbor: Center for Chinese Studies, University of Michigan, 1988.

Bell, Lynda Schaefer. "From Comprador to County Magnate: Bourgeois Practice in the Wuxi County Silk Industry." In *Chinese Local Elites and Patterns of Dominance*, edited by Joseph W. Esherick and Mary Backus Rankin. Berkeley: University of California Press, 1990.

———. "Merchants, Peasants, and the State: The Organization and Politics of Chinese Silk Production, Wuxi County, 1870–1937." Ph.D. diss., University of California, Los Angeles, 1985.

Belloni, Frank, and Dennis C. Beller. "The Study of Factions." In *Faction Politics: Political Parties and Factionalism in Comparative Perspective*, edited by Frank P. Belloni and Dennis C. Beller. Santa Barbara, Calif.: ABC Clio, Inc., 1978.

Benton, Gregor. *New Fourth Army: Communist Resistance Along the Yangtze and the Huai, 1938–1941.* Berkeley: University of California Press, 1999.

Bergère, Marie-Claire. "Civil Society and Urban Change in China." *China Quarterly* 150 (June 1997): 309–328.

———. "The Chinese Bourgeoisie, 1911–37." In *The Cambridge History of China*, vol. 12, Republican China 1912–1949, pt. 1, edited by John K. Fairbank. London: Cambridge University Press, 1983.

Bernhardt, Kathryn. *Rents, Taxes, and Peasant Resistance: The Lower Yangzi Region, 1840–1950.* Stanford: Stanford University Press, 1992.

Boorman, Howard L., ed. *Biographical Dictionary of Republican China.* 4 vols. New York: Columbia University Press, 1967–1971.

Bosco, Joseph. "Taiwan's Factions: *Guanxi*, Patronage, and the State in Local Politics." In *The Other Taiwan: 1945 to the Present*, edited by Murray Rubenstein. Armonk, New York: An East Gate Book, M.E. Sharpe, 1994.

Brunnert, H. S., and V. V. Hagelstrom. *Present Day Political Organization of China.* Translated from the Russian by A. Beltchenko and E. E. Moran. 1911. Reprint, Taipei: Ch'eng-wen, 1971.

Buck, John Lossing. *Land Utilization in China.* Nanking: University of Nanking, 1937; New York: Paragon Book Reprint Corp., 1964.

Bush, Richard Clarence. "Industry and Politics in Kuomintang China: The Nationalist Regime and Lower Yangtze Cotton Mill Owners 1927–1937." Ph.D. diss., Columbia University, 1978.

Calhoun, Craig. "Introduction: Habermas and the Public Sphere." In *Habermas and the Public Sphere*, by Craig Calhoun. Cambridge, Mass.: The MIT Press, 1992, 1994.

Cavendish, Patrick. "The 'New China' of the Kuomintang." In *Modern China's Search for a Political Form*, edited by Jack Grey. London: Oxford University Press, 1969.

Chamberlain, Heath B. "Review Essay: Civil Society with Chinese Characteristics." *The China Journal* 39 (January 1998): 69–81.

———. "On the Search for Civil Society in China." *Modern China* 19.2 (April 1993): 199–215.

Chang, Chung-li. *The Chinese Gentry: Studies on Their Role in Nineteenth Century Chinese Society.* Seattle: University of Washington Press, 1955.

Chang Kuo-t'ao. *The Rise of the Chinese Communist Party, 1921–1927.* 2 vols. Lawrence: University of Kansas Press, 1971–1972.

Chauncey, Helen R. *Schoolhouse Politicians: Locality and the State During the Chinese Republic.* Honolulu: University of Hawaii Press, 1992.

Ch'en Hung-ch'in. "Land Division Through the Land Development Companies in Northern Kiangsu." In *Agrarian China: Selected Source Materials from Chinese Authors,* translated and compiled by the Research Staff of the Secretariat, Institute of Pacific Relations. Chicago: University of Chicago Press, 1939.

Ch'en Li-fu. *The Storm Clouds Clear Over China: The Memoir of Ch'en Li-fu, 1900–1993.* Edited and compiled by Sidney H. Chang and Ramon H. Myers. Stanford, Calif.: Hoover Institution Press, 1994.

Ch'en Yung-fa. *Making Revolution: The Communist Movement in Eastern and Central China, 1937–1945.* Berkeley: University of California Press, 1986.

———. "The Making of a Revolution: The Communist Movement in Eastern and Central China, 1937–1945." 2 vols. Ph.D. diss., Stanford University, 1980.

———. "The Wartime Communists and Their Local Rivals: Bandits and Secret Societies." *Select Papers From the Center for Far Eastern Studies* 3 (1978–1979): 1–69.

Ch'i, Hsi-sheng. *Nationalist China at War: Military Defeats and Political Collapse, 1937–45.* Ann Arbor: University of Michigan Press, 1982.

China Industrial Handbooks: Kiangsu: First Series of the Reports by the National Industrial Investigation. Compiled by the Bureau of Foreign Trade, Ministry of Industry. 1933. Reprint, Taipei: Ch'eng Wen Publishing Co., 1973.

Chow, Tsetsung. *The May Fourth Movement: Intellectual Revolution in Modern China.* Cambridge, Mass.: Harvard University Press, 1960.

A Chronology of Twentieth Century China, 1904–1949. Washington, D.C.: Center for Chinese Research Materials, Association of Research Libraries, 1973.

Chu, Samuel C. *Reformer in Modern China: Chang Chien, 1853–1926.* New York: Columbia University Press, 1965.

Ch'ü T'ung-tsu. *Local Government in China Under the Ch'ing.* Cambridge, Mass.: Harvard University Press, 1962.

Coble, Parks M. *The Shanghai Capitalists and the Nationalist Government, 1927–1937.* Cambridge, Mass.: Council on East Asian Studies, Harvard University, 1980.

Coleman, Maryruth. "Municipal Politics in Nationalist China: Nanjing, 1927–1937." Ph.D. diss., Harvard University, 1984.

Cressey, George B. *Land of the 500 Million: A Geography of China.* New York: McGraw-Hill Book Co., Inc., 1955.

Curran, Thomas Daniel. "Education and Society in Republican China." Ph.D. diss., Columbia University, 1986.

Davenport, F. Garvin. "Resistance is State-Building: The GMD's Attempts at Political Consolidation of Zhejiang, 1937–1945." Unpublished paper presented at annual meeting of Association for Asian Studies, Washington, D.C., March 1998.

Dittmer, Lowell. "Chinese Informal Politics." *The China Journal* 34 (July 1995): 1–34.

Duara, Prasenjit. *Culture, Power, and the State: Rural North China: 1900–1942.* Stanford: Stanford University Press, 1988.

———. "Knowledge and Power in the Discourse of Modernity: The Campaigns Against Popular Religion in Early Twentieth-Century China." *Journal of Asian Studies* 50.1 (February 1991): 67–83.

———. *Rescuing History From the Nation: Questioning Narratives of Modern China*. Chicago: University of Chicago Press, 1995.

Eastman, Lloyd E. *The Abortive Revolution: China Under Nationalist Rule, 1927–1937*. Cambridge, Mass.: Harvard University Press, 1974.

———. "The Kuomintang in the 1930s." In *The Limits of Change*, edited by Charlotte Furth. Cambridge, Mass.: Harvard University Press, 1976.

———. "New Insights into the Nature of the Nationalist Regime." *Republican China* 9.2 (February 1984): 8–18.

———. *Seeds of Destruction: Nationalist China in War and Revolution, 1937–1949*. Stanford: Stanford University Press, 1984.

Esherick, Joseph W. *Reform and Revolution in China: The 1911 Revolution in Hunan and Hubei*. Berkeley: University of California Press, 1976.

Esherick, Joseph W., and Mary Backus Rankin. "Introduction." In *Chinese Local Elites and Patterns of Dominance*, edited by Joseph W. Esherick and Mary Backus Rankin. Berkeley: University of California Press, 1990.

Fewsmith, Joseph. *Party, State, and Local Elites in Republican China: Merchant Organizations and Politics in Shanghai, 1890–1930*. Honolulu: University of Hawaii Press, 1985.

Fitzgerald, John. *Awakening China: Politics, Culture, and Class in the Nationalist Revolution*. Stanford: Stanford University Press, 1996.

Fung, Edmund S. K. "Anti-Imperialism and the Left Guomindang," *Modern China* 11.1 (January 1985): 39–76.

Gamble, Sidney. *North China Villages: Social, Political and Economic Activities Before 1933*. Berkeley: University of California Press, 1963.

Geisert, Bradley Kent. "Power and Society: The Kuomintang and Local Elites in Kiangsu Province, 1924–1937." Ph.D. diss., University of Virginia, 1979.

———. "Probing KMT Rule: Reflections on Eastman's 'New Insights.'" *Republican China* 9.2 (February 1984): 28–39.

———. "Toward a Pluralist Model of KMT Rule." *Chinese Republican Studies Newsletter* 7.2 (February 1982): 1–10.

Goodman, Bryna. *Native Place, City, and Nation: Regional Networks and Identities in Shanghai, 1853–1937*. Berkeley: University of California Press, 1995.

Habermas, Jürgen. *The Structural Transformation of the Public Sphere: An Inquiry into a Category of Bourgeois Society*. Translated by Thomas Burger. Cambridge, Mass.: The MIT Press, 1989.

Harrison, James Pinckney. *The Long March to Power: A History of the Chinese Communist Party, 1921–72*. New York: Praeger, 1972.

Hays, James. *The Hong Kong Region, 1850–1911*. Hamden, Conn.: Archon Books, The Shoe String Press, 1977.

Ho Ping-ti. *Studies on the Population of China, 1368–1953*. Cambridge, Mass.: Harvard University Press, 1959.

Henriot, Christian. *Shanghai, 1927–1937: Municipal Power, Locality, and Modernization.* Translated by Noel Castelino. Berkeley: University of California Press, 1993.

Hofheinz, Jr., Roy. *The Broken Wave: The Chinese Communist Peasant Movement, 1922–1928.* Cambridge, Mass.: Harvard University Press, 1977.

Honig, Emily. *Creating Chinese Ethnicity: Subei People in Shanghai, 1850–1980.* New Haven: Yale University Press, 1992.

Hsiao, Kung-ch'üan. *Rural China: Imperial Control in the Nineteenth Century.* Seattle: University of Washington Press, 1972.

Huang, Philip C. C. *The Peasant Economy and Social Change in North China.* Stanford: Stanford University Press, 1985.

———. "'Public Sphere'/'Civil Society' in China? The Third Realm between State and Society." *Modern China* 19.2 (April 1993): 216–40.

Hunter, Guy. *Modernizing Peasant Societies: A Comparative Study in Asia and Africa.* New York: Oxford University Press, 1971.

Ichiko Chuzo. "The Role of the Gentry: An Hypothesis." In *China in Revolution: The First Phase, 1900–1913*, edited by Mary Clabaugh Wright. New Haven: Yale University Press, 1968.

Iriye, Akira. *After Imperialism: The Search for a New Order in the Far East, 1921–1931.* Cambridge, Mass.: Harvard University Press, 1969.

Isaacs, Harold R. *The Tragedy of the Chinese Revolution.* 1938. Stanford, Stanford University Press: Second Revised Edition, 1961.

Israel, John. *Student Nationalism in China, 1927–1937.* Stanford: Stanford University Press, 1966.

Jacobs, J. Bruce. *Local Politics in a Rural Chinese Cultural Setting: A Field Study of Mazu Township, Taiwan.* Canberra: Contemporary China Centre, Research School of Pacific Studies, Australian National University, 1980.

Johnson, David. "Confucian Elements in the Great Temple Festivals of Southeastern Shansi in Late Imperial Times." *T'oung Pao* 83 (1997): 126–61.

Jordan, Donald A. *The Northern Expedition: China's National Revolution of 1926–1928.* Honolulu: University of Hawaii Press, 1976.

Jowitt, Kenneth. *The Leninist Response to National Dependency.* Berkeley: Institute of International Relations, University of California, 1978.

Keenan, Barry C. *Imperial China's Last Classical Academies: Social Change in the Lower Yangzi, 1864–1911.* Berkeley: China Research Monograph, Institute of East Asian Studies, University of California, Center for Chinese Studies, 1994.

Kipnis, Andrew B. *Producing Guanxi: Sentiment, Self, and Subculture in a North China Village.* Durham, N.C.: Duke University Press, 1997.

Klein, Donald W. and Anne B. Clark. *Biographic Dictionary of Chinese Communism, 1921–1965.* 2 vols. Cambridge, Mass.: Harvard University Press, 1971.

Kotenev, Anatol M. *New Lamps for Old: An Interpretation of Events in Modern China and Whither They Lead.* Shanghai: 1931; Reprint, New York: AMS Press, 1971.

Kuhn, Philip A. "Local Self-Government Under the Republic: Problems of Control, Autonomy, and Mobilization." In *Conflict and Control in Late Imperial China*, edited by Frederic Wakeman, Jr. and Carolyn Grant. Berkeley: University of California Press, 1975.

———. "Local Taxation and Finance in Republican China." *Select Papers from the Center for Far Eastern Studies* 3 (1978–1979): 100–136.

———. *Rebellion and Its Enemies in Late Imperial China*. Cambridge, Mass.: Harvard University Press, 1970.

Kwok, Daniel W. Y. *Scientism in Chinese Thought, 1900–1950*. New Haven: Yale University Press, 1965.

Landé, Carl H. "The Dyadic Basis of Clientelism." In *Friends, Followers, and Factions: A Reader in Political Clientelism*, edited by Steffen W. Schmidt, Laura Guasti, Carl H. Landé, and James C. Scott. Berkeley: University of California Press, 1977.

Lary, Diana. *Region and Nation: The Kwangsi Clique in Chinese Politics, 1925–1937*. Cambridge: Cambridge University Press, 1974.

Liu, Chi Hung. "A Study of Modern Education in Jiangsu Province, China." M.A. thesis, University of Washington, 1932.

Ma, Amy Fei-man. "Local Self-Government and the Local Populace in Chuansha, 1911." *Select Papers From the Center for Far Eastern Studies* 1 (1975–1976): 47–84.

Miner, Noel R. "Agrarian Reform in Nationalist China: The Case of Rent Reduction in Chekiang, 1927–1937." In *China at the Crossroads: Nationalists and Communists, 1927–1949*, edited by F. Gilbert Chan. Boulder: Westview Press, 1980.

———. "Chekiang: The Nationalist's Effort in Agrarian Reform and Construction, 1927–1937." Ph.D. diss., Stanford University, 1973.

Myrdal, Gunnar. *Asian Drama: An Inquiry Into the Poverty of Nations*. Abridged by Seth S. King. New York: Pantheon, 1971.

Nathan, Andrew J. "A Factionalism Model for CCP Politics." In *Friends, Followers, and Factions: A Reader in Political Clientelism*, edited by Steffen W. Schmidt, et al. Berkeley: University of California Press, 1977.

———. *China's Transition*. New York: Columbia University Press, 1997.

———. *Peking Politics, 1918–1923: Factionalism and the Failure of Constitutionalism*. Berkeley: University of California Press, 1976.

North China Herald. Shanghai, 1927–1930.

North, Robert, with the collaboration of Ithiel de Sola Pool. *Kuomintang and Chinese Communist Elites*. Stanford: Stanford University Press, 1952.

Ocko, Jonathan K. *Bureaucratic Reform in Provincial China: Ting Jih-ch'ang in Restoration Jiangsu, 1857–1870*. Cambridge, Mass.: Council on East Asian Studies, Harvard University, 1983.

Paulson, David M. "Nationalist Guerrillas in the Sino-Japanese War: The 'Diehards' of Shandong Province." In *Single Sparks: China's Rural Revolutions*, edited by Kathleen Hartford and Steven M. Goldstein. Armonk, New York: M. E. Sharpe, Inc., 1989.

Perry, Elizabeth J. *Rebels and Revolutionaries in North China, 1845–1945.* Stanford: Stanford University Press, 1980.

Polachek, James M. *The Inner Opium War.* Cambridge, Mass.: Council on East Asian Studies, Harvard University, 1992.

Prazniak, Roxann. *Of Camel Kings and Other Things: Rural Rebels Against Modernity in Late Imperial China.* Lanham, Maryland: Rowman and Littlefield Publishers, Inc., 1999.

———."Tax Protest at Laiyang, Shandong, 1910: Commoner Organization Versus the County Political Elite." *Modern China* 6.1 (January 1980): 41–71.

———. "Weavers and Sorceresses of Chuansha: The Social Origins of Political Activism Among Rural Chinese Women." *Modern China* 12.2 (April 1986): 202–229.

Putnam, Robert D. *The Comparative Study of Political Elites.* Englewood Cliffs, N.J.: Prentice-Hall, 1976.

Rankin, Mary Backus. *Elite Activism and Political Transformation in China: Zhejiang Province, 1865–1911.* Stanford: Stanford University Press, 1986.

———. "Local Reform Currents in Chekiang Before 1900." In *Reform in Nineteenth-Century China*, edited by Paul A. Cohen and John E. Schrecker. Cambridge, Mass.: Harvard University, East Asian Center, 1976.

———. "State and Society in Early Republican Politics, 1912–1918." *China Quarterly* 150 (June 1997): 260–81.

Remer, C. F. *A Study of Chinese Boycotts.* 1933. Reprint Taipei: Ch'eng-wen, 1966.

Rowe, William T. *Hankow: Commerce and Society in a Chinese City, 1796–1889.* Stanford: Stanford University Press, 1984.

———. "The Problem of 'Civil Society' in Late Imperial China." *Modern China* 19.2 (April 1993): 139–57.

Rozman, Gilbert, ed. *The Modernization of China.* New York: The Free Press, 1981.

Schmidt, Steffen W., Laura Guasti, Carl H. Landé, and James C. Scott, eds. *Friends, Followers, and Factions: A Reader in Political Clientelism.* Berkeley: University of California Press, 1977.

Schoppa, R. Keith. *Chinese Elites and Political Change: Zhejiang Province in the Early Twentieth Century.* Cambridge, Mass.: Harvard University Press, 1982.

———. "Contours of Revolutionary Change in a Chinese County, 1900–1950." *Journal of Asian Studies* 51.4 (November 1992): 770–96.

———. "Local Self-Government in Zhejiang, 1909–1927." *Modern China* 2.4 (October 1976): 503–530.

———. "Shen Dingyi and the Western Hills Group: 'What's a Man Like You Doing in a Group Like This?'" *Republican China* 16.1 (November 1990): 35–50.

Schwartz, Benjamin I. *Chinese Communism and the Rise of Mao.* Cambridge, Mass.: Harvard University Press, 1951.

Selden, Mark. *The Yenan Way in Revolutionary China.* Cambridge, Mass.: Harvard University Press, 1971.

Sheridan, James E. *Chinese Warlord: The Career of Feng Yü-hsiang*. Stanford: Stanford University Press, 1966.

Sinai, I. Robert. *The Challenge of Modernization: The West's Impact on the Non-Western World*. New York: W.W. Norton and Co. Inc., 1964.

Skinner, G. William. "Marketing and Social Structure in Rural China." *Journal of Asian Studies* 24.1 (November 1964): 3–43; and 24.2 (February 1965): 195–228.

―――, ed. *The City in Late Imperial China*. Stanford: Stanford University Press, 1977.

Smith, Arthur Henderson. *Village Life in China: A Study in Sociology*. New York: Fleming H. Revell Company, 1899.

So, Wai-chor. *The Kuomintang Left in the National Revolution, 1924–1931*. Hong Kong: Oxford University Press, 1991.

Stranahan, Patricia. *Underground: The Shanghai Communist Party and the Politics of Survival, 1927–1937*. Lanham, Md.: Rowman and Littlefield Publishers, Inc., 1998.

Strand, David. *Rickshaw Beijing: City People and Politics in the 1920s*. Berkeley: University of California Press, 1989.

Stross, Randy. "A Hard Row To Hoe: The Political Economy of Chinese Agriculture in Western Jiangsu, 1911–1937." Ph.D. diss., Stanford University, 1982.

T'ang Leang-li. *The Inner History of the Chinese Revolution*. New York: E.P. Dutton and Co., 1930.

Thompson, Roger R. *China's Local Councils in the Age of Constitutional Reform, 1898–1911*. Cambridge, Mass.: Council on East Asian Studies, Harvard University, 1995.

―――. "Cultural Imperialism and the Modernizing State: Re-viewing Rural China, 1861–1911." Unpublished paper prepared for annual meeting of Association for Asian Studies, Washington, D.C., March, 1998.

Tien, Hung-mao. *Government and Politics in Kuomintang China, 1927–1937*. Stanford: Stanford University Press, 1972.

Tsai, David. "Party-Government Relations in Kiangsu Province, 1927–1932." *Select Papers From the Center for Far Eastern Studies* 1 (1975–1976): 85–118.

Tsou, Tang. "Chinese Politics at the Top: Factionalism or Informal Politics? Balance-of-Power Politics or a Game to Win All?" *The China Journal* 34 (July 1995): 95–156.

Tung, William L. *Revolutionary China: A Personal Account, 1926–1949*. New York: St. Martin's Press, 1973.

Walker, Kathy Le Mons. *Chinese Modernity and the Peasant Path: Semicolonialism in the Northern Yangzi Delta*. Stanford: Stanford University Press, 1999.

Wakeman, Jr., Frederic. "The Civil Society and Public Sphere Debate: Western Reflections on Chinese Political Culture." *Modern China* 19.2 (April 1993): 108–137.

―――. "A Revisionist View of the Nanjing Decade: Confucian Fascism." *China Quarterly* 150 (June 1997): 395–432.

Wang, Ke-wen. "The Kuomintang in Transition: Ideology and Factionalism in the 'National Revolution', 1924–1932." Ph.D. diss., Stanford University, 1985.

Wang, Richard Tze-yang. "Wu Chih-hui: An Intellectual and Political Biography." Ph.D. diss., University of Virginia, 1976.

Wang, Y. C. *Chinese Intellectuals and the West, 1872–1949*. Chapel Hill: University of North Carolina Press, 1966.

Welch, Holmes. *The Practice of Chinese Buddhism, 1900–1950*. Cambridge, Mass.: Harvard University Press, 1973.

Who's Who in China, 1918–1950. Compiled by Jerome Cavanaugh. Hong Kong: Chinese Materials Center, 1982.

Wilbur, C. Martin. "The Nationalist Revolution: From Canton to Nanking, 1923–28." In *The Cambridge History of China*. Vol. 12, pt. 1, edited by John K. Fairbank. London: Cambridge University Press, 1983.

Wilbur, C. Martin and Julie Lien-ying How, eds. *Documents on Communism, Nationalism, and Soviet Advisers in China, 1918–1927*. New York: Columbia University Press, 1956.

Wong, Young-tsu. "Popular Unrest and the 1911 Revolution in Jiangsu." *Modern China* 3.3 (July 1977): 321–42.

Wright, Mary Clabaugh Wright, ed. *China in Revolution: The First Phase, 1900–1913*. New Haven: Yale University Press, 1968.

Xu Youwei and Philip Billingsley. "Behind the Scenes of the Xi'an Incident: The Case of the *Lixingshe*." *China Quarterly* 154 (June 1998): 283–307.

Yang, C. K. *Religion in Chinese Society*. Berkeley: University of California Press, 1961.

Yang, Martin M.C. *Chinese Social Structure: A Historical Study*. Taipei: The National Book Company, 1971.

Yang, Mayfair Mei-hui. *Gifts, Favors and Banquets: The Art of Social Relationships in China*. Ithaca: Cornell University Press, 1994.

Yu, George T. *Party Politics in Republican China: The Kuomintang, 1912–1924*. Berkeley: University of California Press, 1966.

Yung, Teh-chow. *Social Mobility in China: Status Careers Among the Gentry in a Chinese Community*. New York: Atherton Press, 1966.

Zheng, Shiping. *Party vs. State in Post-1949 China: The Institutional Dilemma*. Cambridge: Cambridge University Press, 1997.

Zonis, Marvin. *The Political Elite of Iran*. Princeton, N.J.: Princeton University Press, 1971.

INDEX

agricultural associations, 22
Alitto, Guy, 253n96
Anhui Rectification Committee, 292n8
Anti-CC Clique, 77; under Directorate, 217–20; factional rivalries and, 88–91; leaders jailed, 96–98, 101, 222; members of, 88, 223; Organization Clique and, 92, 185; under Provincial Executive Committee, 220–22; radicalism of, 92, 98, 114; rectification and, 98–101; Reorganization Clique and, 78, 97; Yang-Ma-Cao coalition with, 85
anti-Japanese campaigns, 112, 145–47, 156
antisuperstition campaigns, 148–63; CCP and, 112, 158; and chambers of commerce, 156, 158; in Feng County, 128, 154; intellectuals and, 3, 161–63; in Lianshu County, 112; party-elite tensions and, 124; party-government tensions and, 159–61; property confiscations and, 155; in Songjiang County, 160; in Suining County, 180; women's resistance to, 159; and Yangcheng Massacre, 150–54, 159. *See also* religious practices and institutions
appointments to office, 19, 81–82, 196–97, 207
assemblies, 16–21, 131–32
Autumn Harvest Uprisings, 107, 116
Averill, Stephen, 35, 37, 45

Bai Baoshan, 136
Bailey, F. G., 237–38n13

banditry and bandits, 12, 24, 36, 93
Bao Faction, 81–82
Baoshan County, 9, 20, 239n19
Baoshan County Guomindang, 149, 276n4
Barkan, Lenore, 113, 130–31, 133, 240–41n19
Benton, Gregor, 298
Bernhardt, Kathryn, 57
Big Sword Society, 55, 93–95
Blue and White Society, 73, 268n26
Blue Shirts (*Lanyishe/Fuxingshe/Lixingshe*), 75, 97, 252n89
Borodin, Michael, 43
Bosco, Joseph, 31, 264n3
brawls and beatings, anti-GMD, 171, 181; elite factions and, 138; factional infighting and, 80–81, 87–89, 125–26; leftists against rightists in GMD, 48, 50–51, 259n24; merchants and, 146–47; peasants and, 60
Buck, John Lossing, investigator for, 8, 12, 249n54
bursaries, 29–30
Bush, Richard, 26
businesses, as factional tools, 87–88

Cai Hanyu, 93, 95
calendar reforms, 155
Cao Binggan, 223
Cao Minghuan, 76, 223, 274n83, 299n7
CC Clique (provincial), 75, 220, 265n6; factional rivalries and, 88–89, 90, 92, 100, 299n8; members list, 223; rectification and, 98. *See also* Organization Clique

Ceng Yangfu, 268n26
censorship, 98, 196
Central Clique, 153–54
Central Club (*Zhongyang julebu*), 215–16
Central Executive Committee. *See* Guomindang organizations
Central Organization Department. *See* Guomindang organizations
Central Party Affairs Academy Clique, 76
Central Party Affairs Academy (later Central Political Academy), 73, 191, 215
Central Political Committee. *See* Guomindang organizations
Central Special Committee (CSC). *See* Guomindang organizations
Central Statistical Bureau. *See* Guomindang organizations
Central Supervisory Committee. *See* Guomindang organizations
Central University, 160
chambers of commerce: and antisuperstition campaigns, 156, 158; appointments to, 197; as elite group, 22–23, 133–34; GMD and, 142–44, 146, 192–96; leaders of, 58, 61, 85, 122, 125, 136; members as "local bullies and evil gentry," 114, 140; merchant associations and, 53–54; militia and, 22, 24, 172; propaganda against, 53; religious institutions and, 94. *See also* merchants
Changshu County, 9, 26
Changshu County Guomindang, 62–63
Chauncey, Helen, 82, 110
Chen Boming, 131–32
Chen Cheng, 176
Chen Clique, 78
Chen Gongbo, 77, 197–98
Chen Guofu: administrative views of, 165, 191; anti-Communist purge and, 51, 73, 211; antisuperstition campaigns and, 161; Chiang Kai-shek and, 73, 215, 266n17; decline of party power and, 189, 191; offices held by, 74, 176; Organization Clique and, 72–74, 185; post-purge Communist suppression and, 91, 199; protégés of, 74, 76, 98, 176, 218; on Qidong land reforms, 228; Sunist Practice Society and, 75
Chen Jianbo, 123
Chen Jinju, 61
Chen Kanghe, 223
Chen Lifu, 72–73, 76
Chen Qimei, 73
Chen Qubing, 44, 47–48, 223, 259n26
Chen Ruyi, 78
Chen Sibai, 223
Chen Weishan, 11–12
Chen Xiekun, 94
Chen Yaxuan, 131–32
Chen Zhongming, 223
Cheng Clique, 136
Cheng Ruyuan, 223
Cheng Zhaoshi, 136–42
Chiang Kai-shek: anti-Communist purge by, 50–52, 73, 103, 104–8, 199, 211; Chen Guofu and, 73, 215, 266n17; and intervention in Baoshan County, 276n4; on "local bullies and evil gentry," 109; merchants and, 145; Miao Bin and, 97, 219; Organization Clique leaders and, 191; relieved of Northern Expeditionary leadership, 51; retirement of, 215; reunification of GMD centers and, 213; Wang Jingwei and, 113, 198. *See also* Nationalist Government
Chinese Communist Party (CCP): antisuperstition campaigns and, 112, 158; armies of, 200–1, 298; attempts to control GMD, 47, 109, 238n16; —Central Committee, 112; factionalism in, 252n89; failure in Jiangsu

Province, 2, 198–203; landlord policies of, 54; local uprisings and, 200–1; party-government tensions and, 289n202; "speak bitterness" sessions and, 60; turncoats in, 199–200; war with Japan and, 209. *See also* Communists; Guomindang-Communist alliance
Chinese Nationalist Party. *See* Guomindang
Chongming County, 9, 226–27, 239n19
Christians, 149, 162, 254n102
Chu Shuxin, 196
Chuansha County, 9, 11–12, 19–20, 245n18
City Faction, 82–83, 87
civil service examination system, 20, 33
civil society. *See* public sphere/civil society debate
class struggle, 65–66, 78
Communist Party, Chinese. *See* Chinese Communist Party
Communist Party, Russian, 35
Communists: decline in activity of, 199; GMD branches controlled by, 112–13, 141, 171–72, 207, 289; party-government tensions and, 169, 289n206; post-purge conditions of, 90–91, 113, 141–42, 198, 199, 225–26; purged from GMD, 1, 50–52, 73, 103–8, 112, 175, 211, 274n77; reeducation institutes and, 201–2; in Suining County, 180
Concealed Brightness Society (*Weiguangshe*), 72
confiscation of property: antisuperstition campaigns and, 155; control over, 188; of "local bullies and evil gentry" by GMD, 110, 119–21, 124, 128, 130, 142, 180
Confucianism, 74, 111–12
corporatism, 33–34
cotton textile industry, 11, 26

counterelites. *See* Guomindang
county assemblies, 16, 18–21, 132–33, 171, 194
county-town(ship) tensions, 30, 82–84, 106
courts. *See* special courts
Curran, Thomas, 38, 161–62

Dai Faction, 83–84
Dai Jitao, 65, 221
Dai Jizhi, 83–84
Dajiang University, 40
Dantu (Zhenjiang) County, 9, 40, 63
Danyang County, 9
Danyang County Guomindang, 58–59
Davenport, F. Garvin, 297n6
DD Faction, 272n60
degree-holders. *See* gentry
denunciations, 51, 60, 88, 172
Di Kan, 257n1
Di Ying, 99, 217
Ding Weifen, 269n32
Dittmer, Lowell, 252n89
Dong Hancha, 127
Donghai County, 30, 118–23
Dongtai County, 113, 132–33
Dongyue Temple, ransacking of, 155
Duan Muzhen, 223, 271n51
Duara, Prasenjit, 2–3, 149–50, 287n174

East Clique (Haimen County), 90
East Faction (Jinjiang County), 87–88
East Faction (Shuyang County), 136
East Faction (Tongshan County), 84–85
Eastman, Lloyd, 2, 209
education: of assembly members, 19–20; degrees, earned or purchased, 16–17; of gentry, 16–17; of GMD members, 16, 20–21, 37–38, 111, 148; government oversight of, 206; local elites as reformers of, 15, 112, 153, 156; of merchants, 25–26;

modern, Western-style of, 34–35, 38, 157, 161–63; patronage in, 34–35; and schools as cover for revolutionary activities, 36–37, 44
education associations, 22, 110, 124
Eight Local Bullies, 136
elites, economic, 16, 25–30, 53–54
elites, local, 2; and anti-Communist purge of GMD, 104–8; and county assemblies, 16; definition of, 16, 243n5; factionalism among, 6, 30–35, 78–79, 134–35, 135–42; gentry as, 12, 16–17, 19–20, 62; government-sponsored institutions as, 17–22; personal connections and, 23–25; political leaders as, 16, 53–54, 63–64; professional associations as, 22–23; and radicalism, 1, 70–71; as reformists, 2, 15, 112, 156; religious institutions and, 149–50; taxation and, 15. *See also* gentry; landlords; "local bullies and evil gentry"; merchants; oligarchies
elites, political: definition of, 16; leftist views on, 63–64; as "local bullies and evil gentry," 114; local GMD control by, 130; as revolutionary targets, 53–54, 118; and Yancheng Massacre, 153–54
elites, precinct 134–35
entrepreneurial brokers, 2–3
Esherick, Joseph W., 156, 242n1
examination degrees, 16–17, 19–20
executions, 61, 124–25, 128
Extraordinary Conference, 198

factionalism: in CCP, 252n89; definition of, 31, 237–38n13; in GMD, 5–7, 40–41, 46–52, 69–71, 101–2, 166, 209; of Jiangsu Guomindang, 5, 69–102, 211–22; of local elites, 6, 30–35, 78–79, 134–35, 135–42; of Organization Clique, 5; and provincial-local relations, 89–91; pyramidal structure of, 71–72; self-government system and, 33–34; tactics of, 86–91
Fan Xiongyi, 44, 47–49, 223
Feng County, 125–28, 132, 142, 154
Feng County Guomindang, 38–40
Feng Jufen, 121
Feng Shaozhan, 79
Feng Shiqi, 223
Feng Ti, 217
Fengxian County, 9, 131
feudalism, 27, 111–12, 192
feuds, 20, 63
Fewsmith, Joseph, 192
FF Clique, 75–76; factional rivalries and, 90, 92, 100, 299n8; members of, 191, 223; rectification and, 98
Fitzgerald, John, 35
footbinding, 121, 124, 179
Fourteenth Army (CCP), 200–201
Funing County, 154
Funing County Guomindang, 83–84, 102, 131–32

Ganyu County Guomindang, 113, 123–24
Gao Fang, 300n15
Gao Juemin, 181
Gao Yuesheng, 223
Gaoyou County, 159
Ge Jianshi: arrest of, 97–98; clique membership of, 77, 223, 266n17, 269n29; and intervention in Baoshan County, 276n4; on "local bullies and evil gentry," 109–10; November 22 Massacre and, 301n31; offices held by, 221, 300n15, 302n46; protégés of, 92; on Zhu Jixun, 257–58n5
Ge Jincheng, 132
generational differences, 20, 36–37, 40, 111, 168
Geng Xuannian, 142

gentry, 16–17; conferences of, 21; in county assemblies, 19–20; "Eight Local Bullies" as, 136; leftist attacks on, 62; lower degree holders, 16, 19–20, 127, 137, 156; party-elite relations and, 187; as peasant movement targets, 60; upper degree holders, 16, 84, 124. *See also* oligarchies
gentry-merchants, 12, 20
Goodman, Bryna, 4
government-sponsored institutions, 17–21, 23, 53, 63–64
Grand Alliance, 267n21
Green Gang, 55, 88, 105
Gu Nancun, 122
Gu Renfa, 266n17
Gu Xiping, 223
Gu Zifang, 61
Gu Ziyang, 45–46; as Anti-CC Clique member, 77, 223, 264n5; arrest of, 97· 98, 99; county-level factions and, 84–85; dropped from Jiangsu Special Committee, 212; as National Congress delegate, 257n1; offices held by, 44, 100, 217–18, 221–22, 302n46; leftist leanings of, 259n26; protégés of, 77, 92; recruitment strategy of, 36
Guangdong Province, 54, 143
Guangxi Military Clique, 213–14
Guangzhou Uprising, 217
Guanyun County, 30, 132
Guo Fuzeng, 300n15
Guo Yin'gao, 181
Guomindang (GMD): anti-Communist purge in, 1, 50–52, 73, 103–8, 112, 175, 211, 274n77; and decline in power, 7, 189–97, 207; factionalism in, 5–6, 46–52, 69–71, 101–2, 166, 209; funding of, 164; headquarters location disputes and, 48–51, 139, 213; left v. right wings in, 6, 40–41, 46–50, 64, 106; and party-government tensions, 4–5, 123, 134, 182, 188–89, 206; propaganda lines of, 36; public sphere debate and, 235–37n10; radicalism and, 1, 112–17; reorganization of, 35–36, 43–46, 52, 79; reregistration of members, 82–83, 85–86, 212; reunification of, 213; social background of members, 15–16, 20–21, 35–41, 46–47, 86, 111, 143, 148; as tool of local elites, 2; uprisings against, 104–8, 150–59; urban influence of, 120. *See also* Jiangsu Guomindang
Guomindang-Communist alliance, 5, 6, 40, 44, 46, 51
Guomindang National Congresses: First, 43–44; Second, 45, 53–54, 143; Third, 186, 218–19, 220;
Guomindang organizations: Central Executive Committee: appointments and, 73; on attacks against "local bullies and evil gentry," 186; center divisions and, 50–51, 213; and Jiangsu Special Committee, 211–12, on propaganda functions of local branches, 190; rectification and, 98; and Western Hills Conference, 50; Central Political Committee, 165; Central Special Committee, 213–16; Central Statistical Bureau, 73, 76; Central Supervisory Committee, 47, 51, 213; Investigation Section, 73, 76, 199–200; Merchant Department, 143–44; Organization Department, 51, 70–74, 76, 79, 168; Peasant Department, 60
Guomindang party centers: in Guangzhou, 48–50, 54; in Nanjing, 51, 103, 139, 213; in Shanghai, 50–51; in Wuhan, 50–51, 139, 213

Habermas, Jürgen, 233–37n10
Haimen, 239n19
Haimen County, 9, 90–91

Haizhou County, 30
He Haiqiao, 44, 48, 223
He Minhun, 97, 300n15
He Xuyou, 223
He Yingqin, 274n77, 290n212
He Yushu, 266n17
Hou Shaoqiu, 44–45, 56, 60, 260n31
Hu Hanmin, 97, 165, 276n4
Hu Yinjie, 58
Huai River Conservancy Committee, 73
Huai'an County Guomindang, 89–91, 174
Huaiyin County, 39, 147
Huang, Philip, 27
Huang Jinrong, 94
Huang Lisan, 144
Huang Renyan, 223
Huang Zhian, 88
Huangpu (Whampoa) Clique, 77
Huangpu (Whampoa) Military Academy, 46, 75, 218

imperialists and imperialism, 36, 65, 192
intellectuals, 3, 74, 161–63, 180
Investigation Section. *See* Guomindang organizations
Isaacs, Harold, 54

Jacobs, Bruce, 31–32, 253n96
January 6 Massacre, 135–42
Japan: and anti-Japanese campaigns, 112, 145–47, 156; self-government models in, 17; war with, 1–2, 208–9, 298
Jiading County, 9
Jiading County Guomindang, 124
Jiang Ziying, 300n15
Jiangdu County, 9, 216
Jiangdu County Guomindang, 85
Jiangning County, 241n20, 299n7
Jiangsu Critic, 114
Jiangsu dangwu zhoukan, 186

Jiangsu Farmer's Bank, 73, 144, 266n18, 267n20
Jiangsu Guomindang: central control over, 101–2, 109, 115–17; education levels of members, 20; factionalism in, 5, 69–102, 211–22; headquarters disputes of, 49–50, 139; "local bullies and evil gentry," prosecution by, 63, 108–15, 131–35; public sphere debate and, 236; social background of members, 36–37, 111; subsidies for, 48
Jiangsu Guomindang organizations: Party Affairs Maintenance Committee, 216–17; Party Affairs Preparatory Committee, 257n2; Party Affairs Rectification Committee, 76, 89, 98–100, 186; Party Purge Committee, 76, 108, 211–12; Peasant Department, 55; Provincial Executive Committee, 46, 76, 98–100, 220–22, 302n46; Provincial Party Affairs Directorate, 82–83, 89, 217–20; Provisional Executive Committee (JPEC), 110, 168, 213–17; Provisional Party Committee, 44, 47–49; Special Committee (JSC), 108–9, 110, 116, 173, 211–12
Jiangsu Peasant Association Preparatory Committee, 215
Jiangsu Province, 8–14; assemblies in, 18; CCP's failure in, 2, 198–203; Communist uprisings in, 238n16; as Organization Clique stronghold, 5
Jiangsu Provincial Amalgamated Chambers of Commerce, 193
Jiangsu Provincial Congresses: First, 219–20; Second, 99; Third, 100
Jiangsu Provincial Directorate, 292n4
Jiangyin County, 9, 147, 212
Jiangyin County Guomindang, 110
Jianye University, 40, 47
Jile Temple, 156
Jin Hesheng, 211, 268n25

Jin Pinsan, 151–52
Ji'nan Incident, 145
Jingjiang County, 9, 196–97
Jingjiang County Guomindang, 87–88
Jinshan County, 9, 64
Jinshan County Guomindang, 45, 105–7

Kipnis, Andrew, 253n94
Kunshan County, 9, 29, 135, 174–77, 214
Kunshan County Guomindang, 38, 40, 45, 55, 72

labor movements: leftist/rightist views of, 55, 66; Reorganizationists and, 114; suppression of, 116–17, 269n34; unions and, 122, 124. *See also* mass organizations
Lan Bohua, 85
land reclamation companies, 28, 59–60
land reform movements, 28, 66–67, 196, 225–29, 279n39
landholders' associations, 22
landlords: anti-Communist purge and, 107; economic opportunities of, 12–13, 26–30; "Eight Local Bullies" as, 136; "feudalism" of, 27; GMD as tool of, 2; and land reclamation companies, 28, 59–60; leftist assaults on, 54, 60–62, 114; militia leaders as, 24, 27; and rent collections, 13, 116; rightists' approach to, 66–67; and sharecropping, 119–20; title deeds and, 154. *See also* land reform movements; rent reduction campaigns
Li Dazhao, 47
Li Houji, 128
Li Jingzhai, 100–101
Li Mingyang, 124
Li Shouyong, 75; anti-CSC activities of, 215; clique membership of, 223, 265n6, 272n60; county support for, 84; and factionalism, 252n89; and FF Clique, 268n25, 300n8; and JPEC, 214, 300n15; on "local bullies and evil gentry," 114–15; offices held by, 211–12, 216–17; protégés of, 98, 218
Li Tiping, 195
Li Tongfu, 88
Li Xinglian, 276n4
Li Yafei, 170–73
Li Yicheng, 151–53
Li Yi'e, 106
Li Zifeng, 177, 181–82, 292n8
Li Zongren, 298
Liang Cunren, 223
Lianshui County, 112–13, 174
Limen, 55
Lin Biao, 98
lineages, 23, 31, 107
Ling Shaozu, 85, 98, 100, 223
Liu Bingchen, 300n15
Liu Chengrui, 223
Liu Chuanjing, 85
Liu Jihong, 268n25
Liu Menghou, 156–57
Liu Shengping, 88
Liu Shirong, 158
Liu Tianzhan, 85
Liu Xifan, 91
Liu Xiuqing, 226
Liu Yanxiang, 126
Liu Yazi, 56, 259n24
Liu Yunzhao, 44, 48, 223, 257nn1–2, 259n23
Liu Zhendian, 122
Liu Zihou, 85
Liu Zisheng, 87
Liuhe Guomindang Congress, 190
Liyang County, 93–96
Liyang Critic, 94
lobbying, 89
local autonomy movement, 7, 142

"local bullies and evil gentry" (*tuhao lieshen*), 4, 205–7; anti-Communist purge and, 104–8, 276n4; central GMD and, 103, 115–17, 185–87, 206; chambers of commerce members as, 114, 140; Chiang Kai-shek on, 109; Eight Local Bullies as, 136; elites' reaction to campaigns against, 139, 153; equated with Communists, 108–9; identification of, 129–30, 212; individuals attacked as, 58–62; as label for factional enemies, 32–33, 122, 131–35; leftist assaults on, 54–56, 198; Ni Bi and, 1; and party-government tensions, 167–70, 173–74, 177; peasant movements and, 53, 60–62, 107; property confiscated by GMD, 110, 119–21, 124, 128, 130, 142, 180; prosecution of, 61, 63–64, 108–15, 117, 127–35, 142, 177, 279n41; rectification and, 185–87, 197; rightist views on, 65–66, 263–64n79; self-government office holders as, 114; sword societies and, 155–57. *See also* elites, local

local self-government: attacked as "local bullies and evil gentry," 114; in Chuansha, 245n18; development of, 7, 17–18; factionalism and, 33–34; GMD and, 110, 196; militia and, 24; personal connections in, 33; revolts against elite dominated, 15, 53
Loyal Comrades Club, 211
Lu Donghao, 175
Lu Dun, 223
Lu Wenfeng, 171–73
Lu Yinquan, 223, 270n37
Luo Jigang, 223

Ma Yuanfang, 76, 223
magistrates, 18–19, 21, 34, 168, 174, 243n5
management committees, 19

managers (*xiangdong, shidong, dongshi*), 21; attacks on, 63–64, 119, 130, 133–37, 140; government control by, 65, 177; militia leaders as, 24; powers of, 19, 21–22; replaced by village self-rule, 110
Mao Zuquan, 257nn1–2
marketing system, 22
mass organizations: leftist/rightist uses of, 55, 61, 66, 114, 209; National Assembly elections and, 99; Organization Clique and, 78; and rectification, 116–17; in war with Japan, 2. *See also* labor movements; merchant associations; peasant movements
May Fourth Movement, 56, 111
media, control of, 87, 98, 295n47
Meng Guangtai, 181–82
merchant associations: autonomy of, 4; end of, 192–96; factionalism and, 34; in Ganyu, 124; GMD establishment of, 53–54, 143–44, 148; leaders of, 122; taxation and, 144–45
Merchant Department. *See* Guomindang organizations
Merchant Movement Academy, 143
merchants: economic opportunities of, 13, 26; education of, 25–26; as "gentry-merchants," 12, 20; GMD and, 2, 142–48; harassment of, 121–22; leftist assaults on, 53–54; peasant attacks on, 62; sword societies and, 156; as "traitor-merchants," 143, 146. *See also* chambers of commerce
Miao Bin: as ally of local elites, 132, 180–81; Anti-CC/Reorganizationist leaders punished by, 96–99; as Chiang Kai-shek's protégé, 97, 219; impeachment of, 97; offices held by, 96, 300n15; Organization Clique and, 302n45
militia: chambers of commerce and, 22, 24, 172; GMD and, 53, 62, 196, 200; individual control of,

114, 122, 125–27, 131–32, 136–37, 140–41; landholdings of, 24, 27; merchant-controlled, 53, 143–44; Reorganization Clique and, 93; their leaders as unofficial elites, 23–24
Miner, Noel, 164, 185
Ministry of Interior (Qing), 17
Mo Baichou, 106
modernism, 149–50
modernization campaigns, 2, 74, 205–6
municipal township assemblies, 19

Nanhui County, 9
Nanjing, 8, 37, 240n19
Nanjing government. *See* Nationalist Government
Nanjing Municipal Guomindang, 47–49, 51, 211
Nantong County, 9, 147, 203, 216, 239n19
Nathan, Andrew, 31, 72, 73, 75, 101
national assemblies, 19
National Congresses. *See* Guomindang, National Congresses
National Revolutionary Armies (NRA): factionalism in, 64; First Army, 105–6; and importance to GMD, 44, 192; movements of, 60, 63, 69; mutinous troops in, 93, 96; political departments of, 64, 105–7; Twenty-first Army, 175–76; Twenty-sixth Army, 106–7, 141, 175, 276n4
National Salvation Societies, 146–47
Nationalist Government: centralization in, 7, 206–7; firing of Chiang Kai-shek by, 51; religious policies of, 159–61; and Reorganizationist coup attempt, 78, 92–98, 101; taxation in, 2–3, 145
Nationalist Party. *See* Guomindang
New China Revolutionary Society, 267n21
New China Study Society, 267n21

New Culture Movement, 111, 148
New Fourth Army (CCP), 298
New Suqian Daily, 87
New Zhenjiang News, 40
newspapers, control of, 87, 98
Ni Bi: as Anti-CC Clique member, 223, 269n32; arrest of, 97–98; labor suppression and, 269n34; on "local bullies and evil gentry," 1, 111; offices held by, 217–18, 221, 302nn38, 46; on party-government tensions, 167–68; radicalism of, 77, 114
Ni Bingruo, 105
Niu Changyao, 223
Niu Jianchu, 91
Niu Minhua, 300n15
Niu Yongjian, 97, 99, 104, 126
North, Robert, 38
North Township Faction, 90
Northeast Faction, 83–84
Northern Expedition, 43, 50–51, 149
Northern Faction, 125, 128
November 22 Massacre, 215–16
Number One Faction, 79, 81, 166
Number Two Faction, 79, 81, 166
Number Three Faction, 79, 81

oligarchies, 11–12, 15–16, 23, 36. *See also* gentry; elites, local
Organization Clique (CC Clique), 72–74, 215; factionalism in, 5; members of, 211–12, 220; party control and, 100–101, 190–91; and post-purge Communist suppression, 91; provincial factions and, 75–76, 92, 185–86; and radicalism, 114, 225–26; rectification and, 70–71, 98–102; relationship to other cliques, 223
Organization Department. *See* Guomindang organizations
Overthrow Dai Faction, 83–84

Pan Guojun, 223

Pan Juemin, 189
party-government tensions: antisuperstition campaigns and, 159–61; CCP/Communists and, 289nn202, 206; GMD and, 4–5, 123, 134, 182, 188–89, 206; "local bullies and evil gentry" and, 167–70, 173–74, 177–82; rectification and, 182–83, 188–89
Past and Future Weekly Lecture Society, 40
patronage: control over, 188; in county appointments, 81–82; in education, 34–35; by factions, 86; by Organization Department, 73–74; by purge committees, 212; by Republican Party, 180
pawner's associations, 59
pawnshops, 26, 58–59
Peasant Advancement Society, 59
peasant associations, 116–17, 170, 175, 226, 280; —preparatory committees, 215–16; —rectification committees, 116, 124, 276
Peasant Department. *See* Guomindang organizations; *see also* Jiangsu Guomindang organizations
peasant movements: and land reclamation companies, 59–60; and "local bullies and evil gentry," 53, 60–62, 107; and pawner's associations, 59; post-purge continuation of, 112, 124; and rent reduction campaigns, 54, 56–57; Reorganizationists and, 114; rightist views on, 66–67; secret societies and, 55; suppression of, during purge, 104, 116–17. *See also* mass organizations
peasants: alternative livelihoods for, 12; intellectuals' alienation from, 161–63; rich, as village elites, 27, 29
People's Rule Study Society, 47
Perry, Elizabeth, 14

personal connections (*guanxi*), 23, 31–33, 46, 63, 72
petitions, 89, 122
Pi County, 125, 154
Pi County Guomindang, 79–81, 166
pluralism, 232n5
Political Academy Clique, 223
Political Science Clique, 266n17
Prazniak, Roxann, 243n3
price stability, 148
professional associations (*fatuan*), 22–23
propaganda lines: against imperialists and warlords, 36, 44; against local elites, 40, 57, 108–9; party-government tensions and, 190; of Reorganizationists, 78; of rightists' land reform plans, 67; of the Second National Congress, 53
Prosperous Farmer Pump Company, 59
protégé networks. *See* personal connections (*guanxi*)
provincial assemblies, 17–19, 125–28, 131–32, 194
provincial government: conflicts with GMD, 134, 160, 164–83, 191; religious policies of, 159–61
Pu Rongqian, 133
public sphere/civil society debate, 3–4, 233–37n10
purchased degrees, 16–17, 19–20

Qi Shuzu, 223
Qi Xiyong: as CC Clique member, 75, 98, 223, 268n25; offices held by, 216, 221, 302n46
Qian Sunqing, 194–95
Qidong County, 9, 113, 196, 225–29, 279n39
Qin Xiaolu, 44, 48
Qing period: education in, 34–35; elites of, 3, 16; factionalism in, 33–34; militia in, 23; professional associ-

ations in, 22; religious institutions and concepts in, 148–49, 254n102; self-government in, 7, 17–18, 33–34; taxation in, 53, 149
Qingpu County, 9, 59
Qiu Youzhen, 223
Qiu Yugu, 61
queues (hairstyle), 179–80
Qiu Fu, 174–77

radicalism: of Anti-CC leaders, 92; and attacks on local elites, 1, 107; party-government tensions and, 5, 182; post-purge continuation of, 70, 103, 107, 112–17, 130; rectification and, 71; of Reorganizationist leaders, 92; Shuyang Massacre and, 135–42
Rankin, Mary, 3, 112, 234–35n10
rectification: and attacks on "local bullies and evil gentry," 185–87, 197; county committees of, 85; and GMD influence on administrative policy, 185–92, 207; impact on Jiangsu factions, 98–101, 208; mass organizations and, 116–17; Organization Department and, 70–71; party-government tensions and, 182–83, 188–89; peasant association committees of, 116, 124, 276
Rectification Committee. *See* Jiangsu Guomindang organizations
Red Gang, 55
Red Spears, 55
Reeducation Institutes, 201–2
religious leaders: Huimen, 155; Pan, 151–52, 159
religious practices and institutions, 3, 149–50; landholdings of, 25; leaders of, as elites, 24–25, 154–56, 159; Qing policy on, 148–49, 254n102; and sword societies, 156; temples of the city god, transformation or destruction of, 94, 128, 149, 151–52, 180. *See also* antisuperstition campaigns; Christians; Confucianism
rent reduction campaigns, 54, 56–57, 62, 116, 124, 170
Reorganization Clique, 77–78; and Anti-CC Clique, 78, 269n29; Central Clique and, 154; coup attempt by, 78, 92–98, 101; members list, 223; militia and, 93; Organization Clique opposed by, 92; under Provincial Executive Committee, 220, 222; radicalism of, 78, 92, 114, 197–98; rectification and, 208
Republican Daily News, 214
Republican government: elites of, 3; factionalism under, 31–32; militia in, 23–24; religious institutions and concepts in, 148–49; self-government in, 7, 18; taxation in, 53
Republican Party (Pi County), 79
Republican Party (Suining County), 178–80, 182
reregistration of GMD members, 82–83, 85–86, 212
rice dealers, 147–48
Rong Zongjing, 194
Rowe, William T., 234–35n10
Rugao County, 9; anti-"bully" campaigns in, 130–31, 133; CCP uprisings in, 200, 238n16; landlords in, 26; religious confrontations in, 163; urbanization of, 239–41n19
Rugao County Guomindang, 113

salt-land reclamation companies, 28. *See also* land reclamation companies
Sanwu she (Marxist society), 44, 48
schoolmate personal connections, 31–32, 46
Schoppa, Keith, 239n18, 244n11, 245n19, 253n98, 263n79
scientism, 149, 163
secret police, 73, 76
secret societies, 55, 73, 105

self-government. *See* local self-government
Sha Bingyuan, 57
Shan Xintian, 140–41
Shanghai (city), 8, 9, 11; autonomy of organizations in, 4; CCP in, 295n48; GMD members in, 37; labor movement in, 55, 145; landlords in, 29
Shanghai (county), 9, 135
Shanghai Guomindang, 47, 49–50
Shanghai Guomindang, Executive Committee, 44, 49–50, 259n25
Shao Lizi, 257n3
sharecropping, 119–20
Shen Baixian, 266n17
Shen Dingyi, 66, 264n79
Shen Jing, 44, 47, 259n23, 259n26, 300n15
Shen Susheng, 223
Shen Yi, 112, 170–73
Sheng Xiru, 88
Shi Yiqian, 90
Shi Yousan, 96
Shuyang County, 27, 113, 135–42, 166–67, 193
silk industry, 11, 30, 148
Siyang County Guomindang, 78
Skinner, G. William, 14, 22, 238n18
Small Sword Society, 154, 156
Smith, Arthur H., 254n100
Song Zhenlun, 223
Songjiang County, 9, 60–62, 105, 160, 216
Songjiang County Guomindang, 37, 39
Soong, T. V., 219
Southeast Townships Study Society, 57
Southeast University, 40
Southern Faction, 125, 127
Southwest Clique, 153
Southwest Faction, 83–84
"speak bitterness" sessions, 60

special courts (*tezhong xingshi fating*), 115, 117, 279n41; individuals tried by, 127–29, 132, 135, 142; and reversal of verdicts, 132, 142
Star Society, 56
Star's Rays, 56
Stranahan, Patricia, 295n48
strikes and lockouts, 147
Stross, Randy, 240
study societies: leftist, 56; May Fourth generation, 138; rightist, 47, 65, 214; as rudimentary political parties, 35, 44–45
Suining County, 154, 177–82, 180
Suining County Guomindang, 62, 81–82, 180
Sun Chuanfang, 43, 57, 59, 63, 126, 141–42
Sun Dachen, 223
Sun Gong, 85
Sun Jingya, 66
Sun Jishi, 125–28, 279n39
Sun Yat-sen: brawls at memorial service for, 50; death of, 49; and GMD reorganization, 43, 52; land reform and, 66–67; and Nanjing GMD, 47; on party-government relations, 165; as provisional president, 80; rightists' appropriation of, 65
Sunist Practice Society, 75, 98
Sunist Study Society, 65, 77, 214
Suqian Citizen's Report, 87
Suqian County, 154–58
Suqian County Guomindang, 82–83, 87
Suqian Daily, 87
Suzhou Merchant Association, 145
sword societies, 55, 93–95, 154–58, 181

Tai County, 9
Taicang County, 9, 134
Taiwan, 31–32, 264n3

Taixing County, 9, 170–74, 200, 238n16
Taixing County Guomindang, 112
Tan Pingshan, 79
Tang Qiyu, 223
taxation: collection officials, 2–3; and county assemblies, 19; exemption of Christians from, 149; GMD plans for, 53; by local elites, 15; merchant associations and, 144–45
teachers, 35, 37–38, 40
teacher-student personal connections, 31–32, 46
temples. *See* religious practices and institutions
Tenant's Cooperative Self-Salvation Association, 56
Teng Gu: arrest of, 97; clique membership of, 77, 176, 223; offices held by, 217–18, 221, 302n46; and Reorganizationist coup attempt, 270n37
Teng Yangzhi, 223, 264n5
Third Faction, 84
Thompson, Roger, 33–34, 246n26
Tongshan, 10–11
Tongshan County: CCP decline in, 203; chamber of commerce in, 85, 193–94; landlords in, 27; political appointments in, 197; sword societies in, 154
Tongshan County Guomindang, 84–85; —Rectification Committee, 193
township assemblies, 19–21
Township Faction, 82–83, 87
towns/townships, 30, 83–84, 106, 133–34. *See also* managers
trade associations, 193, 195
traitor-merchants, 143, 146
Tsai, David, 164–65
Tsou, Tang, 275n101

urban reformist elites, 15, 156
urbanization, definition of, 239–41

verdicts, reversal of, 132, 142
vocational associations, 117
Voice of Shuyang, 138–39
voting: irregularities in, 178; qualifications for, 18–19, 48

Wakeman, Frederic, 267n22
Walker, Kathy, 239–340n19
Wang, Y. C., 161
Wang Baoxuan, 75; as CC Clique member, 223, 265n6; offices held by, 217–18, 222, 302n46
Wang Bingheng, 152
Wang Changhao, 121
Wang Changjiang, 152
Wang Gongyu, 126–28, 279n39
Wang Jingwei: and Chiang Kai-shek, 113; democratic concepts of, 198, 236–37; impeachment of, 50; party reunification and, 213; rebukes of, 217–19; Reorganization Clique and, 77, 96
Wang Lantian, 80–81
Wang Shan, 223
Wang Shuhuai, 255n103
Wang Xianghe, 140–41
Wang Yushu, 179
Wang Zuoliang, 123–24
warlord-dominated governments, 15, 43; collusion with, 132–33; funds for, 22–23; leftist/rightist views on, 54, 65; May Fourth movement and, 111; Northern Expedition against, 50; social ills attributed to, 36
West Clique (Haimen County), 90
West Faction (Jingjiang County), 87
West Faction (Shuyang County), 137–40
West Faction (Tongshan County), 84–85
West Township Faction, 90
Western Hills Clique: Dai Jitao and, 65; expulsion of, 211, 216–17; factionalism and, 92; headquarters

disputes and, 50–52, 213–15; members of, 213–14, 223; and Sunist Practice Society, 75
Western Hills Conference, 49–50, 263n79
women's movements, 121, 124, 159, 179
workers' associations. *See* labor movements
Wu Baofeng, 98, 176
Wu Baojin, 223
Wu County, 9, 240–41n19
Wu County Guomindang, 45
Wu Qiang, 282n100
Wu Shaoxi, 135
Wu Yicang, 211
Wu Zhihui, 274n77
Wuhuading Temple, 155
Wujiang County, 9
Wujin County, 9, 64, 113, 146, 174
Wuxi County, 9; anti-Communist purge in, 107; commercial organizations in, 194–95; elite factionalism in, 134; managers in, 64; merchants in, 26, 145, 147; party-government tensions in, 173–74; peasant organizations in, 116; silk industry in, 30
Wuxi County Guomindang, 38, 125, 133

Xi Yutang, 156
Xia Lin, 58
Xia Zicheng, 178–79
Xiao County, 187
Xiao Jishan, 97
Xiao Zheng, 228, 279n39
Xie Dengyu, 223
Xie Lunxian, 139, 141
Xu Faction, 81–82
Xu Wentian, 94, 223
Xu Ximing, 85

Yan Xishan, 198
Yancheng County, 88, 144, 174, 193
Yancheng County Guomindang, 81, 84, 151–52
Yancheng Massacre, 150–54, 159
Yang, Martin, 25
Yang, Mayfair Mei-hui, 32
Yang Fang, 223
Yang Sili, 223, 300n15
Yang Tongshou, 122
Yang Xingqin, 76, 223, 274n83
Yang-Ma-Cao Clique, 76, 85, 99, 223, 299n7
Yangzhong County, 9
Yangzhou County, 113
Yao Erjue, 179–81
Yao Heling, 134
Ye Chucang: absences of, 218, 220; as GMD sponsor, 257n3; offices held by, 217–18, 220–21, 259n25, 302n46; on party-government tensions, 166; and relations with Chen brothers, 74; and Sun Yat-sen memorial service, 260n31
Ye Xiufeng: anti-CSC activities of, 215; and county-level factions, 85; as FF Clique member, 75–76, 223, 300n8; offices held by, 76, 98, 212, 216
Yixing County, 9, 113, 116, 239n19
Yixing County Merchant Association, 144–45
Yu Huaizhong, 223
Yu Jingtang, 266n17
Yu Xiaqing, 145
Yu Yichen, 134–35
Yuan Shikai, 18, 45, 79, 137, 178

Zhang Baopei, 60–61, 105
Zhang Daofan, 98, 268n26
Zhang Fakui, 98
Zhang Guotao, 38
Zhang Hongye, 79–81
Zhang Jian, 28, 138
Zhang Jingtong, 123–24
Zhang Jiren, 280n64

Zhang Laifang, 124
Zhang Minquan, 182
Zhang Naiyan, 220
Zhang Renjie, 223
Zhang Shishi, 223
Zhang Shouyong, 219
Zhang Shushi, 79; brawl involving, 259n24; on enemies of GMD, 54; as National Congress delegate, 257n1; as Provisional Party Committee member, 44, 47; as Zhu Jixun's confidant, 48
Zhang Xiaoyou, 223
Zhang Yimin, 232n5
Zhang Yuanyang, 76, 98, 223
Zhang Zhi, 105
Zhang Ziqin, 156–57
Zhao Ruheng, 264–65n5
Zhao Yuzheng, 223
Zhejiang Province, 8, 245n19; — Guomindang, 185
Zhejiang Revolutionary Comrades Society, 265n10
Zhenjiang County, 9, 40, 63

Zhou Faction (Shuyang County), 137
Zhou Faction (Siyang County), 78
Zhou Fengjing, 223
Zhou Houjun, 83, 191–92, 216, 223
Zhou Huapeng, 78, 223
Zhou Jieren: as CC Clique member, 75, 223, 271n50; offices held by, 211, 221, 302n46
Zhou Ruqian, 225–26, 279n39
Zhou Shaocheng, 75, 223, 225
Zhou Shuiping, 56–57, 60
Zhou Xiaoshi, 137–42
Zhou Xu, 80
Zhou Zhongchen, 84
Zhu Ji, 88
Zhu Jianbai: clique membership of, 223, 267n21, 271n50, 272n60; offices held by, 98, 221, 302n46
Zhu Jixun, 44–49, 107, 257nn1–2
Zhu Limin, 84–85
Zhu Shaoliang, 215
Zhu Shoushi, 124
Zonis, Marvin, 255n109

HARVARD-YENCHING LIBRARY

This book must be returned to the Library on or before the last date stamped below. A fine will be charged for late return. Non-receipt of overdue notices does not exempt the borrower from fines.